Modern English Society

Modern English Society

HISTORY AND STRUCTURE 1850–1970

JUDITH RYDER &

HAROLD SILVER

Methuen & Co Ltd 11 New Fetter Lane London EC4

First published 1970
by Methuen & Co Ltd
11 New Fetter Lane, London EC4
© *1970 by Judith Ryder and Harold Silver*
Printed and bound in Great Britain by
Butler & Tanner Ltd, Frome and London

S B N 416 41770 1 Hardbound
S B N 416 41780 9 Paperback

This book is available in both hardbound and paperback editions. The paperback edition is sold subject to the condition that it shall not, by way of trade or otherwise, be lent, re-sold, hired out, or otherwise circulated without the publisher's prior consent in any form of binding or cover other than that in which it is published and without a similar condition being imposed on the subsequent purchaser.

Distributed in the USA
by Barnes & Noble Inc.

Contents

Illustrations

TEXT FIGURES

Preface

We should like to acknowledge with gratitude the comments and suggestions we have had from Carole Sathyamurthy, Raymond Brown, Colin Falck and Ray Holland. None of these, of course, is in any way responsible for what has finally appeared in print.

Both of us have had the pleasure of teaching on Extension Courses for the Diploma in Sociology of the University of London. Judith Ryder would like to thank all her students on the Social Structure of Modern Britain courses at Hendon, Westminster, Dulwich and Ewell, and Harold Silver his students on the History of Modern Britain courses at Croydon and Wandsworth, for many hours of discussion in which the teachers learned at least as much as the students. It is, in fact, to them that our book is dedicated.

J. R. and H. S.
Centre for Science Education,
Chelsea College,
University of London
March 1970

Acknowledgements

The authors and publishers wish to thank the following for permission to reproduce the illustrations appearing in this book:

Aerofilms Limited, for Nos. 21, 29, 31, 32 and 35
Henry Grant, for No. 36
British Railways Board, for the frontispiece
Keystone Press Agency Limited, for Nos. 34 and 38
The Mansell Collection, for Nos. 1, 3, 5–7, 9, 11–14, 16, 17, 20, 23, 24, 28
Radio Times Hulton Picture Library, for Nos. 2, 4, 8, 10, 15, 18, 19, 25–27, 30, 33 and 37
Michael St Maur Sheil, for No. 39

The authors and publishers would also like to thank the following for permission to compile the statistical appendices and text figures in this volume from the following sources:

Cambridge University Press for statistics from Mitchell and Deane, *Abstracts of British Historical Statistics*, 1962
The Controller of Her Majesty's Stationery Office for statistics from *Annual Abstract of Statistics*, 1967 and 1969; *Statistics of Education (Schools)*, Vol. I, 1969; *Board of Inland Revenue Statistics*; *Registrar-General's Statistical Review of England and Wales*, 1960; *Census, London County Reports*, 1951 and 1961; *Monthly Digest of Statistics*, August 1967
The Longman Group Ltd for statistics from T. K. Robinson, *Population of Britain*, Key Discussion Books, 1968; and G. C. Allen, *British Industries and Their Organization*, 1959
Macmillan & Co. Ltd and St Martin's Press Inc. for statistics from Butler and Freeman, *British Political Facts*, 1969
Routledge & Kegan Paul Ltd and Humanities Press Inc. for statistics from D. C. Marsh, *The Changing Social Structure of England and Wales, 1871–1961*, 1965

Introduction · Sociology and Social History

We have aimed in this book to offer a sociological account of some of the more distinctive features of the contemporary English social structure, and to outline some related aspects of nineteenth- and twentieth-century English history.

Although our historical starting point is the process of change taking place at the beginning of the nineteenth century, we are concerned more centrally with the social transformations of the Victorian period: the growth of industry and towns; changes in the structure of employment; the development of rationalized, large-scale systems of public administration, commerce and finance; the emergence of popular social movements and a democratic franchise; the appearance of public health and welfare policies; and the rapid expansion of communications. All of these had their origins in the disruption of the more settled order of communal existence in the eighteenth century, a disruption which resulted from the complex events we have come to know as the Industrial Revolution. They are developments which have had a continuing influence on English life, and we have tried to account for the changing nature of this influence at different stages in the late nineteenth and early twentieth centuries.

Implicit in this approach has been our interest in demonstrating the links between the methods and emphases of the social historian and those of the sociologist. We have tried to show that, in their common preoccupation with the changing network of relations connecting particular social institutions to characteristic forms of social activity and thought, the social historian and the sociologist can benefit greatly from a sharing of each other's terminology, data and techniques. It may be useful, therefore, at this point to offer some explanation of what we understand by social history and sociology. There are, of course, difficulties in doing this briefly, particularly if it is borne in mind that almost every word in the title of this book is open to, and indeed has been subjected to, far-reaching analysis and prolonged dispute.

We take social history to mean more than an antiquarian interest in the manners and appearances of society, and more than an effort merely to make history reconstruct a 'fabric' of the past. While it may do this, we take it to be concerned more fundamentally with significant human behaviour and action, with underlying changes in ideas, ideologies and attitudes. It entails an interest in the emergence and influence of ideas in relation to other social phenomena; labour history has provided some of the best examples of this interrelation. Social history in this sense, therefore, is normally coupled with, and is to some extent a break-away from, economic history. The point of divergence between the two, Asa Briggs has suggested, has been the change in economic history itself. 'The increasingly close link between economic historians and theoretical economists', he wrote in 1962, 'has induced many historians, who previously thought of themselves as economic historians, to seek greater freedom by proclaiming themselves to be social historians.' [1]

R. H. Tawney warned the historian against being over-preoccupied with problems and not enough with people: 'To view an individual or a society primarily as a problem is to make certain of misconceiving them.' [2] Social historians are not likely to misconceive in this sense because their priorities include, in fact, a concern with human relationships. Economic historians look primarily at 'the record of the economic choices which appear to the historian to have been the most interesting and important that men have made'. [3] Social historians are aware of these industrial, economic and commercial choices, but are more centrally concerned with the record of individual behaviour and collective action, and their relation to a wider spectrum of social changes, including relationships, processes and institutions which are crucial to the interests of sociologists.

The historian, it has been pointed out, is not unlike the psychoanalyst, in that both aim 'to liberate man from the burden of the past by helping him to understand that past' — i.e. both are ultimately concerned to understand the individual consciousness and motive in its wider context. [4] The part played by social history in this explanation of motive is primarily concerned with the group, with the evolution of group relationships and with the adjustment of policy, action and principle to social realities. It is that part of history which is predominantly concerned with man's setting, one with which he has an active relationship (and it is with various aspects of that evolving relationship, and of men's relationship with one another, that other kinds of historian and other kinds of social scientist are concerned).

The sociologist in particular is concerned with 'the analysis and understanding of the organized structure and operations of society and the basis in values and attitudes on which individual participation in social life rests'. [5] He asks the following kinds of question: What are the relationships between different individuals and groups in a particular society? How are these relationships organized into institutions (the family, the economic and educational system, the political and legal system, custom and morality)? How are these institutions interrelated within a given social order? How does this order differ from other varieties of social order? What are the mechanisms by which it is changing? What are the consequences of changes in the structure of one set of institutions on the structure of other parts of the social system? Of course, in investigating such questions the sociologist often finds himself having to cope with economic, political or psychological considerations. But because of his own distinctive viewpoint he approaches these topics with quite a different frame of reference from that of the economist, the political scientist or the psychologist – even though he may sometimes wish to utilize the observations of other specialists in order to amplify or support his own analysis.

Although the sociologist's preoccupations can be readily distinguished from those of workers in the related social disciplines, it is important to remember that within the field of sociology itself practitioners have never all employed the same methods or shared the same assumptions. In the second half of the nineteenth century, for example, organic models of society and developmental or evolutionary morphologies were prominent. Borrowed loosely from Darwinian biology, these theoretical systems reflected a prevailing concern with the re-establishment of social order after the unsettled period of political and social upheaval earlier in the century. At the same time there was a growing preoccupation with exact scientific measurement, arising out of the urgent need to quantify and then control the social evils of industrialism and urbanization. This concern is typified in a spate of major government reports and in the pioneering survey work of Booth and Rowntree. In the twentieth century many of these early positivist models are still employed. However, important refinements in the vocabulary of sociological analysis have been introduced – notably by the American sociologists Talcott Parsons and R. K. Merton. Great advances have also been made in the sophistication of statistical techniques. On the other hand, Marxist sociologists and more recently, existentialist writers, for example, have developed a rather different approach. They have been keen to explore the more dynamic aspects of social existence, focusing for instance on the social-psychological implications of human interaction and particularly on tension and conflict situations.

It is evident that sociology shares at many points the concerns of social history. Indeed, as soon as he turns from a preoccupation with the supposed 'regularities' and 'uniformities' of a given social order to investigate the wider cultural and historical context out of which such 'uniformities' have arisen, the sociologist is obliged to take account of the range of continuities and discontinuities suggested by the social historian. Thus, as Peter Berger claims, 'a humanistic understanding of sociology leads to an almost symbiotic relationship with history'. [6] But, as Berger also demonstrates, whatever the value of historical insight, the sociologist cannot allow himself to abandon scientific principles altogether. If he were merely to pick up haphazard scraps of data it would be just as useful for us to get our information about society from poetry or novels. This is not to say that the only problems the sociologist can study are those which are capable of 'exact' measurement or which give him 'true' conclusions. On the contrary. What it means is that the sociologist's methodology is based on foundations of scientific rigour – and these must always be remembered, even in the analysis of the most subtle forms of social behaviour. For some purposes the necessary rigour may be that of exact statistical analysis, for others that of careful concept definition or theory construction. Most important of all – whatever the school to which the sociologist belongs – is the observation of definite rules of evidence. These allow other researchers to check his findings and to repeat his procedures.

The social historian is concerned constantly to piece together his details into a picture of the significant – that which describes and explains changes in the growth of institutions and the direction of human action. Involved in his work is an effort at objectivity ('something towards which the historian should strive, even if he cannot fully attain it' [7]), but history's ambiguous affiliation with both literature and the social sciences leads to what Stuart Hughes describes as 'the half-scientific, half-artistic nature' of the historians' pursuit. [8] The procedures of the historian are certainly different from those of the sociologist, but they are just as rigorous. Like those of all social scientists, the methods of the historian are open to question as to their 'scientific' character. We cannot here discuss at length the problems of defining science or classifying history or the social sciences. We can do no more than assert our commitment to a view of science which also involves a use of imagination, and to a view of method in the social sciences which is broadly scientific.

The use of such words as 'science', 'scientific' and 'rigour' should not, however, mask our view of all such analysis, in all of the social sciences, as the product of interpretation. In the early chapters of this book, for example, our aim is to point to the determinants of contemporary society. In doing so we shall, of course, be imposing a simplified structure, an interpretation. The writing of history is bound to be a highly selective operation, producing arbitrary and provisional patterns.

Men in society recognize decisive events, but it is rare for such events to represent a total end or an absolute beginning, enabling the historian with certainty to look across the whole range of human activities and say, 'Here begins a new age' or 'Here ends a form of society'. The Reformation, the Civil War and the Industrial Revolution can in some ways be described in such terms, but attention to discontinuities of this kind must not be allowed to conceal the continuities which also exist across major historical landmarks. In looking at some features of contemporary Britain we shall impose one kind of pattern. In looking at some of the processes at work in nineteenth-century English society we shall be equally selective.

E. H. Carr, discussing history as 'a process of selection in terms of historical significance', explains that the historian is, in fact, constantly selecting from 'the multiplicity of sequences of cause and effect'. In selecting those which are historically significant, 'the standard of historical significance is his ability to fit them into his pattern of rational explanation and interpretation'. [9] The historian (and the same is true of the sociologist) is holding what Carr describes as a constant 'dialogue' with facts. 'Facts' only exist at all in response to interpretation, but reality determines what kind of interpretations are possible. A historical sequence and a sociological model are approximations to reality, and both involve the hazardous pursuit of simplification and the search for 'significance'. These are hazardous processes because they are open to the subtle and unsubtle influence of ideology – that is, to the apparent certainties which derive from all attempts by society to explain and justify itself. Ideologies may be useful approximations, or they may be rigid, distorted and self-perpetuating. It is a common quality of history and sociology that they are both centrally concerned to establish relative viewpoints (relative in time and space) and are capable therefore of undermining the rigid certainties of common prejudice and overreaching ideology. They are both, in this sense, what Peter Berger proudly describes as 'debunking'. [10]

In the pursuit of 'significance' the important characteristic shared by the social historian and the sociologist is that each of them is concerned with throwing light on common phenomena. The historian, as E. H. Carr argues, 'will not in ordinary circumstances need to take cognizance of a single discontented peasant or discontented village. But millions of discontented peasants in thousands of villages are a factor which no historian will ignore.' There may be few leaders, but the multitude is essential to their success. 'Numbers', he comments, 'count in history.' [11] The social historian, more than other historians, is by definition concerned with the measurement of such numbers. The sociologist also attempts to organize evidence through 'an appeal to arithmetic where this is possible'. [12] While some features of method and approach are shared, however, the individual insights and preoccupations of the two disciplines can also enrich each other, deepening the sociologist's grasp of the present and clarifying the historian's assumptions about society and social action in his approach to the past. The sociologist is better able to guard against false cause-and-effect assumptions, and to identify what we have referred to as the 'significant' features of the social situation with which he is concerned. As C. Wright Mills points out: 'If we have a sense of real problems, as they arise out of history, the question of truth and significance tends to answer itself.' [13] The historian is also better able to guard against over-simplified assumptions about cause and effect, and about the validity of certain types of historical evidence.

With these considerations in mind, therefore, we believe it possible and right to attempt to analyse contemporary 'social structure'. The notion of social structure runs into the criticism of being conceptually static. You cannot, it is objected, pin society down as a structure; an engine or a house has a structure, but not a society. Nor can you, the criticism continues, be usefully concerned with such an insular concept as a nation's social structure, amid the increasing internationalization and interrelatedness of phenomena. The attempt to expose a structure, not of *society*, but of *a given society*, seems to us justified, however, on two main grounds. First, social theory, comparative analyses and an awareness of vast historical processes do not conjure away the realities of any given society or the obligation to contribute to an understanding of how it works. Secondly, however inaccurate a given piece of social description may be, it is a necessary effort at approximation. We consider it important to organize this kind of conducted tour of our contemporary society, in spite of the theoretical hurdles involved and the danger of tendentious description. Sharper and more reliable descriptions than those which are common currency need to be available.

We are concerned, then, with social description as an awakening, a critical (or, in Berger's term, a 'debunking') activity. Not unlike poetry, as defined by Shelley in *The Four Ages of Poetry*, such descriptions make 'familiar objects be as if they were not familiar'; they purge 'from our inward sight the film of familiarity which obscures from us the wonder of our being'. Professor Tom Burns pursued a similar point in an inaugural lecture on 'Social Explanation'. Sociology, he considered, pursues not so much the right kind of knowledge as the right kind of questions – questions which arise from doubt, which in turn 'arises from a discrepancy between facts, or between accepted interpretations'. From that starting point, sociologists attempt to build an elusive but eventually obvious portrait of reality, and Burns points to the many examples of research which demonstrate what – it appears afterwards – should have been pretty obvious at the time (for example, Booth's efforts to show that a third of the working-class population of London was living in poverty, or Rowntree's to show the proportion of families living below subsistence level):

> The astonishing feature of the *Our Towns* report on the condition of children evacuated from city slums in 1940 was not the squalor and unseemliness of the children but the blank ignorance of all other sections of society about them and the circumstances of urban life which had produced them. Within the last few weeks, Professor Townsend's survey of the millions of families in Britain living at or below the subsistence level represented by national assistance has come, again, as a shock. The results of Harrington's survey of the incidence of poverty in the United States three years ago came as a shock. Now, they are the stock in trade of the week-end political speaker.

The traditional role of descriptive sociology, Burns therefore deduces, has been 'to point out what is immediately obvious to everybody as soon as the task of collecting and presenting the facts has been done'. It is in this sense that sociology is a critical activity. It enables the familiar objects of everyday living to be seen from another angle of vision. The purpose of sociology, Burns decides, 'is to achieve an understanding of social behaviour and social institutions which is different from that current among the people through whose conduct the institutions exist; an understanding which is not merely different but new and better. The practice of sociology is criticism.' [14] It lifts the film of familiarity.

This, of course, does no more than suggest our avenue of approach to the landscape of sociology. We have not attempted to account fully for the different kinds of theoretical models which are available in contemporary sociological thought. Nor have we been able to give an adequate description of the main concepts which sociologists use. We have throughout, however, in our deliberate adoption of an eclectic approach to the selection of material and in choosing between different kinds of evidence and explanation, tried to be alert both to our own biases and to the rival ideological claims implicit in the various types of sociological analysis and theories of history that we have used. We have accepted the Webbs' view that history, 'to be either interesting or significant, must be written from a point of view; and this is less likely to be harmful the more plainly it is avowed'. [15]

It would be impossible here to 'avow' in any detail our own points of view. It is only fair, however, that we should give some broad hints. We accept, to begin with, the inevitability of intellectual 'commitment'. At its most straightforward this means a commitment to unprejudiced analysis in order to combat prejudice, a form of commitment illustrated by a famous study of *The Authoritarian Personality*, the authors of which declared that they did not believe

> that there is a short cut to education which will eliminate the long and often circuitous road of painstaking research and theoretical analysis . . . the authors are imbued with the conviction that the sincere and systematic scientific elucidation of a phenomenon of such great historical meaning can contribute directly to an amelioration of the cultural atmosphere in which hatred breeds. [16]

Such a commitment also means a refusal to bow before empiricism pure and simple, a constant attempt to detect the conceptual, ideological framework within which we all work. 'To denounce ideologies in general', says E. H. Carr, 'is to set up an ideology of one's own.' [17]

Our avowed commitment is to a scepticism about efforts to demonstrate that we are moving steadily into a homogenized form of society troubled only by international economic and financial maladjustments, intruding ideologies, indolent workers and doctrinaire radicals of one variety or another. Somewhere embedded in our analysis is a suspicion that radical students, child poverty campaigners, convention-breakers, rebels and protesters of many kinds are closer to understanding the reality of our society than are their critics (not all of whom are on the political right). We do not believe that we are all middle-class now, or that our society has come near to solving the problems of democracy or welfare which demanded solution after the Second World War. We believe that, in spite of the considerable advances made in specific directions, our society continues to tolerate major injustices, in-humanities and distorted priorities. We are cynical enough to consider that the system of government has been distorted to the point at which democracy as it is and might be has been seriously undermined. The responses of parties and authorities have fallen so far short of that merited by the challenge (social, national and international) of recent decades that cynicism about political processes and public attitudes has inevitably become an entrenched feature of our society. The international (including British) student protest movement, for instance, has in part been a response to this situation – an attempt to reassert, sometimes blindly and arrogantly, the possibility of ideals which have disappeared under the postures and hallucinations of American and Soviet power-mania, sectarian ideologies of many kinds, and Labour and Conservative party routines.

We are not, however, writing a manifesto: we are merely responding to the injunction to declare ourselves. To some questions of the strengths and weaknesses of our society we shall return in our final chapter. Perhaps it is enough for us to confess here that the world we analyse in this book seems to us a disappointing place.

NOTES

1 'Sociology and history', in A. T. WELFORD et al. (eds.) Society, pp. 91–2 (London, 1962).
2 Social History and Literature, p. 12 (Leicester, 1959).
3 W. H. B. COURT 'Economic history' in H. P. R. FINBERG (ed.) Approaches to History, p. 20 (London, 1962; 1965 edition).
4 H. STUART HUGHES 'History and psychoanalysis', History as Art and as Science, pp. 47–8, 63–4 (New York, 1964; 1965 edition).
5 M. STEIN and A. VIDICH (eds.) Sociology on Trial, p. 1 (New Jersey, 1963).
6 Invitation to Sociology, p. 191 (New York, 1963; 1966 edition).
7 E. H. CARR The New Society, p. 102 (London, 1951; 1965 edition).
8 History as Art and as Science, p. 3. Hughes's chapter on 'What the historian thinks he knows' is an excellent discussion of this theme. See also 'History as science and art' in A. L. ROWSE The Use of History (London, 1946).
9 What is History?, p. 105 (London, 1961; 1964 edition).
10 Invitation to Sociology, pp. 51–5.
11 What is History, p. 50.
12 G. KITSON CLARK The Making of Victorian England, p. 14 (London, 1962).
13 The Sociological Imagination, p. 72 (New York, 1959).
14 'Sociological explanation', British Journal of Sociology, Vol. 18, December 1967, pp. 362–7.
15 Quoted in H. L. BEALES 'The new Poor Law' in E. M. CARUS-WILSON Essays in Economic History, III, p. 181 (London, 1962).
16 T. W. ADORNO et al. The Authoritarian Personality, I, p. ix (New York, 1950; 1967 edition).
17 The New Society, p. 16.

Note on Contents and Layout

The combination of historical and sociological description could have been organized in two ways: (*a*) thematically, following through the progress of particular ideas, structures and institutions; or (*b*) in broadly historical and contemporary divisions. Both present difficulties, the first in separating related phenomena too sharply, and the second in presenting apparent breaks between the historical and contemporary analyses. We have chosen, we believe in the interests of clarity, the latter arrangement.

Chapters 1 to 5 are, generally speaking, concerned with social history, and Chapters 6 to 10 with sociology, but within each chapter we have tried to anticipate or refer back to relevant discussions in other chapters. At the end of each chapter we have indicated where else in the book a discussion of the themes of that chapter can be found. It should, therefore, be possible to refer across easily from the historical to the sociological discussion of, for example, urban growth, social class or education.

It should be emphasized, however, that the book is intended to facilitate the progress from historical to contemporary analysis and to relate the two.

We have confined ourselves fairly strictly to the implications of the word 'English' in the title of this book. Major historical differences in, for example, the administrative, Poor Law and educational systems of Scotland have made it impossible to try to trace the story alongside that of English society. Wales has, by and large, shared the administrative structure of England, but an account of the particular history of, for example, Welsh education and culture would have involved us in discussion far beyond a manageable frame of reference. In broad outline the basic trends in urban and population growth, and the main aspects of contemporary society we have considered, apply to a considerable degree throughout the United Kingdom.

There are other omissions. We have found it necessary to omit any real consideration of the history of agriculture and crime and punishment, or any serious concern with religious beliefs and forms of worship. Similarly, we have had to omit any detailed account of the contemporary social services, although their earlier history is discussed as part of our effort to illustrate the forces which have influenced modern attitudes towards social analysis and social policy.

Our earlier chapters refer more frequently to dates, laws and statistics than do later ones – because of the need to take short cuts through detailed historical material – but we have tried throughout to focus attention on broad developments and realities, and to suggest some useful perspectives, historical and contemporary, on modern English society.

THE  CRISIS.

[Institution of the Industrious Classes, Gray's-Inn Road.]

THE CRISIS; OR THE CHANGE FROM ERROR AND MISERY, TO TRUTH AND HAPPINESS.

"IF WE CANNOT YET RECONCILE ALL OPINIONS, LET US NOW ENDEAVOUR TO UNITE ALL HEARTS."

VOL. I.—No. 1.]   EDITED BY ROBERT OWEN.——SATURDAY, APRIL 14, 1832.   [ONE PENNY.

PROSPECTUS.

IT is now evident to every one who observes passing events, and who reflects upon the new public opinion which is arising throughout the various Nations of the World, that some great Change in the condition of man, either for good or for evil, is about to take place—in fact, that a *momentous* CRISIS is at hand. Be it our task to discern the signs of the times—to watch the progress of this Crisis, and to direct it for good instead of evil. For good and evil, in a pre-eminent degree, are now before the world; and it cannot longer defer making a choice whether it shall adopt general measures to attain and secure the former, or to ensure a continuance and increase of the latter.

The time is immediately before us, when either reason, or physical violence of the worst character, must attain the mastery in the future direction of the governments which are now deemed the most civilized.

This is the important Crisis now before us. Calm reflection, devoid of prejudice in favour of old errors, will convince every one, that the real, substantial, permanent interest of mankind will be promoted, by now substituting reason for our guide and director, instead of mystery, fraud, or violence.

It is our intention not only to watch the symptoms of the great change now in active progress, but to aid and assist to the utmost of our power in giving it such a direction as we believe will ensure the well-being, the well-doing, and the happiness of all ranks equally, without regard to the artificial divisions which now separate and divide man from man throughout the world, greatly to the injury of all, and without real benefit to any.

"THE CRISIS" will therefore be no party paper: it will be occupied in developing, in plain simple language, the great principles of human nature, and the means of applying them, with equal simplicity, in practice, to all the affairs of domestic life, and to society in all its ramifications.

"THE CRISIS" will upon all occasions *discourage religious animosities, political rancour, and individual contention: its fixed purpose being to promote real charity, kindness, and union among all classes, sects, and parties.*

All we require from our readers is, that they will endeavour to divest their minds of early prejudices or prepossessions, and candidly judge for themselves, from the data we shall place before them, of the truth of our opinions, and of the beneficial consequences to which they will lead in practice.

We do not mean to offer to our readers any of the excitabilities arising from personal contests, or criminal proceedings; but we hope to create a more lively and lasting interest, by exhibiting the mode by which a new world of happiness is to be attained and secured for the human race.

We must not, however, conclude this Prospectus without stating, most distinctly and unequivocally, that one great object which we have at heart, is first, *to put a stop to the rapid sinking of the Industrious Classes into poverty, crime, and wretchedness,* which the progress of science injudiciously directed has produced, and then to explain the mode by which they may be gradually elevated in the scale of society, in proportion as they can be placed under better circumstances, to be well educated and beneficially employed.

Thus shall we aid in removing Error and Misery, and in pro-

1

The Making of Nineteenth-century Society

The sequence of events which marked the transition from pre-industrial, predominantly rural, eighteenth-century Britain was a complex one. There are symbolic events which act as milestones in the process: the various technical advances in the cotton industry in the 1760s and 1770s, the harnessing of steam power to drive machinery in the 1780s, the first population census of 1801, the end of the Napoleonic wars in 1815, the opening of the Liverpool–Manchester railway in 1830, the first Reform Act of 1832, the Poor Law Amendment Act of 1834, the beginnings of Chartism in 1836, the repeal of the Corn Laws in 1846 and the Great Exhibition of 1851. The Industrial Revolution of the late eighteenth and early nineteenth centuries was not, however, as abrupt and as all-pervasive as the term (and some of these events) make it at first sight appear.

There is, of course, an inevitable time lag between discovery and application in a society with poor technology and communications, and in which human beings are not adjusted to the expectation of constant change. Watt's steam engine, for example, was built in 1769: a steam engine was first used to operate a spinning mill in 1785. The power loom was invented in 1787 and became economic in the cotton industry at the beginning of the nineteenth century, but the climax of the hand-loom weavers' fight for survival did not come until the 1830s and 1840s. The first Factory Acts, covering pauper apprentices, were passed in 1802 and 1819, but not until the Act of 1833 introduced the principle of inspection were even the beginnings of a wide and effective system of factory regulation laid. In many important respects industry disrupted family economy and family structure. Child employment, for example, was nothing new, but its intensification, in factory conditions, made it a representative, socially disruptive feature of early industrial Britain. There was at work here what Neil Smelser discusses in terms of the 'structural differentiation of the family', and yet the process, he stresses, was drawn out long beyond the establishment of the factory system. Parental control over children *in factories* was still a reality into the 1830s. [1] The ripples of abrupt events are not always as large and as far-reaching as might be expected. Agriculture remained the largest single employer of labour for most of the nineteenth century. The first 'middle-class reform' of Parliament, in 1832, did not materially alter its class composition. Nor, it must be remembered, is change itself always as abrupt as it appears. There were manufacturing industries and factories before the Industrial Revolution. There were local Improvement Acts (and improvements) before the first national Public Health Act in 1848.

In a number of critical respects, however, we are dealing in the early nineteenth century with a *changing* society of an entirely new kind. Pre-industrial society was not without social mobility, although such mobility was only marginal, and in very real ways this was a static society. Peter Laslett argues that what he calls the 'one-class society' of pre-industrial England knew a certain amount of mobility, and yet *structural* change was negligible. [2] Although the eighteenth century was not a totally static society, people behaved predominantly as if it was. After, say, 1790, Britain did not suddenly become a mobile or an open society, but the ripples of radical ideas and action made it clear that more people were beginning to behave as if it ought to be.

Pre-industrial society was, to begin with, economically stagnant. Economic growth was 'either painfully slow or spasmodic' or 'readily reversible'. Before the second half of the eighteenth century 'people had no reason to *expect*' growth. The ordinary man

> saw little evidence of economic growth within his own lifetime and no improvement that could not be eliminated within a single year by the incidence of a bad harvest or a war or an epidemic. Thus in pre-industrial England, as in many of today's pre-industrial societies, the normal long-term rate of growth in real incomes per head was under half of one per cent per annum, and it was almost as common for the economy to slide into decline as it was for it to grow. [3]

Eighteenth-century Britain had none of the national movements and organizations which in the nineteenth century became agencies of change. 'In the eighteenth century the characteristic instrument of social purpose', says T. S. Ashton, 'was not the individual or the State, but the club.' [4] Nor was it, he could have added, the *movement*. The radical tradition of the eighteenth century did not find form in the organized popular political and social movement typical of the nineteenth, but in the extra-parliamentary association, aimed at the correction of an abuse, and accompanied on occasion by crowds and riots. Although the society which produced these phenomena was not entirely static, the eighteenth-century labour disputes, riots and reform agitation were not imbued with the sense of purpose and solidarity which marked, for example, political radicalism, Chartism or trade unionism in the nineteenth century.

SOCIAL AND POLITICAL CHANGE

The breakdown in the stability of English society can be traced most clearly in and from the 1790s. We shall return to the economic bases of this change; it is with aspects of social and political change that we are first concerned. The outbreak of the French Revolution in 1789, whatever routes it later took and whatever responses it later provoked, was the point around which not only new radicalisms but new ideas in many fields began to take coherent shape. Political radicalism, the programme of principled argument for the reform of the ossified aristocrats' and landowners' parliament, and for a wider measure of popular representation, had its most recent roots in the agitation which had begun at the end of the 1770s, and which had been directed towards the enfranchisement of the property owners. 'Representation co-extensive with direct taxation' had become, together with annual parliaments, one of the main slogans of the more radical reformers. No one had contributed more than Major John Cartwright to the demand for 'pulling down a Despotism and reinstating public Liberty', [5] but the appeal was to ancient rights, to a concept of 'the People' which nineteenth-century reality profoundly altered, and to 'reform from discussion . . . a recovery of lost liberties from a diffusion of knowledge'. [6] This was an eighteenth-century Enlightenment approach that was to run down into the sands of working-class experience, especially in the 1830s. It was part of the disappearing world of the extra-parliamentary association and the political club. [7]

With the organized, vociferous political movement, including the pioneer London Corresponding Society founded in 1792, the modern political world began. A tradition of popular radicalism was born and a step towards a more alert society was made. With the realization that it was possible for the popular will to assert itself, for tyrannies to be overthrown, for democratic principles to prevail, new aspirations became possible and explicit in the 1790s. Tom Paine's *Rights of Man* (1791–2), William Godwin's *Political Justice* (1793) and Mary Wollstonecraft's *Vindication of the Rights of Woman* (1792), for example, were public and influential expressions of a range of newly activated responses to a lack of rights and justice. Popular, organized political radicalism was one of the results. The body of rational analysis and objectives built up by the eighteenth-century Enlightenment, together with emergent Benthamite efforts towards social reform, came to be accompanied by popular movements, formulating new, precise and far-reaching aims. Action and Utopia became, for a long moment of British history, intertwined.

Human aspirations began to be defined on a wider front. The movements which, in the 1830s and 1840s for instance, sought to humanize industrial society and to achieve a greater measure of popular democracy were torn between two priorities – political action and social organization, parliamentary reform and, for example, the re-ordering of society on the basis of co-operative communities or trade-union co-operative production. It was too early in the 1790s for alternatives to be defined in this way, but alongside (and very frequently within) political programmes, objectives were being defined which indicated how far and how quickly it was possible to travel from the stable society. Around subjects like landownership, popular education, marriage and the status of women, the role of the press and the nature of power – not only in the State, but also, for example, in the Church – new forms of articulate opinion made a dramatic appearance. Society as a whole was not, of course, captured by such opinion. Articulate attacks on aristo-cracy, privilege and landownership, Mary Wollstonecraft writing on women, Godwin on the State and Paine on human rights, for example, were heard by significant percentages of the population, widely enough to make it impossible for assumptions about a hierarchical or pyramidal society ever to be held so impregnably again. Social mobility was no longer a fact of marginal transition from landownership to aristocracy, from commerce to landownership, from aristocracy to the Church or the Church to aristocracy, from craftsman to master: it was now an idea in the market place. You are no longer, men were told, trapped within the limits of a prescribed status. You have rights, and you can, as men in society, aspire to be educated, to change your conditions, to make independent judgements and contest the rules and usages that paralyse you. The response showed that the new political and social radicalisms were making explicit the objectives which men were already beginning to formulate for themselves. The responses, of course, were twofold: broadly speaking, they were those of the unprivileged, whom they suited, and among sections of whom traditions of radical ideas continued to be strengthened into the nine-teenth century, and those of the privileged (with distinguished exceptions), whom they did not suit, and who framed, or acquiesced, in the reactions and oppressions of 1794 and after.

Out of these responses and situations came compromises and failures. Harold Laski, looking at the relevance of the French Revolution for the western world, considered that the precise outcome of that 'gigantic upheaval' was to bring 'the middle-class business man to power; and its chief con-sequence has been the abolition of that political privilege which was the chief obstacle to his ascent'. [8] Though some of the radicals were conscious of this possible outcome, the movements towards the Reform Act of 1832 in England had a wider understanding of political privilege – though in the event what they ultimately achieved was the limited shift of power which Laski described. Popular reform, therefore, was impregnated at different stages with a sense not only of idealism or protest, but also of failure and betrayal.

SOCIAL ATTITUDES

By the end of the eighteenth century social tensions had taken on a new dimension. The trials of the radical leaders in 1794, the organized antiradicalism of the following years and the Combination Acts of 1799 and 1800 were the reverse side of the development from the isolated calls of 'Wilkes and Liberty!' to the organized effort of popular reform. They both mark the opening of new political and class confrontations. In addition, however, to political organization, social aspirations and the opposition they encountered, an important new focus of discussion is also to be found at this point – the need for social conciliation, the need to guard against the upheavals that would result from allowing new developments to run their course. The new developments were, in this respect, not just new ideas and objectives, but the unregulated growth of new industries and towns; and the focal point of the early discussion was education.

Amid the bewilderments and uncertainties of the new tempo of social change, discussions of education had entirely new terms of reference. The increasing diversification of skills taking place as a result of new forms of organization in agriculture and industry, the harnessing of new technologies and the exigencies of urban life were leading to social interdependence on a wider scale. The emergence of nation-wide popular movements, the increasing importance of the press as a means of mass communication, and the new scale of social administration needed to cope with the new problems, were only some of the associated factors influencing the discussion. Urban growth and urban poverty, in particular, provoked the question of social defence against urban ignorance. This was the first crude debate about mass communications.

The debate took place between those who argued that popular education fomented discontent and taught people to aspire beyond their stations, and those who argued that a measure of education, enabling children to read their scriptures and to learn the rules of social obedience, was a necessary form of social self-protection. The Sunday School movement which spread at the beginning of the 1780s, and the monitorial schools which grew out of the beginning made by Joseph Lancaster in Borough Road in 1798, were attempts to come to terms with the realities of the new society. The Charity Schools of the eighteenth century had been a limited exercise in the education of the children of the worthy poor in elementary literacy, simple skills and obedience. The monitorial schools, in which a single teacher, spreading rudimentary knowledge downwards through child-monitors, could teach, or rather govern, a school of hundreds, even a thousand, were more appropriate symbols of the onset of mass society. Sponsored by the Church (through the National Society for Promoting the Education of the Poor in the Principles of the Established Church) and the Dissenting bodies (largely through the British and Foreign School Society), they set the scene for the later debate between the advocates and antagonists of State intervention in education. Involvement by the State did not, in fact, occur until the first vote of government funds in 1833, and did not result in a consensus between the parties involved until the first national Elementary Education Act in 1870. Against every effort to promote popular education in the period from 1790 to the 1830s, however, some form of resistance was offered. The Methodists, for example, who ran Sunday schools and interested themselves in education were labelled insurrectionaries. During and following the Napoleonic wars all who educated were accused from some quarter or other of undermining the stability of society. The expansion of the provision of elementary education, therefore, from the end of the eighteenth century, was a matter of voluntary effort.

Adjustment to all these new social realities was not easy; the dimensions of the problems were unprecedented, and the scale of the response required new ingenuities and imaginations to begin to cope with them. The Speenhamland Poor Law system of 1795, which sought primarily to relieve agricultural poverty by supplementing wages on a scale of benefit adjusted to the price of bread, was one of the symbolic gestures of the old society, a society which could still see itself bound by the responsibilities of community. The period between 1795 and the new Poor Law of 1834 was that of the Napoleonic wars and their aftermath, of slowing down or breakdown in handicraft industries, of towns mushrooming beyond the credibility of men, and problems which seemed almost insoluble. It was consequently the period of the Utopian solution, of the millennium-round-the-corner. In religion, in political reform, in social organization, there were men searching for *the* answer. For all radicals, there was The Vote. For Joanna Southcott and Richard Brothers there was a Second Coming. For Robert Owen there was Co-operative Community. For phrenologists there was a proper understanding of the Mental Faculties. All were fanciful, but in their proper context none was ridiculous. And after the Berkshire Justices in 1795 had made Speenhamland synonymous in the eyes of some with the encouragement of idleness, the millennium which relentlessly gained the ascendant among influential philosophers, economists and Whig and radical politicians in their discussions of poverty and the road to a more just society, was *laissez-faire.*

The important point about *laissez-faire,* with its philosophy of State

2 Lancaster monitorial school, 1829.

non-intervention and the self-adjustment of relationships (in industry or in the market), is that it evolved, through Adam Smith, Bentham, Malthus, James and John Stuart Mill, with various convolutions, as British society's first widely accepted philosophy of *change*. It recognized the changing society, and offered what it considered a rational, humane basis for social policy. It was never total in its opposition to collective intervention (and usually, for example, considered education a proper subject for State action) and never courageous enough to pursue the full logic of its views (both Malthus and Edwin Chadwick would have liked to abolish poor relief, but could only bring themselves to advocate a policy of deterring people from applying for it). The utilitarian philosophy of *laissez-faire* was a philosophy of change and of progress, of efficiency and happiness. It was a complex compromise. Men should be left free. Legislation should enable them to be left free, and prevent interference with their freedom. A framework of rational central government and legislation was therefore necessary, even if it appeared to contradict the doctrine of self-interest. A. V. Dicey, in his *Law and Public Opinion in England in the Nineteenth Century* (1905), a book which for a long time dominated analyses of social policy in the nineteenth century, saw it as a philosophy of individualism, in contrast with the collectivism which grew out of the legislation enforced by 'Tory humanitarianism' (of which Lord Shaftesbury was the prototype), and which was ultimately, Dicey considered, to turn into the misguided doctrines of socialism. But Dicey did not see the flaw in Benthamite *laissez-faire*. [9] It was not thoroughgoing:

> There is no real reconciliation between the argument of the natural, and the argument of the artificial, identity of interests. The one supposes that every individual by promoting his own interests promotes those of the whole society. The other supposes that there are some individuals who by promoting their own interest damage those of somebody else. The maxim, 'the greatest happiness of the greatest number', was a confession that the two arguments could not be reconciled, for it admits by implication that the interests pursued by each individual do not necessarily lead to the 'greatest good for all'.

Benthamism therefore had a 'great internal contradiction': it led 'either to complete bureaucracy or complete anarchism'. [10] In practice it led to an inescapable compromise, encouraging the individual to pursue his own interests, but national and local government to promote collectivist solutions. The 1834 Poor Law Amendment Act, the 1835 Municipal Corporations Act, and the Factory Acts of 1833 and after were *laissez-faire* compromises of this kind. Bentham had said in effect that existing forms of State regulation were harmful because they did not promote a harmony of interests. 'He wanted to sweep most of the existing regulations away, and he believed that most things would be better unregulated than ill-regulated as they were'. [11] Or, it should be added, as they *might be*. Any form of regulation, therefore, was a departure from pure doctrine, and departures were many in the society which saw itself to a large degree as a *laissez-faire* State.

The features we have suggested so far offer a tentative picture of some of the processes of change, largely in terms of human aspiration and assumptions about status and mobility; they also indicate some of the awareness of these new processes of change, which had not been present to any significant extent in the Britain of, say, 1780. They indicate some of the sources of the momentum of modern Britain. There were, of course, other sources, and an intricate point of historical discussion is the relative priority to be given to one factor or another in determining the growth of industrial Britain. This attempt to establish priorities is characteristic of any historical or sociological discussion. The role of will and consciousness, of the religious and philosophical assumptions by which people's lives are or have been governed, the role of economic laws and of the ownership of the means of production – all such widely different considerations are involved in the discussion of, for instance, the causes of the Industrial Revolution or the existence of class in the twentieth century. The role of Marxism has been to stress economic-productive determinants as decisive in social change. The role of modern sociology, both Marxist and non-Marxist, has been to suggest a wider range of determinants that need to be considered in this process.

THE INDUSTRIAL REVOLUTION

The economic facts of the Industrial Revolution, suggested Max Weber, are meaningless without an understanding of the framework of belief in which it took place. He sees the central fact of modern capitalism as having its foundations in certain, largely Calvinist, assumptions about the desirability of profit – assumptions which make worldly activity possible, and which therefore explain the important role of nonconformity in early industrial and commercial expansion. The kernel of the argument about Protestant asceticism runs as follows:

> . . . asceticism looked upon the pursuit of wealth as an end in itself as highly reprehensible; but the attainment of it as a fruit of labour in a calling was a sign of God's blessing . . . the religious valuation of restless, continuous, systematic work in a worldly calling, as the means to asceticism . . . must have been the most powerful conceivable lever for the expansion of that attitude toward life which we have here called the spirit of capitalism.

What this attitude did, Weber suggests, was sanction the acquisition of wealth, at the same time as *imposing restraints on its consumption*. The inevitable result was the accumulation and productive investment of capital. 'The Puritan outlook . . . stood at the cradle of the modern economic man.' [12]

This is one factor – and in sketching early developments towards an industrial society, and the reasons for these developments, there are many others, notably the factors directly affecting industrial improvement and expansion.

Changes in agriculture affected developments in a series of ways, most obviously in making it possible to supply a larger population, differently distributed. Historians have had to modify some of the ideas that used to be held about the reasons for the dramatic improvements in agriculture that took place in the second half of the eighteenth century, and about the effects of the enclosures movement. Neither, it is certain, took place so abruptly or had the abrupt effects that were for a long time assumed. The agricultural revolution of the eighteenth century released 'the latent powers of the soil on a scale that was new in human history; but it was not accomplished by means of a mechanical revolution'. Nor, it is suggested, was this achieved through 'a ruthless reduction of the rural population as a prelude to the formation of an industrial proletariat . . . there is no reason to think that the labour force engaged in agricultural operations fell'. The revolution lay in the manner of farming, the spread of 'alternate' agriculture, a process accelerated in the second half of the eighteenth century. Even though the processes were perhaps more cumulative and less dramatic than previously thought, this departure from traditional practice

> marks a new agricultural epoch, and its acceleration in the second half of the eighteenth century in the form of the classical enclosure movement and the first unmistakable steps by the agricultural pioneers towards 'high farming', mark the opening of the Agricultural Revolution just as surely as factory production marks the dawn of a new industrial age. From this time, the Agricultural Revolution reveals itself as an indispensable and integral part of the Industrial Revolution . . . [13]

Of the Industrial Revolution itself we can do no more here than construct a simple economic-historical model. The cotton industry, unlike the woollen industry, was unhampered by regulations; it had available supplies of raw material, available supplies of labour, a suitable climate in both Lancashire and Scotland, and convenient resources of water and fuel. It made the leap forward which was most dramatic in social terms. Cotton was also the industry in which technical innovation was most sought and achieved, and it was able, slowly, to harness the power of steam. Coal was a traditional industry and capable of expansion. Estimated production in 1750 was 4·8 million tons, and by 1800 it had more than doubled (to 10 million tons). By the end of the eighteenth century cotton had made a visible impact on the economic geography of Britain, and precipitated the great concentration of population in northern England that was an outstanding feature of Britain's nineteenth-century history, affecting both the redistribution of population inside England, and immigration into England, most notably from Ireland. The impact of coal was in this respect less direct, although it became increasingly a focus of awareness of the nature of industrial society. By the 1860s Matthew Arnold could complain that coal had been spoken of as 'the real basis of our national greatness; if our coal runs short, there is an end of the greatness of England ... what an unsound habit of mind it must be which makes us talk of things like coal or iron as constituting the greatness of England'. [14]

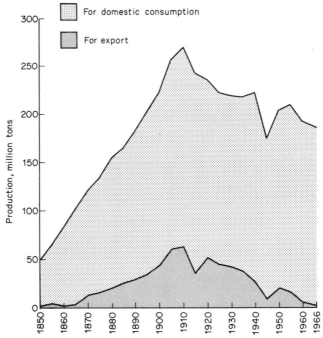

Fig. 1 Coal production in Great Britain, 1850–1966. (See also Table 18, p. 326.)
After Mitchell and Deane, 1962, G. C. Allen, 1959, and Annual Abstract of
Statistics, *1967.*

The role of the iron industry was, in the short run, less spectacular, but in the long term more fundamental to industrial growth than cotton. Henry Cort's puddling process made cheap wrought iron available from the beginning of the 1780s, enabling fifteen times as much iron (of high quality) to be produced by the same amount of power, in the same time. The ancient use of timber gave place to coal; coal and iron together made a fundamental contribution to the new sort of 'greatness of England'.

Innovation and invention obviously played crucial parts in the cumulative processes that led to the industrial break-through of the last decades of the eighteenth century. Equally obviously, each of the industrial developments we have mentioned, and all of the technical developments within them, had repercussions of a major order inside and outside the industry concerned. Arkwright's water frame (1769) for spinning meant factory production in an entirely new sense. Watt's steam engine (1769), later developed with rotary motion (1781), made it possible to erect mills in towns. Cort's puddling process not only contributed to the expansion of the coal industry, but, at a later stage of industrial growth, made railways possible. There was, therefore, at the end of the eighteenth century a cluster of inventions and technical developments, in agriculture as well as industry, which contributed saliently to the processes we describe as the Industrial Revolution.

There is, however, a complex of other economic and commercial factors to be borne in mind. There were skills and resources available to be utilized, experience of banking (the number of country banks rose from 100 in 1780 to 370 in 1800) and business enterprise to be drawn upon. There were during the eighteenth century periods of accelerated capital formation. There were periods of good harvest, and there was an upward trend in population.

A vital link in this interwoven set of developments was transport. On the basis of roads industrialization could not have gone so far so quickly. From the first Turnpike Act of 1663, attempts at improvement in road conditions had been slowly made, but the results were uneven, often short-lived and frequently non-existent. The completion of the Duke of Bridgewater's canal linking Worsley and Manchester in 1761, reducing the price of coal in Manchester by half, and then of the extension (in 1767) linking Manchester and Liverpool, opened an era of canal construction which was long enough to play a considerable part in the process of transforming Britain's undeveloped 'interior'. With the advent of the canals 'England ceased to be hollow'. [15] Britain in general also ceased, economically, to be a confederation of relatively self-dependent regions. The history of industrialization, in the view of H. L. Beales, 'is the history of integration – the unification of the single society'. [16] The construction of a canal network did more than anything else to fill up the 'hollow' and at the same time made a major contribution to economic development by providing a source of experienced manpower for the building of the railways. The industrial Revolution may have been, in its first phase, predominantly a change in methods of production, but the canal system was an indispensable feature of it.

The details which add up to the Industrial Revolution, therefore, included but were not entirely conditioned by scientific and technical advances. Such advances do not in themselves explain the revolution. Only in conjunction with other considerations, including the history of British overseas trade, the Protestant ethic and resources of human ingenuity, do these advances explain what made Britain the first industrial nation. [17]

POPULATION

As the first population census was taken in 1801 and as information culled from sources before that date is defective, the related and vitally important discussion of population trends at the end of the eighteenth century presents us with a double set of problems. The first is simply to try to reconstruct population changes, and the second is to account for them. [18]

Attempts to use numerical techniques in studying the history of population and social structure in pre-industrial (and to some extent nineteenth-century) England are now being seriously pursued, and the results are hoped to be of

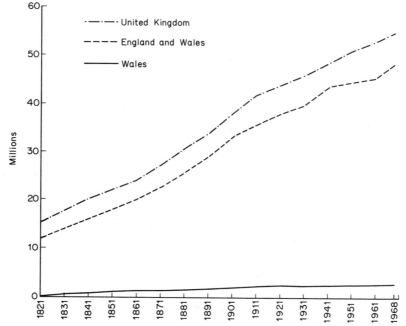

Fig. 2 Population growth, 1821–1968. (See also Table 1, p. 310.) After Mitchell and Deane, 1962, and Annual Abstract of Statistics, *1969.*

significance to intellectual and political, social and economic historians. Population trends in their broad contours, and in their implications for family and social structure, the relevance of the growth of towns, occupational patterns and styles of life, are of central importance to analyses of social change. [19]

It is likely that the population of Great Britain at the beginning of the eighteenth century was of the order of 6·5 million. In 1750, at the beginning of the upward trend that was to be maintained right through the nineteenth and twentieth centuries, it was about 8 million. The census of 1801 reported a population of 10·5 million. In the next twenty years over 3·5 million were added to the population. The significance of these facts, if facts they are, is that conditions conspired from approximately the 1740s to produce the possibility of a sustained increase in population. There had been increases in population, of course, in previous centuries, but these had been 'speedily cancelled by a single peak in the death rate. The difference was that the growth that we date from the 1740s was *not* reversed and indeed it accelerated to unprecedented levels in the 1780s and went on accelerating to a peak rate of growth in the decade 1811–21.' [20]

An increase (or decrease) in population can be the result of only two summary factors – birth rate and death rate (leaving aside here the third and less significant factor of migration). Prolonged controversies have raged around the likely contribution of one or both of these factors to the upward population curve of the eighteenth century. For a long time it was held that significant influences towards a fall in the mortality rate were the most likely explanation, especially as only a slight fall is necessary to have considerable long-term repercussions. It was held that improved food supplies, resulting from a sequence of good harvests, partly from improved farming methods, as well as improved hygiene and medical facilities, were the main contributory causes. Medical history no longer upholds this view, although attempts are still made to demonstrate that health factors influenced, or may have influenced, a decrease in the death rate. [21] The more likely explanations appear to be related to a higher birth rate, since it is known that population grew in this period even where there was no improvement in or access to any medical facilities:

> It would seem ... that increase in population, even in England, must have been largely a rural phenomenon deriving from causes to be found in the countryside, where access to doctors, hospitals and clinics would be least easy. This endorses the lesson, not only of Connaught but of other parts of Ireland as well, that there could be large increases of population in areas in which the improvement of medical facilities in the late eighteenth and early nineteenth centuries were unlikely to have had much effect. [22]

The demand for agricultural labour, the 'family allowances' built into Speenhamland poor relief, as well as greater resistance to epidemic, were likely factors in raising the birth rate, although earlier marriage was the most likely. Edward Thompson, pointing to the weakening of taboos against early marriage, the decline in 'living in' among farm servants and apprentices, genetic selection of the most fertile, and other possible explanations, reflects that 'the arguments are complex and are best left, for the time being, with the demographers'. [23]

INDUSTRIALIZATION AND DEMOCRACY

Industrializing (and, as we shall see in the next chapter, urbanizing) Britain was rooted, therefore, in profound processes of social change. We have glanced at some of the starting points of the enormous developments that were to take place in population, the economy and society between the end of the eighteenth century and the period with which we are primarily concerned, from the middle of the nineteenth century onwards.

Between 1801 and 1851 the population of Great Britain doubled, to attain nearly 21 million. In 1780 some 40 to 45 per cent of the labour force was employed in agriculture, and some 25 per cent in mining, manufacture and building. By 1851 the figures were 21 per cent and 42 per cent respectively. Urban problems were coming more and more into prominence. By the end of the 1830s government had committed itself to the regulation of poor relief, to the assistance and inspection (though not control) of education, to the protection of child and female (though not adult male) labour. By the 1850s the growing commercial and professional middle class had added new public schools and London University to the traditional public and grammar school network (plus Oxford and Cambridge), which was unable, or unwilling, to cater for the new demands. Scotland, of course, had its parochial schools and four universities, though all of these underwent their decline, crises and inquiries in the early nineteenth century.

The date chart of the first half of the century would be, to cover the range of our interests, immense and meaningless. Even to look for the stepping-stones across the 1840s, for example, would take us through the Improvement Acts, particularly in Lancashire, to the Public Health Act of 1848. It would take us through the Mines Act of 1842, prohibiting labour by females and children below the age of ten underground, the Ten-Hour Act of 1847 (and the related Act of 1850), and the attempts to regulate the employment of boy chimney-sweeps (one of the many Acts was passed in 1840, although the practice was not successfully ended until 1875). It would take us through the Bank Charter Act of 1844, which restricted note-issue in England and Wales to the Bank of England and strengthened Britain's role as the commercial and financial centre of the world. A detailed look at the first part of the century would take us through periods of economic activity which have been described in the following terms:

1815–21, *peace and breakdown*: after mounting prosperity from 1811, a hectic postwar boom, followed by a crash in 1819.

1821–36, *recovery and expansion*: the biggest relative increase in industrial output of the century, a rise in real incomes, the vigorous promotion of trade and industry, a decline in prices (continuing until 1853).

1836–42, *critical depression*: the boom in railway and ship-building breaks in 1836, a fall in real incomes (followed, from 1842–73, by a period of 'growth by leaps and bounds'). [24]

By mid-century Britain, as it has been variously described, was the 'Industry State', the 'Fuel State', the 'Workshop of the World'.

An economy, a society, in the early stages of industrialization, does not move forward uniformly or rhythmically. Across the early nineteenth century stretch the trails of enormously uneven economic and social developments. There are forms of social improvement and of social disaster, subtle and brutal changes in patterns and standards of life. The ways in which the growth-points we have established carry through into mid-Victorian Britain will emerge if we take one example, that of the notion of democracy.

Without defining this concept in detail, we take it to refer to three things: the way power is, or is not, diffused through society, and the extent to which those who exercise it are accountable; the right and ability of individuals and groups of individuals to dissent; and the ability of the individual to develop and express himself adequately within that society. 'I do not know of any society', said C. Wright Mills, 'which is altogether democratic', but by acting '*as if* we were in a fully democratic society . . . we are attempting to remove the "as if".' [25] In terms of the major changes in the half-century or more from the departures of the 1780s and 1790s, such a definition and discussion reveal some of the most uneven of the developments. The central fact of power, for example, was the expansion (not, as it used to be called, the 'rise') of the middle class. We will postpone discussion of the concept of 'class', but in the early nineteenth century those who belonged to the middle class had no difficulty in identifying themselves. The expansion of old industries and the inauguration of new led to more widely based industrial and commercial prosperities, to the relentless growth of new clerical and managerial occupations, and of new professions. The profession of architect, to take a single instance, is closely related to the new order. The Industrial Revolution had led to the involvement of industrialists and men of commerce in town government, and the middle class

> was making its voice heard in architectural matters through the medium of the building committees. Theatre shareholders, prison boards, the committees for new public buildings, all became important clients, and their influence on the development of professionalism was considerable.

Architects now dealt not with patrons but with committees. Their status and interests needed some protection. The Institute of British Architects, founded in 1834, 'rigidly defined the relations of its members not only with other architects but with clients and builders'. [26] The profession of civil engineer, or of solicitor, could also illustrate the scale of growth of the professional wing of the middle class. If the middle class was a reality and wielded industrial power, as well as social power of many kinds, it did not wield power in the obvious political sense, in the first half of the century. Its involvement in the fight up to the 1832 Reform Act was a conscious bid for such power, at least in the negative sense of removing some of the prominent bars to its

3 Robert Owen (1771–1858).

participation in it. The Act disfranchised some rotten boroughs and created new parliamentary seats (Sheffield and Manchester, for example), gave the vote in the boroughs to owners of property of a value of ten pounds or more, and (to balance the urban increase) increased the number of seats in some counties and extended the county vote. A quarter of a million new, for the most part urban middle-class, voters were admitted. The middle class was closer to the centre of power, but parliament continued to be a landowners' parliament. The old order did not collapse – it fought back, adapted itself, absorbed its challengers. To Cobden or Bright the old landed order was 'feudalism', and neither of them 'disguised their desire to see the whole "feudal order" disappear along with the Corn Laws'. The Corn Laws went in 1846, but in 1863 Cobden was still meditating 'that feudalism is every day more and more in the ascendant in political and social life'. [27]

The central argument of Major Cartwright's reform movements of the 1780s had been that property should qualify for the vote. The central argument of Cobden and Bright and the Manchester School of Liberal politics was that the middle class had the greatest right and the greatest ability to govern. In 1850 they were masters of urban society, but they did not, in the fullest sense, govern.

The way in which power was exercised in early nineteenth-century Britain is bound up with the second part of our discussion of democracy – the right to dissent. Working-class dissent and organization is the most important index of the consciousness of change, not only of *response* to change but of awareness of the need to *control* it. Working-class and popular movements are in this period an extension, through the zigzags of economic growth, of the aspirations formulated in the 1790s. They reach out, not towards the kind of political adjustments sought by the radical associations of the eighteenth century, but towards a complete revision of the terms of social progress. The popular political radicalism which preceded the Reform Act of 1832, and the radicals' sense of betrayal which accompanied and followed it, were of a new scale and passion. With increasing momentum through the early century, in defiance of stamp tax and the law, the popular radical press self-consciously fought to change the framework of democratic discussion. Chartism, as a popular movement for political reform, on a scale and with a basis of organization and propaganda quite new in history, pursued with varying success the right to participate in the nation's affairs, in a major way to 1848, and in a diminishing way beyond. For his *Political Register* William Cobbett fled the country after the Habeas Corpus Act was suspended in 1817; for his publishing and bookselling Richard Carlile went to jail in 1819; for selling O'Brien's *Poor Man's Guardian* scores went to jail in the early 1830s; and for being militant Chartists men went to jail in 1839, and after.

The organized demand for a share in political power was not, however, the only form of popular dissent. The Owenite co-operative movement from the late 1820s looked towards co-operative production and community settlement, in an attempt to turn its back on the chaos of capitalist industrialism. Trade unionism in different phases, after the repeal of the Combination Acts in 1824, looked towards wider forms of self-protection, and even, in some cases, in an Owenite phase in the early 1830s, the by-passing of capitalist forms of production. By 1850 co-operation, in the form that had come out of Rochdale in 1844, was a growing network of consumers' organizations, and trade unionism was about to enter the New Model phase, with a sophisticated form of the organization of such skilled workers as engineers, carpenters and joiners, and iron-founders. If the middle class had not achieved its full share of power, the working class had achieved, in any obvious sense, none of it. Not until 1867 was the urban working man, generally speaking, admitted to the franchise. Not until 1855 were the 'taxes on knowledge' finally removed from the press, although already the trend towards mass communications had given the advantage in reaching the minds of men to the larger, the more efficient, organization (such as the *Daily Telegraph*, selling at one penny after the

4 *Hardware at the Great Exhibition, 1851.*

removal of the final tax in 1855, and at a rate of 141,000 copies a day by 1861).

The discussion of democracy reaches out in all directions, and the third factor — the position of the individual in society — must be left as an implication of the discussion so far. All we have done is to hint at some of the dynamic of a Britain which by 1850 had come to operate within quite different terms of reference, but in which the major processes of political and social change were still far from complete. Implied in the change that we have suggested is the major contrast between Britain as a nation in 1850 and in the late eighteenth century — a contrast between the essentially local, regional or metropolitan activities of society at the earlier point, and the substantially nation-wide ones at the later. Chartism itself, for example, was in every sense a *national* movement, reaching into every corner of Great Britain, with its Chartist churches in Scotland and Chartist insurrection in Wales. The *Daily Telegraph* was a *national* newspaper, carried on a nation-wide network of railways. The economy was a *national* one, developing national economic responses, possible with national communications and a single national market (resulting in new forms of standardization, as bricks and foodstuffs, for example, were carried throughout the country). Organization, from trade unions to banks (there were 554 of the latter in 1826 and, by a process of unification, 311 in 1842), was becoming more national in scope. Thomas Cook, on 5 July 1841, took 570 people from Leicester to Loughborough by rail for a temperance convention. The fare was one shilling, and the excursion age had opened. Social tension, poverty and deprivation were still facts, but a belief in a never-ending, ever-widening prosperity was a pervasive mid-century view.

THE GREAT EXHIBITION

All of this, and more, was symbolized in the Great Exhibition and, for this reason, 1851 is probably the most useful date to use as the doorway into

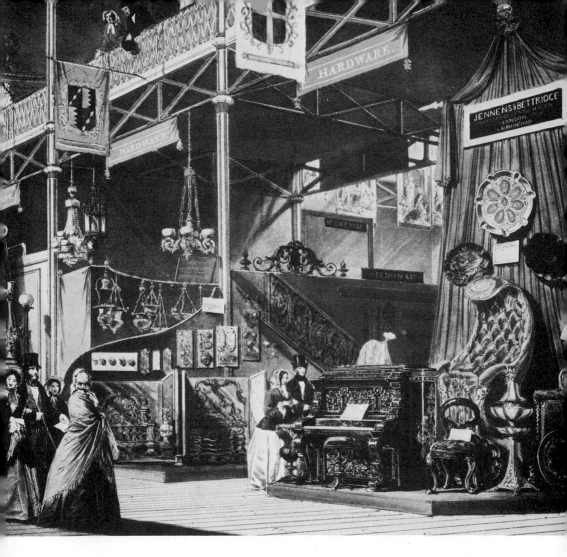

Modern Britain. The Great Exhibition in Hyde Park was designed to demonstrate the confidence of Britain's manufacturers, the supremacy of British trade, manufacture and finance. It was intended to be, and was, a symbol of British material progress. In itself it was a feat of technology. It contained nearly a million square feet of glass (the window tax had just been lifted), 3,300 iron columns and over 2,000 girders. It showed the produce of 7,381 British and Empire, and 6,556 foreign, exhibitors to over six million visitors, between 1 May and 11 October 1851 (including the thousands brought on excursions by Thomas Cook). Daily tickets ranged in price between one shilling and five shillings; 934,691 bath buns and 870,027 plain buns were sold. Sunday opening was not allowed. Nor were alcohol, smoking or dogs. [28] The Exhibition is so complete a symbol that it must be an indispensable preoccupation for any student of Victorian Britain. Prince Albert's 'model dwellings' were reminders that all was not well with the existing non-model ones in which vast numbers of the British people lived; *Punch* (and not only *Punch*) reminded its readers of the realities of the working conditions in which the exhibits were produced. But the Exhibition went its course as an immense achievement. And workers, to the surprise of many, bought shilling tickets and alcohol-free drinks, and broke no windows. The result is that

> We can see the Crystal Palace as a most elegant shelter for exhibiting steam-engines, *or* as a useful iron structure for housing very bad sculpture. In both cases the fundamental Victorian incongruity is there. We can never make up our minds whether – like the age to which it belonged – the Crystal Palace was supremely great or rather comic. Remembering the sincerity, the optimism and the prayers, it was also supremely pathetic. Above all it was a miracle. [29]

NOTES

1 See *Social Change in the Industrial Revolution*, Ch. X (London, 1959).
2 In the preliminary findings of the Cambridge Group for the History of Population and Social Structure, as outlined by Peter Laslett in *The World we have Lost*, Ch. 8 (London, 1965).
3 PHYLLIS DEANE *The First Industrial Revolution*, pp. 11–12 (London, 1965).
4 *The Industrial Revolution 1760–1830*, p. 127 (London, 1948; 1964 edition).
5 *Six Letters to the Marquis of Tavistock on a Reform of the Commons House of Parliament*, p. 23 (London, 1812).
6 *An Appeal to the Nation by the Union for Parliamentary Reform according to the Constitution*, p. 61 (London, 1812).
7 The best account of this world (though with a strong anti-radical bias) is E. C. BLACK *The Association, British Extraparliamentary Political Organisation, 1769–1793* (Harvard, 1963). See also GEORGE RUDE *The Crowd in History, 1730–1848* (New York, 1964).
8 'A plea for equality', *The Dangers of Obedience*, p. 209 (New York, 1930).
9 For a critical dissection of Dicey's assumptions see J. B. BREBNER 'Laissez-faire and state intervention in nineteenth-century Britain', in CARUS-WILSON (ed.) *Essays in Economic History*, III.
10 S. E. FINER *The Life and Times of Sir Edwin Chadwick*, pp. 24–5 (London, 1952). There is an interesting discussion of this theme in HENRY PARRIS *Government and the Railways in Nineteenth-century Britain*, Ch. 7, 'Railways in the theory of government' (London, 1965).
11 G. D. H. COLE 'Ideals and beliefs of the Victorians', *Essays in Social Theory*, p. 196 (London, 1950; 1962 edition).
12 MAX WEBER *The Protestant Ethic and the Spirit of Capitalism* (published in German 1904–5, English 1930). Quotations are from Ch. V, 'Asceticism and the spirit of capitalism'.
13 J. D. CHAMBERS and G. E. MINGAY *The Agricultural Revolution 1750–1880*, pp. 3–5 (London, 1966).

14 *Culture and Anarchy*, p. 12 (London, 1869; 1906 edition).

15 G. D. H. COLE 'Roads, rivers and canals', *Persons and Periods*, p. 98 (Harmondsworth, 1937).

16 *The Industrial Revolution 1750–1850*, p. 13 (London, 1928; 1958 edition).

17 For a survey of attitudes to all these factors, see R. M. HARTWELL 'The causes of the Industrial Revolution', *Economic History Review*, 1966, pp. 164–82.

18 For a recent summary of the evidence, see DEANE *The First Industrial Revolution*, Ch. 2. The largest compilation of evidence and argument can be found in D. V. GLASS and D. E. C. EVERSLEY (eds.) *Population in History* (London, 1965).

19 See F. A. WRIGLEY (ed.) *An Introduction to English Historical Demography* (Cambridge Group for the History of Population and Social Structure, Publication No. 1, London, 1966). Articles on the numerical study of English society, family reconstitution, the study of social structure and the early census returns are particularly useful in relation to our discussions here.

20 Ibid., p. 24.

21 For a recent discussion of the older evidence on death rate, see the chapter on 'The increase in population' in KITSON CLARK *The Making of Victorian England*.

22 KITSON CLARK *The Making of Victorian England*, pp. 69–70.

23 *The Making of the English Working Class*, pp. 323–4 (London, 1963).

24 Summarized from S. G. CHECKLAND *The Rise of Industrial Society in England 1815–1885*, Ch. 2 (London, 1964).

25 *The Sociological Imagination*, pp. 188–9.

26 FRANK JENKINS 'The Victorian architectural profession', in PETER FERRIDAY (ed.) *Victorian Architecture*, pp. 40–1 (London, 1963).

27 Quoted in ASA BRIGGS 'Cobden and Bright', *History Today*, VII, 8, August 1957, p. 503.

28 C. H. GIBBS-SMITH *The Great Exhibition of 1851* (London, 1950).

29 ROBERT FURNEAUX JORDAN 'Sir Joseph Paxton' in FERRIDAY (ed.) *Victorian Architecture*, p. 159.

The discussion of industrial and economic growth is continued in Chapters 3, 5 and 6. Radicalism and reform are discussed in Chapters 3 and 5, social mobility in Chapters 3 and 8, education in Chapters 4 and 8, social attitudes and policy in Chapters 4 and 5, population in Chapters 4 to 7, and democracy in Chapters 3 and 10.

2

Towns, People and Problems

URBAN GROWTH

Neither towns nor urban problems were a product of the nineteenth century. Industrialization, however, generated new energies of urban growth. Industry and transport may create entirely new towns – as the canals did at Stourport and Goole, the railways at Swindon and at first coal transport and then iron-ore mining at Middlesbrough: more frequently, however, they confirm the status of the larger existing urban centres. Generally speaking, the largest towns in 1801 have remained among the largest.

The processes of urban growth, particularly across the middle reaches of the nineteenth century, highlight changes in social conditions and attitudes to social policy: the scale of growth is itself an important factor in such changes. This growth and its attendant problems help to explain some of the patterns of life, relationships and attitudes which were projected into twentieth-century Britain, and which we shall try to analyse in later chapters.

In the period between 1801 and 1891, the population of England and Wales increased by roughly 20 million. The rural population (living in places with less than 5,000 people) in this period increased from 6·6 to 9·2 million, and urban population from 2·3 to 19·8 million. Eighty per cent of the total increase went, therefore, to the towns. Not only, however, did urban Britain increase disproportionately to rural Britain – there were also disparate increases in the rate of growth of the towns themselves. Towns with a population of over 20,000 increased at a rate approximately double that of towns of 5,000 to 20,000. As natural increase (excess of births over deaths) was not larger – and in fact in the early years of the century was considerably smaller – in the towns than in the countryside, the more rapid growth of towns in general and large towns in particular could have been caused only by migration.

The balance of urban to rural population in Britain was roughly equal at mid-century. By 1891 the ratio was roughly 21 million to 8 million for Great

Britain as a whole. The highest percentage growth rates of the major cities tended to occur roughly between the 1820s and 1850s. Migration to cities had been a not uncommon, and frequently pronounced, characteristic of pre-industrial Britain (and not only Britain, of course), although cities, almost always coastal, were small in number, and the extremely high death rate kept down their actual rate of expansion. The growth of towns in the nineteenth

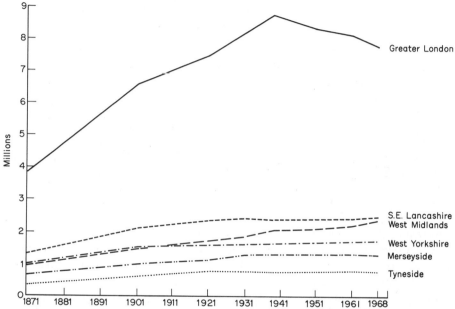

Fig. 3 Growth of conurbations in England and Wales, 1871–1968. (See also Table 14, p. 322.) After Mitchell and Deane, 1962, and Annual Abstract of Statistics, 1969.

century cannot be attributed automatically to the overall increase in population. The increasing population was a *condition* of such growth, but

> it has not necessarily been a positive cause of their *relatively* rapid growth as compared with the remainder of the population – a cause, that is, of the phenomenon of concentration. Positive forces may exist to drive a larger proportion of people into the rural districts notwithstanding an all-round increase in population . . . the growth of cities must be studied as a part of the question of distribution of population, which is always dependent upon the economic organisation of society. [1]

The factors which induce a redistribution of population in this way are both negative and positive. Men may leave the countryside because there is surplus labour; and in fact they did so. Increased agricultural efficiency, together with a rising population, caused city-ward migration, contributing to a larger growth rate for the cities (though not a depopulation of the countryside in absolute terms).

The positive attraction of urban centres was, of course, the demand for labour. Machinery and factory organization were central factors in the new patterns of the distribution of the population, although in many cases (particularly in centres with natural communications and trading advantages) industrial developments led to higher densities in existing urban areas. Once a momentum of expansion has been established, the process is self-sustaining:

> When an industry has been established in a region it creates conditions favourable to its own growth; concentration brings advantages and these advantages in turn strengthen the attraction not only of the region but also of the locality in which the industry has started. Thus, regional concentration, due in the first place to natural advantages, fosters local concentration and the growth of large urban areas. But these, in turn, not only offer further advantages to the 'basic' industries but also offer advantages to other industries. Thus the chosen district tends to grow like a snow-ball and become a large conurbation. [2]

When an industry has become established it gives rise to what economists call 'external economies'. An industry such as the cotton industry produced workers with the appropriate skills, and provided a market for them. Groups of factories, of industries, create 'general' external economies, by evolving a network of industrial and urban services, notably transport, which themselves act as focal points of attraction. This was the basis for the growth of towns with a dominant industry, such as the steel trades in Sheffield and cotton in Manchester. Sheffield, for example, grew from 45·8 thousand in 1800 to 135·3 thousand in 1850 and 324·2 thousand in 1890 (though, in addition to natural increase and migration, the extension of boundaries to incorporate other villages and townships was an important factor). Manchester and Salford between 1800 and 1890 grew from 90·4 thousand to 703·5 thousand. This was the basis also of the growth of towns like Liverpool, Hull, Birmingham and Glasgow, with more 'general external economies'. Glasgow, with 77·1 thousand in 1800, had reached 329·1 thousand in 1850.

The intensity and direction of city-ward migration was not a constant pattern, but was affected by varying factors, such as the revolution in transport caused by the railways from the 1830s, the pull of different regions at different times, with the disparate growth rates of different industries, and the presence of opportunities (including those for immigrant Irish labour) on a new scale in new situations. In the early nineteenth century the largest towns, we have suggested, gained most population; London, though not directly involved in the most immediate economic developments of the Industrial Revolution, was no exception. Its expanding population, commerce and 'external economies' were in every sense the result of the economic and social mobilities we have seen projected into the nineteenth century. The 'million-mark cities', commented the Barlow Commission in 1940, had in the past century 'tended to increase their populations at rates at least twice as great as the mean rate of increase for their respective countries, and especially is this characteristic of the capital cities'. In every intercensal period of the nineteenth century the percentage growth in the population of Greater London was substantially greater (at its greatest nearly double) than the national percentage. The population of Great Britain was in 1911 roughly four times what it had been in 1801. In the same period the population of Greater London had grown from 1·1 million to 7·3 million. [3]

TRANSPORT

Britain's progress towards urbanization was in many respects most clearly confirmed by the achievement of an unprecedented transport system.

The canals, as we have indicated, had contributed to the efficiency of movement required by early industrialization, to the expansion of industries dependent on efficient transport for marketing (the Staffordshire potteries are an outstanding example), and even to the mushroom growth of certain towns. The canals and railways shared in common the fact that, through their speculative construction, they opened up new areas to industrial expan-

5 Weaver's home, showing Jacquard loom, 1850.

sion, at the same time as they both 'often assisted industries to remain in their traditional centres'. [4]

By mid-century the railways had made it impossible for social advance to be effectively discussed, as it had often been in the early decades of the century, in terms of nostalgic glances backwards to pre-industrial society. The railways in a sense ultimately helped to make it possible for Englishmen to remain country-dwellers, or at least seaside homers, at heart by offering increasingly long-term and long-distance opportunities for ritual holiday-making. Their most conspicuous achievement by mid-nineteenth century, however, was the final unification of the economy through the cementing of a pattern of inter-urban relationships.

The fact that the railways were large-scale units was in itself important. Britain opted, under the dominant Benthamism, for private railway ownership. The sponsorship of railway companies was an elaborate and expensive business, involving a private Act of Parliament. Their importance lay in making the joint-stock form, with limited liability, familiar. Short of State intervention and ownership, which no one in Britain (unlike, for example, Belgium) seriously advocated, it became accepted as socially necessary for the pooled resources of the joint-stock company to be developed. The formation of such companies was, therefore, one of the main steps along the road to the large-scale enterprises which became readily possible throughout the economy after the crucial limited liability and joint-stock legislation of the 1850s.

The fact, also, that the promotion of a railway company was a public enterprise, raising share-capital, and above all requiring an Act of Parliament, was of equal importance. *Laissez-faire* had no railway policy, and government in the 1830s vacillated, unwilling to regulate or leave alone. [5] The State, however, was involved in railway developments in a way in which it was involved in nothing else. It had to sanction the building of lines, had to choose between rival schemes, had to be concerned with problems of competition and co-ordination. Factors affecting the safety and convenience of the public at large had to be borne in mind. A Railway Department was first established in 1840. In 1844 parliament legislated for companies to provide one train each week-day at a speed of not less than twelve miles an hour and at a fare of not more than a penny a mile (the 'Parliamentary Trains'). Inspection of track, design of carriages, speed of trains, were accepted as legitimate concerns of a department of government (at a time when the principle of government inspection had also been accepted, in education, for example, from 1839, and in factories from 1833, and at a time when other forms of regulation were beginning to be admitted). The railways, therefore, mark an important step towards the acceptance of the idea of the Responsible State.

The history of railway expansion in Britain has been divided into five periods: (1) the period of experiment, 1820–30; (2) the period of infancy, 1830–45; (3) the period of mania, 1845–8; (4) the period of competition by great Companies, 1848–59; (5) the period of contractors' lines and Com-

6 Waiting for the excursion train, 1880.

panies' extensions, 1859–65. [6] By the end of the third of these periods the main trunk system was completed or about to be completed, and only the regional networks remained to be filled out. Long before the middle of the century London had Euston Station with its great classical portico (completed in 1836 to celebrate the completion of a railway line from London to Birmingham, 'rightly considered an overwhelming achievement of the human intellect'). [7] Trains were running from Paddington to the West Country from 1841. Victoria Station was opened in 1850 and King's Cross was built in 1851–2 (incorporating the clock from the Crystal Palace, which was moved to Sydenham when the Great Exhibition closed).

The establishment of the railways meant doom for the canals, which had in any case by the early decades of the century taken advantage of their monopoly position to raise charges, and had become incapable of carrying the volume of freight efficiently and rapidly. The railways spelled doom also for the increasingly rapid and efficient coaching and posting network, which could not stand up to the competition. Economically, of course, the impact of the railways in increasing the speed of delivery (of goods and passengers), in lowering costs, and in cementing the nation-wide market, was considerable. When, in addition, are added their effect on a whole complex of related industries (building, iron and steel, engineering, etc.) and the accelerated export of railway track, rolling stock, engineering know-how and experienced labour, there can be no doubt about the impetus given to the second phase of industrialization.

Socially also, the consequences of railway expansion were vast. The railways carried post and newspapers, providing a new and radically different outlet for the book and periodical trade in the station bookstall, which started life as a concession 'to injured employees or their widows, who vended an unappetizing stock of newspapers, magazines, beer, sandwiches and sweets to jaded travelers'. [8] By the end of the 1850s, however, the trade was virtually a monopoly in the hands of W. H. Smith. The railways led to the introduction of Greenwich Mean Time (in order to cope with the need to standardize time-tables) and provided facilities for expanding the electric telegraph. They also brought new crafts, a renovation of the hotel and inn industry, and new standardizations in goods, architecture and manners.

On balance, it is not at all clear whether Professor Simmons is right to argue 'that of all classes in the community, the railway brought most benefit to the poor'. [9] It is certainly clear that the changes wrought in ordinary people's lives by this sophistication of transport were, especially in the long run, immense. Britain ceased, in senses other than the economic one, to be hollow. Slowly, but inevitably, the age of the tour, the heroic discovery of North Wales, the Lakes or the Scottish lochs, and the elegance of the spa, Brighton and Scarborough, was replaced by the age of public transport and the day-trip. Although cheap fares, from Gladstone's Regulation of Railways Act of 1844 (and later the Cheap Trains Act of 1883) were an incentive to suburban growth, the importance of their impact on working-class housing before the end of the nineteenth century must not be exaggerated. Such lines as the London and Greenwich Railway, partly opened to traffic in 1836, and similar railways built in the neighbourhood of London, affected only those strata of the community which could afford to travel and to build homes at a greater distance, or buy those built speculatively. Small margins of extra cost and distance were of crucial importance to people in the lower income groups. This was true even with London's improved transport system (the first underground line was opened in 1863), and a particularly striking example occurred in 1877, when the London Metropolitan Board of Works proposed in a bill to try to accommodate people displaced from the West End (by road and other improvements) in Gray's Inn Road, a mile or so from their previous dwellings. The Board considered this reasonable, given the small distance involved, and the fact that most of the workers concerned were migratory. It was shown in evidence, however, that these allegedly migratory workers often remained 'weekly tenants in one house for ten or twenty years, and in some cases have been known to occupy the same room as weekly tenants for forty or fifty years'. What was more important, however, was that:

Their employment obliges them to remain stationary. The fashionable shops of Regent Street, Bond Street and St James's do not move, and they require their workmen near at hand. The numerous coach factories are still about Long Acre. The large warehouses of Crosse & Blackwell in Soho Square, where over 1,000 hands are employed – men, women, boys, and girls – are supplied from the neighbouring streets. Covent Garden, with all its dependents of coster-mongers and labourers, who have to begin work at four in the morning, is still flourishing, and therefore these working people now living on the West-End line of improvement must continue to live there, or in many cases they would be thrown out of employment . . .

The extra mile represented 'an hour a day in time lost, to say nothing of the fatigue'. The loss of an hour a day, at a wage rate of 5d an hour, meant 2s 6d a week, 'a tax that would be put on the workmen by removing them to a distance'. [10] The growth of towns and transport had helped to loosen traditional obstacles to geographical mobility, but had created others.

HOUSING

There remained, then, in the middle of the century, considerable obstacles to the growth of new working-class residential areas, though the middle-class suburban villa now became a reality. More immediately from our point of view here, however, was the impact of the railways on, for example, food supplies to the urban population. Transportation of perishable food was transformed, market gardening on the fringes of cities became of critical importance, fish and meat could be transported greater distances inland (becoming of even greater importance in the 1860s and 1870s when the steam trawler and the use of ice for preservation put fish imports on a new footing, and from the 1870s the large-scale trans-oceanic transportation of frozen meat and grain was made possible). [11] Nuisances, similarly, could be removed from town centres, and 'slaughtering, like cow-keeping and other trades dependent on perishable produce, naturally tended to move from the City [of London] as the use of the railways for transporting such produce increased'. [12]

If Goole and Birmingham are rooted in the canal age, towns like Crewe and Swindon, both created in the 1840s to serve railway needs, are more totally products of their age. Given the arrangements for company housing, and the organization or financing of the building of churches and social amenities, they show how the growth of the railways was related to the history of ideas about town planning. More often than not, however, the construction of a railway, and more especially a railway station, meant a further disturbance in an already chaotic urban environment. Railway construction, like street widening, meant the displacement of some of the poorest of the population from one area to another. Not until well into the twentieth century was the notion of alternative accommodation a serious part of social policy, or slum clearance part of a positive programme – and even then stumblingly and inadequately.

The overriding considerations in the field of housing throughout the nine-teenth century were those of the sanctity of private property and the need for everything 'to pay'. With few exceptions, housing was an entirely private or speculative affair. The picture one must have in mind is of towns which never really recovered from a profound shock. Eighteenth-century towns contained elegant homes, and squares and wide streets, but also miserable cottages and squalid alleys: nevertheless there was a certain urban decorum, visible still in Britain's Roman and medieval towns. The towns of industrial Britain were faced with a bigger task and registered a greater failure, in attempting to cope with the aggregate of problems. They were less aware of, and less equipped to deal with, their corporate responsibilities.

Even by the 1850s the wealthier home, the elegant Georgian or Regency house or the newly built, individually styled, suburban terraced or detached house, was relatively primitive so far as its services were concerned. A cold-water tap was still the height of luxury in 1840. Flush toilets were known in the eighteenth century, but did not begin to come into use in even very wealthy homes until after the 1830s. The privy and the cesspit, and water drawn by servants from the stand-pipe and the rain-tank, were still the rule. The fitted bath was not to become common for the wealthy until the 1870s. Planning, for the wealthy, was a question of new self-protective residential areas like Birkenhead or the Regency or early Victorian squares of Belgravia or Bloomsbury, continuing the traditions of the co-ordinated elegance of the Georgian areas of London and the provincial market towns. The work of Thomas Cubitt, for example, who built for expensive tastes from the fashion-able districts of West London through to the one he created in Clapham, was 'characterized by broad and airy streets, spacious squares and formal design'. His development schemes, many still surviving, 'contrasted markedly with much higgledy-piggledy development at the same time in other districts cater-ing for less wealthy residents'. [13] By mid-century, with growing middle-class affluence, the scale of wealthy 'higgledy-piggledy' had increased, at the expense of wealthy 'formal design', as is shown by a glance at unrelated, in-dividual house-building in the once-superior streets of mid-century urban development. For the rapidly growing lower middle class also, the large house, perhaps with basement, ground floor and two upper floors, had become com-mon by mid-century. Middle-class housing of all kinds, its scale, design and architecture, proclaims the economic position of the occupiers, the size of the families and the number of the servants (an income of £1,000 a year in 1857 would support at least five servants, from butler to nursery maid, and £500 a year would support three). Such housing was not, however, the Victorian prob-lem (whatever problems it was to cause in many areas in the middle of the twentieth century).

We need not here look in detail at the kind of unplanned, minimal house building commonly provided by mill and mine owners, around which towns frequently mushroomed. Generally speaking, in company-built, or speculatively built, housing of this kind, housing standards for the bulk of new urban dwellers were elementary at best. In existing and expanding towns industrialization and urbanization brought increased population density and the proliferation of overcrowded and slum districts. In the centres of towns,

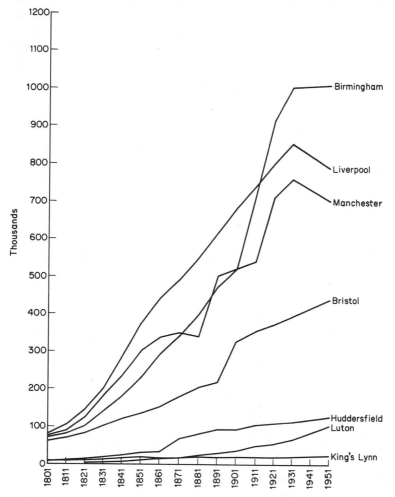

Fig. 4 Population increase in selected English towns, 1801–1951. (See also Table 16, p. 324.) After Mitchell and Deane, 1962.

the effects of these processes could be seen in the insoluble problems of areas completely without sanitation. The problems ranged from the cholera epidemic to the homeless sleeping in stairways and to the overstocked graveyard. There were attempts at philanthropic housing, and even working-class self-help in housing, but in the 1850s none of this had yet become of any consequence (and in any important sense it had not yet done so by the end of the century). Edwin Chadwick's *Report on the Sanitary Condition of the Labouring Population* (1842) and Engels's *Condition of the Working Class in England* (1845) were only two of the more famous documents which, in early Victorian England, presented the desperate picture of the housing conditions (and their related mortality) of London and Manchester. Engels describes St Giles's, close to the fashionable West End, with its narrow roads, street-markets 'in which baskets of rotting and virtually uneatable vegetables and fruit are exposed for sale', foul smells and fantastic overcrowding. He describes the narrow alleys and courts, with 'hardly an unbroken windowpane to be seen, the walls are crumbling, the door posts and window frames are loose and rotten ... piles of refuse and ashes lie all over the place and the slops thrown out into the street collect in pools ...' [14] Even the less poor contended with conditions which made improvement impossible. A description of Manchester in 1805, written by Dr Ferriar, would be equally true of conditions in the 1830s or 1840s, and includes a description of the cellar-dwellings:

> The number of damp, and very ill ventilated cellars inhabited in many parts of the town, is a most extensive and permanent evil ... they consist of two rooms under ground, the front apartment of which is used as a kitchen, and though frequently noxious by its dampness, and closeness, is generally preferable to the back room: the latter has only one small window, which, though on a level with the outer ground, is near the roof of the cellar, it is often covered with boards or paper, and in its best state, is so much covered with mud, as to admit little either of air or light. In this cell, the beds of the whole family, sometimes consisting of seven or eight, are placed. The floor of this room is often unpaved: the beds are fixed on the damp earth ... I have seen the sick without bedsteads, lying on rags; they can seldom afford straw. [15]

These were the conditions which helped to bring about the cholera epidemics of 1831–2 and 1848–9. Of the 4,000 houses in the Low Town area of North Shields in 1849 only 300 had a piped water supply from the mains. They housed 7,000 people, and contained sixty-two lavatories (mostly in tradesmen's houses). [16] Water supplies were widely, in some towns universally, polluted by sewage, and were irregular and inadequate. The Commission which reported in 1844 on the State of Large Towns found innumerable cases of contaminated water. In Newcastle the principal supply from the Tyne and springs was 'impure from the drainage of the sewers'. In Portsmouth the 'poor beg water of the neighbours'. It was bought widely from hawkers and private pumps and was polluted in every conceivable manner. [17]

From mid-century it is possible to trace a higher rate of involvement by government and municipal authorities in the problems of urban living. It is not possible, of course, to separate problems of housing from those of health and of poverty. The domestic environment of the poor offended the ideals of the Victorian moralist in relation to the family and morality; it was the despair of the reformer: 'The housing ruins all.' [18]

Working-class housing ranged from the improved dwellings of New Lanark or Saltaire to the cellars of Liverpool and Manchester, the rural (though in many respects equally insanitary) cottage, and the desperate wretchedness of St Giles, of the courts of the City of London, and of those of Sunderland where, in 1831, cholera first set foot in Britain. The urban environment of the

7 'A Court for King Cholera', 1852. Such scenes were still to be found at the rear of New Oxford Street in the 1860s.

poor was, it must be remembered, more than a purely physical environment susceptible to various, and necessary, forms of social engineering. The improvements in conditions of health which we shall be discussing must not divert attention from the fact that, for the poor, improvements in health and hygiene, drainage and refuse disposal, water supply and the range and purity of food supplies, did not mean any spectacular change in the environment itself, or in their style of life. It was an environment which throughout the century blocked both escape and the imagination of anything different for enormous numbers of people. Built into it was the inevitability of many of the attendant features of poverty – charity, the Poor Law, the workhouse, dirt, disease, early death and almost total defencelessness against the machinery of society, whatever form it might take. To imagine that improved sanitation, greater attention to the problems of disease and greater national prosperity rapidly or substantially altered the conditions of poverty would be to make the same mistake as the generations at the end of the century made, who were *surprised* at the revelations of the extent and conditions of poverty.

Attempts to legislate for housing improvement were, of course, made. The earliest of consequence were in the 1850s and 1860s. With the City of London Sewers Act of 1851, John Simon, the City's Medical Officer of Health, extracted from both the City and parliament 'the first and unequivocal recognition of the right of compulsory clearance of unhealthy housing'. In 1864 Liverpool and Glasgow acquired 'much more elaborate and effective compulsory purchase powers', but 'the City and John Simon deserve the credit for the initial step in controlling a major social evil'. [19] Also in 1851 came the first national housing legislation in the form of Shaftesbury's Labouring Class Lodging Houses Act and Common Lodging Houses Act, the first of which permitted local authorities to build lodging houses, and the second of which made inspection of lodging houses compulsory. Inspection did in fact begin to take place, and to produce improvements, but the other Act was a dead letter. Acts concerned with wider health and sanitary problems, including the great Public Health Act of 1848, were by implication concerned also with housing. The Sanitary Act of 1866, for example, declared overcrowding to be a nuisance and enabled local authorities to take action. Definitions and enabling clauses did not, however, always and everywhere produce results.

The first real housing act as such, the 1868 Artizans' and Labourers' Dwellings Act (the first of three 'Torrens Acts'), was concerned with the individual insanitary house, enabling local authorities to compel its owner to demolish or repair it at his own expense. The Cross Acts, the first of which was passed in 1875, were concerned with the insanitary *area*, and enabled authorities to make compulsory purchases, for redevelopment schemes, involving the erection of houses for sale. Both sets of acts were permissive, both were aimed at maintaining adequate standards without excessively drastic action. Both were relatively ineffective, in that, although they looked ahead (a long way ahead) to firmer powers and wider consequences, the only result was demolition and prohibition, as remained substantially true of all such legislation until after the First World War. Even the 1890 Housing of the Working Classes Act (following on a Royal Commission on the Housing of the Poor in 1884–5) achieved little. It gave the newly created councils powers to deal with unhealthy areas, erect new houses, and buy land compulsorily, but only the new London County Council made a start with the use of such powers. By-laws were increasingly being introduced and taking effect, in regulating such things as the height of buildings and ceilings, sanitation and the size of rooms. Given the prevalent view of housing as a commodity, however, the public authorities themselves continued to condemn and to demolish, but not to erect.

LOCAL GOVERNMENT

The absence of any comprehensive system of local government can be inferred from every aspect of mid-nineteenth-century British society that we have looked at so far. In general, urban England inherited as constituents of local government a medley consisting of the ancient city corporations, various *ad hoc* Improvement Commissioners, the parish vestries and local justices. The corporate towns had won their degree of independence as a result of being at some point rich enough to bargain for it or powerful enough to win it. The Municipal Corporations Act of 1835, following a Royal Commission set up by the Reform Parliament, tackled the abuses of a self-perpetuating, corrupt system, altered the composition of 178 incorporated towns, and destroyed or undermined the power of the exclusive groups. Although a wider measure of democracy was introduced in this way into local than existed in national government, it was not to be until well into the twentieth century that a pattern of elected local government was finally cemented. It was the new corporations, where Harold Laski's 'middle-class business man' came most demonstrably to power, in the large, self-conscious industrial and commercial towns like Manchester, Leeds, Bradford and Liverpool, that were to find it impossible to adjust their thrift-conscious philosophies to *public* needs. Tempted as they were to respond to the needs of civic dignity and build town halls, urban overcrowding and disease were responded to only under legislative pressure from central government, and then more often than not with reluctance and delay. David Roberts demonstrates this effectively in his discussion of the growth of social policy between 1833 and 1854 by taking the case history of Macclesfield, 'the silk manufacturing capital of England'. All the improvements that took place in local conditions (including, for example, child labour, education and the treatment of criminals and the insane) were, he concludes, 'largely owing to the intervention of central government', and all met with local resistance:

> The mill-owners, the wealthiest and most respected citizens of Macclesfield, had petitioned Parliament in 1844 to allow those 4 to 12 years of age to work ten hours a day in the silk mills ... The nonconformist *Macclesfield Chronicle*, which called the Factory Act a great abomination and oppression, described the Government's education plan in 1847 as 'hostile to economic and civil freedom'. The same *Chronicle* and Macclesfield's 150 police commissioners, along with the town's two M.P.s and 4,000 ratepayers, protested vigorously in 1851 against the General Board of Health's plans for sanitary improvement, considering them too expensive. Apathy

and an antagonism to higher rates led them to tolerate the old lockup and to put pauper lunatics in the workhouse. All this would have continued but for the new acts of Parliament and the new civil servants from London. [20]

Another of the ancestors of modern local government was the system of Improvement Commissioners, appointed as a result of the passing of individual local Improvement Acts, particularly in the late eighteenth century, to take responsibility for such matters as paving and clearing nuisances. Open, like the corporations, to corruption and abuse, the Commissioners were in most of the older towns the only vehicle for attempting to cope with the problems of early industrialization, and very often their powers came to conflict among themselves and with other organs of local government. The parish vestry, in its 'open' form, was an ancient democratic institution, a local assembly with the right to impose taxation and responsible for ensuring the appointment and proper conduct of such local officers as constable, overseer of the poor and surveyor of highways. This, too, had often degenerated over the centuries into a self-perpetuating abuse of the system.

The early years of the nineteenth century had, however, destroyed the logic of these forms of local administration. The towns grew beyond them, in two senses; they grew beyond their ability to cope, and beyond their geographical confines. The problem after the 1830s was to improve and extend the machinery of borough incorporation begun in 1835, and to define authorities for the two precise and most important considerations of health and the poor.

The gradual elimination of contradictory powers, the incorporation of new boroughs and the extension of their machinery, did in fact take place slowly. The role of the justices, traditionally country gentlemen appointed by the Crown, became of diminishing importance. They were normally Tory in politics, and strongly opposed by the radicals and utilitarians who shaped the legislation after 1832. That the justices began to lose many of their powers as a result of it is, however, not only a political fact. They became increasingly unable to handle the growing weight of legislation – relating, for example, to mining and industry – and in any case urban expansion undermined their authority. They continued to supervise the operation of the laws in the country districts, and remained identified with local power and rule until the enfranchisement of the rural labourer and the creation of county councils in the 1880s.

PUBLIC HEALTH

Questions of health encompassed all these aspects of environment and administration. Even though germ theory was unknown until the late 1860s, it was obvious enough that disease had *something* to do with dirt. It was also clear from the beginning of the 1840s that urban concentration and conditions were more lethal, more liable to epidemic, more productive of disease, than non-urban conditions. The areas of greatest poverty coincided with those of the highest mortality. Expectation of life, it was clear at the time, was also directly related to social class. Edwin Chadwick's famous *Report on the Sanitary Condition of the Labouring Population* demonstrated that in 1839 in Bethnal Green, for example, the average age of death could be tabulated as follows:

No. of deaths		Average age of deceased
101	Gentlemen and persons engaged in professions and their families	45 years
273	Tradesmen and their families	26
1,258	Mechanics, servants and labourers and their families	16

Similar demonstrations were made for towns like Leeds and Liverpool. [21] The vast class differential in the infant mortality rate was, and continued to be, a considerable factor.

Suspicion of the general findings of Chadwick's *Report*, based on the work done by a select committee and initiated by Chadwick from his position as Secretary to the Poor Law Board, led to the appointment of the Royal Commission on the State of Large Towns (the Health of Towns Commission) in 1843. One of the Commissioners appointed was Lyon Playfair, already an eminent scientist. Playfair was given the large towns of Lancashire to investigate, and he later wrote:

The effects of bad sewerage, defective or intermittent instead of constant water supply, overcrowded tenements, bad construction of streets, and the abuse of opiates among the working-classes, were traced to their sources. In 1844 the sanitary condition of the kingdom was deplorable. Lancashire was especially bad. One-tenth of the population of Manchester and one-seventh of that of Liverpool lived in cellars. In the streets occupied by the working-classes two rows of houses were often built back to back, so that there could be no efficient ventilation; the supply of conveniences was altogether insufficient, and their condition and drainage were shocking ... Civic powers were split up into a number of discordant and often conflicting authorities, constantly overlapping each other in their duties ... The mortality was great, and the average age of death was low in manufacturing towns.

All the features of urban growth we have discussed come together in Playfair's recollection. His precise findings – and those of the Commission – in fact bore out Chadwick's picture. Playfair compared the average age at death in

8 Sir Edwin Chadwick (1800–90).

different Lancashire towns in 1844 with that in Kendal, Westmorland, a healthy agricultural town', where it was 36: at Manchester it was 22, Liverpool 20, Preston 19 and Ashton 16. [22]

All these factors in ill health and early death were discussed and in some respects acted upon most strikingly in the cholera epidemics of 1831–2 and 1848–9. The Public Health Act of 1848, setting up the General Board of Health, resulted from the imminent danger of cholera. In the words of a writer in the *Edinburgh Review* in 1850, 'Cholera is in truth a Health Inspector who speaks through his interpreter, the Registrar General, in a language which reaches all ears.' [23] The dominant local attitude, at least until new terms of reference were established in the 1870s, continued to be indifference. So far as infant mortality was concerned (more than 57 per cent of working-class children in Manchester, reported Chadwick, died under the age of five), it was not until the twentieth century that any substantial progress was made. Three things were required for headway to be made on health problems: changes in social policy, adequate national and local machinery, and improvements in medical knowledge and care.

Those responsible from the 1830s for shaping changes in social policy spanned the range from the evangelical Tory, Lord Shaftesbury, to the utilitarian Benthamite, Edwin Chadwick. Chadwick was the central figure, and he was concerned exclusively with the environmental factors involved in health reform. His position at the Poor Law Commission enabled him to see the dimensions of the health problem, to have it investigated, and to publicize it. His 1842 *Report* was a product of the processes which brought about the parliamentary reform of 1832, and it is important to note, as Playfair was acutely aware, that Chadwick was entirely committed to national policy and central planning:

> Chadwick . . . is the father of modern sanitary reform. He had the faculty of seizing upon an abuse with the tenacity of a bulldog, and never let it go till the abuse was worried to death. But this self-absorption in a subject carried him into extremes, and he failed to see both sides of a question. Thus, seeing the evils which had arisen in local self-government, he could not recognize its benefits, and magnified the power and capabilities of centralized government.

Playfair urged on him the need to throw greater responsibility on the local authorities and reduce the functions of central government, to which Chadwick replied: 'Sir, the Devil was expelled from heaven because he objected to centralization, and all those who object to centralization oppose it on devilish grounds!' [24] Perhaps the most succinct summary of Chadwick's career was G. M. Young's view that its mainspring 'seems to have been a desire to wash the people of England all over, every day, by administrative order'. [25] Chadwick was unable – and in this differed most emphatically from the more open-minded John Simon – to accept new medical evidence as to the causes and treatment of disease, but the fact that his tenacious views on the atmospheric causes of disease led to an equally tenacious dedication to the improvement of ventilation, sanitation and environmental conditions generally meant that 'he inaugurated the first era of English public health as one concerned more with the physical environment than with the personal health of the individual'. [26] His work altered the framework of discussion of social policy as the mid-nineteenth century approached. The 1848 Public Health Act symbolized the strengths and weaknesses of the new situation. This was a more restricted Act than Chadwick had hoped for, and was surrounded by hostility from many quarters, including many liberals, because of the centralization it entailed. *The Times* was implacably against Chadwick and the Act. Nevertheless the Act did give the General Board of Health real powers, including that of ordering an inquiry in a town if a tenth of the ratepayers petitioned for it, or if the annual mortality in the town exceeded 23 per 1,000. A local Board of Health, however, whether set up voluntarily or not, was exempt from national inspection or control. The General Board of Health lasted, in that form, only until 1854. Alternative approaches to public health were by now taking clearer shape.

The City of London, in gaining exemption from the operation of the 1848 Act, framed the terms for the first really full-scale experiment in effective local health administration. John (later Sir John) Simon, its first Medical Officer of Health, was ultimately more influential than Chadwick partly because the techniques he evolved (again, in the teeth of prolonged opposition from the forces of apathy and vested interest) could be seen to be viable and effective, and partly because British experience clung to the policy of local independence and initiative on which Simon relied. After seven years spent in building the first local health machinery of any importance, Simon became medical adviser to the government's reconstituted Board of Health in 1855, and in 1871 Chief Medical Officer of the newly formed Local Government Board. He was himself an eminent medical figure, and worked towards a conception of public health administration dominated by medical considerations. By 1870 he had made the Privy Council's Medical Department supreme in the formulation and operation of public health policy. It was to the doctor, not the sanitary engineer, that Simon delivered the direction of health policy at the beginning of the 1870s.

The policy that prevailed, therefore, was that of reliance on medical expertise (which made great strides in the 1870s) at national and local level, combined with local machinery for investigation, medical and environmental improvements. It can be seen, then, that of the three factors necessary for change – new policies, administrative machinery and medical knowledge – the first two made visible, though far from spectacular progress between the 1840s and 1870s, and it was after 1870 that the main impact of the changes began to be seen in the mortality statistics. The anaesthetics and free vaccination of the 1840s, sanitary improvements from the 1850s in particular, and the lessons learned from epidemics, all contributed to the developments. And yet during the period 1841–75 the death rate remained almost constant, at just over 22 per thousand. The major killers, such as tuberculosis, scarlet fever, diphtheria and the numerous infectious diseases connected with maternity and childhood, were still far from being conquered. [27]

POOR RELIEF

Although all these questions are closely bound up with that of the poor, influential Victorian Britain preferred not to recognize the presence of poverty as such. New directions in social policy at the turn of the twentieth century were to be very closely connected with the conception of poverty. Public policy for the major part of the nineteenth century was, in the sector of poor relief, based on the concept of pauperism. Poor relief had, since Elizabethan

9 Field Lane Refuge for the Destitute, 1859.

England, been accepted explicitly as a moral responsibility, and two of the
elements of local government inherited by the nineteenth century, the vestries
and the justices of the peace, were involved in its administration. Parish
officers were responsible for raising and distributing the local poor rate, and
the justices to one degree or another established the rate and supervised the
procedure. They were torn between the relative merits of 'out-relief'] and the
'workhouse'. Parishes were responsible for their own poor (the 'settlement',
as it had always been called, was to continue to operate to some extent right
through the nineteenth century and, in veiled forms, through to today); a
distinction was made between the able-bodied (out-relief) and non-able-bodied
(workhouse) recipients of relief. An Act of 1782 (Gilbert's Act) had aimed at
the creation of workhouses by unions of parishes. The Speenhamland decision
of 1795 to supplement wages on a sliding scale according to size of family
and price of bread was the last major Poor Law development of the old
dispensation.

What Chadwick's Poor Law Amendment Act of 1834 sought to achieve
was to put a stop to a system under which, it was held, the pauper obtained
advantages without penalties. It tried to deter him from seeking aid, by insist-
ing that he receive *in* and not *out* relief, at a lower level of comfort than the
poorest worker in employment. Benthamite economic orthodoxy held that the
right level of wages was the one dictated by the market, and that interference
by legislation or combinations of workers or employers distorted the market.
Similarly, in a free market situation poverty had nothing to do with the

economic system and could not be regulated; there was nothing *in the situation* to prevent the industrious from prospering. Relief of the Speenhamland variety merely discouraged industry. The Act of 1834 went as far as its authors felt they could persuade the public to follow, and they expected by it to be able to bring outdoor relief for the able-bodied to an end sooner or later. Relief from now on was to be minimal – that is, to prevent actual starvation – but the conditions in which it was to be given were to deter people from applying for it. The doctrine of 'less eligibility' was the crux of the Act. The Report of the Commission on which the 1834 Act was based explained that it was necessary to impose conditions in the administration of relief, the most essential being that the situation of the person relieved

> shall not be made really or apparently so eligible as the situation of the independent labourer of the lowest class . . . in proportion as the condition of any pauper class is elevated above the condition of independent labourers, the condition of the independent class is depressed; their industry is impaired, their employment becomes unsteady, and its remuneration in wages is diminished. Such persons, therefore, are under the strongest inducement to quit the less eligible class of labourers and enter the more eligible class of paupers . . . Every penny bestowed that tends to render the condition of the pauper more eligible than that of the independent labourer is a bounty on indolence and vice. [28]

Restrictions on poor relief were the result both of utilitarian philosophy and of cost. The mounting cost of relief can be seen in the case of London, for example, from Lambeth. In the first two decades of the century the population of the parish of Lambeth St Mary's, in which machinery, earthenware and tiles, for example, were manufactured, more or less doubled. [29] In 1800, 413 people were admitted to Lambeth Workhouse and 347 outdoor relief payments were made. The total cost to the rates was £11,691. By 1818 the numbers had risen to 1,250 workhouse inmates, 1,867 payments, and a rate of £47,870. [30] The new national administration from 1834, with a Central Board of Commissioners (from 1847 the Poor Law Board) supervising the Boards of Guardians, administering 600 to 700 unions (into which the 15,000 parishes of England and Wales were combined), was designed to end the indiscriminate element in relief. Chadwick and the 1832–4 Commission intended that separate workhouse provision should be made by local Boards of Guardians for different categories of pauper, but this did not happen. The general mixed workhouse prevailed. The Commissioners, in recommending separate buildings for children, able-bodied males, able-bodied females and the sick, were in fact trying to combat the concept of the mixed workhouse, and they – and others – were dismayed at its continuance. The Minority Report of the Poor Law Commission in 1909 explained that the intention of 1834 *had been* to follow these emphatic recommendations, but the intention had foundered on the structure of the system itself:

Parliament had placed the care of all these classes of poor in each Union under a single Local Authority, and had charged that Authority, not with the treatment of any one of these classes, not with the education of the children or the prevention and cure of sickness, but generally, with the relief of the destitution of all of them.

To the local Boards it seemed a waste of money to maintain separate institutions. 'Within a few months we see the attempts given up, and all the classes

Agricultural labourer's family budget, Lavenham, Suffolk, 1843

Name	Age	Earnings		Expenditure		
		s	d		s	d
Robert Crick	42	9	0	Bread	9	0
				Potatoes	1	0
Wife	40		9	Rent	1	2
				Tea		2
Boy	12	2	0	Sugar		$3\frac{1}{2}$
				Soap		3
ditto	11	1	0	Blue		$\frac{1}{2}$
				Thread etc.		2
ditto	8	1	0	Candles		3
				Salt		$\frac{1}{2}$
Girl	6	—		Coal and wood		9
				Butter		$4\frac{1}{2}$
Boy	4	—		Cheese		3
	Total earnings	13s	9d	Total expenditure	13s	9d

'But there are numbers of families who, although in the possession of the same amount of wages shown above, do not dispose of it with such frugality, but appear in the greatest state of destitution; many others, with the same number of children, do not get the wages this man's family have. The family I have given as an example is more to show you that with industry and frugality, their diet consists principally of bread and potatoes. There are, however, some who, when their families are grown up, by putting their earnings together, occasionally get a piece of meat at their supper-time, and their Sunday dinner.'

From: Reports of Special Assistant Poor Law Commissioners on the Employment of Women and Children in Agriculture (1843), quoted in JOHN BURNETT *Plenty and Want*. pp. 26–7 (London, 1966).

of poor huddled into a single building.' [31] Husbands and wives were separated, and even though in 1847 an Act permitted couples over sixty to occupy a separate bedroom in the workhouse, 'few had the courage, or the knowledge of the regulations, to take advantage of the concession, and it was not until 1885 that it was made obligatory'. Not until 1868 'were Guardians compelled to provide such minor comforts as backs to the benches on which old people sat or little chairs for children's sick-wards . . .' [32] Inmates were subjected to every conceivable major and minor tyranny. Paupers in Lambeth

Workhouse were not allowed to receive gifts of money, their letters were opened and even their newspapers confiscated. [33] As late as 1895 a Royal Commission on the Aged Poor was urging masters and mistresses of workhouses to abandon uniform times of going to bed and getting up for old people, and again recommending that they should be allowed their separate cubicles, to be allowed (if well behaved and within 'reasonable limits') to go out for walks, visit friends and attend their own places of worship.

Although the central aim of Poor Law administration was to stop outdoor relief for the able-bodied (an aim which was never achieved), it had never been intended to stop outdoor relief for the aged and infirm. Many unions, however, did refuse it to the aged, and indeed to all applicants. Across the whole field of relief spread the stigma of pauperization. The general mixed workhouse was throughout the century the principal method of destitution relief for every kind of contingency. The Minority Commissioners of 1909 pointed out that the authors of the 1834 Report failed to make a distinction between able-bodied pauperism and able-bodied destitution. The men of 1834 had considered that they were dealing with pauperism only, that is, with a condition about which moral judgements could be made, and over which control needed to be exercised. Benthamite economic orthodoxy blinded them to the fact that whole sections of the population in the 1830s (hand-loom weavers, millwrights and workers deprived of employment by seasonal hazards, for example) were unemployed or underemployed. With such able-bodied destitution 'the Royal Commission of 1832–4 chose not to concern itself. We find in its voluminous proceedings no statistics of Unemployment, no statement as to fluctuations of trade, no account of the destitution produced by the new machines.' The Commissioners, in fact, 'concentrated their whole attention on one plague spot – the demoralization of character and waste of wealth produced in the agricultural districts by an hypertrophied Poor Law'. [34] The Poor Law Commission, its Report, and the 1834 Act were intended as answers to 'the degradation of character' caused by the Speenhamland system of subsidized agricultural wages. The new Poor Law policy did not match the reality of forms of poverty which were now endemic and which – as those who suffered it were able to realize and make explicit – directly related to the conditions of industrial growth. The authorities struggled to maintain the purity of the system. The awareness of its unreality and cruelty drove northern working men in particular to emphatic and even spectacular protest against the new Poor Law and its representatives when it began to be implemented in the towns. Out-relief, in fact, did not die. The Act drove a wedge between the middle-class radicals who subscribed to utilitarian philosophy and their former working-class allies, and created, momentarily, an alliance between a generation of Tory reformers and working-class radicals, which at one and the same time was aimed against the mill-owners and for wider rights for working men. The fight against the Poor Law was of major importance in the growth of Chartism.

10 *Scripture reading in a night shelter, 1872. From a print by Gustave Doré.*

During the middle decades of the nineteenth century, therefore, the (for the most part unsolved) problems of urban scale and administration, and most of the individual but related urban problems of housing, health and poverty, were explicit and prominent features of social affairs. These were not, of course, the only urban problems, and mid-Victorian society as a whole was not obsessed by them. The philosophy underlying prevailing middle-class attitudes towards social policies remained that of do-nothing. In restricted fields, restricted legislation was seen to be necessary, and a restricted amount of machinery, spending a severely restricted amount of money, was being created. Administrative authority was frequently vested in *ad hoc* bodies (the Poor Law Commissioners, for example) which, it was felt, might ultimately efficiently organize themselves out of existence. Other authorities (like the Committee of the Privy Council on Education of 1839) crept awkwardly and uncertainly into existence. A constant fight was waged to keep down the size and functions of departments of State and some (the Education Department and the Railways Board, for example) proved far more formidable and far-reaching than their creators could have envisaged. Machinery was being created, and within it the expert was taking his place. The specialist adviser and administrator, in the shape of the inspector of schools or factories, or the medical officer of health, for instance, was making his appearance. Within the individualism of Victorian Britain were taking shape forms of social planning and responsibilities, which, in David Roberts's summary, 'however meagre compared to the responsibilities assumed by Whitehall today . . . did mark the beginning of the welfare state'. [35]

We have looked, in fact, only at some of the most prominent features of the environment and policies of mid-Victorian Britain. And although in later chapters we shall not be concerned in the same way with contemporary developments in these areas of policy and social administration, it has been important here to illustrate something of the context from which modern social development began. We shall not, for example, be following through the details of developments in water supply, health or the railways; they have been intended as illustrations of the processes which governed people's lives, their social relations, their attitudes to themselves and to society and, above all, the levels of human concern beneath those of formal political and economic structures. They point to the forces which helped to shape a particular society, operating on the basis of particular sets of assumptions. They indicate that social evolution is the product of intricate processes of tension and struggle. The structure of mid-Victorian Britain was not static. Neither is that of Britain today. A social situation is the product not of a sequence of automatically changing contexts, but of changes in which social attitudes and decisions play an important part. Modern Britain is as much the product of attitudes towards housing as of attitudes towards machinery. Within the kind of situations we have described there were constant struggles to understand and to ignore, to describe and to misinterpret, to conserve and to alter, to uphold and to jettison. We have so far seen aspects of this struggle in terms of, for example, health and housing. In the next two chapters we shall look at other aspects of the transition to the Britain of recent years, in terms of the broadening of organization for action, and attitudes to social change.

NOTES

1 ADNA FERRIN WEBER *The Growth of Cities in the Nineteenth Century*, p. 157 (New York, 1899; 1963 edition).
2 ROYAL COMMISSION ON THE DISTRIBUTION OF THE INDUSTRIAL POPULATION (BARLOW COMMISSION) *Report*, p. 29 (London, 1940).
3 BARLOW COMMISSION *Report*, p. 12, and *Minutes of Evidence*, p. 399.
4 BARLOW COMMISSION *Minutes of Evidence*, p. 182.
5 See PARRIS *Government and the Railways in Nineteenth-century Britain*, Ch. 1 (London, 1965).
6 R. DUDLEY BAXTER 'Railway extension and its results', in CARUS-WILSON (ed.) *Essays in Economic History*, III, p. 33.
7 NIKOLAUS PEVSNER 'Victorian prolegomena', in FERRIDAY (ed.) *Victorian Architecture*, p. 27.

8 RICHARD D. ALTICK *The English Common Reader,* p. 301 (Chicago, 1957).

9 JACK SIMMONS *The Railways of Britain,* p. 17 (London, 1961; 1965 edition).

10 MAUDE STANLEY 'West-End improvements', *The Nineteenth Century,* May 1881, pp. 852–3.

11 JOHN BURNETT *Plenty and Want,* Ch. 6 (London, 1966).

12 ROYSTON LAMBERT *Sir John Simon 1816–1904,* p. 189 (London, 1963).

13 WILLIAM ASHWORTH *The Genesis of Modern British Town Planning,* p. 38 (London, 1954).

14 F. ENGELS *The Condition of the Working Class in England,* p. 34; trans. W. O. HENDERSON and W. H. CHALONER (Oxford, 1958).

15 Quoted in FRANCES COLLIER *The Family Economy of the Working Classes in the Cotton Industry 1784–1833,* pp. 20–1 (Manchester, 1965).

16 NORMAN LONGMATE *King Cholera,* p. 45 (London, 1966).

17 *First Report,* 1844, I, pp. xxv–xlvii.

18 JAMES H. RIGG *National Education in its Social Conditions and Aspects,* p. 33 (London, 1873).

19 LAMBERT *Sir John Simon,* p. 175.

20 DAVID ROBERTS *Victorian Origins of the British Welfare State,* pp. 310–15 (New Haven, 1960).

21 Quoted from E. N. WILLIAMS *A Documentary History of England,* 2, p. 230 (Harmondsworth, 1965).

22 WEMYSS REID *Memoirs and Correspondence of Lyon Playfair,* pp. 65–6 (London, 1899).

23 Quoted in ASA BRIGGS 'Cholera and society in the nineteenth century', *Past and Present,* April 1961, p. 85.

24 REID *Memoirs and Correspondence of Lyon Playfair,* p. 64.

25 *Portrait of an Age,* p. 11 (London, 1936; 1960 edition).

26 LAMBERT *Sir John Simon,* p. 61.

27 Playfair points out proudly that the death rate attributable to 'zymotic diseases' (arising from filth) fell from 4·52 per thousand in 1841–50 to 2·71 per thousand in 1880–4, but the major gains were at the latter end of the period.

28 Quoted from the ROYAL COMMISSION ON THE POOR LAWS, Majority *Report,* 1909, I, p. 103.

29 The figures were 27,985 and 57,638 in the 1801 and 1821 censuses respectively. *Victorian History of the County of Surrey,* p. 447 (London, 1912).

30 AILEEN DENISE NASH *Living in Lambeth 1886–1914,* p. 52 (London, undated).

31 Minority *Report,* III, p. 19.

32 MAURICE BRUCE *The Coming of the Welfare State,* p. 99 (London, 1961; 1965 edition).

33 NASH *Living in Lambeth,* p. 54.

34 Minority *Report,* III, pp. 437–9.

35 ROBERTS *Victorian Origins of the British Welfare State,* p. 315.

The discussion of the growth of towns is continued in Chapters 4 (suburbs) and 6, transport in Chapter 4, housing in Chapters 4 to 6, local government in Chapters 5 and 10, public health in Chapter 5 and the Poor Law in Chapters 4 and 5.

3

Democracy and Social Movements

The British economy in the Victorian 'Golden Age' was, of course, susceptible to setback and crisis, but the picture of the third quarter of the century is over all one of astonishing economic and industrial expansion. Britain's industrial revolution had established for her a paramount position in the world's economic development and trade. Britain supplied railways at home and abroad and British ships carried British consumer and capital goods to overseas customers. Metal and machinery were of central importance in the developments, but cotton and – increasingly – woollens played a major part in exports. By 1851 cotton spinning and weaving had become very largely mechanized mill activities; in the 1860s over 80 per cent of cotton manufacturing output was being exported. Imports of raw cotton almost doubled between 1850 and 1870, and those of wool increased almost fourfold. The 1860s and 1870s saw the consolidation of steam and iron as the basis of shipbuilding, and the amount of merchant shipping powered by steam rose sharply by comparison with sail. In 1851 British yards produced 3·6 million tons of shipping, and in 1871 the figure was 5·7 million. The number of workers employed in shipbuilding, iron and steel more than doubled between the two dates.

The advances which thrust Britain's economy into the industrial dominance of the nineteenth century came, as we have seen, from defined industries. The economic development of the second half of the century could not have taken place in the same way without important changes in the very basis on which industrial firms could establish themselves, and by which the economy could be diversified. These changes were to an important extent connected with developments in limited-liability and joint-stock organization. Before 1844 such organization was virtually prohibited, except by special charter, as in the case of the railways. Partnership was the most common basis of large-scale organization, although even on this basis the large, even the enormous, firm was possible. To form partnerships at New Lanark, in the early years of the century, Robert Owen had had to rely at one stage on family investors and at another on London connections. Acts between 1844 and 1862, making joint-stock organization possible, recruited the funds of the small investor impersonally. The effect on industrial organization was quite dramatic: in the six years following the 1856 Act, for example, nearly 2,500 companies registered. What was demonstrated was that 'limited liability was needed for local enterprises of a useful kind, financed by numerous passive small investors . . . The great increase under this Act of 1856 . . . shows the popularity of the limited form and clearly demonstrates both the need and usefulness of this form as a factor of enterprise.' [1] The eagerness with which small investors had flocked to invest in railways in the 1830s and 1840s was a demonstration of the availability of savings for investment purposes. Railway, banking and joint-stock developments illustrate how closely connected the rise in and spread of middle-class domestic standards were to the economic conditions in which it took place.

The effect of these changes on the size and structure of industrial firms, and on social relations within them, was considerable. In the small firm of the early phase of industrialization, relations between man and master, however cordial or brutal they may have been, were direct. At one level they were, of course, class-divided, as the ferocities unleashed by trade union activity demonstrate, but at another level they were organic: there was a common destiny that could be felt to be involved in the fate of the firm, and the success of the factory owner depended not only on his ability to market his products, but on his ability directly to handle his men, to conciliate or to tyrannize over them. The expansion of firms led gradually to specialization at the level of management as well as to a finer division of labour among workers. The workers' relationships with management (including hiring, firing and wages) came increasingly to be through the all-powerful foreman. In a South Wales valley, as Phelps Brown points out, the difference in the new situation was noticed 'when the miner who had had a dispute with the deputy or under-manager could no longer walk across the fields and see the owner at the door of his house, but must deal with a manager who was tied down by instructions from the head office of the combine in Cardiff'. Remote power (as likely as not to be malevolent) became more common, and workers had to deal with 'a poker-faced man whose relation with you was dehumanized and strait-jacketed'. [2] Employers became different types of people, hedged around with considerations of education and class position. Social distance increased. The role of the trade union official began to change, London headquarters and national negotiations assumed greater importance, and the pattern of modern British industrial social relations began to take shape in the conditions of the joint-stock, impersonal financing of industrial development.

By the beginning of the 1870s Britain had for a quarter of a century or so been reaping, as a nation, major benefit from the second phase of her industrial revolution. The advantages of having been the first to industrialize were obviously immense; economically, however, there were to be disadvantages. Other nations were to see more readily than Britain the need to readjust old methods and techniques, to invest in newer forms of capital equipment; British industrialists were reluctant to invest in modernization, so long as old plant and old routines continued to be profitable. Capital for newer industries, taking advantage of new materials and inventions, was to be slower to come forward in Britain than in newly industrializing countries. Many of the problems of the decline of the staple industries after the First World War derive from the very fact of their dominance in the late nineteenth century. Similarly, with established industrial techniques and a hitherto successful basis of apprenticeship and practical skills, Britain fell steadily behind other nations in scientific and technical education (and education in general). The tradition of the amateur scientist and the uneducated inventor of the George Stephenson type died hard. A young boy visiting Stephenson's house was shown his 'cyphering book', the contents of which 'extended as far as the "rule of five", from Tinwell's Arithmetic. I don't think he went much beyond this in his arithmetical education.' [3] This had been a successful tradition in the early stages of industrialization, although it is possible that this tradition has been exaggerated in past efforts to assess the role of education and science in the Industrial Revolution. Efforts at technical education did exist, from the early decades of the nineteenth century, largely – in the first place – through the Mechanics' Institutes; they were encouraged by government departments and grants after the Great Exhibition. The results, however, were meagre and the radical reorganization necessary in the approach to the basis of industrial skills did not take place. New competitors were entering the world's markets, on which the British economy – by dominating them – had come to be dependent.

From the early 1870s the British economy entered a phase deceptively described as the Great Depression, a period, through to roughly the end of the century, in which it was widely felt that parts of the economy were running down. Foreign competition and free trade were held by many to be responsible. Lord Randolph Churchill strongly expressed this view in 1884, tracing the depression back a decade:

> Your iron industry is dead, dead as mutton; your coal industries, which depend greatly on the iron industries are languishing. Your silk industry is dead, assassinated by the foreigner. Your wool industry is *in articulo mortis,* gasping, struggling. Your cotton industry is seriously come to a standstill ... Well, but with this state of British industry what do you find going on? You find foreign iron, foreign wool, foreign silk and cotton pouring into the country, flooding you, drowning you, sinking you ...

Although such rhetoric on behalf of tariffs was never in the late nineteenth century able to disturb the basic British confidence in her ultimate supremacy through free trade, it nevertheless reflects the growing uneasiness. Churchill was as sure that free imports were murdering British industry 'as if I found a man standing over a corpse and plunging his knife into it'. [4] A Royal Commission Appointed to Inquire into the Depression of Trade and Industry reported categorically in 1886 that Britain was in all fields of production falling behind Germany. The Commission found that those giving evidence were in general agreement on four points: that trade and industry were 'depressed', that this meant smaller profits and less employment, that it was the value of trade and not its volume that had declined, and that since 1875 the depression had more or less consistently affected trade and industry, and especially agriculture. [5] There were indeed serious realities behind the exaggerations of Churchill and the anxieties of the Commission. It was not only a question of German steels and skills. America was now able to supply herself (and others) with railways. The Paris Exhibition of 1867 was a major shock to British industry, demonstrating that in important fields Britain was falling behind and that entirely new ones, such as electricity and chemicals, were being pioneered by other countries. British products – though not British finance – were no longer indispensable. The search for compensatory markets was seriously engaged: the British Empire was buying 35·4 per cent of Britain's home-produced exports in the period 1909–13, and almost half by the Second World War. International competition was now a question that involved, among other things, Africa. It was to mean war.

Despite the sense, however, of the passing of the Golden Age, the period was not in any precise sense one of depression. Increases in production were offset by falling international prices. The so-called Great Depression was, in the formulation of H. L. Beales, 'a period of progress in circumstances of

11 Wolverhampton, 1866.

great difficulty. It might be dubbed a period of "lean years" in contrast with the preceding good years, if profits were the main criteria of welfare. In no final sense, however, was that period one of retrogression.' The fall in prices was, in fact, enough to cause the return on investments to stagnate or fall, and in many sections of industrial and commercial activity, therefore, the sense of 'being depressed' was acutely felt. The change in 'business psychology' did not come until 1896, when prices began again to rise. [6] By this time, as we shall see, fundamental aspects of British social life had been affected. In addition the future international dangers for Britain's economy were growing distinct. The decline of British dominance coincides with the beginning not only of more complex economic relations, but the increasing internationalization of many aspects of industrial and social activity. From the late nineteenth century it becomes more and more impossible to discuss British social conditions in isolation from those of other countries.

Accompanying the picture of the 'depression' as a period of slower speed is one of increasing real incomes. The evidence, says Ashworth, that these 'rose rapidly in the late nineteenth century does not seem ... to have been seriously undermined, though the sources of the rise may not have been accurately traced and its amount may have been slightly over-estimated'. [7] Falling prices, if production and sales do not adequately compensate for them, mean lower dividends. They also, if no significant changes in employment take place, mean higher purchasing power for wages. The late 1870s and early 1880s, in fact, mark important changes in the value of working-class incomes. Agricultural prices fell, largely under the impact of the opening up of North American wheat lands and the ability to transport frozen meat. Frozen lamb from Australia arrived in London for the first time in 1880. In the last quarter of the century 'significant improvements are observable in the general standard of working-class diet'. [8]

SOCIAL CLASS

We shall see in a later discussion that the concept of social class is notoriously difficult to use and define. We have, however, come to the point at which it is important to examine briefly what was happening to the composition of British society in the economic circumstances of the 1870s and 1880s. We have already assumed a good deal about this composition in our use of terminology, and, to clarify the picture fully, it will be necessary to look at class composition, the industrial and occupational classification of the population, its regional distribution and aspects of its age, sex and family composition. Before we approach these in outline, and class composition in particular, there are two points that need to be remembered. The first is that in one crucial respect the examination of problems of class in the nineteenth century remains unaltered today: that is, despite the development in social mobility that has taken

12 Rotten Row, 1872. From a print by Gustave Doré.

place, the element of inheritance in people's social position has not disappeared. The boundaries of class, in T. B. Bottomore's view, may have become blurred and some expansion of opportunities may have taken place, but 'there is no general sense of greater "classlessness", nor of great opportunities for the individual to choose and create his way of life regardless of inherited wealth or social position'. [9] It was certainly true of Victorian society that men did not 'choose and create' their way of life, and were aware that they did not.

The second point to remember is that the very process of mobility reminded men in Victorian Britain of the reality of class. Mobility does not, and men were then conscious that it did not, alter the fact of an overall class relationship. Edward Thompson emphasizes that class is a historical phenomenon. The concept is meaningful only in terms of the interaction between real people in a real context. We do not start with 'two distinct classes, each with an independent being, and then bring them *into* relationship with each other'. Class happens, he suggests, when 'some men, as a result of common experiences (inherited or shared), feel and articulate the identity of their interests as between themselves, and as against other men whose interests are different from (and usually opposed to) theirs'. [10] Thompson's view is that the attempt of some sociologists to stop this process dead 'at any given moment and anatomize its structure' is impossible: the relationship is too elusive. Late nineteenth-century society illustrates, however, that with Thompson's historical reality in mind such an analysis can, in fact, be made. The attempt to stop history dead and anatomize it fails only if sociology itself is unaware of, or rejects, the reality of historical movement and direction contained within the phenomena it investigates. There is no reason why sociology should be so unaware, or should reject such a reality. How sociologists consider this question in terms of contemporary Britain is matter for our later discussion. Here the point is that, against the background we have described, men did not fail to see themselves in relation to other men, and to use the terminology of class in so doing.

Behind the complexities of nineteenth-century politics lay a continued concentration of major areas of power in the hands of what Kitson Clark calls the 'nobility and gentry – old style'. The 1832 Reform Act was not a symbolic arrival at the ultimate position of power by the middle class; nor did it mark the decline of the ancient English aristocracy. The eighteenth century 'lingered at the top of society as obstinately and as self-confidently as it did anywhere in the social pattern of Victorian England'. Until the new patterns of power that emerged as a result of political pressures before and after the 1867 Reform Act and the economic situation from the early 1870s, parliament continued to be dominated by the old 'feudalism', the 'landed interest'. Politics was still in the middle of the century 'to a remarkable extent the plaything of the nobility and gentry'. [11] What was true of parliament was also true of other aspects of national life, including the Civil Service, although the introduction of competitive examinations (following the

Trevelyan-Northcote Report of 1854) began slowly to make inroads into aristocratic patronage and domination in the Civil Service. Certainly until then it was normal for the top administrative positions to be occupied by the aristocracy, giving England what David Roberts calls 'a rule of patricians' – a rule which was 'in general conscientious, honorable, and enlightened'. Eighteenth-century traditions persisted in administration as well as parliament. The virtues of the 'patricians' were those 'of the eighteenth-century grandee, or as some of them fancied, of Roman senators'. [12] Their power and influence were great, and the subsequent history of power in Britain is to a large degree concerned with the way in which the centres of hereditary power were able to continue relatively unmolested past the first exercise in parliamentary democracy in 1832 and its sanctification as a principle in the Act of 1867, and survive the social readjustments of the late century. The position of the gentry was undermined in very direct ways – in, for example, the loss of the traditional powers of the country justices, greater taxation, and the emergence of modern political parties to cut back the traditional ascendancy of hereditary influence. But the gentry 'old style' intermingled with the 'new gentry' born of industrial and commercial expansion. Influence found new ways to operate, and hereditary positions found new ways to reassert themselves. New strengths were found for the traditional qualities of England's aristocratic 'grandees'.

For a prolonged period, therefore, the new middle class, or middle classes, had the problem of defining themselves in terms of their relationships across both an upper and a lower frontier. The middle-class Liberals of the 1860s were as aware of the 'feudalism' above them as they were of the slippery but important boundary which delimited them from the other nation below. The perpetuation of aristocratic power and the attacks on its positions offer a clue to the agonies of self-definition through which the middle class went in the second half of the century.

If class can only be seen as a relationship, it is imperative to realize that the relationship existed across a wide range of social processes. The most obvious relationship downwards was in terms of employment, the economic basis on which Marx's analysis of class identities and class struggle was primarily (though not exclusively) made. This was the relationship of factory owner to factory worker, of mistress and servant. The relationship involved in class self-consciousness was also apparent, however, in the class differentiation of towns as middle-class suburbia spread, in the differentiation of shopping and consumption, education and religious worship. For example, the Board Schools created by the 1870 Education Act were as categorically working-class as the revivified grammar schools were middle-class. The complex definition of the concept of middle-class people would, in fact, have to compound not only the economics of their income and the status evaluation of their occupations, but increasingly their postal district, religious affiliation, schooling and – in the case of new professions and the changing status of older ones – their relationship to inferiors. For those at lower levels of the middle class, particularly in small business and clerical positions, the definition was of poignant importance.

The expansion of the world of commerce and trade is, of course, the central fact of the Victorian middle class. The merchant and the middle class were not phenomena created by industrial Britain, but the nature of the nineteenth-century economy meant a sharply widening catchment area of population involved in middle-class economic activities; the expansion of joint-stock enterprises, the increase in the scale of industrial (and public) administration, and the growing territory of industrial invention and production skills, meant a considerable growth in the numbers of managers, shopkeepers and industrial entrepreneurs. The ideals of the new middle class (that is, those who grew out of the accepted reality of a way of life committed not only to affluence but to a display of affluence) were a long way from the Protestant ethic described by Weber as a feature of the origins of industrial society. When *The Times* in 1919 reviewed the difficulties of the middle class it traced its history in miniature:

> ... the plight of the middle classes is undoubtedly partly due to a disposition for the last twenty or thirty years to aim at a standard of living which has been far too high, to seek expensive pleasures, and to neglect the more irksome duties of citizenship. In the Victorian era, which it is now the fashion to despise, the middle classes lived far more simply and frugally. They did not frequent costly restaurants, went to the theatre once a month, travelled comparatively little, rarely sought a continental holiday, and were more interested in domestic life ... [13]

What *The Times* was deploring was a process which, in Edwardian England, had grown out of tendencies within Victorian society itself. The Great Exhibition, for example, had been 'a monument to middle-class endeavour and success'. The middle class had initially been driven by 'the gospel of hard work', which, in preaching and organizing for others, they had accepted for themselves: 'the middle classes set the example in work and austerity; the manufacturers led a protesting nation into the factories, preaching that its reward would be in the next world – while reaping a considerable interim dividend for themselves in this.' [14]

New foods, new consumer products, new luxuries, new services, new styles of living, were all part of the breakdown of the old ethic, and the adoption of new suburban shopping-centred, home-centred, child-centred, comfort-centred standards. In this situation there is a marked example of what Veblen described as rising standards of possessions – as 'conspicuous consumption'. Veblen explains how human beings, from primitive society onward, become involved, by virtue of the very existence of a leisure class, in processes of social emulation.

13 'Boulter's Lock: Sunday Afternoon', 1897.

Position becomes identified not only with the possession of leisure, but with the possession of its symbols — most obviously servants. A leisure class develops an 'instinctive repugnance for the vulgar forms of labour' and abstention from labour 'is not only an honorific or meritorious act, but it presently comes to be a requisite of decency'. Leisure and evidence of wealth become 'means of gaining the respect of others'. Conspicuous consumption of valuable goods 'is a means of reputability to the gentleman of leisure'. Veblen's thesis up to this point does not apply directly to the Victorian middle class in general in the first half of the century. It becomes relevant, however, when we remember, from our discussion of industry and industrial relations, that the increased scale and changing structure of industrial and commercial organizations made it possible for the middle class in greater numbers to strive after and attain the trappings of leisured life. The availability of a widening range of 'conspicuous' domestic goods, including the bric-à-brac stimulated by the Great Exhibition, intensified the process. Veblen, still discussing the leisure class, goes on to explain how, in the modern urban community in particular, greater involvement in large gatherings (theatres, ballrooms, shops, etc.) places people in front of 'transient observers', and to impress them

and to retain one's self-complacency under their observation, the signature of one's pecuniary strength should be written in characters which he who runs may read. It is evident, therefore, that the present trend of the development is in the direction of heightening the utility of conspicuous consumption as compared with leisure.

Leisure, therefore, in the second half of the century, became subsidiary to the 'struggle to outdo one another'. The city population especially 'push their normal standard of conspicuous consumption to a higher point ... The requirement of conformity to this higher conventional standard becomes mandatory ... this requirement of decent appearance must be lived up to on pain of losing caste.' [15] The commitment of the Victorian middle class to this battle to raise standards, to emulate the class above and differentiate themselves from the class below, is apparent in everything from the changing habits and demeanour of the Victorian owner and manager, to the crinoline, the architecture of the villa and the clutter of the drawing-room. It was, as we shall see in the next chapter, an important aspect of the crisis of incomes and family size in the last decades of the century. What *The Times* was deploring in 1919 was the fact that the battle for conspicuous consumption and conspicuous leisure had been taken out of the home.

The complex structure of the middle class changed during the century to incorporate the newly expanding and newly aspiring professional groups necessary to industrial and public administration. The rulers of the old order understood, within limits, the virtues of the new middle-class professionals, although the failure to appoint Chadwick one of the Poor Law Commissioners provides an illustration of the limits. In answer to Chadwick's protests at not being appointed, Lord Althorp reminded him in 1841 of the social realities: 'I must frankly admit', he told him, 'that your station in society was not such as would have made it fit that you should be appointed one of the commissioners.' [16] It was the middle class, however, which provided the growing mass of administrators, civil servants, factory and school inspectors. Into it came some of the growing clerical and supervisory occupations. Between 1881 and 1901 the numbers employed in 'general and local government' rose from 97,000 to 172,000. Old and stigmatized occupations, from the apothecary to the dissenting minister, acquired firm middle-class status. The new duties and relationships of members of some sections of established professions, such as the law and engineering, also achieved the raised status. The position of the relatively new occupation of architect and the element of training or impersonal consultation involved in such occupations as that of the civil engineer gained, as we have seen, both accepted status and the cachet of the professional association. The expansion of the middle class, therefore, rests on the morality of impersonal investment, the growth of the larger production unit and bank, and the concomitant need, in an increasingly urban environment, for reliable administrators and experts. It rests also on the rising scale of private consumption and the production and commercial opportunities it offered. On the basis of the 1851 census it has been estimated that rather less than one and a quarter million adult males, about 18 per cent of the labour force, were in middle-class occupations. About half of these were in commercial occupations, about a quarter were farmers, and the remainder 'members of the professional, administrative and employing classes' in commerce or industry. 'Most of the middle class', it is pointed out, in the singular, 'was literate.' [17] Those of the middle class who were not involved in a direct relationship with the working class through the process of production, were engaged in a constant comparative and explicit relationship in terms of housing and style of life, consumer consumption and educational and cultural values.

Working-class identity was a product of the conditions of early industrialization. In factory conditions, and in the unanimity of protest and ideal, the coherence of an industrial working class was born. Within it, as the century progressed, powerful groups of skilled manual workers emerged, able to improve their wages and conditions and achieve – within the working class – a special status. In the later part of the century a more and more substantial stratum of semi-skilled machine-minders – especially in the metal and engineering industries, and chemicals – grew up between the highly skilled and the unskilled. The process was to result eventually, as science was applied more widely to methods of production, in a decline in the proportion of workers employed directly on production, and an increase in the proportion of service or 'tertiary' groups of workers. In 1851 just over a million people were employed in domestic service. Machine and boiler making accounted for under

64,000, but 'blacksmiths' for over 112,000, and iron workers 80,000. Some 150,000 were employed in different types of transport. In 1881 the number employed in 'domestic' occupations had risen to over one and a half million. 'Metals, machines, etc.' now absorbed some 813,000, and 'conveyance of men, goods, etc.' approached 800,000. [18] The proportion of workers employed in agriculture steadily declined, from 21·7 per cent of the labour force in 1851 to 8·7 per cent in 1901. While the occupational balance of the population was tilting continuously towards industry, mining, building and transport, it should be remembered that the standards of middle-class prosperity led to a high proportion being constantly employed in the 'domestic and personal services' category (15·3 per cent of the labour force in 1871, and 13·9 per cent in 1911). 'Industrialization or no industrialization,' comments Phyllis Deane, 'the army of domestic servants, the host of housemaids which served the Victorian middle-class home, was still growing faster than the labour force, until towards the end of the nineteenth century it reached its peak.' [19]

The occupational structure of the working class was changing, therefore, to reflect both expanding older industries and employment in new ones. The old staple industries continued to expand up to 1914. British coal exports, for example, dominated world markets until the First World War. Although Britain was to pay the penalty of her pioneering status in these industries, the end of the century saw aspects of modernization which were important for future industrial development and indicative of occupation trends. At the close of the century industries such as hosiery, footwear, clothing, flour-milling and brewing were almost completely mechanized. [20] Greater precision was achieved and cheaper machinery available, the small steam-engine was brought into use, and new light industries (for example, large-scale bicycle manufacture – an important prelude to the manufacture of cars) were created. The geographical as well as the occupational distribution of the population was to be substantially influenced by these changes. An efficient gas mantle, invented in the 1880s, staved off the doom of gas lighting (which had been universally available since the 1820s) until beyond the end of the century. The electricity industry expanded only slowly in the second half of the century. The first modern power station was opened at Deptford in 1889 and by 1900 the incandescent lamp was unchallengeable. British electrical engineering, however, lagged considerably behind that of the United States and Germany.

These are only some indications of the industrial context within which the changes in working-class occupational structure were taking place in the late century. In the middle of the century wage differentials between skilled and unskilled workers had increased, and were either steady or increased up to 1914. Eric Hobsbawm describes the wage and status gap between the working-class 'aristocrats' and the rest, and also the important 'transfer of the centre of gravity within the labour aristocracy from the old pre-industrial crafts to the new metal industries'. [21] The real wages of all workers in full work rose considerably in the second half of the century. The wide differences in the wage rates of skilled and unskilled workers were reduced in the 1890s, but widened again between the turn of the century and the First World War. In 1867 a skilled engineer earned on average approximately twice as much as a labourer; in 1914 he earned perhaps 50 per cent more.

It is difficult to generalize about so complex a phenomenon as the structure of the working class over so long a period. The working class was never homogeneous, although in many senses it tended to become less and in others more so. There were, as recent historians have been at laborious pains to demonstrate, differences in methods of work, traditions, levels of income and status. [22] Such differences of economic and social position, of course, point to differences in response to such things as industrial bargaining and disputes, suffrage demands and political representation. Rises in the incomes of some lower groups brought them closer to groups above them, but generally speaking economic differentials were real and acutely felt. This did not, however, preclude a growing sense of working-class identity which accompanied the establishment of specifically working-class institutions, such as the Trades Union Congress (in 1868) and the working men's clubs (most of them combined in the Club and Institute Union, founded in 1862). Trades Councils at one level and the T.U.C. at another were vehicles through which this sense of identity was cemented. Chartism and suffrage agitation in the 1860s were forms of awareness of identity in action. The fight for the reform of trade union legislation was another form and 'the successful campaign from 1867 to 1875 gave the movement a new unity, expressed in the establishment of the Trades Union Congress'. [23] The Webbs saw the T.U.C. as 'an outward and visible sign of that persistent sentiment of solidarity which has . . . distinguished the working class'. [24]

In many ways, some hazy, some intensely practical, this unification, this sense of working-class solidarity, was strengthened in these decades. There was contained in working-class experience throughout the century an approach to society, to social organization and purpose, and to concepts of democracy and community, fundamentally different from that which rested on the individualism of the middle class. Where middle-class values were predominantly those of consumption and emulation, competition and the supremacy of individual endeavour, working-class survival and advance depended in general on collective action, on the erection of objectives and ideals from the starting point of common experience, shared deprivation. This growing unification – embodied in working-class institutions encompassing independent trade union and co-operative, political and educational activities – pointed towards many of the critical disputes about politics, culture and society in the twentieth century. Raymond Williams has, in *Culture and Society*, analysed some of the achievement and promise of this tradition. In *The Long Revolution* he has discussed some of its disappointments. What working-class experience and organization in the nineteenth century offered, he suggests, was not only a system of 'sectional defence', but a

steady offering and discovery of ways of living that could be extended to the whole society, which could quite reasonably be organized on a basis of

14 Lock-out in South Wales, February 1875. A pawn-office at Merthyr Tydfil.

collective democratic institutions and the substitution of co-operative equality for competition as the principle of social and economic policy.

What in fact happened was that this challenge was eroded, under strong pressure from the existing organization of society for the co-operatives to 'be simply trading organizations, the trade unions simply industrial organizations with no other interests, each union keeping to its own sphere, and the Labour Party simply an alternative government in the present system'. [25]

POWER AND POLITICS

From social class, therefore, it is a short step to questions of the diffusion of power and participation in the process of social progress, that is, to the concept of democracy. Given the situations and relationships of classes in the nineteenth century, it is useful to ask here what is the nature of social change, seen as a result of forces which include purposeful social action. We are concerned in this respect with public opinion, with social movements and political agitation. Social history is concerned, when it is concerned with politics, with popular politics, representative movements and the effects of political change on social assumptions and behaviour. It is concerned with movements not only for the suffrage, but for industrial legislation and trade union rights, for co-operative organization, a free press and the specific political, legal and social rights of women. In its concern with influential action, the meaningful and widespread responses and initiatives of men, social history is concerned with all of these contributory aspects to the structure of democracy, although it is possible here only to suggest their barest outlines.

The prime feature of a social movement is its desire to arouse and sustain public opinion in such a way as to effect change. A diffuse movement like Chartism and a tightly organized movement such as the National Education League both aimed to stimulate public concern and to attain precise targets. Rarely can action and achievement be directly correlated; widespread public concern is matched, however, by corresponding shifts of opinion and response on the part of policy-makers. The 1867 Reform Act and the 1870 Education Act were the product of such changing responses – in these cases over long periods of time. The important new feature of nineteenth-century social development was precisely, as was shown outstandingly by Chartism and the Anti-Corn-Law League in one respect and the popular press in another, a new dimension in the marshalling and organizing of opinion.

The 1832 Reform Act disfranchised some rotten boroughs, created new boroughs and enfranchised a quarter of a million new property-owning voters. It deliberately left the working class outside the structure of power. Working-class support for the reform movement went unrewarded. Before the Bill was passed the radical working-class press made it clear to working men that 'the measure gives nothing to you':

> . . . it is considered that it will be a 'stepping-stone to something which will do you good'; now the only ground upon which it can possibly be so considered is that the 'reformed constitution' will be more favourable to your interests than the present, or rather, that £10 house-holders or 'middle-men', who will acquire a voice in the government, will be more inclined to admit your right to Universal Suffrage, &c.: we have already exhausted all our argument to prove to you that the 'middle-men' are the 'master-men', and that you are the 'serving-men', and that the interest of the former is to depress the latter . . .

The Bill would not benefit 'the degraded mob'. It 'may perhaps benefit a few, but it will still be at the expense of the many. It will benefit none but the proud and arrogant "shopocracy".' [26]

There were already strong traditions of working-class independence born in the system of Methodist study classes, trade unionism, political and Luddite agitation, and Owenite co-operation. The experience of the Chartist movement, which reached its peaks in 1842 and 1848, confirmed this sense of a need for independent working-class political and social action. The working class had defined its aims in relation to the 'middle-men'. Chartism aimed formally at annual parliaments, universal male suffrage, equal electoral districts, the removal of property qualifications for membership of parliament, the secret ballot and payment for members. The middle class in (or holding some of the strings of) power did not feel strong enough to absorb a new democratic development towards the working class and resisted the strong Chartist pressures. Growing national prosperity, the alliance between skilled trade unions and Liberalism, and the internal uncertainties of working-class radical programmes, made it possible for working men to be kept outside the

Voters as a percentage of the population aged over 20 years

1831	5·0%
After 1832 (First Reform Act)	7·1%
After 1867 (Second Reform Act)	16·4%
After 1884 (Third Reform Act)	28·5%
After 1918	74·0%
After 1928 (Equal Franchise Act)	96·9%

After S. GORDON *Our Parliament*, Cassell (London, 1964).

structure of political democracy until the middle class felt capable of containing and indeed benefiting from its further extension. Chartism made universal suffrage ultimately inevitable, projecting important social ideals into the national consciousness, but this, the first major organized political movement of the working class, was unable to dictate the speed and terms on which the political and social concessions were finally to be made.

Reform came in 1867, with an Act which took seats from small boroughs and gave them to large ones, gave the suffrage in boroughs to all householders and to lodgers paying ten pounds a year or more, and added one million voters to the registers. The Act was not an immediate outcome of the Chartist movement, but new pressures had built up between the decline of Chartism and the late 1860s. Trade union pressures especially had been strong in the early 1860s, and even when agitation for reform was not taking place there was a sense of its imminent possibility. In 1866 and 1867 agitation for reform was firm and influential. [27] With the Act of 1867, working men in towns were largely admitted to the franchise. The 1884 Act created another two million voters by putting the vote in the countryside on the same basis as the urban franchise.

The history of parliamentary reform comprises other considerations. It has to answer the question: what difference did these developments make to political life and public opinion? Apart from their reflection of changes in the centres of political power, they also reflect profound changes in the very nature of political awareness. The pressures towards the 1867 Act, for example, and the Act itself, demonstrated the new need to 'capture' the working-class voter. Out of the confused alliances which had hitherto characterized political groupings was emerging the concept of the modern political party, which needed to try to enlist mass support. Before 1867 Gladstone had become leader of a Liberal Party profoundly different from the old Whig and Radical alliances. 1867 marks the appearance of nation-wide leaflet circulation, and for the first time in the late 1870s Gladstone established the practice of making speeches in his constituency during the parliamentary session, and courting press publicity. It was Disraeli and the Conservatives who, after much manœuvring, had promoted what he called the 'leap in the dark' of the 1867 Act. The working-class vote went, however, in the election that followed, to the Liberals. For the next five years Disraeli worked to set up the first efficient centralized English party organization – the National Union of Conservative and Constitutional Associations. It won him seats at by-elections and 'had candidates ready in every constituency which he could conceivably hope to win. The general election of 1874 was the first triumph of the Conservative Central Office.' [28]

The impetus to local organization was given by the need to recruit and retain the popular vote, to dominate local government with its growing powers, and to manipulate the voting system in constituencies with more than one member. The result, in the mid-1870s, was the Birmingham 'caucus'. Joseph Chamberlain, using the experience of the 1868 election and of School Board elections, built a local Liberal organization which was the first effective local political machine of its type. A complex machinery of ward and committee organization was established, combining democratic features with strong central control. Two results ensued: first, Chamberlain's 'caucus' dominated Birmingham local government; secondly, other local Liberal organizations, and then the powerful National Liberal Federation, came into existence, confirming the arrival of the age of mass political organization and appeal. [29] From within the parliamentary parties pressures had been exerted which resulted in the creation of Liberal and Conservative constituency organizations. The Labour Party, at the beginning of the twentieth century, was to work in the reverse direction, with organizations outside parliament seeking to build a parliamentary representation. National and local politics were a two-way process. All major legislation in the field of parliamentary representation was followed by important legislation affecting the structure and operation of local government and affairs. The 1832 Act, as we have seen, was followed by Acts directly affecting factory conditions (1833), school building (1833) and municipal government (1835). The 1867 Act was followed by the

15 Bloody Sunday, 13 November 1887. The Life Guards hold
Trafalgar Square.

reconstruction and expansion of the basis of elementary education (1870) and the machinery of central and local sanitary administration (1871–2). The 1884 Act was followed by the 1888 Local Government Act, bringing the country districts into line with urban administration by the establishment of county councils. In very many cases such legislation followed on the work of Commissions appointed by incoming governments elected on the basis of new franchise conditions.

Working-class efforts to achieve a wider measure of political participation continued through the century to lie uneasily between the necessity to use Liberal machinery to exercise political influence and the necessity for independent action. The rival socialist organizations of the 1880s (including the Social Democratic Federation and the Fabian Society), and the hostility during the 1890s between the old unionism of the skilled workers and the new unionism of the organized unskilled, reflect some of the tensions in the labour movement before the Labour Representation Committee was – with many hesitations – created in 1900 (changing its name to the Labour Party after the election of 1906).

Throughout the century the thrust towards independent action vacillated between different forms. The working class had its own radical political organizations, its own radical press, a long history of involvement in organized political protest, and experience of various forms of repression. The working-class co-operative movement had begun in the 1820s with the aim of creating communities for production and a better way of life. Co-operative store-keeping grew from the beginnings at Rochdale in 1844 through to the establishment of a nation-wide network of shops offering cheap, unadulterated food, and the creation of the Co-operative Wholesale Society in 1860. The co-operative movement in its first phase was a design for an alternative way of living; in its second phase it was a way for working-class families to participate in some of the benefits of rising material standards.

The trade unions of the 1830s were also involved to a considerable extent with ideals of social reorganization which went far beyond the immediate problems of the trade unionist – though it was frequently the bewilderments of the immediate situation that led to the identification of trade unionism with wider ideals, including those of Owenism. The New Model unions from the 1850s, with high rates of subscription and benefit, aimed explicitly to organize the craft labour aristocracy. The unions of skilled workers played a dominant part in the early history of the Trades Councils, and their officials played a skilful and successful part in pressing for improved legislation affecting the unions. Conciliation and expert political pressure on the one hand could be accompanied by decisive strike action on the other. The New Model, however, in the conditions of the 1880s, had become old unionism. The New Unions, organized for the most part by socialists, covered the unskilled across whole industries, offering low subscriptions and effective militancy as the stimulus to membership. Unionism among the unskilled had been alive in places like the ports of Hull and Liverpool from the 1870s, but the union and strike of the Bryant & May match-girls in 1888, the organization on a larger scale in 1888 and 1889 of unions among the gas workers and dock workers, and the London dock strike of 1889, demonstrated the arrival of general unionism. These developments in trade unionism, though they were not consistent in the 1890s, pointed (as did the foundation of the Independent Labour Party in 1893) towards the future coalescence of working-class organizations into the Labour Party.

FACTORY LEGISLATION

The kind of social and political movements we have been considering both reflected and shaped changes in social consciousness. Many of the settled assumptions of mid-Victorian Britain were crumbling by the final decades of the century, and we have been glancing ahead to some of the new frameworks of discussion and action. Discussion of social problems and even awareness of social realities are conditioned not only by what *is* but by what is *pointed out to be*. By the end of the Golden Age settled assumptions had been assailed by the demonstration of fact and the campaign for change. By the 1870s these changes had begun to take place against a background of at least one set of assumptions in which firm changes had already taken place – that relating to industrial conditions. From the late 1860s trade unionism was not only placed in a new situation of political influence, but also found itself having to adjust to new responsibilities and accommodations with the law and the employers. The nature of the regulation of factory conditions is obviously related to the strength and purpose of the working-class movement, but it is also related to technical and structural changes within industry, to assumptions about social and economic organization, to complementary legislation (on, for example, education and health), and to differing attitudes towards the economic and social roles of male and female, adult and child. We have not traced the earlier history of factory conditions and legislation, and we can do so now only in the barest outline. It is important, however, to establish how far this process had gone, indicative as it is of some of the contradictions in the Victorian scheme of things. There are two important facts about the situation to bear in mind: factory reform throughout the century was concerned almost exclusively with women and children; and the subject of legislation was not wages, but hours of work.

The first Factory Acts of 1802 and 1819 were concerned with pauper apprentices in cotton mills. The first effective Act (that of 1833) limited hours to nine a day for children under thirteen, and twelve a day for young persons between thirteen and eighteen. Pressure for a ten-hour Bill covering adult males had been evaded and, by organizing children in shifts, firms could in fact work adults fifteen hours a day. The Act involved a number of gains:

textiles other than cotton were included, schooling was made a requirement for factory children for two hours a day, six days a week (the first form of compulsory schooling in England) and the principle of compulsory holidays for children and young persons was introduced. The appointment of four factory inspectors – not in itself enough to check abuses – was an important departure for the whole development of the structure of public responsibility. The 1842 Mines Act prohibited the employment of women and of children under the age of ten underground (a measure evaded for a long time in some places) and introduced safety restrictions. Other legislation gave mining by the 1870s a basic legislative code (the first national miners' union had been formed in 1858).

Textiles, however, continued to be the area of main legislative attention until the 1870s. An Act of 1844 made a further step towards industrial safety and the protection of children; women and young persons were now classified together, with the maximum working day remaining at twelve hours, and a schooling requirement of fifteen hours a week for children. This 'half-time' system (applauded by Marx, who considered that it provided a proper combination of learning and industrial experience) continued until after the First World War. The direction of the legislation was now clearly to protect workers in general by restricting the work of women and children, on whom – in the textile industries – the operations performed by adult males depended. The Ten Hours Act of 1847 was the culmination of nearly two decades of agitation for such an Act, agitation which had brought together Shaftesbury-type 'social Tories' and ten-hour committees organized by the workers in the northern textile counties. This agitation interlocked with Chartism, trade unionism and other protest movements. The Act set the pattern for subsequent factory legislation. The basic provision was a ten-hour day (and a fifty-eight-hour week) for women and young persons. The manufacturers found a loophole by organizing irregular relays, and a compromise Act of 1850, which defeated the relay system, stipulated a twelve-hour period within which the hours had to be worked, but extended the working day by half an hour. Dicey's agonized verdict on these two Acts was that they laid the basis 'for a whole system of governmental inspection and control'. Their success 'gave authority, not only in the world of labour, but in many other spheres of life, to beliefs which, if not exactly socialistic, yet certainly tended towards socialism or collectivism'. [30] This is an exaggeration, but it does locate some of the importance of the Acts, and by the time the 1860s and 1870s arrived the history of factory legislation had become interlinked with the history not only of industrial and economic conditions, but also of the changes in political and social assumptions we have discussed. Legislation from then on widened the range of industries covered and intensified the system of inspection. By the First World War it had taken in wider considerations. Employers' liability and compensation for accidents, the conditions of shop workers and the supervision of dangerous industries had become, albeit in some cases timidly,

16 Children's hiring fair, London, 1850.

subjects of legislation and controls. The Coal Mines Regulation Act of 1908 regulated hours for *male* labour, and the 1909 Trade Boards Act represented another new departure in legislation by seeking – as a result of a campaign against 'sweating' – to protect the ill-organized workers in trades such as tailoring (there were fifty-two Trade Boards by 1945, when they became Wages Councils). Joint Industrial Councils (Whitley Councils) came into existence in 1919.

We have looked ahead at this point to some scattered moments of legislation in order to see how, in the special case of industry, a process of broadening social responsibility, covering an increasing range of persons and interests, can be discerned. The process demonstrates how interrelated were factors such as the direction of economic expansion, the strength of popular organization and public opinion, the educational machinery and the economic status of women. It demonstrates how far parliamentary and public involvement was seen to be necessary or inevitable. It illustrates some of the changes taking place in social institutions and social relations, some of the ways in which social assumptions and expectations were being subjected to pressure. It was not only the precedents of previous industrial legislation, but the campaigns to obtain and implement it, that produced responses. Political reform Acts and industrial legislation were surrounded by an awareness that popular organizations, social pressure groups and popular action were now important elements in social change.

NOTES

1 H. A. SHANNON 'The coming of general limited liability', in CARUS-WILSON (ed.) *Essays in Economic History*, I, pp. 375–9.

2 E. H. PHELPS BROWN *The Growth of British Industrial Relations*, pp. 105–13 (London, 1959; 1965 edition).

3 THOMAS SUMMERSIDE *Anecdotes, Reminiscences and Conversations of and with the late George Stephenson*, p. 7 (London, 1878).

4 Quoted from KEITH HUTCHISON *The Decline and Fall of British Capitalism*, pp. 19–22 (London, 1951).

5 The relevant extract can be found in HERMAN AUSUBEL *The Late Victorians*, p. 106 (New York, 1955).

6 'The "Great Depression" in industry and trade', in CARUS-WILSON (ed.) *Essays in Economic History*, I, pp. 406–15.

7 WILLIAM ASHWORTH 'Changes in the industrial structure: 1870–1914', *Yorkshire Bulletin of Economic and Social Research*, Vol. 17, No. 1, May 1965, p. 68. This also provides a useful survey of interpretations of economic developments in the last quarter of the century.

8 BURNETT *Plenty and Want*, p. 156. See also HELEN MERRELL LYND *England in the Eighties* (New York, 1945).

9 *Classes in Modern Society*, p. 41 (London, 1965).

10 THOMPSON *The Making of the English Working Class*, p. 9.

11 CLARK *The Making of Victorian England*, pp. 206–14.

12 *Victorian Origins of the British Welfare State*, p. 138.

13 Quoted in ROY LEWIS and ANGUS MAUDE *The English Middle Classes*, p. 70 (London, 1949).

14 Ibid., pp. 52–3.

15 THORSTEIN VEBLEN *The Theory of the Leisure Class*, pp. 37–88 (New York, 1899; 1912 edition). See especially Chs. III, 'Conspicuous leisure', and IV, 'Conspicuous consumption'.

16 Quoted in ROBERTS *The Victorian Origins of the British Welfare State*, p. 146.

17 DEANE *The First Industrial Revolution*, pp. 264–5.

18 See J. H. CLAPHAM *An Economic History of Modern Britain, Free Trade and Steel 1850–1886*, p. 24 (Cambridge, 1932; 1963 edition); and DAVID C. MARSH *The Changing Social Structure of England and Wales 1871–1961*, pp. 112–18 (London, 1958; 1965 edition).

19 *The First Industrial Revolution*, pp. 255–6.

20 See WILLIAM ASHWORTH *An Economic History of England 1870–1939*, Ch. IV (London, 1960), for a discussion of technological changes in the final decades of the century.

21 E. J. HOBSBAWM 'The labour aristocracy in nineteenth-century Britain', *Labouring Men*, p. 284 (London, 1964).

22 See H. A. CLEGG, ALAN FOX and A. F. THOMPSON *A History of British Trade Unions since 1889*, Vol. I, 1889–1910 (Oxford, 1964), particularly the chapter on 'The trade union movement before 1889'.

23 Ibid., p. 48.

24 Quoted in ibid., p. 250.

25 *The Long Revolution*, p. 302 (London, 1961). See also the conclusion in *Culture and Society 1780–1950* (London, 1958).

26 *The Poor Man's Guardian*, 3 December 1831 and 26 May 1832, pp. 185 and 401.

27 See ROYDEN HARRISON *Before the Socialists* (London, 1965).

28 J. L. HAMMOND and M. R. D. FOOT *Gladstone and Liberalism*, pp. 124–5 (London, 1952).

29 For a brief account of these developments and questions of parliamentary reform in general, see H. J. HANHAM's pamphlet *The Reformed Electoral System in Great Britain 1832–1914* (London, 1968).

30 *Law and Public Opinion in England*, pp. 239–40 (London, 1905; 1962 edition).

Industrial and economic growth (previously discussed in Chapter 1) is discussed in Chapters 5 and 6, radicalism and reform (discussed in Chapter 1) is also discussed in Chapter 5, social mobility (discussed in Chapter 1) is continued in Chapter 8, and democracy (discussed in Chapter 1) is continued in Chapter 10. Trade unions and industrial relations are discussed in Chapters 5 and 6, social class in Chapters 7 and 8, social status in Chapter 7, power and politics in Chapters 7 and 10, and leisure in Chapters 5 and 6.

4

New Dimensions, New Attitudes

The Great Depression, as we have seen, amounted to a crisis of confidence. If, by the end of the century, 'Britain's easy leadership among the industrial nations of the world was over', [1] so also were many of the assumptions and social relationships that went with the industrializing society of the early nineteenth century. Although the economy of early industrial Britain had had certain acute effects on ways of life, family and class relations, there were, as we have also seen, continuities with pre-industrial Britain. From the 1850s the picture is clearer, and from the 1880s it can be discussed in terms which have a recognizable ring to modern ears. By the 1920s the entire range of discussion of social problems had been reordered.

By the final decades of the century the very process of growth, in population and cities, industrial output and the scale of industrial, commercial and social organization, had brought about widespread changes in attitudes towards the problems which these things represented. Growth and scale do not affect our attitudes and emphases alone and unaided: human agency is involved. People have to learn to recognize facts before they can act in the light of them. It is important to remember how surprised people were in the 1840s by Chadwick's 'revelations', or Simon's of the state of the City of London, and how shocked they were by what Booth revealed at the end of the 1880s. Recognition and surprise, as well as the conditions themselves, play a part in the reshaping of social assumptions and social policy.

What men were prepared to believe about the role of human agency in social affairs in the 1840s was something quite different by the 1880s. *Laissez-faire* doctrines, as our discussion has shown, were never applied consistently, even when they were most influential; the dominant *assumption* about human agency in the middle of the century was certainly, however, that it should be allowed to operate unhampered in social matters. It implied the operation of self-help, production for a free market, the absence of interference between employer and employee, and minimal intervention by the collective agencies of society, even in such matters as health. Resistance continued throughout the century to any form of collective action in situations where it was thought that personal or family responsibility should be paramount. Even after 1900, to take one example, when none of the general hospitals had maternity wards, the proposal that St Thomas's in London should introduce one 'was carefully considered with great anxiety, so common at that date, as to whether it might not demoralize those who ought to be able to make provision for the birth of their children at home'. [2]

Where collective agencies did exist and operate successfully, they were generally anxious to keep their activities and expenditure to a minimum. It was a constant and unwelcome surprise to the Victorians to see how relentlessly some of these agencies grew. By the middle of the century a wide range of them had, in fact, been created, including independent commissions in the fields of the Poor Law, charities and the registration of births, deaths and marriages, inspectorates for factories, prisons and mines, Privy Council departments to deal with problems of education and railways, and a variety of more temporary commissions of inquiry. The powers granted to such agencies, however, were intended 'to regulate social and economic matters. Economic freedom was infringed only to correct scandalous evils . . .' [3] Every such development had to overcome resistance. Even in the 1880s the Treasury was asking the Education Department irritably if it foresaw any end to its constant requests for more inspectors. The Department replied that the limit of this demand had 'been very nearly reached'. [4]

Chartism, trade unionism, co-operation and collective self-help on a variety of levels had made prominent contributions to the available range of attitudes to social development; however, the nature of economic development, the type of political reform which took place, the dominant vision of what the British economy could achieve if left unfettered – all these things helped to preserve for Victorian Britain an underlying philosophy of society in which all aspects of social existence were subordinated to the concept of individual responsibility. Doctrines of individual responsibility and individual effort came together at a variety of points in high-Victorian England. In the field of ideas it was Herbert Spencer who embodied the doctrines at their sharpest. A latter-day utilitarian and liberal, Spencer rejected completely the path towards legislative, collective solutions, to which he felt Liberalism and Toryism were both increasingly committing themselves. In *The Man versus the State*, first published in 1884, he catalogued the long and – for him – criminal list of State legislative interference in social processes, interference which meant that the citizen was being gradually 'in the growth of this compulsory legislation deprived of some liberty which he previously had'. The assumption was everywhere being fostered in Spencer's view, that government should step in whenever anything was not going right, a view which took it for granted first 'that all suffering ought to be prevented, which is not true: much

17 Saturday night at a London hospital, 1879.

suffering is curative'. It took it for granted, secondly, that all evils could be removed, which, given the existing defects of human nature, was also untrue. It took it for granted, thirdly, that evils of all kinds should be dealt with by the State, ignoring the proper role of other agencies. [5] *The Man versus the State* is typical of Spencer's general appeal for the limitation of the powers of parliament, and for the enhancement of the value of individual exertion. The State could not cure, and suffering was a stimulus to effort. For Spencer, therefore, the doctrines which had underlain Victorian prosperity, and which were being eroded, needed to be reaffirmed. At the end of his enormous contribution to the literature of education, sociology and popular science, that was the message he had in mind.

From the 1880s onwards, social problems began to attract attention in a new way – although it is important, when examining end-of-the-century forms of 'collectivist' growth, to avoid the danger of assuming too drastic and total a shift away from earlier attitudes. The individual, it was becoming more widely and uncomfortably realized, could not bear full responsibility for his status in society. Was it always possible – it was seriously asked – for the individual, however talented, however industrious, to be the agent of his own success? Was self-help meaningful when it was suspected that there might be structural defects in the economy? How much of what had been interpreted as pauperism was in fact poverty? Was it, after all, undesirable to admit the intervention of collective agencies to set limits on the 'freedom' of the individual, by relieving him of responsibilities which he could not in any case properly bear? Were not housing, health, education, hours of work and the quality of food, for example, already to one extent or another subjects of legislation, and should not the range and scale of this kind of 'interference' be extended? Not everyone in the closing decades of the century asked these questions, and there was certainly no wide measure of agreement even among radicals and liberals on how to answer them. The momentum of change in attitudes had, however, become powerful by the 1890s. The Poor Law illustrates how, in relation to one of the main structural defects in society, the older attitudes clung tenaciously.

Poor Law arrangements after 1834, as we have seen, were a machinery for the protection of the community against what was assumed to be the irresponsible and feckless nature of pauperism. The workhouse, in order to deter, was self-consciously forbidding. It was what one sociologist has called a 'total institution' – that is, 'a place of residence and work where a large number of like-situated individuals, cut off from the wider society for an appreciable period of time, together lead an enclosed, formally administered round of life'. He explains that 'their encompassing or total character is symbolized by the barrier to social intercourse with the outside and to departure that is often built right into the physical plant, such as locked doors, high walls, barbed wire, cliffs, water, forests, or more'. Those immured tend for the most part to be the incapable and the dangerous, but also those whose work qualifies them (e.g. soldiers) or whose way of life requires it (e.g. monks). [6] Although the indigent appear in the list of candidates, in modern British society indigence is not a qualification. In the nineteenth century it was. Poverty, in the final analysis, required as 'total' a treatment as

18 A London workhouse interior.

crime, insanity or military training. Despite relaxations in regulations, the workhouse remained a persistent fact and a symbol of a basic continuity in the dominant forms of social action, at least until after the First World War. George Lansbury, the Labour leader, describes his first visit to a workhouse in the 1890s as follows:

> Going down a narrow lane, ringing the bell, waiting while an official with a not too pleasant face looked through a grating to see who was there, and hearing his unpleasant voice . . . made it easy for me to understand why the poor dreaded and hated these places, and made me in a flash realize how all these prison or bastille sort of surroundings were organized for the purpose of making self-respecting, decent people endure any suffering rather than enter . . . Officials, receiving ward, hard forms, whitewashed walls, keys dangling at the waist of those who spoke to you, huge books for name, history, etc., searching, and then being stripped and bathed in a communal tub, and the final crowning indignity of being dressed in clothes which had been worn by lots of other people, hideous to look at, ill-fitting and coarse — everything possible was done to inflict mental and moral degradation. [7]

Conditions remained arbitrary; cruelty was common. A writer in 1886, pointing to improvements in infirmary nursing, emphasized by contrast the continuing workhouse cruelties, the maltreatment of the mentally and physically sick and the aged, the brutality of the workhouse rulers: 'the days of such tyrants are not yet over, and it is well that we should be reminded of this fact, and aroused from a pleasant dream to the terrible reality'. [8]

The late-century development which revealed this general approach as clearly in the field of social action as did Spencer in the field of ideas was the establishment of the Charity Organisation Society. The C.O.S., founded in 1869, made important contributions to forms of social work, but its main role was to carry over into the charitable field the philosophy of deterrence. Although it intended to co-ordinate and even to supersede existing charitable organizations which, it believed, handed out charity too indiscriminately, it failed from the start to obtain sufficient co-operation from rival charitable bodies. What it did achieve, however, was a prominence in charity work which made the C.O.S. symbolic of a particular view of poverty and the poor. Its aims included 'the promotion of habits of providence and self-reliance, and of those social and sanitary principles, the observance of which is essential to the well-being of the poor and of the community at large', and also 'the repression of mendicity and imposture, and the correction of the maladministration of charity'. [9] The Society withheld, and tried to persuade others to withhold, charity for purposes which the poor ought themselves to have planned and provided for. Although in emergency, and to restore independent endeavour, it was prepared to help with a sewing machine, a horse or training, it strongly resisted any form of action which might seem to encourage idleness. It fought undeviatingly against old age pensions. In the view of its Secretary, C. S. Loch, 'to supplement low wages is to prevent wages from rising: even a postponed supplementation, old age pensions, will have the same effect by discouraging thrift'. [10] One of the first lady almoners, recommended to St Thomas's Hospital by Loch, was greatly relieved in 1908 when Lambeth failed to implement a proposal to open a subsidized meals centre for mothers (as Chelsea had done). 'Fortunately,' she wrote, 'this scheme was not adopted. Any movements of this kind would be disastrous to the neighbourhood and would undermine much of the present effort to raise people from pauperization.' [11]

What this type of philosophy meant in personal terms was recalled indignantly by George Lansbury. His mother used to do little things for the poor of the neighbourhood, including the sending of a Sunday dinner to an old couple living in an East End slum. His wife's mother also visited the sick and needy, and in both cases they came up against the 'malignant work' of C.O.S. policy and the Board of Guardians:

> On at least two occasions these wretched experts in rate saving actually had the impudence to write and request us not to help certain people, as our assistance prevented the Guardians – the Guardians, mind you – from sending them to the workhouse, which in the judgment of these Christians was the best place for them. [12]

For the C.O.S. and its supporters there were two kinds of pauper: those who could be helped back to independence by properly applied, short-term, conditional remedies; and those who could not be helped. The proper organ of support for this latter residue was the Poor Law Board of Guardians with its workhouse. 'There is a subtle and constant influence,' moaned the Majority Poor Law Commissioners in 1909, 'fostered by the kindly instincts of impulsive humanity, which is ever at work sapping and undermining restrictions upon the grant of public relief.' [13] Such instincts, inside or outside the Poor Law machinery, damaged it. Indiscriminate dinners were a distraction from the process of deterrence, and for the sake of the whole apparatus they must be discouraged!

We cannot at this point pause to see in detail how resistance to this particular philosophy grew. There were in general two principal factors in the emergence of organized resistance to social attitudes of this kind, and of alternative policies. The first was the growth of a labour movement better equipped to formulate political and social policies and to take significant action; the second was, partly for this very reason, the elaboration by various social thinkers of alternative policies. The simple fact is that an element in social consciousness after the Reform Acts of 1867 and 1884 was the realization that the working man and his movement were to be reckoned with. As a historian of the growth of the social services has put it: 'politicians could see before the turn of the century that something would have to be done about unemployment. No matter what was the cause of the idle man's condition, after 1885 he was a man with a vote.' [14]

SOCIAL INVESTIGATION

Coupled with this consciousness was the elaboration of new policies rooted in sociological investigation and analysis. Social investigation was not, of course, created in the 1880s by Charles Booth. The collection of social data had become in the nineteenth century an important and influential activity. Since 1801 the compilation of census data had been refined. Henry Mayhew (*London Labour and the London Poor* was written between 1849 and 1862) had been outstandingly preoccupied with precise data as well as with moral demonstration. We have already looked at Chadwick's efforts to discover and confront the facts. Statistical societies attempted – notably in education – to draw accurate guide-lines. Out of the reports of inspectors slowly emerged a realization that social policy and action needed to be based on something more than haphazard information. Industrial reformers understood the role of precise evidence. Engels (in *The Condition of the Working Class in England in 1844*) and Marx (in *Capital*, the first volume of which appeared in 1867) understood the value of detailed documentation. The tradition of 'the discovery of fact' made it possible for Booth, in the more self-conscious conditions of the 1880s, to grasp the importance and relevance of extending the scale of discovery. This preoccupation with problems and facts has continued to be the distinguishing feature of British sociology, by contrast with its more theoretical counterparts in other countries.

Booth, wealthy shipowner, Liberal, rooted in the C.O.S. tradition, began in the second half of the 1880s to organize a series of surveys, first in Tower Hamlets, then in Hackney, and then on a widening basis to cover what the seventeen volumes of his great work (completed in 1903) described as *The Life and Labour of the People of London*. In 1887, seven months after his inquiry began, he read a paper to the Royal Statistical Society in which the only conclusion he was prepared to offer was that 'an unexpectedly high proportion of the total population (of Tower Hamlets), 35 per cent, had been found to be living "at all times more or less in want".' [15] The word 'unexpectedly' is crucial. His inquiry in Hackney, to his own dismay, confirmed these findings. A second paper to the Society in 1888 expressed the view that about one third of the population of London was 'sinking into want'.

The magnitude of this discovery for Booth and for liberal opinion generally cannot be over-stressed. When his work began to appear its impact was considerable, being the focus of widespread discussion in the press; its 'significance was immediate and immense, and the first edition was quickly exhausted'. [16] Booth had set out, in fact, hoping to demonstrate that British social conditions were not as bad as some commentators – particularly the socialists – had claimed them to be. He set in motion machinery, using census material and detailed material collected from School Board Visitors. He ended by changing the whole context of discussion of social realities. The information he collated was in itself dramatic enough: one-quarter to one-third of the population was demonstrated to be living 'in poverty' (including 'the poor' with regular family earnings of eighteen to twenty-one shillings a week, and 'the very poor', earning less). The breakdown of social categories he gave in the second volume of *Life and Labour* (1891) indicated that 8·4 per cent fell into classes A (lowest) and B (very poor), and 22·3 per cent into C and D (poor); 51·5 per cent were in E and F (working class, comfortable) and 17·8 per cent in G and H (middle class and above). [17] The crisis of opinion which the findings entailed for Booth himself was considerable. He had accepted the reality and the need for emphatic social action to alleviate the distress which, he had become convinced, was on a scale which made individual responsibility no longer an adequate answer to the deficiencies in the fabric of society. He came to a conclusion which marks a real turning point in social policies, from the world of nineteenth-century reluctant involvement to that of twentieth-century considered action. 'The individualist community on which we build our faith', he admitted at the critical stage of his dilemma in 1888, 'will find itself obliged for its own sake to take charge of the lives of those who, from whatever cause, are incapable of independent existence up to the required standard . . . and will be fully able to do so.' [18]

If there is a representative text for the new search for directions in social policy this could well be it. Policy was to remain 'individualist', but society was to 'take charge'. Poverty, it was recognized, could result from a variety of causes, and there were definable and 'required' standards. The community as a whole would be 'able'. There is a survival of confidence in all this, but also a recognition of deep difficulties: a sense of inevitability goes along with a new sense of the possibility of change and control. The need for social intervention was exhibited most clearly in Booth's assessment of the actual cause of pauperism: old age, he computed in his survey of Stepney, accounted for 32·8 per cent of pauperism, sickness for 26·7 per cent. [19]

The acceptance of social control over extreme poverty was signalled by Booth's conversion to the idea of old age pensions. This was one of the battlegrounds for old and new views of social action. If Liberal policies for responsibility from 1906 have any recognizable sources they lie not only in the pressing need to conciliate the 'man with a vote', but also in the crisis of conscience of Charles Booth. If the conflicts in the Poor Law Commission of 1905–9 and between its Majority and Minority Reports are to be understood, and if the measures taken in the field of pensions, health and unemployment insurance by a revived Liberalism are to be properly assessed, the sharpness of the crisis which Booth had precipitated and typified needs to be borne in mind. [20] British traditions of social analysis had now resulted in the elaboration of sophisticated new survey techniques, and an interest in new types of data. Booth's questions, answers and techniques were reflected in other inquiries. A Royal Commission on Labour in the early 1890s, for instance, was inciting those who gave evidence to collate detailed information. Men like Sir Robert Giffen, Permanent Secretary to the Board of Trade, and Professor Leoni Levi were deeply concerned with labour statistics; Giffen computed to the Royal Commission that 23·6 per cent of 'the actual earnings of adult males engaged in manual labour' in Great Britain and Ireland in 1885 were twenty shillings a week or less, and 35·4 per cent were between twenty and twenty-five shillings. [21] Seebohm Rowntree's investigation of poverty in York, begun in the spring of 1899 and published in 1901, followed directly from the work of Booth – 'the second great exercise in basic fact finding, a kind of modern social Domesday Book'. [22] Booth's principal contribution to social analysis was the sheer pioneering courage of it, and not so much 'the discovery of particular facts, but the elaboration of an adequate technique for expressing qualitative concepts and arguments about society in precise numerical terms'. Rowntree's work was important in that it obtained more of its information directly from working-class families, and 'gave new precision to the concept of poverty. He constructed in money terms, a quantitative standard of minimum family needs in respect of food, clothing, fuel and rent.' [23] A family of five, he calculated, needed 21s 8d if they were not to fall below the Poverty Line. He found that in York 10 per cent of the population were not earning enough to meet this standard of living and were therefore living in what he called 'primary poverty'. Another 18 per cent failed to achieve the standard because, although earning this amount, expenditure on anything from drink to furniture meant that the minimum necessary for such things as food and clothes was lacking. These were living in 'secondary poverty'.

The refinements of other investigators like Rowntree marked an important advance, but Booth stands out as one of the most important and influential figures in the history of social analysis and policy. The reception given to his statistics and conclusions forced a consideration of broad aspects of social progress, and of specific items of social reform. If, however, old age pensions became for this reason a central feature of intensive social debate, other items were at the same time achieving prominence, and as a result of other activities and cumulative processes. The discussion of housing and living conditions, for example, found new terms of reference from the late 1870s onwards. The first Cross Act of 1875, the activities of Joseph Chamberlain (including as Mayor) in Birmingham, the gradual growth of regulations covering building density and construction, and the Housing of the Working Classes Act of 1890 – all these indicated a changing climate of opinion over housing. The Local Government Act of 1888 and the creation of the London County Council were crucial growth points in the administrative framework and added powers and example to the good intentions of legislation. In housing, as in town planning, Poor Law reform, health and unemployment insurance, achievements by the advent of the new century were sporadic and often minimal, but the climate in which these things were discussed was quite different from what it had been when the C.O.S. was founded. To complete

Menu of meals provided during the week ending
22 February 1901

	Breakfast	*Dinner*	*Tea*	*Supper*
Friday	Bread, butter, tea	Bread, butter, toast, tea	Bread, butter, tea	
Saturday	Bread, bacon, coffee	Bacon, potatoes, pudding, tea	Bread, butter, shortcake, tea	Tea, bread, kippers
Sunday	Bread, butter, shortcake, coffee	Pork, onions, potatoes, Yorkshire pudding	Bread, butter, shortcake, tea	Bread and meat
Monday	Bread, bacon, butter, tea	Pork, potatoes, pudding, tea	Bread, butter, tea	One cup of tea
Tuesday	Bread, bacon, butter, coffee	Pork, bread, tea	Bread, butter, boiled eggs, tea	Bread, bacon, butter, tea
Wednesday	Bread, bacon, butter, tea	Bacon and eggs, potatoes, bread, tea	Bread, butter, tea	
Thursday	Bread, butter, coffee	Bread, bacon, tea	Bread, butter, tea	

For a lorry driver receiving 20*s* per week, his wife and two children. From
B. SEEBOHM ROWNTREE *Poverty. A Study of Town Life*, 1901, quoted in JOHN
BURNETT *Plenty and Want* (London, 1966).

our picture of this overall transition, there are some aspects of nineteenth-century social developments, most notably education, which need to be brought into perspective.

EDUCATION

The history of education in the nineteenth century is the history of two quite distinct systems, consciously shaped to fit the fact of class relationships. Even the system which comprised the endowed grammar schools, the public schools and the Universities of Oxford and Cambridge was diversified along class lines. The major public schools had separated themselves off from the local grammar school system, and had become predominantly old-style gentry preserves; the expanding middle class found it necessary to establish new public schools, embodying similar values, but more readily accessible to their children. By the middle of the century this whole system was being subjected to pressures which made changes and adaptations inevitable. Prolonged criticism of the public schools led to the appointment of the Clarendon Commission in 1861 to inquire 'into the nature of the endowments, funds and revenues' of the major, ancient public schools. Its Report, in 1864, was followed by the appointment of the Schools Inquiry Commission (the Taunton Commission), which reported four years later on the state of the endowed grammar schools generally. What followed was a gradual improvement in the use of available endowments, the reinvigoration of decrepit and inefficient grammar schools, and attempts to modernize curricula. The secondary education of girls was improved. The second half of the century saw, in fact, a considerable sophistication of the system of middle- and upper class education based on privately endowed, fee-paying institutions.

It is important to emphasize the class-connotation of this system: the public school headmaster and the grammar school reformers alike were self-consciously defining educational values in terms of class needs. When the Bryce Commission came to review progress in secondary education (it reported in 1895), it could find no better way of defining different types of secondary school than by continuing to use a classification introduced in the Taunton Report over a quarter of a century earlier. The Taunton Report had distinguished between three 'grades' of secondary school; the Bryce Commission suggested the preservation of the classification, but the relaxing of class frontiers. The 1895 definition of 'first grade' schools, for example, reads:

> 'First Grade' Schools are those whose special function is the formation of a learned or a literary, and a professional or cultured class. This class comprehends the so-called learned professions, the ministry, law, medicine, teaching of all kinds, and at all stages, literature and the higher sciences, public life, the home and foreign civil service, and such like. This is the class whose school life continues till 18 or 19, and would naturally end in the universities. The more highly organized our civilization becomes, the more imperative grows the need for men so educated and formed, the more generous ought their education to become and the greater the necessity for recruiting their ranks with the best blood and brain from all classes of society.

Higher education should be 'open and accessible to capable and promising minds from every social class'. British society had not yet, however, organized its educational system in such a way as to enable children of non-middle- or non-upper-class parents to gain access to any of the components of this system. The Bryce Commission was advocating a 'ladder' (as T. H. Huxley had called it in the 1870s) for the middle class, in clear knowledge of the class rigidities of the existing system. Although a ladder, with narrow and widely spaced rungs, was shortly to be constructed for working-class children, in the

1890s it scarcely existed. Under the Technical Instruction Acts of 1889–91 counties and county boroughs were beginning to aid grammar and secondary schools, and some also awarded scholarships (the Bryce Commission discovered that forty-two out of forty-eight counties and fifteen out of sixty-one county boroughs were making scholarship grants, but the sums involved were for the most part very small). [24] A Joint Scholarships Board was set up in 1895 'to frame conditions of examination for the scholarships enabling children to pass from the elementary through secondary schools to the Universities'. [25] The 1902 Act provided the framework within which this aim could be implemented.

The social definition of this educational system can be seen most clearly, in fact, in its total separation from the other system, the machinery of 'popular' education. The elementary school system of the nineteenth century was consciously designed, in all its forms, for the children of the poor. Up to 1870 the system was dependent on private initiative, although from 1833 it was supported to some extent by parliamentary grants, and from 1839 was subject to public inspection. There are, therefore, two main threads to the story of popular education up to 1870, the expansion of the network itself (the providing bodies, the kinds of school, the system of school organization), and the nature of public involvement.

The establishment of the system is directly attributable to the new departures in British society we have previously examined in the final decade or so of the eighteenth century. New ideas were abroad, and new concentrations of population involved threats to the very structure of society. Against enormous resistance, day schools for the poor on an extensive scale (supplementing the Sunday Schools founded from the 1780s and the century-old Charity School movement) were being founded by the end of the first decade of the nineteenth century. The largely nonconformist British and Foreign School Society and the National Society for Promoting the Education of the Poor in the Principles of the Established Church were spreading parallel networks of schools based on the use of monitors. One teacher could teach as many as a thousand children, with a minimum of cost, by the efficient organization of children to teach other children. The intention was to spread rudimentary literacy, for purposes always defined in religious and moral terms. Although there were more generous interpretations of education, the dominant system was a socially protective mechanism. The Report of the National Society in 1844, for example, discussed recent disturbances in mining and manufacturing areas. Inquiry had shown, said the Report, that 'discontent and insubordination were most rife in quarters which least enjoyed the advantages of education under the superintendence of the Church; whose office it is to teach men, even when suffering under the sorest trials, to possess their souls in patience'. So convinced was the Society that agitation could be prevented by 'the benign influence of an education conducted upon the principles of the Established Church', that it had determined to increase its efforts to 'imbue the minds of our manufacturing population more effectually with the principles which result from good early training', and had established a special fund 'for the extension and improvement of education in the manufacturing and mining districts'. [26]

The rivalry between the two Societies, and the inability of legislators to reconcile the positions of Church and Dissent, of supporters and opponents of State intervention, meant that the main burden of school provision until 1870 fell upon the various religious denominations and the educational societies they sponsored. The system was in serious respects inefficient. Even improvements in teacher supply, the gradual replacement of the monitorial system by a pupil-teacher system from the mid-1840s, rising government grants and improved conditions of inspection, meant only imperceptible improvements in the quality of the education provided. A constant struggle was waged to improve the efficiency of the schooling, and the Newcastle Commission of 1858–61 was commanded to investigate the state of popular education in England and suggest measures 'for the extension of sound and cheap elementary instruction to all classes of the people'. The scheme of payment by results which followed was intended to improve the 'soundness' of the basic teaching in schools (as well as cut the mounting cost). The amount of grant was to be dependent upon the results of inspectors' examinations in the

19 Nature class at an elementary school, c. 1908.

three Rs. One of the most critical of modern commentators on the Newcastle Commission has described it as representing 'the attitude of the landed gentry and the bourgeoisie of the time, not only towards the "independent poor", but also towards the very idea of education whether for rich or poor . . . They understood cheapness, but perhaps they very well represented the England of 1860 in failing to understand soundness as a quality of education.' [27]

The emphasis of the events of 1861–2 is of considerable importance in the indication it gives of the view of the providers about the *content* of education for the poor. Matthew Arnold, as an inspector of schools, understood very clearly what payment by results meant. Inspectors had previously been able to judge – and contribute to – the overall cultural and intellectual standards of classes and schools; under the new code they were concerned with the examination of individual children, in a situation in which the school's income depended upon the results of his tests. 'I know', he said in 1863, 'that the aim and object of the new system of examination is not to develop the higher intellectual life of an elementary school, but to spread and fortify, in its middle and lower portions, the instruction in reading, writing, and arithmetic, supposed to be suffering.' If this was being achieved, and it was not at all certain that this was the case, it was at the expense of proper concentration on raising the general intellectual level of teachers and children, of strengthening learning across a wide range, and of efforts that needed to be made to obtain more consistent attendance. For several generations, therefore, payment by results concentrated attention, in the schools described by the Newcastle Commission as being for 'the independent poor', on the mechanical attainment of certain basic routines. Children needed to be able to read and take dictation from prescribed texts. 'The circle of the children's reading has thus been narrowed and impoverished all the year for the sake of a *result* at the end of it, and the *result* is an illusion.' [28] The history of the content of the elementary system of education in the remaining years of the century is the history of a slow evolution away from the restricting concept of rudimentary attainment.

It would be wrong, in spite of these considerations, to pretend that the system of popular education before 1870 was inefficient in every sense. The attainment was considerable if we look, not at the content of education, and opportunities missed, but at the *extent* of elementary literacy. In the two decades before 1870, for example, the literacy rate for males had increased by 11·3 percentage points and that for females by 18·4 points, reaching figures of 80·6 and 73·2 per cent literacy respectively by 1871 (it had been 67·3 and 51·1 per cent respectively in 1841). What the 1870 Act did was 'to insure that the rate at which literacy had increased in 1851–71 would be maintained. Had the State not intervened at this point, it is likely that the progress of literacy would have considerably slowed in the last quarter of the century, simply because illiteracy was by that time concentrated in those classes and regions that were hardest to provide for under the voluntary system of education.' [29] The chapbooks of the eighteenth century, the radical press of the early nineteenth century, and the penny fiction of the middle of the nineteenth century are useful reminders that active literacy was well established before the State intervened in 1870.

Schools and curricula had come to be shaped, therefore, in the nineteenth century, to suit particular interpretations of what was necessary for a Bible-reading, docile working population. It was a closed system. It provided, with only the rarest exceptions, no route to secondary education or university. The 1870 Act did not directly concern itself with the content, but only with the supply, of education for working-class children. The central feature of the Act was its declaration that:

> There shall be provided for every school district a sufficient amount of accommodation in public elementary schools . . . available for all the children resident in such district for whose elementary education efficient and suitable provision is not otherwise made . . . Where . . . the deficiency is not supplied . . . a school board shall be formed for such district and shall supply such deficiency . . . [30]

Local School Boards were formed by direct election, and their responsibilities covered only elementary school provision. The network of voluntary schools was not superseded, but supplemented, and voluntary bodies were given six months to apply for grant aid to build new schools. The religious question was settled by laying down that 'no religious catechism or religious formulary which is distinctive of any particular denomination shall be taught'. Although local powers were made available to provide for compulsory attendance, education was not made compulsory. The Act simply ensured the provision of places. The efforts during the remainder of the century were directed towards securing regular attendance, making schools free and raising the leaving age. The leaving age in 1870 was theoretically thirteen, with a half-time system operating between ten and thirteen, and exemptions based on attendance and performance making the effective leaving age ten. By-laws making education to the age of ten compulsory were made obligatory in 1880, and the age was raised to eleven in 1893 and twelve in 1899. School fees were limited under the 1870 Act to ninepence a week. In 1891 parents were given the right to demand free education, and in 1918 fees for elementary education were abolished.

The fact that the two educational systems of the nineteenth century were parallel and not convergent can be seen most clearly in the events leading up to the second of the outstanding education Acts in England's history – that of 1902. The reforms of the nineteenth century had confirmed the classical-literary emphasis in the grammar school. Science and modern subjects had gained a foothold, but the classical-literary tradition continued to be considered the right kind of intellectual discipline, and the right kind of cultural and moral contribution to the preparation of an educational and social élite. Out of the elementary system, however, the later decades of the century saw the emergence of an alternative pattern of – if not *secondary*, at least *post-primary* – education. 'Higher grade' schools for pupils wishing to remain beyond the statutory leaving age were established under some Boards, especially in northern towns, and served the purpose – as some of the witnesses demonstrated to the Bryce Commission – of providing a completion to the elementary course. 'The pride of the higher grade school', it was pointed out, 'is that it has engrafted a system on the system already in existence in connexion with, and in continuation of it.' [31] The relaxations effected in the system of payment by results, the adventurous policies of some Boards, and manifest local needs for a supply – among other things – of a better-trained technical and clerical labour force, led to these experiments in senior classes and central schools which would cater for the demand. Scientific, technical, commercial and vocational subjects played a large part in the curricula of these classes and schools. The logic of the 1870 Act itself, when a generation of children had gone through the Board schools, led to many of these developments in higher day (and evening) classes. The Boards, in making such a departure, exceeded their mandate, according to the letter of the law. In 1900, Robert Morant, a towering figure in the establishment of the pattern of education in the twentieth century, engineered a court verdict to the effect, and himself chiselled the features of a new education Act in 1902.

The Act had, in fact, two main purposes. The first was to demolish the School Boards and place all education under the multi-purpose county and borough authorities; in doing so it completed the demolition of the nineteenth-century tradition of *ad hoc* authorities. Balfour, the Conservative, in sponsoring the 1902 Act, was implementing a policy which, through Morant, was urged and shaped by Fabian Socialist Sidney Webb, the enthusiastic advocate of efficient local government. The second purpose was to ensure that, whatever developments in secondary education might occur, it should be within a single system, in which the dominant values would remain those of the traditional grammar school and its curriculum. The legal judgement of 1900, the Act of 1902, and Secondary Regulations issued by Morant in 1904 were aimed at holding back what he considered excessive concern with science and modern subjects in the higher grade schools and classes. If there were to be an educational ladder it should lead into the traditional values of the grammar school. Olive Banks, who tries to exonerate Morant from responsibility for this development, describes nevertheless how the higher grade schools under the new dispensation turned, like the grammar schools, to languages and mathematics. The two kinds of school 'grew steadily closer together sharing not only the same curriculum, but also the pride in an old tradition and common ideals for the future'. The disappearance of the practical curriculum of the higher grade schools, in her view, was the responsibility both of Morant and of the teachers and administrators who welcomed the Regulations of 1904 'as a means of reinstating the literary and linguistic elements in the secondary schools'. [32] The Regulations of 1904 appeared to aim at a balanced curriculum, but it is clear that the higher grade innovations were being discarded. The new Regulations, in the words of Professor Eaglesham, 'certainly effectively checked any tendencies to technical or vocational bias in the secondary schools. They made the schools fit only for a selected few. Moreover they proclaimed for all to see the Board's interest in the literary and classical sides of secondary education. For the future the pattern of English culture must not come from Leeds and West Ham but from Eton and Winchester.' Morant and Balfour shared, in fact, 'similar middle-class educational values, similar doubts about the abilities of the masses ... Such were the two architects of the educational system which has largely survived to the present day.' [33] The definitions and appeals of the Bryce Commission, the activities of Morant, the Act of 1902, and the Free Place system which formally inaugurated the policy of the scholarship 'ladder' to secondary education, all attempted to open out the secondary school frontiers at the same time as preserving 'middle-class values'. They were successful. From this point begins the story of secondary school selection in the process of widening the boundaries of what the Bryce Commission called 'blood and brain'.

That the battle for the place of scientific and technical subjects in secondary curricula had been set back considerably is highlighted by other educational departures in the second half of the nineteenth century. From the creation of London University (from the starting point of University College in 1826) to the beginnings of new provincial universities in towns like Manchester, Birmingham, Leeds, Bristol and Sheffield in the latter part of the century, new concepts of university curricula had begun to be formulated and acted upon. Commissions on technical education sat in the 1870s and 1880s. Out of the Mechanics' Institutes grew Technical Colleges. Others, especially in the 1880s and 1890s, were created. Grants to encourage science and art teaching were available from 1853, and rate aid was available for the same purpose from 1889. Oxford and Cambridge reform began in the 1850s, and from the beginning of the 1870s the University Extension movement carried adult education into towns like Derby, Leicester and Nottingham (and out of some of these activities grew universities). Within the schools themselves there were pressures towards the acceptance of new ideas. Ideas of education in social science and health gained some momentum. New movements in infant and nursery education took shape in the second half of the century. It was demonstrated in 1902 that none of this was to be allowed to influence the basic pattern of English secondary education.

These developments should not cloud the fact that nineteenth-century English society (Scottish traditions were in many crucial respects different) was in fact two societies ('two nations' was Disraeli's phrase), and to all intents and purposes the two societies were educated for different ends, on the basis of different social and cultural assumptions, with different curricula, for different lengths of time, and above all in different schools.

RELIGION

The strengths of the School Board system lay in the towns, and the class-rooms of the Board schools were demonstrations, if demonstration was still needed, of the existence of a working class, and of institutions designed for the working class. The Church, and the churches, were deeply involved in these recognitions and processes, but *as churches* they failed to a large extent to grasp the problems of either towns or class. The churches themselves in the nineteenth century demonstrated class divisions as visibly as anywhere in society. There were polarizations within church bodies into wealthy and poor, autocratic and democratic branches, as the Wesleyan and Primitive wings of Methodism illustrate. Within church buildings themselves the exist-ence of subscribed pews and free 'sittings' marked the class division. In Shef-field in 1841 there were thirteen churches of the Establishment which could accommodate 15,000 people, but 6,000 places at most were free. Of the 25,000 places in the thirty-seven nonconformist chapels less than one third were free. [34] The evangelical wing of the Established Church and the evangelical nonconformist churches themselves, were to one extent or another aware of the problem of 'reaching' the urban working class, in conditions of the relative breakdown of the unitary function of the parish — pre-eminently a rural form of church organization. The churches made various attempts to speak distinc-tively and make appropriate kinds of appeal to the working class, but Professor Inglis has shown the extent and limitations of the appeal. At the back of it lay what Edward Miall, one of the prominent nonconformist spokes-men of the century, considered to be a morbid horror of poverty: 'The service concludes, and the worshippers retire. Communion with God has not dis-posed them to communion with each other, beyond the well-defined bound-aries of class.' In his journal, the *Nonconformist*, he invited working men to write letters on 'The Working Classes and Religious Institutions', and in response they denounced social distinctions in churches, their worship of respectability and contempt for the poor, the 'almost total want of sympathy manifested by the ministers of religion of every denomination with the privations, wants, and wastes of the working classes' and the 'aristocratic character of religious institutions'. [35]

A Religious Census in 1851, and a local count in the borough of Sheffield in 1881, both arrived at the rough conclusion that one person in three for whom there were places attended for worship on an average Sunday. In Sheffield between the two dates the population had slightly more than doubled, so that although the ratio remained the same, the absolute number of non-attenders doubled across the period. Since 1881 the population has again almost doubled, but attendances in 1957 were far less than in 1881: 'It is almost certain we have near doubled the population, and more than halved actual numbers of attendants, and this is probably true for every denomination except the Roman Catholics . . .' [36] The falling off of church

20 *'The Chapel, on the "separate system", in Pentonville Prison'.*

and chapel attendance at the end of the century, however, was from an already narrow basis. Professor Inglis demonstrates both the inadequacy of religious organizations to deal with the problem of winning the support of the working class, and the flimsiness of their interest. 'Before wondering why people stop doing something,' he advises, 'it is worth asking whether they ever started; and the social historian of religion in modern England could find a worse guide than the clergyman who remarked in 1896: "It is not that the Church of God has lost the great towns; it has never had them . . ."' People moving into towns lost the habit of worship, and working-class people born in towns never acquired it. The strength of Primitive Methodism, the most working-class of the nonconformist bodies, was not in the large towns, and it was not, in any case, as numerous as the more aristocratic and highly conservative Wesleyan Methodists, who, as the largest Methodist body, had the smallest percentage of working-class supporters. The nonconformist churches in general were apathetic about the problem of the cities. Some sections of the Established Church did move towards reorganization and special effort to win the working class; in some sections of nonconformity, on the other hand, Professor Inglis concludes, 'scarcely any effort was made before or after 1850 to reach the working classes. The elect were content merely to preserve their own fellowship.' [37] The decline in religious attendance from the 1880s was an important phenomenon in the history of the middle class, and confirmation of the inability of the churches in the nine-teenth century to confront the problems of urban, and later of suburban, life.

BEGINNINGS OF TOWN PLANNING

We have seen a range of areas in which piecemeal or remedial action was taken to cope with the growth of urban society; there were, of course, inside towns and in experimental settings outside, attempts at answers of different kinds. Small-scale attempts at rehousing inside cities gave rise to broader ideas of planning. The intensification of urban problems gave rise to new initiatives in town planning, particularly as London's suburban transport developed, as new and scattered industries arose, and as prospects of the disappearance of accessible countryside increased. As ideas of social responsibility spread, and as local and country instruments for the organization of community existence became more effective (schools and roads, for example), so it is possible to trace a shift towards more widespread ideas of local community planning. Before the end of the nineteenth century, however, the examples of such developments in practice were sporadic and self-contained, and it is easy to exaggerate their importance. The continued confusions, lost opportunities and mistakes of the twentieth century show how important it is not to make such an exaggeration.

Early attempts at industrial planning were confined to relatively remote communities, particularly in connection with textile enterprises dependent upon water supply. The most important was New Lanark, during Robert Owen's management between 1800 and 1824, important not only because it was an attempt to improve industrial conditions and provide community services, but because it was a practical experiment which Owen himself, and other prominent social thinkers influenced by Owen, used as a demonstration of more far-reaching views on community planning. Owen advocated the estab-lishment of self-sufficient communities for the poor, combining an industrial and agricultural economy, and with basic planned communal services. Others pursued and refined the proposals. Some Owenite and other communitarian experiments were made, though with little influence on opinion or practice in the field of planning. Hardly more influential were Titus Salt's model woollen mills and town at Saltaire, built from scratch near Bradford in about twenty years from 1851. This was an employer's town, benevolently administered. In less easy-going conditions from the 1870s, 'changes in the environment and location of industry had become at least a topic for occasional discussion. In most of the basic industries profits were not so easily obtained as in the recent past and the urgent importance of efficient and healthy labour was, as a direct result, beginning to be more widely recognized.' [38]

A beginning was made on the building of Bournville by George Cadbury in 1879, but not until 1895 did the plans really begin to be developed. Port

21 Port Sunlight. The village, looking towards the factory; in the foreground the Lady Lever Art Gallery.

Sunlight was begun by W. H. Lever in 1888, associating a new village with his expanding soap firm, and making the administration of the village an extension of the firm's interest in labour–management relations. The spaciousness and variety of the village still demonstrate, in the proximity of Birkenhead, the boldness of such new approaches to community planning. Joseph Rowntree's interest in such planning at his New Earswick development near York broke away from the enlightened philanthropy of the earlier ventures. The aim of Joseph Rowntree (Seebohm's father) was to provide houses 'artistic in appearance, sanitary, well-built, and yet within the means of men earning about twenty-five shillings a week'. But he was not a paternalist. 'I should regret', he wrote, 'if there were anything in the organization of these village communities that should interfere with the growth of the right spirit of citizenship . . . I do not want to establish communities bearing the stamp of charity but rather of rightly ordered and self-governing communities.' |39| The venture was directly influential in that its architect was later to be involved in new-town planning at Letchworth, and Seebohm Rowntree, on the basis of both his investigation of working-class conditions in York and his involvement in the New Earswick scheme, played a prominent part in the wartime

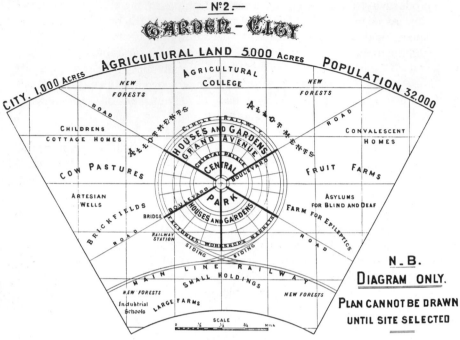

22 *Garden City. From Ebenezer Howard,* Garden Cities of To-morrow.

planning of housing needs, helping materially to prepare the way for the Housing Act of 1919, the first of any major importance.

It was, however, the publication of Ebenezer Howard's book *To-morrow* (later retitled *Garden Cities of To-morrow*), published in 1898, followed by the establishment of the Garden City Association (1899) and the first Garden City at Letchworth (started in 1904), that projected the discussion of town and environmental planning squarely into the twentieth century. Cecil Harmsworth, as Chairman of the Council of the Garden Cities and Town Planning Association, told the Barlow Commission that he had been 'drawn into the movement by the infectious influence of Sir Ebenezer Howard'. [40] The book, Letchworth, and Howard's own later promotion of Welwyn Garden City (in 1920) arose out of his familiarity with the 'grave warnings against the evils of great towns'. The Association summarized what he had stood for as follows:

> ... the revolt of philanthropists and reformers and a large proportion of ordinary people against the size and character of the great town had been endemic since the Industrial Revolution, and had been eloquently voiced by Cobbett, Shaftesbury, and many others of great authority. The emergence of a vast class of city-dwellers who have never known a decent environment, and the fatalism of statesmen who have believed that this herding of the masses was somehow connected with advances in industrial and commercial

productivity, have prevented this revolt from becoming effective. Ebenezer Howard aligned himself with his predecessors in the protest against the squalor and overcrowding inseparable from great towns; but he differed from many of them in accepting whole-heartedly the desirability of the town in itself from the point of view of modern populations . . . he discerned that the essential urban advantages . . . could be provided in a town of limited size and density; and that in addition many of the amenities of the country . . . could be retained in such a town. [41]

Howard's concept was one of 'Town–Country' which would be free of the disadvantages of both. His Garden Cities would be 'Social Cities'. He argued strongly in *To-morrow* that his scheme combined the ideals of individualism ('if by Individualism is meant a state in which there is fuller and freer opportunity for its members to do and to produce what they will, and to form free associations, of the most varied kind') and of socialism ('if by Socialism is meant a condition of life in which the well-being of the community is safeguarded, and in which the collective spirit is manifested by a wide extension of the area of municipal effort'). He argued that he had taken a leaf out of the books of A. J. Balfour on the one hand and Hyndman and Blatchford on the other. [42]

Ideas of this kind were regenerative, however marginal they were to the problems of existing towns. They also forcefully raised problems of the kind of community in which modern urban man was prepared, and wished, to live. In many respects the garden-city, garden-suburb, new-town thinking of the twentieth century can be seen as an evasion of fundamental social problems. In other respects it can be seen as a gesture towards them.

The growing phenomenon of middle-class, and later working-class, suburbanization, and the consequent depopulation of town centres, were accelerated by new developments in transport. Cheaper rail fares began to be introduced in the 1870s, and the Cheap Trains Act of 1883 introduced workmen's fares. The first section of London's underground railway was opened in 1863, and electric trains date from 1890. The train, however, was largely inter-urban and metropolitan. For cities in general the new outward impetus came from the roads. The motor bus and car began slowly in the late 1890s to replace the horse bus and hansom cab, but cycling had already made an important contribution to transport by drawing attention to the state of the roads, and providing the technological basis on which more advanced forms of transport were later to be constructed. The cycling craze dates from the 1860s (and the 'bone-shaker') and the 1870s (and the 'penny-farthing'), reaching a peak in the 1880s with the development of the pneumatic tyre. The creation of the County Councils in 1888 meant a new dispensation for the nation's roads, and motor cars made their first appearance in the 1890s. When the Motor Car Act of 1903 required motor vehicles to be licensed, 18,000 were registered in the first year. By 1914 the number had risen to 389,000.

Buses and trams, however, made the most decisive impact on urban life, making it possible for working men to travel longer distances to work. The early trams were horsedrawn, and these marked 'a substantial advance in the conveyance of large numbers of people in urban areas at low fares'. Electricity applied to trams at the end of the century provided the real break-through to cheap transport in dense urban areas. By 1909 there were some 2,300 miles of electric tramway. [43] An important feature of tramway transport was that it led to municipal involvement in urban transport.

Towns continued, then, to spread, with industries confirming the process of expansion by siting themselves at greater distances from town centres. At the same time as impressive new domestic architecture was appearing in expensive residential districts (such as Bayswater and Hampstead in London),

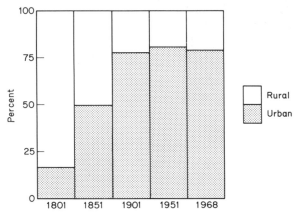

Fig. 5 Geographical distribution of the population in England and Wales, 1801–1968. (See also Table 13, p. 321.) After Adner Ferrin Weber, The Growth of Cities in the Nineteenth Century, *New York, 1899, and* Annual Abstract of Statistics, *1969.*

the regulated 'by-law housing' was creating the architectural deserts of the speculatively built suburbs within widening transport distance from the centres of every major town. New local government responsibilities had led to new surges of public building – town halls, fire stations, public baths, libraries, post offices and – above all – schools, almost all proudly displaying the date of construction. Gaunt and impracticable though many of these buildings now are, many were – and still are – impressive in their scale and ambition.

There had been from the 1840s attempts at philanthropic working-class housing in dense urban conditions. The Improved Industrial Dwellings Co., established in 1863, was the best known of the companies which built at a deliberately restricted rate of interest. Best known of the developments, however, was one which was based on a bequest from the American, George Peabody, and which came to be used for working-class housing. [44] Most of these developments were in London, and in general were available only to the more 'respectable' of the poor. For the housing of the lower strata of the poor, Octavia Hill offered a system of housing management. By raising funds for the purchase of property and recruiting ladies to act as rent collectors, she hoped to establish a system of influence and benevolent incentives to self-improvement and property improvement, a system described by Professor Owen as one for 'transmuting improvident savages into solid citizens'. [45] All such schemes accepted the necessity of high urban density, all were reasonably cheap and in one way or another made tenancy contingent upon cleanliness, regular employment and character. None of them made a significant impact on the basic problems of housing and overcrowding.

THE FAMILY

The population was still increasing, and Britain was, from the middle of the nineteenth century dominantly urban. In the second half of the century the population increased by over 80 per cent, and in the first half of the twentieth century by 34 per cent. The death rate declined steadily in the second half of and nineteenth century (22·5 deaths per thousand of the population in 1861–70; 19·1 in 1881–90; 15·4 in 1901–10). That the population did not increase more spectacularly as a result was due to a parallel decline in birth rate (from over thirty-five per thousand in the 1860s and 1870s, steadily downwards to just over twenty-seven in 1901–10). From the 1870s the rate of population growth began to fall. It is with some of the social realities behind these statistics that we are concerned for the remainder of this chapter.

Of every hundred women who married in the years 1870–9, there were sixty-one who bore five or more live children; seventeen bore ten or more;

23 *'Dwellings for the Working-classes, Peabody Square, Shadwell', 1867.*

only twenty-one of them bore none, one or two. By contrast, of every hundred women who married in the years 1900–9, only twenty-eight bore five or more children; only one in a hundred bore ten or more; the number bearing none, one or two had risen from twenty-one to forty-five. [46] The structure of the family had begun markedly to alter in the last quarter of the century.

In many respects it was the working-class family that was least affected by the new economic and social directions of the nineteenth century. It was disrupted, of course, as an economic unit, but the changes did not, in Ronald Fletcher's view, 'bring about, for the wage-earning classes, a total worsening of an earlier family life which had been altogether more satisfactory, so much as a new and terrible aggravation of existing evils. There was a new degree of family disunity in a situation where new insecurities, new harshnesses of work and environment, new miseries, were added to the old.' [47] Industrial legislation had, of course, improved the conditions of working women. There were frequent attacks in the nineteenth century on the practice of working-class wives being employed in the mills and factories; such married women, even in the second half of the century, would be away from home from something like 6 a.m. to 6 p.m. The number of married women in industry was, however, considerably exaggerated.[48] The working-class family in the nineteenth century was, in fact, subject both to severe instabilities, as a result of physical and economic conditions, and to pressures making for an autocratic family structure. Divorce was not available, the position of the father was dominant, and the woman in the home was committed to a life of considerable drudgery. For the unmarried girl the only escape, for a large part of the century, was into the mill or domestic service. In the twentieth century, with the removal of intolerable burdens by welfare provisions, in Fletcher's opinion, 'the working-class family has achieved a new condition of stability, well-being, security, and opportunity for the development of its individual members, which is unprecedented in our history'. [49] Improvements in the nineteenth century, however, were too slow to impinge on the working-class family to any significant extent. The woman at work, constant childbirth and a high rate of infant mortality, the demoralization of domestic conditions – all these parallel, with few compensations, life in pre-industrial society. Changes in the administration of poor relief merely surrounded the working-class family with additional elements of harshness, disunity and misery.

The nineteenth century did, however, see important changes in the content of middle-class family life. Among farmers and traders in pre-industrial society 'marriage was often a business partnership in which husband and wife worked together in their joint interests'. [50] The cementing of middle-class affluence, the new patterns of middle-class occupation and the new scale of industrial and commercial operations broke these elements of partnership and firmly established the husband as the sole provider. Paid employment for women before the nineteenth century was more widespread than is sometimes imagined. Working-class women had age-old employments in agriculture, textiles, coal and metal mining, straw-plaiting, hat-making, jewellery and fan-making. They worked as 'assistants to masons and bricklayers, as labourers in brickyards and foundries, load carriers to and from markets, as rag sorters and cutters in paper mills, as cinder sifters and collectors of refuse'. [51] Some of the descriptions of women's employment, however, disguise relatively middle-class, entrepreneurial activities. A large number of women's names, for example, appeared in Wren's account books during the building of St Paul's in the late seventeenth century:

> Sarah Freeman undertook some of the plumbing, widow Clare was a joiner, Ann Brooks one of the smiths. It is doubtful how much of the actual work these women did. They may have been contractors employing the actual craftsmen, but the fact that Wren employed them does show that women were running businesses in the City even if they did not work at the trades. [52]

In the early days of the Industrial Revolution, as previously, women — wives, widows and single women — were shopkeepers. English women in the seventeenth century and later managed estates, obtained patents and monopolies, dealt in insurance and supplied clothing to the army and navy. In its early stages, says one writer on population, 'capitalism enhanced the economic value of middle-class women and brought them into co-operative activity with men; in the succeeding period, women's economic value was again depreciated by developments leading to her isolation from productive activity'. [53] The result was that the role of the male head of the household was made paramount, and the middle-class (and upper-class) family became more and more strongly home-centred. The wife had no serious occupation inside or outside the home. The household duties of the middle-class wife 'were limited to supervising, and complaining about, her servants'. [54] Wanda Neff describes how, by the eighteenth century, among the leisure class 'the triumph of the useless woman was complete'. With the Industrial Revolution 'the practice of female idleness spread through the middle class until work for women became a misfortune and a disgrace'. [55] In domestic structure the large clergyman's family was little different from that of the industrialist or businessman. The family of Bishop Moberly was one of the large Victorian families which 'were a world in themselves'. The fifteen Moberlys 'made an immense society with common interests, common tastes, and common memories'. A family like this 'was regulated according to a clearly conceived pattern. It was a constitutional body, based on law, and every member had his own place in the social scheme under the father, who was the supreme head of all . . . Something like this existed in all families, but a clergyman had to set a special example in fatherhood as in everything else . . .' [56] Not all middle-class families had the good fortune of the Moberlys to be united in common interests of an absorbing kind. Victorian women's writings, and particularly diaries, are full of trivialities of conversation and social relations dominated by boredom. 'A daughter', one of them was still protesting in 1894, 'must arrange the flowers, help with the house-keeping, pay the family calls, entertain the family visitors, always be at hand, well-dressed, cheerful, and smiling . . . she can never undertake any definite work or pursuit . . . She never, in fact, has an hour that she can call absolutely her own.' [57]

Victorian young ladies had time to write enormous diaries; a reconstruction from those of two of them, Ellen and Emily Hall, of the lives of young ladies in early Victorian England, illustrates the general situation clearly. [58] West Wickham was a small village, with one public house and one general shop. London, thanks to the railway, was not inaccessible, though in the early trains the girls had to hold 'our handkerchiefs over our noses'; trains were not heated and journeys could be 'unendurably cold'. Distances were not what they now are. Tooting, now an inner suburb of London, was to the girls only 'much nearer London' than Jersey, where they had previously lived. Camberwell was still in countryside which was 'really very pretty'. In their seclusion the girls were busy, busier than they might have been in a city. They drove, rode or walked into Croydon and other neighbouring towns on shopping expeditions. They supervised servants and gardens and rejoiced in the arrangement of flowers. They played music and 'took their fair share in the visits, picnics and the like'. They cultivated guests and read histories, memoirs, sermons and poetry. They enjoyed conversation, and the Church played a large part in their lives. One of them took a part in the Sunday School, made clothes for village children and visited the sick. The same daughter had in 1839 in Jersey helped to dispense soup to the poor, and scolded 'some of the horrid old women who have been telling fibs and getting soup from two boilers at the same time'. The Halls, like the Moberlys, had the advantage of a strong, active culture. Like other Victorian middle-class girls, they found the chess games of courtship and marriage going on about them a subject for constant conversation and, like a high percentage of them, they remained unmarried.

It is not difficult, then, to see why importance was attached in mid-Victorian middle-class England to the large family. Like the Villa, the Crinoline and the Servant, the Family − a 'conspicuous' item in affluence − testified to the solidity and permanence of the middle-class way of life. Wealthier families were the first and most to benefit from improved standards of health and environmental conditions − hence the longer fertility of mothers, the better survival chances of children and the greater size of families. The large working-class family − said the middle-class Malthusian − indicated improvidence. The large middle-class family was a symbol of success.

It is from this starting point that we must see the changes in family size, and in the status of women, in the last twenty to thirty years of the century. The decline in family size, in the analysis of J. A. Banks, is related directly to the fact or the possibility of rising material standards. His thesis is briefly as follows. [59] The average family size of couples married in mid-Victorian

Britain was between 5·5 and 6 live children, and of those married in 1925–9 it was 2·2. The percentage of women marrying while capable of bearing children, however, remained roughly constant. At some time in the 1860s and 1870s a decline in family size had begun among upper- and middle-class families. The earliest signs of the change in reproductive patterns took place amongst the families of, for example, officers, clergymen, lawyers, doctors, authors, journalists and architects, with not far behind them civil servants and clerks, dentists, teachers and people in scientific pursuits. Commercial men followed. Although some signs of family limitation were early visible among textile workers, not until much later did the decline in family size spread amongst less privileged social groups. Birth control, it becomes clear, was taken up with enthusiasm from the 1870s, and given an impetus by the Bradlaugh-Besant trials of 1877–8. Artificial methods of birth control had, however, been known and available very much earlier. Why had they been spurned, for example, in the 1820s, and adopted in the 1870s? The answer lies in the rising standard of middle-class life and the determination to maintain and secure the higher standards of comfort. It had become prudent to postpone the time of marriage in order to ensure that married life began at the proper level of respectability (and this, it should be mentioned, was one of the factors involved in the dual standard of morality, which involved a high incidence of resort to prostitution inside and outside marriage among Victorian middle-class men). [60] The dominant factor, however, Banks continues, was the maintenance of material standards in marriage. Associated with middle-class status were what he calls 'paraphernalia of gentility' (Veblen's 'conspicuous consumption'), including material objects, servants, holidays and travel. The point at which the cost of any of these basic paraphernalia began to rise (e.g. servants' wages), at which new paraphernalia became desirable (e.g. new types of imported luxury foods), or at which income was in any way lowered or threatened, made a reconsideration of the whole basis of family size imperative. If the threat continued over a long period of time the choice available was to cut back on material standards (or fail to raise them) or to maintain them by reducing expenditure in some other way. A further postponement in the age of marriage was not seriously possible, and the possibility of reducing family size was therefore the most acceptable of the alternatives available. The 'Great Depression' and its attendant psychology, in fact, provoked such a reassessment of the cost of raising children. The decline in the hold of the Church, the breakdown of old ideas under the impact of new appeals to science and reason, higher rents – these were additional factors helping towards the ultimate acceptance of two-plus-two as the new ideal of family size. Feminism, as J. A. and Olive Banks demonstrate elsewhere, [61] was not directly responsible for the adoption of birth control. It is obviously true, however, that birth control and smaller families had a major effect on the status of women in the family and in society.

A certain democratization of family life was, indeed, taking place, and the smaller family intensified the process. The new attitude to family size, spreading downwards through the social classes, had other repercussions. It helped to break down the situation in which solemn standards of morality had been combined with pre-marital and extra-marital sexual relations through prostitution. It made earlier marriages possible. It made it possible for new views of sexual relations and marriage to gain ground. With fewer children, fewer servants and more efficient homes (including gas cookers and water closets) a greater domestic role for suburban middle-class housewives was created. [62] Parallel developments for working-class housewives had to await considerable progress in social reform.

EMANCIPATION OF WOMEN

The story of the greater emancipation of women involves both the economic and social facts we have traced, and mounting individual and organized pressures. Women over thirty obtained the vote at the same time as it was finally given to all males over twenty-one in 1918, and all women over twenty-one obtained it in 1928, but the story of their political emancipation is one in which neither the pressures of the campaigning, nor the simple facts of economic development and war, can alone claim credit for the final success.

The principal elements in the changing position of women were fivefold, relating to property, divorce, employment, education and the suffrage.

The existing legal relationship of husband and wife was defined in 1869 by John Stuart Mill, in one of the most famous documents on women in society, as follows:

> . . . the absorption of all [women's] rights, all property, as well as all freedom of action, is complete. The two are called 'one person in law', for the purpose of inferring that whatever is hers is his, but the parallel inference is never drawn that whatever is his is hers . . . I am far from pretending that wives are in general no better treated than slaves; but no slave is a slave to the same lengths, and in so full a sense of the word, as a wife is. [63]

At this date the whole of the wife's income, from whatever source, belonged to her husband. The first of a series of Property Acts was passed in 1870, and it gave a married woman the right to possess her earnings, but not any other property. Millicent Fawcett records how in the 1870s, in the campaign for another Married Women's Property Bill, she approached some of the Liberal electors at a meeting at her father's house in Suffolk with a petition form. 'Am I to understand you, ma'am,' responded one of the farmers, 'that if this Bill passes, and my wife have a matter of a hundred pound left to her, I should have to *ask* her for it?' [64] An Act of 1882 enabled a woman to retain as separate property whatever she possessed at marriage or acquired after. A final Act of 1893 removed anomalies and made all property of a married woman her separate property. From the 1850s a women's movement had been organized, campaigns conducted, signatures collected and discussion aroused. Hostility to any form of action of this kind on the part of women was immense (including among women who saw their femininity undermined), but a beginning had been made and an important shift in status had been achieved in the Acts of 1870–93.

Since the sixteenth century Scotland had had legal equality and cheap divorce. A divorce Act of 1857 (a Matrimonial Causes Act, as it and all subsequent Acts were named) brought divorce for the first time within reach of the English middle class, but, in 'making divorce easier for men than for women, it sanctioned two standards of morality', and the cheaper procedure of the divorce court 'remained so costly that working people were denied the remedy of divorce for their matrimonial difficulties'. [65] An Act of 1878, followed by other Acts through to 1902, gave magistrates powers to grant separation orders with maintenance to a wife whose husband had been convicted of 'aggravated assault'. Not until 1923, however, could a woman obtain divorce on the simple grounds of adultery, as her husband had been able to do. Not until an Act of 1937 were the grounds for divorce extended to include desertion, cruelty and being incurably of unsound mind. Not until the introduction of legal aid in 1949 did divorce become practicable for the poor.

Again, a minority of articulate women had been involved in exerting – with difficulty – pressure for reform. On the related questions of employment and education the basis of action and the range of achievement were wider. Writing in 1886, Millicent Fawcett, already of importance in the movement for emancipation, forecast what factors would come together to achieve it – a forecast of considerable interest:

> Women's suffrage will not come, when it does come, as an isolated phenomenon, it will come as a necessary corollary of other changes which have been gradually and steadily modifying during this century the social history of our country. It will be a political change, not of a very great or extensive character in itself, based upon social, educational and economic changes which have already taken place ... the political change will not be a revolution, but a public recognition by the State that the lot of women in England is no longer what it was at the beginning of the century. [66]

This extremely percipient analysis identifies correctly the relationship in this movement between social and political change. Economic change and women themselves had created new attitudes to employment. New occupations were appearing. There were, for working-class and lower-middle-class girls, new opportunities in post offices, and shops, commerce and industry. The reformers set up women's employment agencies to try to help middle-class girls. The fight was engaged for access to training and the professions.

In the 1840s women's training colleges and Bedford College, London, were founded, the North London Collegiate School for girls was established in 1850,

24 Members of the W.A.A.C. on motor service.

and the Cheltenham Ladies' College eight years later. The Girls Public Day
Schools Company opened thirty-three schools for girls between 1872 and the
end of the century, following the Endowed Schools Act of 1869, which was
described as 'the Magna Carta of girls' education, the first acknowledgement
by the State of their claim to a liberal education'. [67] The Bryce Commission
reported in 1895 that since the Taunton Report of 1868 'there had been more
change in the condition of the Secondary Education of girls than in any other
department of education . . . the idea that a girl, like a boy, may be fitted by
education to earn a livelihood, or, at any rate, to be a more useful member of
society, has become more widely diffused.' [68] Working-class girls may have
entered voluntary elementary schools or Board Schools after 1870 through a
separate gate or doorway from the boys, but they were being 'fitted' as well,
or as badly, as boys for a livelihood or their place in society. Girton College,
Cambridge, was founded in 1869 (although girls were not admitted to Cambridge degrees until the 1920s). Bedford College reached university rank, and
university colleges were opening their doors to women. The University
Extension movement was reaching a female audience. Women were more
widely hankering after and pressing for fuller occupational opportunities.
The sex ratio of the British population in Victorian Britain was tilted towards

women; a basic consideration in looking at the position of women was the fact that a quarter of them did not marry.

There was, wrote one cynic in *Blackwood's Magazine* in 1860 on the subject of women, 'a great waste and over-production of that feminine article. An unnecessary surplus of half-a-million, say the statistics . . .' The only answer to the problem that this writer could see was that women should be made strictly to choose between the careers of worker or mother:

> If England is to be permanently afflicted with an unavailable margin of women, this surplus must either have the courage to make that necessary sacrifice which alone can insure its fidelity to its work, or else stifle its discontent, and make the best of its unlucky position. [69]

For women in general emancipation within the family and opportunities within society were one and the same thing. The most convenient approach to the story of emancipation, suggests George Dangerfield in his fine account of the suffrage movement, is through the wardrobe. The female form, 'as the century progressed towards war, was being released from the distortions and distentions of the Victorian era'. [70] From the crinoline and the bustle and the trappings of uselessness women were to be released by factors ranging from the bicycle to war. Tennis dress (ladies did not *run* after the ball) and swimming costumes would not necessarily have made a great impact on clothing conventions, but the practical and comfortable female cycling costume (and all that cycling itself implied) emphatically did. Edwardian entertainment and the occupations of wartime were for middle-class girls acts of liberation. Poverty, need and the rigours of industry and domestic service still surrounded the working-class girl with considerable obstacles.

We cannot here pursue the outcome of these changes in the shape of the organized fight for the suffrage. It ran from the first recognizable women's suffrage movement organized by Barbara Bodichon in 1865, through the half-way manœuvres of the Primrose League and the Women's Liberal Federation of the 1880s, to the Women's Social and Political Union founded by the Pankhursts in 1903 and the militant suffragette movement in the years leading up to the First World War. The movement, in the eyes of some, did damage to the women's cause [71] and amounted in the eyes of others, to 'pathological posturings'. [72] It is also argued that it was the role of women during the First World War, in civilian employments of all kinds, on buses, in munitions factories and in service occupations, that produced the post-war political settlement. [73] But the very social and political build-up that Millicent Fawcett had described led to the easy acceptance of women as components in the war effort. The nation need not have called on or accepted participation by women to the extent that it did: nations do not necessarily do what is best for their survival. Women had, however, improved their status and asserted themselves to the point at which it was incompatible with national realities for it to be judged unseemly that women should now drive trams, nurse soldiers, make shells or dig graves. War and the bicycle were the only factors not adequately foreseen in Millicent Fawcett's analysis.

The problem of the relationship between the position of women and the content of democracy has been seen to relate, historically, to the removal of legislative and political constraints, to education and employment, and, so far as working-class women have been concerned, to the achievement of adequate standards of economic security and social welfare. All these factors influenced the status of women in society and in the family. All were of central importance in the shifts of attitudes in the quarter of a century or so leading up to the First World War.

NOTES

1 BEALES 'The "Great Depression" in industry and trade', in CARUS-WILSON (ed.) *Essays in Economic History*, I, p. 413.
2 E. MOBERLY BELL *The Story of Hospital Almoners*, p. 70 (London, 1961).
3 ROBERTS *Victorian Origins of the British Welfare State*, p. 95.
4 P. H. J. H. GOSDEN *The Development of Educational Administration in England and Wales*, p. 27 (Oxford, 1966).
5 1950 edition, pp. 16 and 34.
6 ERVING GOFFMAN *Asylums*, pp. 11, 15 (New York, 1961; 1968 edition).
7 GEORGE LANSBURY *My Life*, pp. 135–6 (London, 1928).
8 LOUISA TWINING 'Workhouse cruelties', in MICHAEL GODWIN (ed.) *Nineteenth Century Opinion*, p. 56 (Harmondsworth, 1951).
9 Quoted from the C.O.S. annual report for 1875 in CHARLES LOCH MOWAT *The Charity Organisation Society 1869–1913*, pp. 26–7 (London, 1961).
10 Quoted in ibid., p. 69.
11 Quoted in BELL *The Story of Hospital Almoners*, p. 59.
12 LANSBURY *My Life*, p. 132.
13 Majority *Report*, I, p. 100.
14 BENTLEY B. GILBERT *The Evolution of National Insurance in Great Britain*, p. 233 (London, 1966).
15 T. S. and M. B. SIMEY *Charles Booth, Social Scientist*, p. 90 (London, 1960).
16 Ibid., p. 109.
17 Ibid., p. 116.
18 Quoted in ibid., p. 95.
19 Ibid., p. 161.
20 For an account of and extracts from Booth's work, see also HAROLD W. PFAUTZ *Charles Booth on the City: Physical Pattern and Social Structure* (Chicago, 1968).
21 LYND *England in the Eighteen-eighties*, p. 52.
22 ASA BRIGGS *Social Thought and Social Action: A Study of the Work of Seebohm Rowntree 1871–1954*, p. 30 (London, 1961).
23 MARK ABRAMS *Social Surveys and Social Action*, pp. 41–2 (London, 1951).
24 SECONDARY EDUCATION COMMISSION *Report*, Vol. I, pp. 34–8, 138.

25 PHILIP MAGNUS *Educational Aims and Efforts 1882–1910*, p. 39 (London, 1910).

26 *Twenty-Third Annual Report*, pp. 1–2 (London, 1844).

27 T. RAYMONT *A History of the Education of Young Children*, p. 212 (London, 1937).

28 F. S. MARVIN (ed.) *Reports on Elementary Schools 1852–1882 by Matthew Arnold*, pp. 93, 126 (London, 1889; 1910 edition).

29 ALTICK *The English Common Reader*, pp. 171–2. See also LAWRENCE STONE 'Literacy and education in England 1640–1900', *Past and Present*, No. 42, February 1969.

30 Clauses 5 and 6. The full text is in NATIONAL EDUCATION UNION *A Verbatim Report . . . of the Debate in Parliament* (Manchester, 1870).

31 SECONDARY EDUCATION COMMISSION *Report*, p. 143.

32 *Parity and Prestige in English Secondary Education*, pp. 49–50 (London, 1955).

33 E. J. R. EAGLESHAM *The Foundations of 20th Century Education in England*, pp. 39–40, 59 (London, 1967).

34 E. R. WICKHAM *Church and People in an Industrial City*, p. 80 (London, 1957).

35 Quoted in K. S. INGLIS *Churches and the Working Classes in Victorian England*, p. 19 (London, 1963).

36 WICKHAM *Church and People*, pp. 148–9.

37 *Churches and the Working Classes*, pp. 3–15.

38 ASHWORTH *The Genesis of Modern British Town Planning*, p. 135.

39 BRIGGS *Seebohm Rowntree*, pp. 95–6. See also *One Man's Vision: the story of the Joseph Rowntree Village Trust* (London, 1954).

40 *Minutes of Evidence*, p. 626.

41 Ibid., p. 619.

42 *To-morrow: a Peaceful Path to Real Reform*, pp. 7, 118–28 (London, 1898).

43 Ibid., pp. 193–4, Memorandum of Evidence submitted by Ministry of Transport.

44 For all these developments, see '"Philanthropy and five per cent": housing experiments', Ch. XIV in DAVID OWEN *English Philanthropy 1660–1960* (Harvard, 1965).

45 Ibid., p. 389.

46 A. M. CARR-SAUNDERS, D. CARADOG JONES and C. A. MOSER *A Survey of Social Conditions in England and Wales*, p. 23 (London, 1958).

47 *The Family and Marriage*, pp. 104–5 (Harmondsworth, 1962).

48 See MARGARET HEWITT *Wives and Mothers in Victorian Industry* (London, 1958).

49 *The Family and Marriage*, p. 26.

50 IVY PINCHBECK *Women Workers and the Industrial Revolution 1750–1850*, p. 1 (London, 1930).

51 Ibid., p. 2. See also HEWITT *Wives and Mothers in Victorian Industry*.

52 GEORGE E. EADES *Historic London*, p. 164 (London, 1966).

53 SYDNEY H. COONTZ *Population Theories and the Economic Interpretation*, pp. 160–1 (London, 1961).

54 O. R. McGREGOR *Divorce in England*, p. 65 (London, 1957).

55 WANDA F. NEFF *Victorian Working Women*, pp. 186–7 (London, 1929; 1966 edition).

56 EDITH OLIVER *Four Victorian Ladies of Wiltshire*, pp. 27–8 (London, 1945).
57 ALYS W. PEARSALL-SMITH 'A reply from the daughters', in GOODWIN (ed.) *Nineteenth Century Opinion*, p. 89.
58 O. A. SHERRARD *Two Victorian Girls*, pp. 164–7 (London, 1966).
59 See *Prosperity and Parenthood*, passim (London, 1954).
60 See PETER T. COMINOS 'Late Victorian sexual responsibility and the social system', *International Review of Social History*, VIII, 1963, No. 18.
61 See *Feminism and Family Planning in Victorian England* (Liverpool, 1964).
62 For domestic conditions in middle-class and working-class homes at the turn of the century, see MARGHANITA LASKI 'Domestic life', in SIMON NOWELL SMITH (ed.) *Edwardian England 1901–1914* (London, 1964).
63 *On the Subjection of Women*, pp. 247–8 (Everyman edition, 1929).
64 MILLICENT GARRETT FAWCETT *Women's Suffrage: a short History of a great Movement*, p. 23 (New York, undated).
65 McGREGOR *Divorce in England*, p. 19.
66 'Women's suffrage', in GOODWIN (ed.) *Nineteenth Century Opinion*, pp. 84–5.
67 Quoted from Alice Zimmern in JOSEPHINE KAMM *Hope Deferred: Girls' Education in English History*, p. 213 (London, 1965).
68 ROYAL COMMISSION ON SECONDARY EDUCATION *Report*, p. 75.
69 MARGARET OLIPHANT in Vol. 88, December 1860, pp. 711–13.
70 *The Strange Death of Liberal England 1910–1914*, p. 142 (New York, 1935; 1961 edition).
71 This is ROGER FULFORD'S view in *Votes for Women* (London, 1957).
72 McGREGOR *Divorce in England*, p. 91.
73 For an account of the role of women in the war see ARTHUR MARWICK *The Deluge*, particularly Ch. 3 (London, 1965).

Education (discussed in Chapter 1) is also discussed in Chapter 8, social attitudes and policy (discussed in Chapter 1) are continued in Chapter 5, and population (discussed in Chapter 1) is continued in Chapters 5 to 7. The growth of towns was previously discussed in Chapter 2, housing (previously discussed in Chapter 2) is continued in Chapters 5 and 6, the Poor Law (discussed in Chapter 2) is continued in Chapter 5, town planning is continued in Chapter 6, and the discussion of women and of the family is continued in Chapter 9.

5

Twentieth-century Emergencies

What we have tried to indicate in previous chapters is the complex of nine-teenth-century changes and continuities which helped to shape society in the twentieth century. It would be impossible, without seriously distorting our purpose, to pursue at this point all the threads we have so far traced, or to anticipate all the emphases we shall place in our analysis of society in the second half of the twentieth century. To follow the transitions across the first half of this century means being even more selective than previously. It is, again, partly in an examination of some attempts at social reorganization, and at coping with emergencies, that we may see significant changes relevant to our analysis of the shape of modern society.

SOCIAL LEGISLATION

After the turn of the century the working-class standard of living remained static or declined, working-class political and industrial organization grew stronger, and there was consequently an acute and conscious necessity for the Liberal Party in particular to identify itself as the popular party, by transform-ing a heightened social understanding into practical social policy. The super-ficial prosperity of the pre-war period was what the literary language of one historian calls the 'Indian summer of British capitalism', bringing 'carefree plenty to the well-to-do', but 'for the workers a winter of discontent'. Real wages declined for a large part of the period. If falling prices during the pre-vious decades had obscured economic progress, rising prices now lent to the economy a 'false air of prosperity'. [1] Edwardian developments in social policy arose out of conceptions of communal responsibility, some more altruistic than others. Altruism was, in fact, tempered throughout with a sense of social reality and inevitabilities. Behind concern for the unemployed, for example, at the turn of the century lay the new understanding of the structure of poverty, and of the failure and inadequacy of the Poor Law principles of 1834. It was to 'stop this rot in the Poor Law and its administration' that, according to Sidney and Beatrice Webb, the Poor Law Commission was set up in 1905 'under the confident assumption that the Commission could not do otherwise than recommend a return to the principles of 1834'. [2]

The Poor Law Commission did not report until 1909. Almost immediately after its creation the reforming Liberal government of 1906 had come to power. Old age pensions were introduced in 1908 (resisted to the last ditch by the C.O.S.) on a non-contributory basis, at a maximum level of five shillings per week. Although the National Insurance Act of 1911 was, unlike the pension scheme, a contributory one, and involved the less magnanimous principle of individual insurance, it was in a sense further removed from nineteenth-century thinking on social legislation. The Act consisted of two parts: Part I concerned health and Part II unemployment. The legislation on health insurance accepted (as legislation on school meals, a school health service and midwives had done in a more limited way already) the welfare of the individual as a matter of primary social concern. Unemployment insurance was necessary because, said Lloyd George, whoever was to blame for the great fluctuations in trade which caused unemployment, 'the workman is the least to blame . . . he is not responsible, although he bears almost all the real privation'. [3] 1911 was, therefore, far removed from the philosophy of, for example, the Public Health Act of 1848. Public opinion in 1906 was prepared to accept, and indeed demanded, State responsibility for much more personal aspects of welfare. The pension scheme called seriously into question, as the C.O.S. very clearly understood, the entire basis of the Poor Law. The health insurance of 1911 was more hesitant in its contributory nature but − compulsory as it initially was for everyone earning under £160 a year − it had wider implications for the future shape of the welfare services. The health part of the Act (resisted by the doctors as well as by the Conservative opposition) was operated through approved insurance schemes run by trade unions, insurance companies and others. The unemployment scheme was administered through the new Labour Exchanges. The employee, the employer and the State paid contributions, and the scheme provided sickness and maternity benefits, the services of a doctor and other medical benefits.

Unemployment − a subject to which we shall return − was in Part II of the Act made the target of a more limited exercise, providing through insurance a benefit scheme for workers in what Lloyd George called 'precarious trades', that is, those 'liable to very considerable fluctuations', employing roughly one sixth of the industrial population. The coverage of both parts of the Act was gradually extended.

The important consideration here is that by the outbreak of the First World War a serious accumulation of social commitments had been expressed and acted upon, in relation to children, health, unemployment and old age. The process of State and local government intervention and control was being

25 *London interior, December 1912.*

consolidated. The very process of monopoly organization in the private sector of the economy, and of wider public management of services and bureaucratic controls in the national and local government sectors, contributed to a recognition of the collective needs of a complex society. We have discussed the extension of local authority responsibilities under the general umbrella and impetus of national legislation. By the early twentieth century local authorities were becoming increasingly involved in, for example, transport, electricity, gas and water services. By 1913, 80 per cent of the consumers of water and of passengers on trams, over 60 per cent of consumers of electricity and 40 per cent of those of gas, were catered for by local authorities. The reason for the growth of municipal involvement was not simply socialist doctrine of the Fabian 'gas and water' kind, but largely 'the need to control natural monopolies, in the hope of relieving the rates, and in a praiseworthy measure of civic pride'. [4]

The period between the mid-1890s and the First World War was also the decisive period in the process of industrial amalgamation and monopolization (in fields ranging from tobacco to steel). The first Woolworth's was established in 1909. In an ill-considered metaphor a historian of shopping has described how in the period before the First World War the 'big multiples' in the grocery trade were 'eating up their competitors in every part of the country', though the pace slowed down after 1918. [5] The processes of large-scale production, extensive and intricate commercial operations, widespread public controls, impersonal industrial management and public planning, nation-wide industrial bargaining and the national consolidation of trade union and employer organizations, were all to one extent or another implanted in the national consciousness by the First World War, even though some of them were not finally consolidated until after it. The Federation of British Industries, for example, was born during the war in 1916, and the T.U.C. General Council after it in 1921. Although there had been a national organization of building employers since 1878, it was in 1896 that a full-time general secretary and staff were appointed, in 1901 that it adopted its present title of National Federation of Building Trades Employers, and at the end of the First World War that it consolidated its local and regional organization. The 1902 Education Act had already illustrated the process of transition to more efficient and all-embracing local authority control, a process which, in abandoning some of the disadvantages of the elected School Board system, also jettisoned the opportunity to strengthen the ties between the schools and the community. Education became *one* of the items in the election manifesto, and in this sense the Act was a retreat from opportunities for popular involvement in educational policy-making, a retreat not to be halted until the widespread interest in education of the 1950s and 1960s.

Between 1902 and the outbreak of war Britain acquired, in fact, a considerable body of legislation and machinery affecting a wide range of social services. The concept of social services other than those provided under the Poor Law was in this period effectively implemented for the first time. Legislation related not only to the provision and administration of education, for example, but also, in 1906, to school meals, and in the following year to a school health service. The Children Act of 1908 was concerned with wider problems of the protection of children. A Royal Commission report was followed in 1913 by a Mental Deficiency Act. Free school places, Labour Exchanges, town planning – the range of new departures was wide even if their effectiveness was not always great. They illustrate, however, the extent to which awareness of social realities had sharpened since the end of the 1880s.

THE POOR LAW COMMISSION AND AFTER

That the ground had not been totally cleared for the building of a new kind of welfare society can be seen from both the limitations of the legislation itself and the debates about social policy highlighted by the Poor Law Commission Reports of 1909. The analyses and findings of the Commission demonstrate vividly the scale of reference being established for the approach to poverty and social planning for the next half-century.

The two philosophies battling it out in the Poor Law Commission were broadly that of the C.O.S. (the nineteen-member Commission included the

C.O.S. Secretary, C. S. Loch, and five others of its members) and that of the socialists (with Beatrice Webb representing the extremely influential Fabians). The philosophy of the former was based on the retention of the fundamental principles of 1834, however far these might need to be adapted, and on co-operation between the Poor Law authorities, whatever new name might be found for them, and the voluntary organizations. The Fabians were more concerned with efficient local government, specialized social services and the total abolition of the Poor Law and its agencies. The Commission failed to produce an agreed report, and the Minority Report was signed by four members.

The Majority Report was rooted in the explicit awareness that, in spite of moral and material progress and an 'enormous annual expenditure, amounting to nearly sixty millions a year, upon poor relief, education, and public health, we still have a vast army of persons quartered upon us unable to support themselves, and an army which in numbers has recently shown signs of increase rather than decrease'. The Report sought ways of strengthening the machinery of relief. It proposed changing the name of the local Poor Law authorities to Public Assistance Committees – though this was 'not intended to disguise the fact that those who come within the scope of the operations of the new authority are receiving help at the public expense'. It wished to ensure adequate specialization within the system, in order to strengthen the principle of deterrence. An all-purpose workhouse was inefficient, argued the Report. The 'loafer, the in-and-out, and the work-shy are influenced as to whether or not they accept the offer of the workhouse by the amount of physical comfort, restraint, or inconvenience associated with the particular institution offered them. The more comfortable the house, the less is it a deterrent to this class.' The 'respectable poor', on the other hand, were deterred from accepting the workhouse out of moral considerations, not wishing to 'accept comfort if it involves association with a number of persons of a degraded *status*'. The mixed workhouse, therefore, 'with its higher level of comfort works most unevenly as a deterrent. It attracts the very class it ought to repel, and it may act as a deterrent in the case of the aged and infirm to whom it might legitimately be a refuge.' A streamlined system of classification by institutions would make it easier to provide conditions which could really act as a deterrent to the able-bodied.

The analysis and recommendations of the Report demonstrate repeatedly the continued existence of a social philosophy which refused to accept that what was under discussion was the phenomenon of poverty and not the moral stances involved in the concept of pauperism. Its vocabulary makes no effort to disguise the fact. It saw the poor as 'a vast army' which had *intruded* into the social structure; they were 'quartered' upon 'us'. The sense of poverty as a discrete condition, unrelated to society, outside the society of *us*, is in this sentence absolutely complete. The discussion of the direction to be taken in this period of alert interest in social and individual welfare is here conducted in strident moral terms. The fact that Poor Law institutions had made it easy for paupers to obtain relief on more than one occasion in the year (the 'ins-and-outs') meant that curative treatment was impossible:

> The worst characters may flock into the workhouse to recuperate from the effects of their evil lives, and as soon as they have, at the ratepayers' cost, partially recovered their physical condition, they can leave the workhouse and resume their degenerate careers.

Old persons 'given to drink, or of dirty habits' should not 'be enabled to remove themselves from control either by a pension or by the granting of outdoor relief'. Institutions should have the power to *detain* 'drunkards and persons leading immoral lives . . . after their incapacity to lead a decent life has been proved'. Outdoor medical relief should be conditional upon 'the maintenance of a healthy domicile and good habits'. The Report attacks the school meals Act of 1906 as interfering with the proper processes of relief.

What the Report did, in fact, was to accept the criteria of the C.O.S. and argue, as the Society had argued forty years before, that there were too many agencies dealing indiscriminately with 'a class which is sometimes called ablebodied, sometimes unemployed, regardless of the fact that this class is not really a class at all but a heterogeneous mass of men . . .' which included the honest, the criminal, the unfortunate, the industrious and the loafer, all of whom, 'in the prevailing confusion, are shifting about from one agency to another'. To ensure that they were sifted and classified, and each agency was assigned its appropriate work, the Report urged stronger co-operation between the authorities and the C.O.S. itself:

> As was urged in 1834, and again in 1870, so we once more urge the need of co-operation in this work between the help which is paid for out of the rates, and that which is rendered by voluntary charitable agencies. On these lines the Charity Organisations Movement has worked consistently, and the present moment seems to afford a peculiarly favourable opportunity for securing that co-operation on a wider and more permanent basis. [6]

The vocabulary of the Minority Report is at times not dissimilar in its condescension from that of the Majority. It points out, for example, that destitution authorities rarely bother to ascertain 'how the household is actually being maintained upon the Outdoor Relief . . . The result, as we have grave reason to believe, is that a large part of the sum of nearly four millions sterling is a subsidy to insanitary, to disorderly or even to vicious habits of life.' Children were 'actually being brought up at the public expense in drunken and dissolute homes'. Although the Fabian philosophy was as socially manipulative in its way as was the C.O.S., the differences between the general purposes of this Report and that of the Majority are great. The Minority Report is aware of the failures of past analysis and sees the underlying processes of social change. Beatrice Webb had worked with Booth and had been offered marriage by Joseph Chamberlain. George Lansbury, another Minority

Commissioner, had intimate experience of the working of relief in the conditions of destitution in Poplar. They relentlessly carried the Minority Report through to what, in its considered construction, must have been intended as the most crucial sentence of all:

> For all sections of the Able-bodied, the Poor Law, alike in England and Wales, Scotland and Ireland, is, in our judgment, intellectually bankrupt.

It had been Chamberlain, in fact, 'who, first among statesmen, realized the bankruptcy of the Poor Law and the utter inadequacy of Voluntary Agencies as methods of relieving Able-bodied Destitution'. The Majority's recommendations would work, on its own admission, only if compulsory powers of detention were available. This, said the Minority, would make the destitution authorities 'very nearly akin to the Prison Authorities'. The Minority rejected altogether such principles of deterrence. It had become apparent that:

> the condition of the lowest grade of independent labourers is unfortunately one of such inadequacy of food and clothing and such absence of other necessaries of life that it has been found, in practice, impossible to make the conditions of Poor Law relief 'less eligible' without making them such as are demoralizing to the children, physically injurious to the sick, and brutalizing to the aged and infirm.

The Minority Report demanded the complete break-up of the Poor Law machinery, nationally and locally. It considered, in fact, that no residue of pauperism would need to be dealt with by an unspecialized agency, in conditions of the general workhouse or out-relief, if specialized local authority services were properly organized. The Minority had been horrified by what

26 Distress in London, July 1912. Children waiting outside a hall in Salmon's Lane for a free dinner.

they had seen, for example, of the typical men's day ward in an urban work-house, containing:

> one or two hundred wholly unoccupied males of every age between fifteen and ninety – strong and vicious men; men in all stages of recovery from debauch; weedy youths of weak intellect; old men too dirty or disreputable to be given special privileges, and sometimes, when there are no such privi-leges, even worthy old men; men subject to fits; occasional monstrosities . . . the respectable labourer prematurely invalided; the hardened, sodden loafer, and the temporary unemployed man . . .

This, or any other version of this, was for the Minority unacceptable. Britain now had efficient local government; to it, its sub-committees, and its special-ists, *all* the functions of the destitution authority should be transferred. Only a Registrar of Public Assistance with a staff of inquiry officers and a Receiv-ing House would be needed 'for the strictly temporary accommodation of non-able-bodied persons found in need, and not as yet dealt with by the Com-mittees concerned'. [7]

Eventually, in 1929, the Poor Law became Public Assistance in the hands of the local authorities, nationally administered by the Unemployment Assist-ance Board from 1934, and with extended powers and the title of Assistance Board from 1940. The Poor Law died but a use for its machinery continued to be found. Neither of the Commission's Reports proved in the event directly influential. The Liberal government took no action on the recommendations of either, and by-passed the problem of the relief of the indigent poor by pursuing its attempts to combat indigence. The problem of whether or not to break up the Poor Law was simply evaded.

Our analysis of the philosophies embodied in the Reports has not been intended to suggest that the Reports themselves played a significant part in shaping social institutions but to illustrate, at their sharpest, alternative approaches to social policy in the period when the basis of the 'welfare state' was laid. It is common in histories of this period to use the adjective 'great' of the advances made under the Liberal government from 1906, and it is true that they represented major achievements in a variety of fields. It would be wrong, however, to assume that they marked a total break with the past. If, taking a long view, the Poor Law was to some degree the father of the modern social services, the child was recognizably like the parent. The legislation accepted collectivist notions only so far as appeared strictly neces-sary. Restrictions and hesitations were expressed in the form of moral judge-ments. The old age pension was given on condition that certain criteria were met, including not only age (seventy) and income (full pension if annual income was below two pounds per year) but also worthiness – the five shillings a week would not be paid to those who had habitually failed to work. A person would not be disqualified if he had for ten years up to the age of sixty made provision against old age, sickness, infirmity or want or loss of employment.

The discussion of health insurance and medicine involved a view of the doctor as moral adviser on habits of excessive drinking and unwise eating. National Health Insurance from 1911 provided benefit for the insured, not their families. It should be noted that, although the parliamentary Labour Party supported the 1911 legislation on health and unemployment insurance, Lansbury, among others, opposed it, because he considered the contributory principle anti-socialist. The conclusion arrived at by Richard Titmuss about 'the great collectivist advances at the beginning of the century, with their positive achievements in social legislation' is that although they were aimed at the gradual overthrow of the Poor Law, in the absence of 'new insights into the social phenomena of human needs and behaviour, the ideas and methods of the poor law were transplanted to the new social services'. The way in which the new institutions grew, detaching the needs of the individual from those of the family, partly explains 'the *ad hoc* fragmentary growth of the British social services'. The important point Titmuss makes is that the new services developed 'to cater for certain categories of individual need; for certain categories of disease and incapacity, and for certain special needs of special groups. Classes of persons in need and categories of disease were treated; not families and social groups in distress.' [8] Progress was real, and more may have been possible; we must not credit the policy-makers and legislators with more than they in fact did.

Some redistribution of income was certainly involved (total working-class incomes may have benefited from all the social benefits introduced in 1906–11 by some 6 per cent per year), but the approach was piecemeal and the departures less radical than is sometimes claimed. The notion of 'settlement', of parish responsibility for the problematical and burdensome poor, for example, had continued from Tudor times, through its formalization in the seventeenth century and the changes of 1834, to the events of 1906–11 and the transition to public assistance in 1929, and beyond. It has remained part of the practice of national assistance and social security. Although the Minority Report of 1909 agreed that fewer paupers were being compulsorily removed than at any previous date, it indicated, in its chapter on 'Settlement and Removal', that over 12,000 poor persons were deported annually, under compulsory orders, and often against their will, from one union to another. Although 'settlement' deportations no longer take place in this way, the 'settlement mentality' remains, and Borough X prefers not to have to accept responsibility for the homeless from Borough Y.

The limitations of the collectivist advances with regard to *scope* can be seen most clearly, not only in such fields as family health, but in the failure to tackle adequately such problems as regional industrial decline and housing, both of which affect important aspects of working-class family stability and structure at a fundamental level.

HOUSING

There is an underlying conflict in all thinking and legislation on housing in Britain between, on the one hand, the philosophy of social responsibility, including for the provision of an adequate standard of housing as of right, and on the other hand the baronial-yeoman-bourgeois concept of the Englishman's private (and heavily mortgaged) castle. The rage of the suburban bungalow-owner against the council tenant has become a major factor in political argument only since the Second World War. During approximately the first half of the century the practice of collective responsibility for the raising of housing standards was too limited and irregular in its achievement, and the emergencies in which it was exercised were too bewildering, for an excessive display of rage.

We have already seen that the housing Acts of the nineteenth century, in so far as they were effective at all, were concerned with regulating, but not intervening in, the construction of houses. In both town planning and house building the departures of the early twentieth century were hesitant or ineffective. The Town Planning Act of 1909 made it possible for local authorities to adopt planning schemes, but to all intents and purposes only for new, that is suburban, developments. The philosophy of suburban planning embodied in this Act coincided with and related to the dilution of Garden City ideas into the movement towards the Garden Suburb (as it was called in Hampstead) or the Garden Village (as it was called in Hull). For existing housing the first move did not come until wartime. For the first time restrictions on rent increases were introduced in 1915, with an Act touched off by an outcry against rising rents in Glasgow. Between the wars there were, in Marion Bowley's formulation, three periods of experiment. [9] The first began in 1919 with the Housing and Town Planning Act, which inaugurated the principle of Treasury subsidies and made it necessary for local authorities to survey housing needs, and try to provide for them. Public involvement in housing provision, made possible in 1890 but largely inoperative, had now really begun, though it was widely believed that the Act would need to be only a temporary measure and that the housing programme would rapidly make up the deficit caused by war and establish an adequate supply of new housing. But the homes for the returning heroes did not materialize. It had been estimated before the war that working-class houses needed to be replaced at a rate of 60,000 a year, and simply to catch up with pre-war needs, it was variously estimated, between 300,000 and a million new houses would be needed immediately after the war. Vast promises had been made, and great hopes were pinned on the 1919 Act. The result was derisory. Nowhere 'were suffering and social dislocation more apparent than in the need for houses. And nowhere was the failure to provide relief more clear and calamitous by the end of 1920. The history of the housing programme is the history of a rout.' [10] By 1921 it was decided that the subsidy for house building was too expensive.

Marion Bowley's second period of experiment runs from 1923 to 1934. Neville Chamberlain's Housing Act of 1923 made subsidies again available, but on a more rigid basis. Local authorities could build houses with them only if they could convince the Minister of Health that it would be better for them than for private enterprise to do so. The subsidies were available until 1925, on the continued assumption that the housing crisis could be quickly overcome. The Wheatley Housing Act of 1924, probably the most important piece of legislation of the short-lived first Labour government, firmly restored the responsibility for working-class housing to the local authorities. Subsidies were increased, but were offered only for houses to be let. The Greenwood Slum Clearance Act of 1930, a product of the second Labour government, was designed to clear and to build under the long-term planning introduced in 1924. The Conservative-dominated National Government of 1931, led by the former Labour Prime Minister, Ramsay MacDonald, ended the Wheatley subsidies in 1933 and defined the terms of the third period of experiment. The new policy launched by the Housing Act of that year was intended to continue slum clearance and attack overcrowding, but urged maximum incentive for competitive private building, to be supplemented where necessary by unsubsidized local authority building.

One thing that this story indicates is that the limits on social policy were now vastly different from those of the nineteenth century. Policy and progress were now features of election manifestos and programmes, and the limits to which they became subjected were those of government mis-estimations and economic stringency. The ethics of the struggle between public programmes and private enterprise were being largely dictated by Treasury considerations. Public responsibility and public planning to some extent overtook all political parties, given the magnitude of the social problems of the 1930s, the magnitude of war efforts and the magnitude of international economic competition.

Parties became inexorably committed to public planning in principle, and not until the mid-1960s was any serious attempt made, within the Conservative Party, for example, to retreat from this commitment towards more thorough-going private initiative.

EMPIRE AND WAR

The economic circumstances which, in the first half of the twentieth century, underlay developments in social engineering included both war and the consequences of war, as well as fundamental changes in Britain's trading position. International competition had helped to make the idea of empire widely acceptable in the 1870s, and in the 1880s Britain was involved in the scramble for Africa. The Imperial Idea, for the first time in Britain's history, was strongly justified in terms of tongue, race and destiny. In the 1890s and after the turn of the century – particularly during the Boer War – imperialism became a cause to be fought for, and the relationship between Britain's economic stability and the necessity of empire became a subject for debate. The reluctant political imperialism of Gladstone became the imperialism defended on economic grounds by Joseph Chamberlain, the creation of whose Unionist Party by secession from the Liberal Party in 1886 'may be said to mark the birth of the Imperialism which dominated British politics for twenty years'. [11] Cecil Rhodes, the most forthright of empire builders, contributed to the funds of the Liberal Party, and in 1895 made his sharp defence of empire:

> I was in the East End of London yesterday and attended a meeting of the unemployed. I listened to the wild speeches, which were just a cry for 'bread', 'bread', 'bread', and on my way home I pondered over the scene and I became more than ever convinced of the importance of imperialism . . . in order to save the 40,000,000 inhabitants of the United Kingdom from a bloody civil war, we colonial statesmen must acquire new lands . . . The Empire, as I have always said, is a bread and butter question. If you want to avoid civil war, you must become imperialists . . . [12]

The idea of empire not only captured Chamberlain and inspired Rhodes, but overtook wide sections of the labour movement, and made it popular to believe that 'to us – to us, and not to others, a certain definite duty has been assigned. To carry light and civilization into the dark places of the world; to touch the mind of Asia and of Africa with the ethical ideas of Europe.' [13] The jingoism of the Boer War contributed to the state of mind which made possible the scale of the First World War. Both related to a world in which the internal stability of the great nations depended strongly on raw materials and markets, on success in international competition, and therefore on a new mastery of international relations. Much of the detail of Britain's twentieth-century history is governed, not only by competition and war with Germany, but by the fact that the United States during the First World War replaced Britain as the world's major industrial and financial power, that it was in the empire that Britain found markets to substitute for those lost to the United States and other powers, and that new world economics became bound up with world war. [14]

The First World War, in fact, interrupted many of Britain's traditional export relations, to the benefit of the United States, which changed 'within the short span of the war from a major debtor to a major creditor nation, and there was a sharp increase in the American share of world production of many key commodities'. [15] Although Britain was able to compensate for the lost trade by temporarily improving her share in such things as shipping and insurance, the dangers were now looming more clearly. Not only was the United States in such a strong position, but other competitors (including Japan) were also threatening more urgently, the Soviet Union had come into existence, and more and more spheres of British economic interest (in the Far East, Canada and Latin America, for instance) were weakening – although some lost ground was regained in the 1930s. The war did not, however, cause these developments, it dramatized and accelerated them. Professor Ashworth has summarized the relationship between the war and the range of wartime and post-war developments:

> The most fundamental changes of the nineteen-twenties were not primarily the result of the war, and some of the greatest changes of which the war was one cause were irreversible. Had there been no war the United States would still have become the world's great creditor; industrialization would still have spread in new areas, to the destruction of some British export markets; substitutes for coal would still have grown in importance; the sources and costs of primary commodities would still have changed. Even many of the changes in British society would have come, too. Labour would still have become a stronger and more cohesive political force; women would still have gained the vote and wider social opportunities; there would still have been a larger scale of organization among firms and trade unions; doubtless, many tastes and consumer demands would have changed in just the same way . . . The war did two things. It accelerated many economic and social changes already in progress, carrying them near to completion earlier than otherwise would have happened . . . And it smashed the delicate framework of international economic and financial organization . . . [16]

We shall return later in the chapter to the questions of war and social welfare, and war and the disappointment of social expectations. World war obviously made fundamental inroads into patterns of social assumptions and consciousness. It produced or heightened a basic spiritual dislocation and malaise, over which attempts were made to plaster the post-war 'business as usual' signs. The politics, as well as the philosophy and the literature, of the interwar decades were starkly defined by the experience and the aftermath of the world war. The war also, of course, introduced new factors into the structure of British social organization, in order to meet a new order of emergency. The State became involved in the control of war industries, [17] agricultural production, the running of the railways and the control of a variety of resources and services. Although the end of the war saw the relaxations of these regulations and involvements, extensive State action to meet one sort of emergency meant that it could be called upon to meet another sort.

BETWEEN THE WARS

British society and economy in the 1920s and 1930s were not what they had been before the war. People's level of expectation – as we have seen notably in the case of housing – was higher, even if the level of achievement was disastrously low. Homes for heroes, full employment, the return to industrial and commercial 'normality' – all of these were slogans which, because they were unfulfilled, helped among other things to set the scene for renewed and intensified social conflict.

Economically, Britain's position after the short post-war boom was one of sharp contrasts. The old staple industries like cotton, coal and shipbuilding were hard hit by competition from better-equipped industries, by over-optimistic estimates of post-war demand, and by the lack of demand from saturated or lost markets. The inflated wartime capacity in shipbuilding, for example (followed by a disastrous decline at the beginning of the 1920s), and the steep drop in coal production at and after the end of the war, were two prominent factors which produced the higher level of regional unemployment, especially in the northern counties of England, in South Wales and industrial Scotland. On the other hand, electrical engineering, road transport, building and artificial silk, for example, made rapid advances at the same time. The expansion in electricity consumption and related investments by the State, together with the expansion of the electrical trades, were important examples of growth points; at the moment – in the late 1930s – when the expansion of these and other industries appeared to be past its peak, rearmament stopped any further recession. [18] The annual increase in British industrial output as a whole between the wars was just under 2 per cent: that of electrical goods and motor cars was over 10 per cent, and that of artificial silk over 15 per cent. Given such disparate developments, therefore, the structure of the labour force and the relative prosperity of different regions were inevitably being altered.

The Barlow Commission, whose report on the industrial population was completed in 1939, considered some of the factors which, after 1921, had led to a changed pattern of population growth. Between 1921 and 1937 the population of Great Britain had increased by 7·5 per cent (from under 43 to about 46 million). London and the Home Counties had increased by about 18 per cent, the Midland counties by about 11 per cent. The increase in Lancashire, however, was less than 1 per cent, and counties including Glamorgan, Northumberland and Durham registered declines. London, the Home Counties and the Midland counties contained nearly 70 per cent of the population added during the period. Industrial depression, resulting from the contraction of exports, new methods of working, the use of substitutes (such as rayon), and above all the development of industries not dependent on proximity to sources of power, lay behind the new population patterns, [19] and explain why unemployment and slump did not hit the south in the same way as the north and, even within regions, did not hit West Riding wool in the same way as Lancashire cotton or Yorkshire coal. Between 1921 and 1938, although the percentage of the labour force employed in 'manufacture' fluctuated between about 33 and 36 per cent, individual sectors registered considerable variations. The percentage of manufacturing workers employed in vehicle building rose from 5·75 to 8·85 per cent. The percentage employed in textiles fell from 21·4 to 16·15. Large increases took place at the same time in the numbers of workers employed in the distributive trades, insurance and

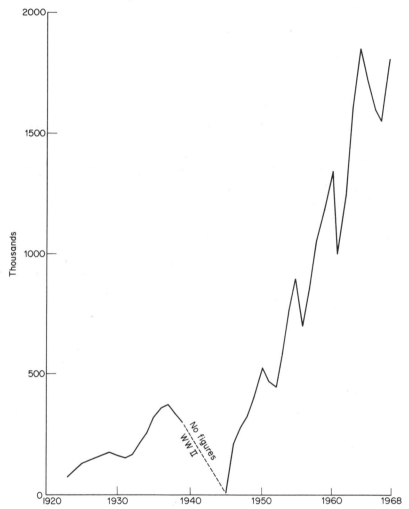

Fig. 6 Motor-car production, 1923–68. (See Table 19, p. 327.) After Annual Abstract of Statistics, *1969, and G. C. Allen, 1959.*

banking, and various local government, professional and other services. Available evidence on this extremely important development of service and tertiary occupations shows that there was

an increase of 1,246,000 salaried persons, or 35%, as against an increase in the number of wage-earners of 1,686,000, or 14%, between 1920–2 and

1937–8. Insurance statistics suggest a rise in the proportion of salaried workers from 22·0% in 1924 to 25·5% in 1938, and a corresponding fall in the proportion of wage-earners from 75·8% to 72·2%, the rest being armed forces. This tendency of the growth of the service industries, and of the growth of the 'salariat' within each industry, was common to all advanced countries. [20]

Changes in industrial and occupation structure were also taking place, affecting, for example, the scale and nature of female employment; many of the trends did not become acute, however, until the Second World War. Domestic service was still, before the First World War and in the 1930s, the largest single category of female employment (dropping from well over a million in 1931 to under 350,000 in 1951). Women were, however, moving into the distributive trades (starting with drapery during the Crimean War) and offices to an increasingly rapid extent by the First World War. By 1951 there were one and a quarter million female clerical workers, and the number has gone on increasingly steadily. It was during and after the Second World War that factory work passed domestic service in social esteem.

By the 1920s and 1930s the scale of economic and commercial organization, industrial production, social debate and conflict, had grown considerably beyond the dimensions discernible even in, for example, the 1880s. If, at the earlier date, new scales of monopoly and amalgamation, of industrial and urban units, had helped to define new attitudes to problems, by the end of the First World War national organization, national planning, national solutions, were a normal dimension of social thought. The national employers' and trade union organizations, party and ministerial policies, and national responsibilities in dealing with social problems which constituted national emergencies – all made this inevitable. Basic aspects of society, such as education or size of family, democratic participation and the planning of town communities and sub-communities, were now more than ever governed or influenced by national decisions, nation-wide services and government policy.

Government policy (in the shape of Neville Chamberlain's reforms) altered the pattern of local government, for example, in 1929. It transferred the powers of the Poor Law Guardians to the local authorities, and the counties received greater powers in the field of public health, welfare, planning and roads. The Ministry of Health had already been created in 1919, and from 1929 the new local authority powers were to extend hospital, maternity and child welfare and other services. An Act of 1933 rationalized legislation relating to local authority structure and powers. In commerce the process of combination and the expansion of multiple grocery and general stores were firm inter-war trends. So were the increased scale and efficiency of public administration and services, increased suburban and inter-urban transport, and the greater scale of postal, telephone, news and distributive services. The B.B.C.

was created in 1922. The 1930s saw both a rapid expansion in the purchase of radio sets, and acute competition among the large-circulation newspapers for readership. This was a period of expansion above all of the national dailies, offering free sets of the novels of Dickens or some other reward for the regular reader. In transport, too, the trends were clear: a Ministry of Transport was created in 1919, a Railways Act of 1921 compulsorily combined the 120 railway companies into four, at the same time ensuring a unified service and system of charges. An amalgamation of rail, tram and bus services in the London area produced the London Passenger Transport Board in 1933. In 1922 there were some 315,000 private cars in Great Britain. In 1930 there were over a million (and in 1967 10·3 million). More local authorities ran their own, and larger, bus services. The first unsuccessful experiments in internal air services took place in 1930. Five years later there were nineteen companies operating services.

INDUSTRIAL CONFLICT

'There can have been few times', says Ashworth, 'when the lot of the very poor was more miserable than in the early years of the twentieth century.' [21] Real wages had risen consistently through the second half of the nineteenth century, but roughly between the turn of the century and the First World

27 *Unemployed in Wigan, 11 November 1939.*

War they fell. They rose again in the 1920s and 1930s when, in spite of heavy unemployment, there was a rise in average living standards – as a result principally of a marked fall in the cost-of-living index, but also increased productivity and the increase in the proportion of higher-paid, salaried employees.

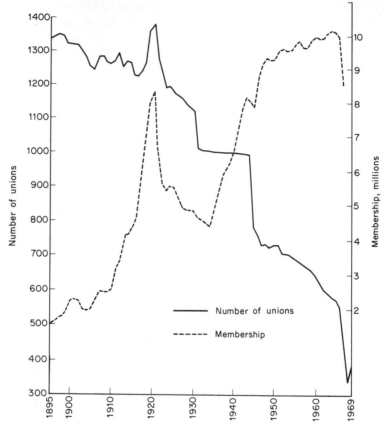

Fig. 7 Growth and consolidation of trade union membership (head offices in the United Kingdom), 1895–1969. (See also Table 12, p. 320.) After Mitchell and Deane, 1962, and Butler and Freeman, 1969.

Averages, however, are deceptive. The distribution of increased national income was uneven, and although the families of men in employment experienced improvements of one kind or another (including shorter working hours and paid holidays), the incidence of unemployment and its attendant suffering makes it difficult to dwell on averages.

Between 1921 and 1938 the percentage of unemployed never fell below 9·6, and at its peak – in 1932 – it reached almost 22 per cent. Unemployment data before the 1920s are not accurate, and have had to be deduced from trade union records of payments to their members when out of work. It is likely, however, that between 1856 and the First World War unemployment fluctuated between 2 and 10 per cent. Between 1921 and 1938 in only one year was the figure less than 10 per cent. Even allowing for the widest margin of error, Lord Beveridge came to the conclusion that unemployment after the First World War was 'most probably nearly two and a half times as severe as before the war'. [22] The two facts of declining real wages before the First World War and mass unemployment in the 1920s and 1930s form the main background to the presence of social conflict in Britain up to the Second World War, and the industrial and social policies and legislation aimed at relief and conciliation. Neither, of course, entirely explains continuing industrial militancy or social tension. Other factors, such as industrial rationalization and eventually automation, social problems relating to housing and a growing percentage of old people in the population, inadequate hospital facilities, responses to international situations, and the problems of particular industries – all contributed to tension and conflict.

At the back of conflict lay also, of course, the fact of political and industrial organization. A critical moment for the future history of trade union organization had been the new unionism of the late 1880s, which not only widened the basis of trade unionism, but also demonstrated the potential of organized militancy. George Howell, writing in 1891, complained mournfully that the distinguishing trait in the conduct of the militant 'new leaders' was 'their persistent, cowardly, and calumnious attacks upon the old leaders, upon men who have borne the brunt of labour's battles . . . The effect of slanders, so ruthlessly and persistently circulated, has been to foment discontent among the members of societies represented by those named . . . Some of the new leaders have openly proclaimed that their mission is to preach the gospel of discontent . . . In so far as discontent leads to emulation, to vigorous effort to better the condition of the workers, it is healthful . . . But there is discontent of another kind, which aims at lawlessness and licence.' [23] Within the working-class trade union and political movements (both becoming increasingly organized) the dispute over forms of industrial action, and over the relationship between industrial and political action, had now become sharp and portentous.

We cannot here attempt to trace the organizational forms of working-class action, and still less the place that the Labour Party came to occupy in British politics. [24] Nor is it necessary to pursue the economic arguments about the reasons for the difficulties of these years ('probably the only considerable period since the Napoleonic Wars in which real wages have not actually risen . . . With real wages falling, it would still appear that the experience of wage-earners was less favourable than that of other classes'). [25] The position in 1910, the background against which the immediate pre-war struggles have to be seen, has been described as follows:

by 1910 declining earnings were raising the temperature of industrial relations throughout the coalfields, with South Wales near to flash-point

Afternoon Edition. Monday May 10.

Ten people, one a small girl, were hurt in a car smash at Ilford to-day, when two motor-cars, one containing four people and the other six people, came into collision head on.

Two prominent Labour leaders, one a former Parliamentary representatives for South Shields, were arrested in County Durham yesterday afternoon under the Emergency Act. They were formally charged and remanded, bail being refused.

The Secretary of the Shoreditch Labour Party has been remanded on bail, charged with sedition.

Eight men have been arrested and charged with sedition in Battersea following a conflict between police and strikers in which a number on both sides were hurt.

Public houses in Poplar were closed to-day owing to a shortage of supplies. A number of public houses in parts of Stepney were similarly affected.

Further to the closing of the public houses in Edinburgh, the Government has asked brewers in Liverpool to cease delivery of beer, and many public houses are running short of supplies.

The Executive of the Miners Federation met in London to-day, and it is understood they discussed the reports of conferences held at Ostend during the week-end by Continental Miners and Transport Workers' Unions, who, rejected the proposal of sympathetic strike action and only passed an embargo on the import of coal to England.

A large number of men made an organised attack on a London dock late last night. The special constable on duty called up police reinforcements and the strikers were dispersed. Four arrests were made.

Nearly half the tram staff at Bath have reported for work, and signed on as non-unionists.

Birmingham tram and bus inspectors returned to work to-day.

Lowestoft electricians returned to work to-day.

The electric power station workers at Stoke Newington have decided to remain at work contrary to the orders of their Union.

Seven arrests have been made at Cricklewood, two at Camden Town.

TRANSPORT

Over 300 London General omnibuses now running, four routes being maintained:- No.1. Ealing Broadway-Oxford Street-Piccadilly-Kensington-Hammersmith-Brentford. No.2. Richmond-Turnham Green-Putney-Chelsea,-Piccadilly-Vauxhall-Clapham Common. No.3 Hendon-Cricklewood-Kilburn-Marylebone-Piccadilly-Marble Arch. No.4 Harlesden-Marylebone High Street-Euston Road-Liverpool Street- Bank-Holborn-Oxford Street-Holland Park. Further routes will be started as soon as possible.

TRAINS. All London termini report additional services at rush hours, Southern Railway instituting service on North Kent line. Cannon Street to Dartford. 700 trains ran on G.W.Rly. yesterday.

Fish plentiful at Billingsgate. Reasonable prices.

PRINTED BY THE NEWS ASSOCIATION. 63a Cliffords Inn, E.C.4.

28 General Strike news sheet, 10 May 1926.

on the abnormal place issue. In the cotton industry fifteen years of industrial peace had been broken by a county-wide spinning lock-out in 1908. The depression of 1908 had robbed the railwaymen of the benefits they had hoped to obtain under their new conciliation scheme. The printing industry was preparing for a battle on craft issues. And on the waterfront, labour was stirring after almost two decades of slumber. [26]

Factors such as these, together with new aspects of working-class political disillusion and militancy, produced a wave of industrial struggles, which a historian of the London Trades Council describes as deriving from 'a sense of power, the will to take charge of working-class destiny'. [27]

Miners, railwaymen, cotton spinners, boilermakers, seamen, dockers and workers in a variety of other trades were, in fact, involved in intense and prolonged struggles – and those involved were not always the groups who were worst off or with the strongest traditions of militancy. Syndicalism, a form of unionism aiming at industrial control through strike action, provided some of the sense of 'working-class destiny'. Economic hardship or the sense of deprivation fostered by the conspicuous affluence of the wealthy provided some of the incentive. The importance of the Great Unrest to the story of modern British society lies in the fact that it contained the combination of factors which was to be present in future industrial struggles: militancy, sensitive relations with Labour parliamentary politics, local, regional and national levels of strike action, attempts at industrial arbitration, and a concern with objectives not always easy to define in terms of money or conditions. It is not only the enormous scale of the strikes and demonstrations, but their implications for future working-class attitudes and action, that make the period important. [28]

Conflict and attempts at industrial conciliation ran in parallel between the wars. In the nineteenth century, as we have seen, industrial relations, in the sense of long-term agreement or co-operation between owners and workers for the achievement of optimal working conditions, were virtually non-existent. Employers, guided by the principles of *laissez-faire* and with their effective power little damaged by industrial legislation, controlled wages, prices and profits. By the early twentieth century, however, a new industrial ethic was taking root. Linked to the scientific management movement in the 1920s, and to research in 'human relations' carried out in the 1930s, the aims of this new ideology were conformity and co-operation – albeit more in the interests of greater managerial efficiency than out of any particular respect for the workers' own interests. With the rise of a new group of industrial consultants and managers, improvements were directed less towards changing working conditions as such than towards developing the morale and effectiveness of working groups.

As unemployment, wage cuts in declining industries (notably mining) and industrial disputes built up towards the General Strike of 1926, doctrines of social harmony urgently took shape. Stanley Baldwin, Conservative Prime Minister from 1924 to 1929, spent his early months in office propounding a simple vision of service to the country, of the ordinary loyalties of ordinary folk. In a speech early in 1925 he confronted the problem of unemployment and conflict. At that moment, with one in ten of the working population unemployed, but with some faint hope of an economic revival, Baldwin watched the signs of an industrial storm gathering. It was inevitable, he considered, that large-scale production should be accompanied by 'great consolidations of capital managed by small concentrated groups, and by great organizations of Labour led by experienced and responsible leaders'. It was suspicion between the two that needed to be eradicated:

> I am whole-heartedly with those men who talk about disarmament on the Continent, peace on the Continent, and the removal of suspicion on the Continent, but far more do I plead for disarmament at home, and for the removal of that suspicion at home that tends to poison the relations of man and man, the removal of which alone can lead us to stability for our struggling industry . . .

He pleaded for peace and harmony:

> I want to plead for a truce. In the Middle Ages when the whole of Europe was in conflict, one part with another and one fragment with another, men of goodwill strove in vain to get what they called a truce of God . . . I want a truce of God in this country . . . [29]

Fourteen months later the breakdown of negotiations between Baldwin and the General Council of the T.U.C. heralded the General Strike.

Conciliation machinery within industry itself had developed in a miniature way late in the nineteenth century. A Conciliation Act of 1896, for example, had made the services of the Board of Trade available for industrial arbitration. The Trade Boards of 1909 and the Joint Industrial Councils of 1919 had more recently lent authority to the process of negotiation on wages and conditions, even though the Councils themselves, and the conciliation powers given to the Ministry of Labour in 1919, were not particularly successful. The Mond-Turner talks between employers and trade union leaders in 1928–9 sought – in the wake of the General Strike – to find approaches to industrial co-operation. 'Mondism', together with the study of management and industrial relations and renewed appeals for a 'truce of God' in the country or in industry, did not, however, remove the reality of unemployment and unrest. They did not remove memories of pre-war struggles, those in which the shop steward movement was born in the First World War, the Clydeside clashes of 1919, and the consequent strengthening of socialist organization and programmes. For all the failures of the General Strike of May 1926, the search for harmony could not break fundamental suspicions, even though the collapse of the strike deepened the divisions within the labour movement between the advocates of industrial action and the advocates of negotiation and parliamentary pressure. Whatever else the General Strike did, it left among the workers, as Mowat puts it, 'a compound of bitterness and pride: pride in the unselfishness of it, in the skill in organization which their people had shown'. The strike initially weakened the labour movement, but helped to strengthen 'the working man's loyalty to his own movement and his own party'. For the leaders, 'it confirmed and strengthened all the conservative, rightward tendencies which were manifest before it'. [30] The election of a Labour government in 1929, the economic crisis of 1931 and Ramsay MacDonald's defection to lead a National government, the election success of the Labour Party in 1945 – and constant struggles within the Party over the definition of socialist policy – mark some of the movement's later developments. The successes and failures of the Party and the movement indicate the reality of social tensions and continuing conflict. The attempts within the labour movement to reconcile divergent views about the tactics of struggle have always presupposed motives for struggle. They are the political expression of social realities.

The Labour Party and the trade unions did not, of course, in the 1920s and 1930s, hold a monopoly of involvement in political and social conflict. They show more clearly than any other kind of reference, however, the relationship between structural and economic changes in society, on the one hand, and the new dimensions of social action on the other. The developments we have briefly mentioned related immediately, perhaps, to defined questions of wages, rights or redundancy. Through these, however, they related also to wider considerations of social relationships, of social expectations. The 1930s were dominated, in fact, by an urgent search for ways of mending, quickly, a broken society, one which had only recently, in the plans and promises of wartime, seemed to be capable of rapid renovation. The First World War had faced Britain with an emergency of a new kind and quickened the awareness of and responses to social change. The problems of the inter-war years, arising from some of these profound economic and social changes, and from the new international contexts, faced British society with an emergency of another kind. The sense of urgency was intensified by the greater sensitivity to world events, to the excitements of the creation of the Soviet Union, the disappointments of its development, and the relentless threat of Fascism, Nazism and war. Alongside the story of industrial action, and closely interwoven with it, is the story of social protest, of hunger marches, of anti-fascist demonstrations, the literature of commitment and protest, the Left Book Club, and death in Spain.

HEALTH AND LIVING STANDARDS

It is important not to allow such real and prominent phenomena as mass regional unemployment and organized protest to conceal some of the changes that were taking place in vital fields of human welfare. Developments in, for example, the related fields of health and living standards need to be brought out clearly, not only to bring our previous discussion more up to date, but also because of their importance for our later analysis of the age structure of the population, the size and functions of the family, and the whole pattern of expectation of marriage, parenthood, employment and length of life.

The Beveridge Report of 1942 offers a summary of the findings of social investigators (including a second survey of York by Rowntree in 1936) about changes in working-class standards of living since the investigations at the end of the nineteenth century. The York Survey of 1936 and a *New Survey of London Life and Labour* conducted in 1929 gave proof of 'large and general progress':

> . . . the average workman in London could buy a third more of articles of consumption in return for labour of an hour's less duration per day than he could buy forty years before at the time of Charles Booth's original survey. The standard of living available to the workpeople of York in 1936 may be put over-all at about 30 per cent higher than it was in 1899 . . . In London, the crude death rate fell from 18·6 per thousand in 1900 to 11·4 in 1935 and the infant mortality rate fell from 159 to 58 per thousand . . . What has been shown for these towns in detail applies to the country generally . . .

Increased real incomes, Beveridge pointed out, were even more marked in the case of people whose earnings were interrupted by sickness, accident or unemployment, or ended by old age. [31] Want had been diminished at least far enough to have, in conjunction with other factors, a serious influence on mortality statistics.

Between 1911 and 1940 the birth rate dropped sharply and consistently (from 21·8 live births per thousand to 14·8 in England and Wales, the lowest figure ever). The death rate in England and Wales, after falling slowly to 12·1 deaths per thousand in 1921–30, has fluctuated only very slightly since. The natural increase in the population in England and Wales in the 1930s was the lowest recorded (2·5 per thousand, compared with, for example, 14·0 in the 1870s). The average annual rate of increase in the 1930s and 1940s was about a third of what it had been a century before. With the possibility of Britain's population beginning to decline, a Royal Commission on Population was appointed, reporting in 1949. With various fluctuations, however, the birth rate rose after the war, and again after 1955. For the United Kingdom as a whole the figure was 18·5 per thousand in 1963 and 17·1 in 1968.

The most significant improvement in the early decades of the twentieth century was in infant mortality figures. Improvements in housing, diet, welfare and medical services had a considerable impact on the figures, which had lagged behind those of other improvements in the late nineteenth century. What is equally significant, however, is that the infant mortality figures indicated continued − and in some cases *increased* - class differentials. We have seen, in Chadwick's analyses, for example, the earlier class differential in mortality statistics in general. We have seen also how, in his and Playfair's reports, the same causes produced differentials between industrial and rural

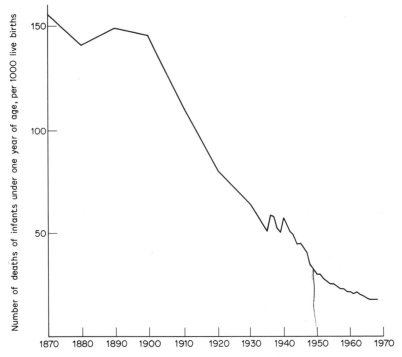

Fig. 8 Infant mortality rates in England and Wales, 1870–1968. (See also Table 5, p. 314.) After Mitchell and Deane, 1962, and Annual Abstract of Statistics, *1969.*

or middle-class residential areas. The differentials continued into the twentieth century. In 1912 the average infant mortality for London was ninety-one per thousand. In wealthy Hampstead it was sixty-two; in congested Shoreditch it was 123. Children's weight, for example, as tabulated in an inquiry into wages and the nutrition of children in Surrey, varied almost exactly in proportion to the average weekly wages of the father. The infant mortality rate among families in L.C.C. housing was less than half that for London as a whole. [32]

For the country as a whole, infant mortality in the Registrar General's Social Class I (Upper and Middle) fell, between 1911 and 1930–2, from seventy-six to thirty-three per thousand legitimate live births. The drop for Social Class V (Unskilled Labour) was from 153 to seventy-seven. The differential had increased. The differential in the same period between towns like Bournemouth, Great Yarmouth and Eastbourne, and towns like South Shields and Newcastle, was also preserved or widened. Evidence submitted to the Barlow Commission showed that infant mortality figures also related directly to the number of persons per room. High density per room almost uniformly meant high infant mortality. [33] It is not always easy to judge from the figures what improvements took place in the death rate for different diseases. In some cases there were enormous regional differences, governed by the state of medical inspection and facilities as well as by housing, diet and sanitation. Actual *increases* in some figures (for diphtheria in the 1930s, for instance) may indicate, not increases in the incidence of a disease, but improvements in the system of notification and diagnosis. Between the mid-1920s and the mid-1930s, however, it is clear that there was a substantial fall (of a quarter to a third in many large cities) in the death rate from tuberculosis, and even more dramatically in the case of deaths from measles, whooping cough and scarlet fever. [34]

The social services and the protection afforded at moments of crisis by unemployment and health insurance were indications of how far the relationship between the individual (particularly the underprivileged individual) and government had been taken even by 1914. The attack on unemployment in particular, suggests Bentley Gilbert, brought the government for the first time into the life of the 'ordinary, adult, male, able-bodied workman'. For such a man, 'who did not pay income tax, who stayed off the poor law, who did not serve in the army, who rarely used the Post Office, His Majesty's Government was a far-off, olympian thing'. Now, however, 'finally, visibly, and intimately, the government was truly his servant. A precedent had been set.' It was one which took the State 'beyond the area of social welfare and into the area of social service'. [35] It would be impossible, henceforward, to consider problems of the individual in modern Britain without close regard to the evolution of a complete, finely organized network of responsible public authorities. Government was from now on in one sense the individual's servant, but in another sense his master. Discussions of the nature of a democratic society, and the details of political programmes, were to become increasingly concerned with the extent and strength of public powers, with the balance between paternal authorities and individual freedom. The spokesmen for nationalization, increased social welfare services and a high degree of public planning, on the one hand, and the spokesmen for private enterprise, individual choice and freedom from controls, on the other, were all to assert that they did so in the name of democracy.

In one important respect the commitment by the State to the principle of unemployment insurance was more than what Gilbert calls a 'precedent'. It was to be made, by force of circumstances, the turning point in approaches to welfare and service. The principle involved was one of insurance, with benefit by right in return for contributions, a principle extended in 1920 to cover all workers. By 1921, however, the magnitude of the unemployment problem had shattered the basis of the principle. For hundreds of thousands, and then millions, of men the benefit entitlement was rapidly exhausted, and the government had to commit itself to 'transitional' or 'uncovenanted' benefits – the dole. More than any other act this response to unemployment

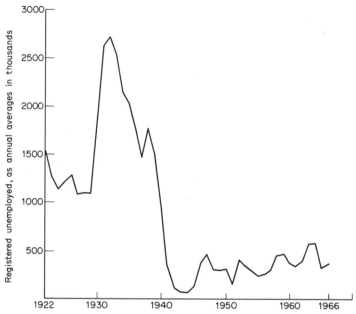

Fig. 9 Persons registered as unemployed in Great Britain, 1922–66. (See also Table 8, p. 318.) After Mitchell and Deane, 1962, and Whitaker's Almanack, *1968.*

interred the principles of 1834. A 'dole' had, in fact, been paid in this way to unemployed, demobilized servicemen for a period after 1918. The 1921 development adopted the principle behind the previous short-term measure, and made it an inescapable feature of social policy. Unemployment benefit was now paid without regard to contributions, as a right, and at a level which made nonsense of the notion of 'less eligibility'. The dole, more than the transfer of the Poor Law machinery to the local authorities in 1929, marks the real turning away from the view of pauperism which dominated the nine-teenth century. Subsequent attempts in the 1930s to return to the pure principle of insurance failed; insurance was retained, certainly, as a basic feature even of the 1948 Welfare State provisions, but it had by then become *social* insurance, entailing a fundamental right to social protection.

After the First World War, therefore, the various improvements in health and mortality statistics, commitments to social welfare and improvements in the social services began to come together to point towards the more comprehensive welfare planning of the Second World War and after. Against the background of considerable unemployment and the poverty, under-nourishment and ill-health associated with it, it is possible to trace the pattern of advance. In the field of health, in addition to developments we have already mentioned, there were such important measures as the Maternity and Child Welfare Act of 1918, which developed services for expectant and nursing mothers and the under-fives. Contributory pensions from 1925 made available a higher rate of retirement benefit. It is not, of course, being suggested that the the real definition of the 1930s is in terms of a dedicated movement towards a welfare society. The slum clearance Act of 1930 did not mean the end of slums, or unemployment benefits the end of unemployment hardship. Acute national and international dilemmas perpetuated and deepened old and bitter problems. Whatever the motives, however − whether humanitarian or, by papering over the ugliness, to preserve the basic structure of capitalism − people's lives and the structure of society were beginning to be affected at many levels by the new concern with welfare. This concern was heightened by the very grimness of poverty in the old industrial areas. Beveridge describes how Britain, after 1918, entered the period of mass unemployment, and yet:

. . . across this waste period of destruction and dislocation, the permanent forces making for material progress − technical advance and the capacity of human society to adjust itself to new conditions − continued to operate; the real wealth per head in a Britain of shrunken oversea investments and lost export markets, counting in all her unemployed, was materially higher in 1938 than in 1913. [36]

This, with a forgivable wartime appeal to the inevitable rightness of things, summarizes the ambiguities of the period.

LEISURE

An interesting specific illustration of this ambiguity in human terms lies in the fact that the decades of heaviest unemployment and distress in some regions and industries also saw the most important break-through in the field of holidays with pay. The widening of facilities for organized leisure had, of course, been a Victorian and largely middle-class phenomenon. Between the 1860s and the 1890s various sports − including tennis, cricket and golf − gained their modern codes of rules, and a new popularity. The urban middle class, as we have previously seen, already had its characteristic forms of social intercourse and cultural activity − its 'conspicuous leisure'. For some there were visits to the resorts, mostly with eighteenth-century or Regency origins −

29 Late Victorian seaside.

such as Brighton, Torquay and Bournemouth in the south, and Scarborough in the north. There were occasional crazes like roller-skating for girls in the 1880s.

Leisure, and facilities for leisure, were obviously of a different order for the Victorian poor. The urban worker was cut off from traditional country pursuits, including the sports which were still popular in country areas well into the nineteenth century. A historian of Pickering, in Yorkshire, for example, lists sports common in the area in the early part of the century:

Fox hunting
Badger drawing
Duck hunting with dogs and sometimes duck and owl diving
Cock fighting
Cock throwing at Eastertide
Bull baiting and sometimes ass baiting
Squirrel hunting
Rat worrying [37]

Cock fighting, for example, took place in the beautiful Norman crypt of Lastingham Church. It is interesting, in considering the urban replacements for these country pursuits, to take a description written in 1870 of one pleasure resort available, among others, to the London lower classes:

> That which made this part of Battersea Fields so notorious was the gaming, sporting, and pleasure-grounds at the Red House and Balloon public-houses, and Sunday fairs, held throughout the summer months. These have been the resort of hundreds and thousands, from royalty and nobility down to the poorest pauper and the meanest beggar. And surely if ever there was a place out of hell that surpassed Sodom and Gomorrah in ungodliness and abomination, this was it. Here the worst men and vilest of the human race seemed to try to outvie each other in wicked deeds. I have gone to this sad spot on the afternoon and evening of the Lord's day, when there have been from 60 to 120 horses and donkeys racing, foot-racing, walking matches, flying boats, flying horses, roundabouts, theatres, comic actors, shameless dancers, conjurers, fortune-tellers, gamblers of every description, drinking-booths, stalls, hawkers, and vendors of all kinds of articles.

These, said the writer, were 'the unmentionable doings of this pandemonium on earth'. [38] The pleasures of the gin palace and then the pub (ubiquitous, spacious and class-divided into public and saloon bars, from about 1890), of the music hall, Battersea Fields, the trip to Margate or Ramsgate, or on some Cook's excursion, grew alongside the legislation which produced shorter hours, free Saturday afternoons, the certainty of a free Christmas Day, Good Friday and Bank Holidays. The first instance of paid holidays for manual workers came in 1884, when Brunner-Mond gave some of their employees an annual week's holiday with pay.

Progress was made, to begin with, largely in public and semi-public enterprises (including the railways and the police); the railways, cycling and other developments made it possible to take greater advantage of available leisure. By 1900 the older seaside resorts were being caught up or outstripped by the new resorts like Southport and Blackpool, Weston-super-Mare and Southend, which were within reach of large urban centres.

J. A. R. Pimlott, the historian of these developments, points out that the question of holidays with pay was never in the forefront of the programmes of the Trades Union Congress or individual unions until the 1930s. It was under collective bargaining that the main advances had slowly taken place. By 1925, and throughout the 1930s, some $1\frac{1}{2}$ million workers were entitled to paid holidays under collective agreements; by 1937 the number entitled under collective agreements and other arrangements was about 4 million (earning under £250 a year, plus another 1 million from higher income groups). With or without pay, about half the workpeople in London took holidays away from home in 1934. The total number of holidaymakers away from home for a week or more in 1937 was about 15 million. Plans for legislation on holidays with pay were pursued between 1925 and 1938, when a Holidays with Pay Act (stopping short of compulsion) gave the Ministry of Labour responsibility for helping to bring about voluntary schemes. There was a big response to the appeal for voluntary action:

> By November 1938, the number of workpeople with £250 a year or less entitled to holidays with pay had risen to about 9 millions, including nearly $4\frac{1}{2}$ millions covered by collective agreements. By June 1939, the total was over 11 millions . . . there was no corresponding increase in the number of actual holidaymakers . . . One reason may have been the international crisis, and others were the beginnings of a slump in some industries and the high pressure in those engaged in rearmament. [39]

What is clear is that, apart from this spread of holidays, the use of leisure in general was moving rapidly in the inter-war years towards the enjoyment of mass-produced or collective forms of activity, ranging from rambling, hiking and jazz to the crossword puzzle – first introduced into Britain in 1924. The mass newspaper, the popular magazine, the twice-a-week visit to the cinema (Chaplin happened in 1915, and sound came in 1928) – all went further towards undermining long-established Protestant ideas, not only about the sanctity of the Sabbath, but also about 'wasting' time. Football (the first Cup Final was in 1923) and football pools in the 1930s together with legalized racecourse betting, also further undermined traditional teaching about gambling. The association of sport and leisure with betting is only a late reminder of the extent to which some of the popular pursuits in urban society – gin drinking, outings, gambling, fantasy literature, theatrical melodrama, the cinema, radio and television – are all in different ways to some extent responses to the need for escape. There are, of course, other ways in which men in society defeat the pressures of routine or ugliness or poverty; and descriptions of forms of 'escape' do not necessarily imply judgements against them.

There are many ways in which it would be possible to relate all these aspects of leisure and holidays to other aspects of social life and social re-lations. The seaside holiday and the picnic, for example, indicate major changes in family relationships, changes in the position of wife and child in the family structure. This use of leisure and holidays was a factor in mental and physical health. The ability to take advantage of holidays, to possess a radio set or to go frequently to the cinema became, in the 1930s, a factor in estimating relative affluence or deprivation. It provided a major stimulus to developments in various types of consumer goods industries, electronics and transport. It helps to explain some of the points of industrial and commercial growth, and in living standards. All these developments point to the increase (in cinemas, light industry, hotels and restaurants, for example) in the number of jobs available to women, and the increased incentive for married women to take employment, in order to provide the additional income, not only to improve standards of accommodation and diet, but also for holidays and family treats. The question of the use of leisure pin-points one of the basic

30 Lord Beveridge, 1943.

dilemmas in seeking to evaluate concepts of social progress and democracy – the central fact that the individual in this period gained greater freedom, greater opportunity creatively to construct his own style of life, and at the same time became more vulnerable to methods of mass persuasion, less active and involved in the processes of entertainment.

BEVERIDGE

The story of leisure, therefore, like the story of economic and industrial growth, urban conditions and social policy, points towards basic features of the central complex of problems with which we are concerned: man in modern society. The historical developments we have chosen have been intended to illustrate some of the types of influence which have shaped our concepts of the individual and society. The Second World War and many of the developments which followed it, most prominently in the fields of industrial organization and welfare, were obviously momentous contributions to this shaping process, and their treatment in detail would make our analysis of contemporary society more complete. We can do no more, however, than take one representative expression of this critical period of change – the principles of Lord Beveridge.

Rowntree and Lavers, in a third York survey in 1951, analysed changes in living standards and the effects of welfare measures between 1936 and 1950. The conclusion they came to was that 'whereas the proportion of the working-class population living in poverty has been reduced since 1936 from $31 \cdot 1\%$ to $2 \cdot 77\%$ it would have been reduced to $22 \cdot 18\%$ if welfare legislation had remained unaltered'. [40] We are concerned not with the niceties of the statistics, but to establish that welfare provisions since 1936, and notably since 1948, had obviously had a considerable effect on standards of life. What the Beveridge Report on Social Insurance and Allied Services of 1942 had aimed to achieve was, in fact, the promotion of a Plan for Social Security 'to win freedom from want by maintaining incomes' – the assurance that no one should be allowed to fall below a subsistence minimum. The Plan rested on three principles, the statement of which is worth quoting at length, offering as it does a comparison with the previous definitions of 1834 and 1909. A document which became one of the twentieth century's best-sellers set out, then, three guiding principles:

> The first principle is that any proposals for the future, while they should use to the full the experience gathered in the past, should not be restricted by consideration of sectional interests established in the obtaining of that experience . . .
> The second principle is that organization of social insurance should be treated as one part only of a comprehensive policy of social progress. Social insurance fully developed may provide income security; it is an attack upon Want. But Want is one only of five giants on the road of reconstruction and in some ways the easiest to attack. The others are Disease, Ignorance, Squalor and Idleness.
> The third principle is that social security must be achieved by co-operation between the State and the individual. The State should offer security for service and contribution. The State in organizing security should not stifle incentive, opportunity, responsibility; in establishing a national minimum, it should leave room and encouragement for voluntary action . . .

The Plan used experience but was 'not tied by experience'. It was a contribution towards a 'wider social policy'. It was 'first and foremost, a plan of insurance – of giving in return for contributions benefits up to subsistence level, as of right and without means test, so that individuals may build freely upon it'. [41]

When Beveridge, in 1944, turned to the problem of unemployment, he was acutely conscious of the implications of social engineering of any kind. In this Report on Full Employment in a Free Society he was anxious to achieve the one without undermining his conception of the other. Protection of basic freedoms meant excluding 'the totalitarian solution of full employment in a society completely planned and regimented by an irremovable dictator'. His proposals 'preserve absolutely all the essential liberties which are more precious than full employment itself'. [42] The 1942 Plan for Social Security, felt Beveridge, was consistent with his belief in active democracy. There were people, he knew, 'to whom pursuit of security appears to be a wrong aim. They think of security as something inconsistent with initiative, adventure, personal responsibility.' That was not his view. The plan was 'not one for giving to everybody something for nothing and without trouble, or something that will free the recipients for ever thereafter from personal responsibilities. The plan is one to secure income for subsistence on condition of service and contribution . . .' It could be carried through, he proclaimed, 'only by a concentrated determination of the British democracy to free itself once for all of the scandal of physical want for which there is no economic or moral justification'. To those who thought the Report did not go far enough Beveridge pointed out that his Plan was intended only as one prong of an attack on the five giant evils. 'Freedom from want', he concluded, 'cannot be forced on a democracy or given to a democracy. It must be won by them. Winning it needs courage and faith and a sense of national unity . . . overriding the interests of any class or section.' [43]

The Beveridge analyses, therefore, produced definitions of acceptable minima, allied with 'service and contribution'. The Welfare State that was constructed after the war sought to achieve these minima along the lines Beveridge had proposed − through social insurance (which guaranteed the right to a minimum income in important contingencies), through social assistance of various kinds, and through basic services in such fields as education, hospitals and medical care. The Beveridge Plan and the Welfare State provisions demonstrated that British society was prepared to accept the implications of precedent (and comparison with systems in other countries) in establishing an integrated, comprehensive system. In doing so it also accepted the limitations of precedent. Areas of welfare either remained untackled (an antiquated medical and hospital system, for example) or inadequately so. Most conspicuous among the latter were the problems relating to old age, which, the Rowntree–Lavers survey of 1950 showed, was the 'greatest contemporary cause of poverty and accounted for $68 \cdot 1\%$ of all the poverty in York in 1950'. [44] Beveridge's appeal, finally, to a unity which could override the interests of class or section could not, even in wartime, and still less after, disguise the continuing prominent social fact of the existence of classes and sections.

The post-war problem, as the planners saw it, was to make radical readjustments in the social framework so as to set the seal on a doctrine of social community. The point in history had been reached, said E. H. Carr, for example, in 1951, when 'the process of transition from the nineteenth-century *laissez-faire* capitalist order offers us no alternative, short of annihilation in war, to a social and economic order which we can call the "welfare state", the "social service state", or simply "socialism"'. Embedded in Beveridge-type planning was a defence against accusations of the infringement of personal liberty. Embedded in 'socialist' planning was a dilemma about the parameters of socialism. Social legislation from 1945 was socialism in the sense that we are 'all socialists now'. It was, Carr also pointed out, the task of combining political and economic aims,

> of reconciling democracy and socialism, which, after the second world war, inspired the social policies of Great Britain and of some of the smaller European countries. The possibility of the attempt to make political liberty compatible with planning for socialism has been challenged from both sides. It is denied by the communists . . . It is equally denied by those old-fashioned democrats whose conception of democracy is still rooted in the derelict philosophy of *laissez-faire*. [45]

We are not concerned, in future chapters, to follow through the details of the accomplishment, or otherwise, of this task, and the political and legislative implications of these concepts of socialism and planning. We are concerned, however, to relate notions of democracy to those of, for example, the various roles individuals are called upon to play in society. We have in past chapters followed the growth of some institutions and policies which will play little apparent part in our discussion of contemporary society. It has been important, however, to see, towering behind any such discussion, the ways in which human understanding of the nature and responsibilities of 'society' and 'government' have changed, and the points of social development around which the battles of concept and interpretation have taken place. We have so far traced, primarily, the path of modern economic, urban growth, and its attendant re-adjustments in fields of social thought. We have tried to establish one of the dimensions necessary for our analysis of modern man in modern society.

NOTES

1 HUTCHISON *The Decline and Fall of British Capitalism*, pp. 86–7.
2 *The Decay of Capitalist Civilisation*, p. 130.
3 DAVID LLOYD GEORGE *The People's Insurance*, p. 28 (London, 1912).
4 SIDNEY POLLARD *The Development of the British Economy 1914–1950*, pp. 75–6 (London, 1962).
5 DOROTHY DAVIS *A History of Shopping*, p. 283 (London, 1966).
6 Majority *Report*, I, pp. 78, 145, 182, 185–6, 232, 260, 281–2.
7 Minority *Report*, III, pp. 69, 382, 386, 389, 431, 468, 529.
8 RICHARD M. TITMUSS *Essays on 'The Welfare State'*, pp. 18–22 (London, 1958).
9 *Housing and the State 1919–1944* (London, 1945).
10 PHILIP ABRAMS 'The failure of social reform: 1918–1920', *Past and Present*, 24 April 1963, p. 44.
11 G. P. GOOCH *History of our Time 1885–1914*, p. 5 (London, 1911; 1946 edition).
12 Quoted from BERNARD SEMMEL *Imperialism and Social Reform*, p. 16 (London, 1960). A classic study of this period is ELIE HALÉVY *A History of the English People*, Epilogue (1895–1905), I, *Imperialism*, 1926.
13 H. F. WYATT 'The ethics of empire', in GOODWIN (ed.) *Nineteenth Century Opinion*, p. 267.
14 For the history and current state of the concept of imperialism, see D. K. FIELD-HOUSE *The Theory of Capitalist Imperialism* (London, 1967).
15 POLLARD *The Development of the British Economy*, pp. 75–6.
16 ASHWORTH *An Economic History of England*, p. 301.

17 The Webbs considered that capitalist industry was 'virtually superseded as a system during the war' (*The Decay of Capitalist Civilisation*, p. 131).
18 See MAURICE DOBB *Studies in the Development of Capitalism*, pp. 339–41 (London, 1946; 1963 edition).
19 See BARLOW COMMISSION *Report*, Ch. IV.
20 POLLARD *The Development of the British Economy*, pp. 287–8.
21 *An Economic History of England*, p. 252.
22 *Full Employment in a Free Society*, pp. 40–7, 72 (London, 1944; 1953 edition).
23 *Trade Unionism New and Old*, pp. 133–5 (1891, 1894 edition).
24 In addition to HENRY PELLING's *Short History of the Labour Party* (London, 1961), RALPH MILIBAND's *Parliamentary Socialism* (London, 1961) is important for the story of the tussle between policies of parliamentarianism versus direct action.
25 CLEGG *et al. History of British Trade Unions*, p. 474.
26 Ibid., p. 465.
27 GEORGE TATE *London Trades Council 1860–1950*, pp. 96–7 (London, 1950).
28 For an account of this 'Workers' Rebellion', see DANGERFIELD *The Strange Death of Liberal England*, Pt II, Ch. IV.
29 STANLEY BALDWIN *On England*, pp. 40–2 (London, 1926; 1937 edition).
30 CHARLES LOCH MOWAT *Britain between the Wars 1918–1940*, pp. 330–1 (London, 1955; 1962 edition).
31 *Social Insurance and Allied Services*, paras 446–7 (London, 1942).
32 GRACE M. PATON *The Child and the Nation*, pp. 38–9 (London, 1915).
33 See BARLOW COMMISSION *Minutes of Evidence*, pp. 966–7.
34 See ibid., pp. 968–71.
35 *The Evolution of National Insurance*, pp. 287–8.
36 *Social Insurance and Allied Services*, para. 447.
37 GORDON HOME *The Evolution of an English Town*, p. 221 (London, 1915).
38 Quoted from the *London City Mission Magazine* in STEEN EILER RASMUSSEN *London: the Unique City*, p. 234 (London, 1934; 1961 edition).
39 J. A. R. PIMLOTT *The Englishman's Holiday: a Social History*, p. 221 (London, 1947). Much of the above material is drawn from this source. For some of the Victorian leisure activities, see JOHN GLOAG *Victorian Comfort* (London, 1961). See also ROBERT GRAVES and ALAN HODGE *The Long Weekend: a Social History of Great Britain 1918–1939* (London, 1940).
40 B. SEEBOHM ROWNTREE and G. R. LAVERS *Poverty and the Welfare State*, p. 40 (London, 1951).
41 *Social Insurance and Allied Services*, paras 7–10, 409.
42 pp. 21, 36.
43 *Social Insurance and Allied Services*, paras 455–6, 461.
44 *Poverty and the Welfare State*, p. 60.
45 *The New Society*, pp. 38–9.

Industrial and economic growth (previously discussed in Chapters 1 and 3) is also discussed in Chapter 6, radicalism and reform was previously discussed in Chapters 1 and 3, and social attitudes and policy were discussed in Chapters 1 and 4. Population (discussed in Chapters 1 and 4) is continued in Chapters 6 and 7, housing (discussed in Chapters 2 and 4) is continued in Chapter 6, local government (discussed in Chapter 2) is continued in Chapter 10; public health was previously discussed in Chapter 2, and the Poor Law in Chapters 2 and 4. Trade unions and industrial relations (discussed in Chapter 3) are discussed in Chapter 6; leisure (discussed in Chapter 3) is also discussed in Chapter 6.

6

Urban and Industrial Changes

We have seen two major processes dominating the course of developments in British society during the nineteenth and early twentieth centuries: the growth of industry and the growth of cities. In previous chapters we have described historically the way in which changes in the structure of the economy and in population distribution, for example, influenced the structure of all the other important institutions of society. We have also examined the way in which these changes were linked, in turn, to developments in the machinery of government, politics and social administration and to the growth of communications and the mass media.

Our task in future chapters will be to examine the present-day structure of English society. We shall aim to demonstrate in greater detail the interconnectedness of contemporary social institutions, as well as to explore the legacy of older traditions and values which still remain. We shall also try to locate the changing ideological assumptions which influence not only social planning but the character and conclusions of historical and sociological research themselves.

POPULATION CHANGES

As a background to our discussion of urban and industrial conditions it will be helpful to consider briefly recent population changes. In the twentieth century, despite a marked fall in the overall rate of population growth, [1] numbers have gone on increasing over each decennial census period. Between 1951 and 1961 alone, for example, the population of England and Wales increased by nearly $2\frac{1}{2}$ million, so that by 1961 the total population was twice that of 1861, standing at just over 46 million. This relatively high rate of

31 Plaistow.

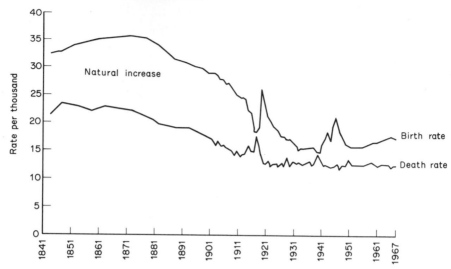

Fig. 10 *Natural increase in the population of England and Wales, 1841–1967. (See also Tables 2 and 3, pp. 311 and 312.) After R. G. O.,* Matters of Life and Death, *1956, p. 7, and* The Population of Britain, *British Information Services, 1968, p. 3.*

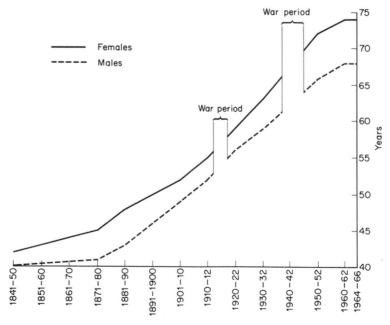

Fig. 11 *Expectation of life at birth in England and Wales, 1871–1966. (See Also Table 4, p. 313.) After R. G. O.,* Matters of Life and Death, *1956, p. 7, and* The Population of Britain, *British Information Services, 1968, p. 3.*

growth continues, largely as a consequence of a new upward trend in birth rates since the end of the war (in 1931 the birth rate was 15·8 per 1,000; it reached a peak of 20·5 per 1,000 in 1947 and, after falling again in the 1950s, climbed to 17·7 per 1,000 in 1966). Lower infant and adult mortality rates have reinforced recent population growth. Infant mortality in England and Wales was reduced from 29·7 per 1,000 in 1951 to 18·3 per 1,000 in 1968. Adult mortality fell over the same period (figures are available only for the United Kingdom as a whole) from 13·4 per 1,000 to 12·4 per 1,000 for males, and from 11·8 to 11·3 per 1,000 for females.

Perhaps the most significant feature of contemporary population structure is the balance of age groups. This is both a cause and a consequence of the changing pattern of overall growth. In 1901 the young (those aged up to fourteen) constituted nearly one third of the total population. By 1966 they accounted for only just over 23 per cent. The elderly (aged sixty-five and over), on the other hand, have increased substantially, both in numbers and as a proportion of the population as a whole. They represented 5 per cent of the population in 1901 and just over 12 per cent in 1966. The greater expectation of life revealed by these statistics (in 1968 men could expect to live to the age of sixty-nine and women to seventy-five, as compared with forty-one and forty-five years respectively in the decade 1871–80) has resulted in a population which is predominantly middle-aged. This is likely to remain the typical pattern until at least the end of the century according to the latest estimates of future demographic trends. But how is this population distributed?

We have seen that in 1851, after a period of unprecedented cityward migration, the population was more or less evenly divided between town and country. Today, four-fifths of the population of Great Britain live in towns of over 50,000 inhabitants. Half of these reside in the seven major conurbations (Greater London, South-East Lancashire, the West Midlands, West Yorkshire, Central Clydeside, Merseyside and Tyneside), and the area covered by London and the Home Counties alone contains one quarter of the total population. The Midlands and the South-East have, in fact, now become the main centres of migration (and of industrial growth), while some of the former nineteenth-century areas of industrial and urban expansion, like the North-East and South Wales, are declining in importance.

URBAN AND RURAL PATTERNS OF SOCIAL ORGANIZATION

Urbanism, then, has become the dominant form of society in Britain – as it is becoming in the rest of the world. [2] It has brought into existence entirely new patterns of social organization, and it has disrupted the relative stability of earlier rural and pre-industrial communities. Sociologists employ a variety of theoretical concepts to describe these two different modes of social organization. Durkheim, for instance, contrasted societies which are characterized by 'mechanical solidarity' (for example, feudal societies) and those whose structure, like that of contemporary industrial societies, is 'organic'. Herbert Spencer, on the other hand, distinguished between the 'indefinite, incoherent homogeneity' of pre-industrial societies and the 'definite, coherent heterogeneity' of the modern urban-industrial state. Perhaps the most useful model of pre- and post-industrial forms of social organization, however, is that provided by Ferdinand Tönnies' contrast between *Gemeinschaft* (community) and *Gesellschaft* (association). Tönnies himself studied several instances of *Gemeinschaft*: the family, the neighbourhood (in village and town), and friendship groups, while the city and the state were chosen for his study of the characteristics of *Gesellschaften*.

In the twentieth century, and in the period since 1930 in particular, there has been a tremendous increase in comparative investigations in urban sociology. [3] Some have focused on whole towns or on particular urban or rural neighbourhoods in countries like Britain and the United States. On the other hand, there has also been a great deal of research into the process of urban and industrial growth (and into its consequences) in the newly developing nations. Whatever their orientation and whether mainly theoretical or mainly empirical in their approach, the essential contrast referred to in all of these studies is the same. It is based on a comparison of the degree of complexity of the different institutional structures found in these two main types of social system. The following brief descriptions of typical patterns of urban and rural social systems indicate what the main differences are.

The traditional rural village was a small community, probably containing no more than a few hundred people in all, many of whom were interrelated through local marriages. Migration was rare and the village was relatively isolated geographically. The occupational structure was closely linked to agriculture, and jobs were commonly passed on from fathers to sons. Home, work and leisure were intimately related, the family often forming a self-sufficient economic unit to which both women and children contributed equally with the men. Within the village there was a fairly rigid social hierarchy, consisting of gentry, craftsmen and agricultural labourers, and social mobility was slight. Nevertheless relationships were face-to-face and people knew each other as 'whole' people, not just as 'segments' of people in specialized roles. The regulation of public behaviour, even in the absence of many formal restraints (there was no police force, for instance), was strong, and social isolation and ostracism operated as very real sanctions.

Today, on the other hand, most people live in large towns and cities where no individual can possibly know more than a fraction of the inhabitants. The significance of relationship by kin and intermarriage has, on the whole, tended to decline in importance and the family has become more a focus of emotional security than of economic necessity. As a consequence of better public and private transport there is a considerable amount of movement from place to place and from one region of the country to another. Occupations are diverse and new skills replace old ones at a rapidly increasing rate. Few jobs are now hereditary (coal mining, the docks and fishing are exceptions) and they possess no such clearly unifying social bond as did agriculture and the land. Social stratification in the city is complex and impersonal, and opportunities for social mobility are much greater. Thus, a person is more likely to be evaluated for what he is or what he does than by the ascribed status he derives from his father and family. Informal social control, however, is less effective since face-to-face relationships and intimate knowledge of others' business cannot operate over large communities of thousands of people. This means that anonymity and independence are more easily obtained in the city centre and its institutions.

These two social systems are clearly quite distinct. One, the traditional rural system (*Gemeinschaft*), is relatively simple and based on intimate primary contacts; the other, the urban-industrial system (*Gesellschaft*), is infinitely complex and based to a much greater degree on secondary contacts between people. The related social-psychological contrasts are equally marked. But striking as these differences are, it is important to remember that they refer to highly generalized ideal types. [4] What is more, they are historical contrasts. It is true that at the extremes the distinctions between city and village life persist (although even in most villages today – especially in the Midlands and South of England – agriculture is a minority occupation). But it is also true that particular neighbourhoods within the city often maintain many of the characteristics of the more simple communities. [5] For most purposes, therefore, it is probably more useful to think in terms of a continuum between the patterns of social organization which characterize these extremes. As Maciver and Page comment,

> In modern society, it is not simply that the techniques of our civilization are inexorably making city dwellers of the majority of the population, but rather that the very techniques that draw people to the cities carry the influence and quality of urban life to all but the remotest recesses of the countryside. [6]

Ruth Glass makes the same point more specifically. In her view it is no longer appropriate to speak, in general terms, of a rural as distinct from an urban culture, since

> The cities draw workers from suburbs, from exurbia, and from even more remote hinterlands. Holidays with pay and the greatly increased speed and provision of public and private transport have resulted in frequent exchanges of visits between town and country. The same media of communication reach everywhere ... The same chain stores which serve urban customers have become accessible to rural customers ... The National Health Service is ubiquitous. Differences between the educational opportunities ... have narrowed considerably. And all this has ... brought

about a good deal of similarity in urban and rural modes of thought, expression, and behaviour. [7]

What is more, there are a large number of extremely different social environments within the city. This makes it quite misleading to treat as unities for the purpose of comparison the less homogeneous and the more homogeneous. Indeed, while most rural communities differ considerably from one another, each one exerts a far greater common influence on its inhabitants than does the city. [8]

URBAN TYPOLOGIES AND REGIONAL DIFFERENCES

In view of these limitations on the usefulness of direct rural–urban comparisons, it is helpful to examine different *types* of urban community and *regional* variations in city life. Moser and Scott, using a multivariate analysis technique based on the criteria of size, region, population structure and social class, have worked out a very detailed classificatory scheme for British towns. [9] Three main types of urban system are featured in their scheme, each having several subdivisions:

A *Mainly resorts, administrative and commercial towns*
  1 seaside resorts
  2 spas, professional and administrative centres
  3 commercial centres with some industry

B *Mainly industrial towns*
  4 traditional railway centres
  5 larger ports
  6 textile centres of Yorkshire and Lancashire
  7 towns of the North-Eastern seaboard and mining towns of Wales
  8 more recent metal-manufacturing towns

C *Suburbs and suburban-type towns*
  9 'exclusive' residential suburbs
  10 older mixed suburbs
  11 newer mixed residential suburbs
  12 light-industry suburbs and towns within the sphere of influence of large conurbations
  13 older working-class and industrial suburbs
  14 newer industrial suburbs

A fourth residual category contains London (i.e. the area covered by the former London County Council) and Huyton with Roby, a Liverpool suburb, both of which were too different from other towns to be included in one of the three main groups.

It is clear that these urban groupings mainly reflect differences in the economic structure of different kinds of community. A detailed analysis of the vital statistics which distinguish their populations also reveals differences in terms of demographic trends, housing, education and social class. Overall, however, the most persistent differences are regional ones. The most striking contrast is between the older heavy-industry towns of the north of the country and those in the south of the country where light engineering and administrative and professional activities are more common. Even here, though, there are a number of outstanding exceptions. In Blackpool and Harrogate, for example, conditions approximate to those of the southern seaside towns; while in London, on the other hand, there are areas like West Ham which are similar in many ways to the industrial cities of the north of England. Moser and Scott summarize north–south differences as follows:

With respect to *population size and structure,* the southern regions, and particularly London, have an older population than the northern, higher sex ratios, [10] and fewer women aged 20–24 who are or have been married. *Population increase* [1931–51 and 1951–58] was highest in London and the South-East, largely due to a relatively high degree of inward migration.

The *household and housing* structure shows significant differences too. The North is particularly marked by the high proportion of small dwellings, while overcrowding is also considerably higher in the northern than in the southern regions. New housing is particularly low in London and the North, while the share of council houses in total new buildings is especially high in the North.

Southern towns have substantially smaller portions of the population employed in manufacturing and higher proportions in all the service trades. They consequently have higher proportions in the upper *social classes* and substantially higher proportions of jurors, as well as lower proportions voting left.

Among the health indices, infant mortality rates are considerably higher in the northern regions, as are bronchitis mortality rates and mortality from cancer other than lung and bronchial cancer.

The *education* figures follow the social class data; the extent of education ... is subsequently higher in the southern than in the northern towns. [11]

Although they did not necessarily expect to reach this conclusion, Moser and Scott found that social class was the most important variable between the different types of towns and between the main geographical regions which they studied. This is perhaps not surprising considering how closely class is connected with all of the other indices. Peter Mann, however, comments on the importance of one other factor – the location of a particular community in relation to a major conurbation. Thus, he contrasts the predominantly 'urban' way of life of the residents of the small commuting town of Forest Row in Sussex (population 3,258) with that of the less sophisticated and more 'rural' way of life in Huddersfield (population 128,000). [12]

In discussing differences between the patterns of social life in various kinds of urban and rural community today, then, we need to bear in mind not only differences in the economic structure of particular communities and in their historical development, but also their locations — both regionally and in relation to large conurban centres. The importance of these factors is made very clear in the various empirical surveys of the structure of family relationships, patterns of neighbourhood organization, housing conditions and so on which have recently appeared. [13] What is more difficult, however, is to integrate this type of empirical and statistical analysis into conventional sociological theory.

THEORIES OF URBAN ORGANIZATION

As we have seen, research on the city exists at both the macro-social and at the micro-social level. [14] In our review of the demographic and social variables which distinguish different types of towns and cities we have been concerned with the latter. We shall later be referring to a number of wider ranging, if locally limited, empirical studies which have been mainly devoted to an investigation of the consequences of changed and changing patterns of social organization in particular cities and rural neighbourhoods. Many of these surveys, like those of Booth and Rowntree, have had an explicit link with a felt need for large-scale social planning. Analyses at the macro-social level,

32 Suburban Chingford.

however, have a different sort of usefulness. They enable us to concentrate on the essential social and social-psychological characteristics that cities have in common. They also enable us to explore more fully the whole process of urban growth.

Urban sociology at the macro-social level has its roots in the response to the early transformation of British society which followed the Industrial Revolution. Since then it has gone through a series of profound ideological shifts. In the latter half of the nineteenth century, despite an overwhelming confidence in progress, particularly in the economic sphere, reaction to urban growth was almost entirely pessimistic – perhaps not without reason. The projects envisaged by the Garden City Movement and by many of the 'De-centrist' planners [15] reflect this basically anti-urban feeling. Two new pre-occupations in urban sociology soon emerged, however. On the one hand more systematic attempts were made to account for the origins and growth of cities, for example by C. H. Cooley and Max Weber, and on the other hand an ecological approach, focusing on the relationship between population and environment, was launched. Originally based on land-use analysis, the main emphasis of the ecological tradition gradually moved towards a more strictly social-psychological or interactional view, represented, for example in the writings of Louis Wirth. [16]

Wirth, following an earlier analysis presented by Georg Simmel, defines the contemporary industrial city in terms of three factors: size, density and heterogeneity. He then proceeds to deduce the typical modes of social inter-action to which these conditions are likely to give rise. He contends that large numbers account for 'individual variability, the relative absence of intimate personal acquaintanceship, the segmentalization of human relationships'. Density gives rise to 'diversification and specialization, the coincidence of close physical contact and distant social relations'. It also leads to the

predominance of formal, as opposed to informal, systems of social control. Finally, heterogeneity tends to result in the disintegration of formerly rigid social structures, thus producing 'increased social mobility, instability, and insecurity'. [17]

Wirth's propositions highlight five major characteristics of social interaction in the urban-industrial environment (some of which we have already referred to above): (1) The agencies of formal control (government, judiciary, police) tend to predominate over informal procedures for regulating social conduct (local gossip chains, traditional religious and sub-cultural codes of values); (2) a high proportion of social relationships are based on secondary contacts between people (for example, salesman–client relationships) rather than on intimate personal ties; (3) large-scale, rationalized bureaucratic structures (in government, industry and education, for instance) replace smaller institutions (like the family firm and the corner shop); (4) mobility is facilitated because of the diversity of economic roles; (5) as a result of the growth in scale, not only of cities themselves and of all their typical institutions, but also of communications and of mass production and mass marketing methods, mass standardizing influences are more effective.

It is possible to argue that Wirth's propositions concerning the characteristic features of city life might have been derived from other criteria than those of size, density and heterogeneity alone. R. N. Morris, for instance, suggests that the technological and communication systems, the prevailing pattern of beliefs and values, and the social and psychological environment of

33 Council housing in Hemel Hempstead New Town, 1953.

the city are equally relevant factors. [18] But whichever indices are preferred, the association between urbanism and the kinds of social conditions described above is not in dispute. The way this relationship operates, however, is likely to be a matter of degree, depending on the type of city and on the degree of industrialization present in a nation. The more difficult question of 'cause' and 'effect', on the other hand, which Wirth himself does not deal with (for example, does 'heterogeneity' cause greater mobility or is it a consequence of population movements?) remains rather obscure and untested. It also seems likely that the many overlapping systems of social interaction in the city operate in a more complex and variable way than Wirth indicates, according to whether or not there are adequate intermediary contacts between the individual and the larger social structure, and to the strength of traditional customs and beliefs.

URBAN PROBLEMS AND SOCIAL POLICY

Urban growth and the new patterns of social interaction to which it gave rise were accompanied in the nineteenth century, as we have seen, by profound social problems. Slowly a more efficient system of administration was evolved to cope with these difficulties and to co-ordinate the various agencies of law, finance, public works and social welfare. The initial tasks of the new public and semi-public planning authorities were extremely basic: to provide streets, water supplies and sewage systems, and to maintain effective police and fire protection. Then came the provision of the other major public utilities, as well as parks, civic centres, schools, libraries and urban transport systems. Unlike the more radical, if sometimes romantic and idealistic, solutions proposed by the Garden City enthusiasts, all of these provisions were essentially remedial and palliative. Developments outside of existing city boundaries were non-existent and the State exercised, until late in the nineteenth century, little or no control over private speculative developments. Even in the first half of the twentieth century little was achieved in the field of major urban planning or replanning.

Since the Second World War solutions involving population dispersal and the building of large blocks of flats rather than semi-detached 'cottage dwellings' have seemed the only alternatives. It is true that the devastation caused by the war provided an opportunity for some important local urban renewal schemes (for example, in Coventry, Bristol, Birmingham and Plymouth). The expectation of improved living standards, a higher birth rate, the backlog of earlier deficiencies and the continued growth of the major conurbations have all, however, contributed to the need for new housing and new types of housing in new areas. They also explain the growth of larger metropolitan authorities. The central planning problems today are these: to check the process of urban concentration and sprawl — particularly in the Midlands and South-East; to speed up the provision of new dwellings and to rehouse the surplus or 'overspill' population in the big cities; to improve traffic and public transport facilities and to plan for future vehicular growth; and to cope with the social consequences of dispersal.

Governments have responded to these needs with a number of interrelated long-term planning policies. On a national level, town planning policies include the establishment of more new and expanded towns (by 1968 a total of twenty-three new towns had been built or were fully planned); the renewal of dead city centres and 'twilight' zones – i.e. areas where large old houses, too good to be classified as slums, have become multi-occupied lodging houses, as in North Kensington and in the Sparkbrook district of Birmingham; and a higher investment in municipal housing. Each year between 300,000 and 400,000 new homes are built, but whereas in the period 1945–51 88 per cent of the new dwellings built were houses, by the late 1950s this figure had fallen to 60 per cent – the remaining 40 per cent of the new homes being in flats. [19] The attraction of migrants back to the declining areas of the North-East and South Wales, and the preservation of the countryside, are complementary national planning aims. At a local level other related policies are being pursued. Most local authorities, for example, have committed themselves to the acceleration of slum clearance projects, to the improvement of road and transport facilities, and to the extension of grants and loans for home improvements and house purchase. The important work of co-ordinated regional planning is as yet little developed, however. Regional planning authorities still do not exist in statutory form, and the present economic councils for the regions can only advise on such questions as the main communications network, the distribution of population and employment, major open spaces and recreational areas, and provisions for services such as water and power.

Two main sociological concepts have underlain these post-war urban planning developments in Britain: the ideal of 'neighbourhood units' and that of 'balanced communities'. Nineteenth-century towns, as we have seen, did not evolve to any significant extent a sense of community, and it was in response to this awareness that the idea of the neighbourhood unit gained currency. This idea has the object of stimulating community life by dividing a town up into groups small enough to encourage neighbourliness. The size of such units may vary from 5,000 to 10,000 but the aim is that no child shall have to undertake more than a five-minute walk to his primary school and that all housewives shall be adequately served by local neighbourhood shops.

Despite the undoubted overall improvement in the quality of life offered by the new towns and the more qualified achievements of post-war housing estates, recent empirical research suggests that neither of these abstract town-planning ideals has met with complete success in practice. Indeed, the assumption that merely by replicating older spatial arrangements in new settings it is possible to achieve the same kinds of neighbourliness and social mixing (even if it were the case that we could adequately measure such phenomena) seems to be completely mistaken. In fact, as Josephine Klein rather wryly comments, all that has happened on the new estates is that 'relationships, instead of being face-to-face, become window-to-window'. [20]

The second key concept in post-war planning has been that of 'balance'. The principal aim was to eliminate class segregation, as had been the intention on a smaller scale in earlier community and new town planning in the nineteenth century. It was also hoped that balanced communities would encourage a more balanced distribution of industry, trade and services and that the middle class would provide a potential source of leaders in the community. Again, however, the ideology has failed – at least in the short run. Thus, the new areas seem in practice to enhance status distinctions rather than the reverse. Even the 'one-class' estates of Liverpool and Sheffield, for instance, were found to have two different sub-cultures: the 'roughs' and the 'respectables'.[21] And the attempt to attract middle-class and professional families to the new towns around London has met with little response.

Ruth Glass attributes the failure of these town-planning ideals to a 'Utopian' and 'anti-urban' bias among British planners. [22] It is a bias which is certainly quite explicit in the writings of Sir Frederick Osborn and Charles Whittick, who claim, for instance, that

Of all the expedients of man in pursuit of satisfactions and power over things, towns have been the least amenable to considered and intelligent human organization. Much of their past record has been indescribably shocking ... And we have to consider whether, in view of the recent evolution of means of communication, physical and mental, close spatial grouping of large numbers of people is any longer necessary or conducive to the further advance of civilization and culture. [23]

Against the anti-urban view, the American writer, Jane Jacobs, has argued in favour of a quite different set of policies. She suggests that urban planning should concentrate not on dispersal of urban populations but rather on the regeneration of existing city neighbourhoods. Her ideal is to foster precisely those elements which make the city city-like: to create more diversity and complexity and a more intensive commercial and social life in the centre of cities. [14]

Whichever of these rival urban policies is pursued in the future – and there is some evidence that the latter is gaining in influence (the designs for the second-stage new towns like Cumbernauld, for instance, rely on much higher densities in the city centre than was the case with the first of the new towns) – and whether or not developments in the future are wholly centrally planned, simple expediency is bound to dictate some of the solutions. For there are still considerable and urgent problems to be dealt with – in the new towns, in the cities, in the suburbs and on new housing estates. Graham Lomas, having these problems in mind, and reviewing the achievements of urban planning and social welfare over the last century, comments that

There have been some remarkable advances: the average length of human life in our industrial towns is now over sixty years; in Liverpool in 1842 it was sixteen . . . Our minimum housing standards allow one person per habitable room; a century ago it was not uncommonly four or five. But the environmental quality of our towns is still not high . . . The faces of most of our cities would seem to deny that they are the foci of 'civilization'. [25]

In most of the new towns, although housing conditions are much better than those to be found in the cities from which their population is drawn, environmental standards are certainly low – particularly in comparison with contemporary urban developments in Scandinavia, for instance, and even compared with the elegant city planning carried out in England in the late eighteenth and early nineteenth centuries. This, however, is perhaps the least of the difficulties facing the new towns. Of much greater importance are the problems created by the untypical age-structure of the population (it is predominantly young and middle-aged), and the consequent pressures which this generates in terms of the demand for schools, colleges, recreational facilities, commercial entertainment and jobs. The lack of normal, fully functioning social services, including transport, particularly in the early life of the new towns, creates further difficulties – as does the leadership of community associations. There is a marked lack of those groups which traditionally occupy such leadership roles, the late middle-aged, middle-class and professional people. [26]

HOUSING

Of urban problems in the city housing is, of course, the most outstanding. For despite improvements – in standards of accommodation, in the proportion of the population who occupy separate dwellings and who have access to various household amenities such as an internal piped water supply, W.C. and baths, and in home ownership – there are still marked regional and social class variations. For example, whereas in 1964 householders in Social Classes I and II were 19 per cent of the total, they accounted for 30 per cent of the owner-occupiers; householders in Social Classes IV and V were 26 per cent of the total but they accounted for 39 per cent of those living in controlled private unfurnished accommodation. Forty-one per cent of local authority tenants, on the other hand, came from among the manual wage earners in Social Class III. [27] At least 25 per cent of the dwellings now occupied are over eighty years old and have thus exceeded the officially defined period of their useful life. Even in 1964 22 per cent of householders either had to share a bath or had no fixed bath at all. Six per cent shared a W.C. and 11 per cent were without a W.C. altogether. [28] Many of the old dwellings lacking in modern conveniences are on the way to augmenting the existing slums, which

34 *Holidaying on the A.20.*

already house over one million people. And if some sections of the population are now better housed than they have ever been, other groups remain in very poor conditions: the 3 million who at present live in conditions of gross overcrowding, for example, the homeless, the old and the disabled. [29]

Compared with the problems of the underprivileged groups of urbanites, the difficulties of suburbanites and of those living on new housing estates seem relatively trivial. They are certainly different. But although the evidence on suburban life would appear to be contradictory so far, it is clear that very real problems do exist. There are also important social class differences in respect of successful or unsuccessful adaptation to life in new kinds of surroundings, as well as cultural differences between England and other countries. Herbert Gans, for instance, in his survey of an American suburban estate in New Jersey, [30] contends that his respondents, who were mostly middle class, reported an accelerated social life after their move. About half of them said that they visited neighbours more often than in their former residence, few reported feeling lonely, a large proportion were involved in community activities, and mental illness was a less common experience than in the cities from which they had come. [31] On the other hand, there was a shortage of ready transportation, adolescents complained of the inaccessibility of entertainment facilities and some somen spoke of feeling isolated (although Gans attributes this latter fact to the general problems of working- and lower-middle-class women, rather than to the effect of suburban life as such).

By contrast, Hilda Jennings in her survey of a mainly working-class housing project on the outskirts of Bristol suggests that there is evidence for 'the existence of a feeling of "not belonging" expressing itself in withdrawal from and antagonism to society'. [32] These are the classic conditions of what sociologists call 'anomie'. [33]

A number of explanations have been suggested to account for this apparent feeling of insecurity on English housing estates. Frankenberg, for instance, believes that 'since rents are relatively high and most council house tenants are manual workers on daily or weekly engagements, there is a sense in which, despite their council house, they are fundamentally and patently insecure'. He goes on to say that this feeling is probably reinforced by the absence of 'gossip chains' and the reliance of the individual on the sanctions of the mass media, in place of strong family and group values. [34] H. E. Bracey, in a comparative survey of English and American new housing estates, adds some further insights into the reasons for loneliness and dissatisfaction on English estates. He comments, for example, on the reticence, unsociability and passiveness of English householders, and on their reluctance to create effective community associations or to argue on equal terms with 'the authorities' when they have justified complaints. His conclusion is that

In a rapidly changing society ... if loneliness is to be prevented, if neigh-bourliness is to be sustained, if social organizations are to flourish, a framework has to be provided for newcomers to establish their status, for new leaders to be identified quickly, for everybody to acquire a sense of belonging in a very short time. American society has recognized and makes provision for this: English society does not. [35]

THE URBAN WAY OF LIFE

Perhaps it is too soon yet to assess the full impact of redevelopment schemes and new housing areas. Certainly many of the problems which have been reported seem to have more to do with the difficulties inherent in the very act of moving, and in the initial adjustments to a new way of life, than with any permanent inadequacies in the new environments or any fundamental incapacity of the newcomers to settle down satisfactorily. In any case, it is impossible to foresee an immediate way out of these kinds of difficulties for, as John Madge comments,

> However much we may lament the loss of traditional solidarities and settled courtesies, our civilization is leading us away from them into the opportunities, and anxieties, of an adaptive future. These are the product of an urban life . . . Even if the ethos of competition which epitomizes this way of life were to be absorbed in a new social solidarity, I doubt whether we could hope, or that we should aspire, to recapture the nostalgic simplicity of an earlier age. [36]

It has been evident at many points in our discussion that there have been both gains and losses resulting from the process of urban growth over the last century. Health and housing standards have improved for the majority, and the urban-industrial way of life has liberated individual citizens to an unprecedented degree. More choices are available in respect of jobs, education, marriage, moral and religious codes, and more people are now in a position to choose not only where they want to live but also how they want to spend their working lives. The city, furthermore, provides a sufficient cross-section of people for everyone to know the kind of people they *want* to know. It also provides an unrivalled range of cultural, educational, recreational and civic amenities. On the other hand, apart from the difficulties which are entailed precisely because of such a wide range of opportunities for personal choice, it is also true that the city imposes regulations and uniformities. It may, moreover, create a considerable strain in terms of traffic conditions, noise and lack of adequate recreational space. Today, about half of the families in Britain own a motor vehicle. By 1980 it is estimated that there will be three times this number of cars on the roads. As the Buchanan Report makes plain, there is only one real solution to such an emergency:

> if we want both to liberate the motor vehicle and to regain cities that are pleasant places to live and work in . . . We shall have to make a gigantic effort to replan, reshape, and rebuild our cities. [37]

We shall later be examining some of the other effects of urbanization on the family and on social stratification, for instance. First we must turn to questions of work and working relationships in England today.

WORK: CHANGES IN THE OCCUPATIONAL STRUCTURE

Changes in the structure of industrial organization and in the typical pattern of jobs and working relations — like those connected with the growth of towns — have had a profound influence on almost every aspect of contemporary life. This is so not only because of the close links between work and family life, and between work and education, social class and politics, but because — for most people — work is the most important source of self-identification:

> every employee is precipitated, by virtue of a given division of labour, into unavoidable relationships with other employees, supervisors, managers, or customers. The work situation involves the separation and concentration of individuals, affords possibilities of identification with and alteration from others, and conditions feelings of isolation, antagonism, and solidarity. [38]

Since the end of the eighteenth century, and at an increasingly accelerating pace in the present century, just as a greater proportion of the population have felt the impact of urban growth and the new conditions of city life, so, in economic terms, has the country become more and more industrialized. These two processes, as we have seen, have been virtually complementary. The associated developments in science and technology have generated continued and rapid changes in production methods, products and working conditions, and these in turn have had a number of decisive consequences — for workers and managers, for the traditional industrial entrepreneur and for the State. By contrast with the work force of traditional societies that of our contemporary industrialized society is highly differentiated — both in terms of the range and degree of skill of the occupations available and in terms of the various rates of pay and relative rights and duties binding on workers. 'Job evaluation and salary plans symbolize the ordering of the industrial work force', [39] just as the traffic signal, in Wirth's view, symbolizes one of the central features of modern urban life.

As we saw in earlier chapters, the most important occupational trend in the last century was the decline in agricultural labour and the parallel growth in the numbers employed in factories, offices and shops in the cities. This trend was accompanied by the growth of new professional and white collar occupations, and by a marked redistribution of workers between various types of industry. David Marsh summarizes the main conclusions to be drawn about the changing pattern of industrial employment between 1851 and 1951 as follows:

The proportion of the occupied population engaged in agricultural, fishing, mining, quarrying, and personal service occupations declined; the proportion engaged in manufacturing, building, transport and communications remained relatively stable . . . there was an appreciable increase in the proportion concerned with administration, defence, commerce and finance, and a slight increase in professional and technical occupations. [40]

In the last twenty years white collar occupations have grown at an even faster rate. Thus, since 1951 roughly two out of every three people added to the nation's total working population have been absorbed by non-industrial occupations: by the distributive trades, by banking and finance, by public administration, by the professional and scientific services and by the 'miscellaneous service trades' (including hotels, laundries, entertainment, garages and so on).

CHANGES IN INDUSTRIAL ORGANIZATION

We have seen that another striking feature of industrial organization over the last 100 years has been the expansion in scale of many manufacturing and commercial enterprises, a development which has affected both the production and distribution sides of industry. This has been a result of economic pressures and policies favouring amalgamation or vertical integration between firms occupied in producing the same end product or in distributing a particular range of products. In the 1870s firms employing more than 200 people were well above average for all but a very few industries. By 1961, however, although more than two-thirds of all manufacturing establishments still employed fewer than 100 people and provided one fifth of all employment, there were 1,206 firms each employing over 1,000 men and these accounted for well over one third of all jobs. These large firms are especially common in the engineering and electronics industries and in vehicle-building.

Developments in technology and the rapid growth of white collar and service occupations in recent years have resulted in a major redistribution of skills within industry. For example, whereas in 1948 about a quarter of the total employees in the chemical industry were administrative, technical or clerical workers, that figure has now risen to well over one third. If automation continues, this trend is likely to become even more marked in the future and to extend to all industries. In the United States, the service sector already accounts for more than half of total employment and for more than half of the gross national product. In Britain, even within manufacturing industry, by the late 1960s more than a quarter of employees belonged within the category 'administrative, technical and clerical'.

The revolution in industrial techniques, new modes of capital accumulation and corporate finance, and the development of new markets which have been responsible for these changes in the structure of industries and occupations, have also had important consequences for the internal structure of industrial organizations. The way in which an organization is run – whether it is a factory, an office or a large shop – depends on three factors: its ownership,

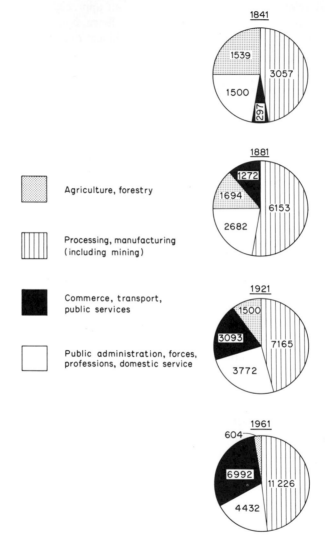

Agriculture, forestry

Processing, manufacturing (including mining)

Commerce, transport, public services

Public administration, forces, professions, domestic service

Fig. 12 Changes in occupational distribution in the United Kingdom, 1841–1961 (in thousands). After Mitchell and Deane, 1962, and Annual Abstract of Statistics, *1967.*

the goals it pursues and the rules of conduct it applies. These, in turn, are closely related to the division of labour and to the degree of specialization of the work process in a particular enterprise. Over the last century there have been major changes in all of these elements of industrial organization.

G. K. Galbraith summarizes some of the contrasts in these terms:

> Machines have extensively replaced crude manpower, and one machine increasingly instructs other machines in the process we call automation. Industrial companies or corporations have become very large. They are no longer directed by great entrepreneurs as a right of ownership. They are guided impersonally by their staff . . . In the world of the large companies they [prices] are set by the sellers and often remain fixed for long periods of time. These companies are also at considerable pains to persuade the customer what he should buy . . . Finally, even in countries such as the United States, where faith in free enterprise is one of the minor branches of theology, the state plays an increasing role in affairs. [42]

OWNERSHIP

Since the latter part of the nineteenth century the most typical form of ownership in England has been the joint-stock corporation. The establishment of public corporations like the B.B.C., and of nationalized industries, however, has altered the overall pattern of ownership to some extent. The main consequence has been a decline in the concentration of private shareholding in private hands, although in over one third of Britain's largest industrial companies, share distribution still permits ownership control. [43] One third of all company assets are now in the hands of public corporations, and around 50 per cent of new investments are financed by public, including local, authorities. Institutional shareholding, by insurance companies, building societies and unit trust companies, for example, is also increasing.

In terms of ownership, then, one of the most significant modern trends is that of public investment. The role of the State and of public authorities is not limited simply to the operation of particular nationalized industries or corporations, however. Their power and responsibilities extend over much wider areas of economic life.

Acting as the Third Party the State is responsible for defending workers from employers (for example, through minimum wage legislation), consumers from manufacturers and retailers (for example, by controlling monopoly and restrictive trade practices, by weights and measures regulations and under the Trade Descriptions Act) and shareholders from promoters and directors (for example, through Company Law). The State is also responsible for keeping the ring round contestants in industrial disputes, for participating with employers and workers in the Industrial Courts and since the late 1960s, under the Labour government, for mediating and supervising wage agreements in the context of prices and incomes legislation. As the Primary Party, the State is responsible for publishing information about industry, for providing unemployment insurance and industrial injury benefits and for maintaining a national network of Labour Exchanges, as well, of course, as actually

operating certain key industries. Less directly, but perhaps equally importantly, the State has control over industry through its fiscal policies and
through the regulation of tariffs, subsidies, purchase taxes, profits taxes,
budgetary policy, Bank Rate, rationing, licensing, the direction of labour and
development incentives.

It is evident from the partial list of State responsibilities in contemporary
economic life that the nationalized industries and public corporations as such
are only one part of a very much wider area of State regulation and control
in English society today. Nevertheless, the public sector of industry is in
itself of considerable importance. In 1960 one person in four was in public
employment of some kind. This is six times as many as before 1940. But the
State is not only a major employer. As William Robson points out:

> In Britain, as in most developed countries, the efficiency of the entire
> apparatus of production, distribution and exchange, and indeed the standard
> of living of the people as a whole, are dependent on the industries con-
> cerned with fuel and power, transportation, banking and credit, iron and
> steel, to a greater extent than on any other factors. [43]

Communications, which are also for the most part in the hands of public
corporations (the G.P.O. and the B.B.C.), are equally important in regulating
economic affairs. Bearing in mind all of these areas of operation of nationalized undertakings, therefore, there is little question that 'the public corporation
in Britain today is a political, social and economic invention of high significance'. And, as Robson suggests, it is probably 'destined to play as important
a role in the latter part of the twentieth century as the joint-stock company has
played in the last 100 years'. [44]

BUREAUCRACY

If the contrast between the predominantly *laissez-faire* economy of the
nineteenth century and that of the more fully 'planned' economy of the mid-
twentieth century is particularly marked in terms of ownership, so it is also in
terms of its typical rules of conduct. Because of changes in ownership and
management, increasing specialization and the growth in scale of industrial
and commercial undertakings in the twentieth century, rational bureaucratic
procedures have come to predominate over earlier paternalistic systems of
authority. There have, of course, been bureaucracies in pre-industrial societies,
as in Egypt, in Rome and in seventeenth-century France. The difference is that
today bureaucratic methods and values pervade the entire fabric of our social
life. They are built into the system of social welfare, education, communications and mass entertainment, just as much as into industrial and commercial
undertakings.

According to Max Weber, the most important theorist to have written on this subject, the main characteristics of a bureaucratic structure (in the ideal typical case) are these. There is a clear-cut division of labour, and a fairly rigidly defined administrative hierarchy. Operations are regulated by a uniform system of rules and standards in a spirit of 'formalistic impersonality'. Employment constitutes a career and there is a recognized system of promotion. Finally, the bureaucratic organization is capable of attaining the highest degree of efficiency. It 'compares with other organizations as does the machine with non-mechanical modes of production'. [45]

Weber's analysis focuses on many of the central goals of modern industrial and administrative organizations. But it tends to give a somewhat misleading impression of the degree of stability and integration of which they are capable. Recent research, for instance, reveals the administrative inefficiency of an over-rigid adherence to organizational rules, secrecy and red tape. It also points to certain 'dysfunctions' — that is, activities which contribute to the disturbance (as opposed to the survival) of the social activities of the bureaucratic system, from the point of view of individual workers or employees. [46] Competing personal loyalties, or 'role incongruence' as some sociologists call this, are particularly evident in the case of the industrial scientist, for example, who is torn between the pursuit of knowledge on the one hand and the need to develop marketable products on the other. The predicament of the teacher, trying to develop a humane relationship with his pupils, while at the same time having to maintain discipline and to subject his pupils to the rigours of a formal examination system, is a similar case. A more radical objection to bureaucracy in the view of Tom Burns and G. Stalker is that the ruling management ideology in such organizations often impedes the implementation of new industrial methods, since it does not allow for the degree of flexibility and adaptiveness which is necessary to cope with modern technological developments [47] (this argument applies equally, of course, to educational institutions, as we shall see below).

AUTOMATION

The 'new industrialism' to which Burns and Stalker refer is founded on automation, a computer-based technology which, in various forms, is rapidly becoming the dominant mode of production in many industries. It is perhaps too soon yet to examine the full implications of automation. A number of consequences do, however, seem to be fairly firmly established. [48] Under automation work in the factory becomes lighter and cleaner; manual skills decline in importance and new technical skills take their place; employee responsibility is heightened. In both the factory and the office, jobs tend to be enlarged rather than further subdivided, and the distance between supervisors and workers is reduced.

These changes, together with new forms of ownership and control, have resulted in significant alterations in the pattern of industrial relations and in management policy over the last twenty years. They have also transformed the role of the trade union movement. We shall consider in turn each of these changes – and their influence on the character of industrial work today.

MANAGERIAL IDEOLOGIES AND INDUSTRIAL RELATIONS

We have previously referred to the relative absence of formal 'industrial relations' and the concentration of exclusive power in the hands of the employers in the nineteenth century. We have also described the growth of 'human relations' policies and industrial conciliation machinery in the twentieth century. [49] Since 1945 increased government intervention in the labour market, research in such new fields as ergonomics, and responses to management and organizational developments in other countries (such as Sweden and Yugoslavia) have resulted in further changes in the character of industrial relations. The prevailing ideology today is more democratic and egalitarian than it was at the beginning of the century, as is reflected, for instance, in the adoption of more refined types of conciliation procedures as well as in the application of wider redistributive measures. This ideology has also led in some sectors of industry to an increase in workers' participation in management and in company profit-sharing schemes. These developments have all, however, been more in appearance than in fact. In most firms where experiments in so-called 'industrial democracy' have been introduced there is very little *real* sharing of power. Thus, in commenting on the achievements of the John Lew Partnership, Allan Flanders and his colleagues conclude:

> Although . . . the existence of representative institutions . . . have made the employment relationship positively attractive for most employees . . . one strong source of discontent among the rank and file was their lack of any direct control over their pay and other working conditions.

A further objection to such an approach to industrial democracy, at least when it is imposed from above, is that it tends to result in paternalism. 'Management, it is assumed, knows what is in the best interests of all the Partners.' [50]

Similar criticisms can be made of the efforts of works study engineers, organization and methods consultants, personnel managers and industrial psychologists – all of whom are charged with keeping things running efficiently and making the workers happy and 'adjusted'. As Amitai Etzioni points out, the approach of these specialists does not take a sufficiently comprehensive view of industrial organizations, and therefore it results in management policies which 'favour the bosses' and 'mislead' the workers. He explains how this happens:

By providing an unrealistic 'happy' picture, by viewing the factory as a family rather than as a power struggle among groups with some conflicting values and interests as well as some shared ones, and by seeing it as a major source of human satisfaction rather than alienation, Human Relations comes to gloss over the realities of work life. Worker dissatisfaction is viewed as indicative of lack of understanding of the situation rather than as symptomatic of any underlying real conflict of interests. [51]

New management ideologies have been paralleled by important modifications in the conduct of the trade union movement. As we saw earlier, not only have the unions achieved many of their basic objectives, but they have also begun to acquire something of a niche in the edifice of public administration. [52] Indeed, today many of the traditional trade union responsibilities overlap with those of the government. This means that the strike, for example, instead of being a conflict between the interests of two disputants – bosses and workers – regulated by a theoretically impartial State, is appearing more and more as a conflict between the interests of overall national economic stability and those of the individual worker. The role of the T.U.C. reinforces this dilemma, for its General Council normally attempts to restrain strikes so as to avoid embarrassing the government – particularly when a Labour government is in office, and more particularly when, as in the late 1960s, voluntary restraint by the unions became a bargaining counter to prevent greater government intervention to impose wage restraints. It is this 'institutionalization of industrial conflict' [53] which perhaps partly explains why, despite the massive increase in trade union membership (in 1931 there were 4·6 million members, but by 1965 this figure had risen to 10·2 million – of whom just over 2 million were women), active participation in union affairs is at a minimum nowadays. When the unions are militant and struggling for recognition, participation can bring psychological as well as material benefits to their members. In the context of the modern Welfare State, however, when the unions act mainly as service agencies, and when most of their work is done by a handful of 'union bureaucrats', the help of the members is not needed in the same way. Amalgamation and affiliation of the smaller unions have, of course, added to the distance between the leadership and the workers and may contribute further to the general mood of apathy. In 1931 there were over 1,000 separate unions, but by 1965 only just over half of this number (580) were left, of which the seven giants accounted for over two thirds of the total membership of the movement. But, while it is true that some of the aims and objectives of the trade union movement have altered in character since the late nineteenth century, the role of the unions as instruments of what Marxists call 'class struggle' remains substantially the same.

WORK SATISFACTION

Changes in the structure of the work process, together with all of the different changes in industrial organization and management policies we have discussed, have had a marked effect on the nature of the contemporary working environment, as well as on the life of the worker away from his work. There have, however, been conflicting interpretations of what these changes mean to the average employee. As Lisl Klein rightly comments, 'Work satisfaction is a very slippery topic.' Mining, for instance,

> is by most standards a terrible job – dangerous, dirty, unpleasant, unhealthy. But because it has existed for a long time, because traditions have grown up round it, because there are social compensations for the arduousness and danger, miners will fight hard for the right to do it.

What is more, she points out, whereas joint consultation is supposed to stimulate a sense of participation,

> nobody ever seems to get a sense of participation from it, and many people don't want a sense of participation. Again, everybody wants more money, but many are prepared to take less money for a job which gives them a sense of purpose and self-fulfilment. [54]

Generalization, then, is difficult here. Alain Touraine, the French sociologist, suggests why:

> Occupational reactions and dissatisfactions are not isolated phenomena and have to be explained by the discrepancies between work situations and attitude systems or objectives in life. Any element of the work situation, wage level, for example, will be interpreted differently according to whether it represents simply the gratification of an economic need or is interpreted by the worker as an indication of the recognition of his occupational competence. [55]

The worker's level of 'adjustment' or 'satisfaction' also depends on the social system of the factory or shop in which he is employed, and on his individual situation in various primary groups – in his work teams, in his family and in his neighbourhood. But if it is impossible to be confident of universally applicable generalizations concerning recent changes in working conditions, a number of overall trends do seem to be fairly clear.

The distance between supervisors and their subordinates has narrowed, punishment has been replaced by more positive disciplinary methods, income differentials between skilled and unskilled workers and between some groups of white collar workers and the more successful manual workers have been reduced, and conditions and hours of work have been improved. Yet some sections of the working population remain much worse off than the rest. In most manufacturing industries, for example, there is still a considerable element of restraint imposed over the workers' conduct. Few enjoy positions of responsibility, and although automation may be expected to bring some improvements in the future, owing to specialization and mechanization, the work of many people remains standardized,

> its pattern and rhythm inflexibly set by machinery, with little scope for individual intelligence or initiative and for spontaneous action ... Monotony is made more dreary by the vastness of production lines which weakens the relationship of each worker to the end product and indeed to production as a meaningful process. [56]

Peter Berger is among those sociologists who have reacted pessimistically to current developments in industrial organization. He contends that whereas 'for most of history men have *been* what they *did*' (although this does not necessarily mean that they *liked* what they did), this is no longer the case with most kinds of work in contemporary society. [57] In his view, increasing fragmentation of the work task and the divorce between work and family life have meant that for the majority work must seem 'meaningless' and problematical. He points to two major consequences of this fact. One has been the concentration of the individual's search for meaning and identity in the so-called 'private' sphere. The other has been a wild scramble for professional status among a large number of occupations – because of the value of 'projecting an image'. To these consequences, both of which would seem to be supported by the evidence of recent empirical research, [58] Nels Anderson adds a third. He suggests that 'modern work, stripped of all transcendental values, except for the fortunate few who have work with which they can become personally identified, has acquired a quasi-commodity character. In the consumer society it acquires exchange value.' [59] In other words, people sell time (i.e. they work) primarily in order to buy products (made by other workers who are selling their time too), which will enhance their free time or leisure.

Three themes link these arguments about the workers' status in modern industry: 'alienation', 'leisure' and 'privatization', and each helps to round off our discussion of some of the main features of modern urban-industrial society.

ALIENATION

We have already referred to the chief signs of alienation in the working environment: work is depersonalized, there is little opportunity for the individual to gain pride in his work or to participate in the running of the industry, jobs are over-specialized and workers are bored and dissatisfied. [60] Such conditions, however, do not apply universally. As Robert Blauner demonstrates, having compared workers in four different settings – print shop, textile mill, automobile factory and automated chemical plant — 'Whether a worker approaches the state of being merely a commodity, a resource, or an element of cost in the productive process depends on his concrete relation to technology, the social structure of his industry, and its economic fortunes.' [61] This explains why it is possible for Ferdynand Zweig to assert that alienation was non-existent among the workers whom he interviewed in the relatively prosperous and expanding steel, motor-car, rubber and electronics industries. [62] Clearly, opportunities for involvement and self-fulfilment for the worker in present-day society vary widely — as between the doctor, the craft printer, the bus driver and the assembly-line operator, for example. There are also differences between industries and between particular firms in terms of the management policies that they adopt. What is more, aspirations and ideal standards — prompted among other things by the examples suggested by the mass media — are continually undergoing change, usually in an upward direction. This means that what might have seemed 'satisfactory' twenty years ago will appear less so by today's standards.

LEISURE

We shall return to the discussion of alienation in our final chapter. A second and related theme in our discussion of 'job satisfaction' here is that of leisure. Since the end of the nineteenth century, as we saw earlier, social life outside the world of work has not merely re-emerged, but it has developed in quite new forms — forms which are themselves a product of modern commercial and industrial growth. Leisure has also acquired a new significance. According to Joffre Dumazedier, for instance, leisure is now 'the very central experience in the life-culture of millions upon millions of workers'. [63] It assumes this importance for several reasons. In the first place, of course, leisure offers a release from the strains and stresses of the working environment, and these affect everybody, however satisfying his job. It also provides an opportunity for alternative sources of self-identification and enables individuals to make significant personal choices. Leisure pursuits may even have an effect on occupational choice itself — at least for those who are in a position to choose at all — since occupations normally provide recognizable reference groups, as well as setting the boundaries of 'free time' for the worker. [64] What is more, in a situation where many employees fail to derive much satisfaction or sense of belonging in their workplace — or indeed in the world at large — the ritualistic aspects of leisure may also be important. Tom Burns, for instance, considers that leisure, and especially commercial entertainment,

> domesticates the unattainable and the threatening and reduces the increasing range and strangeness of the individual's world to the synthesized,

rehearsed and safely repeatable form of a story, a documentary, a performance, a show. The structures of leisure exist as repositories of meaning, value and reassurance for everyday life. [65]

PRIVATIZATION: THE GROWTH OF A 'HOME-CENTRED' SOCIETY

It is the centrality of leisure in contemporary experience which accounts for the presence of the third theme in this discussion of the wider implications of contemporary work patterns: the theme of privatization. Jules Henry summarizes the meaning of this process thus:

> The fact that the majority [of workers] have little or no involvement in the institutions for which they work means that work, which in most *non*-industrial countries is a strong and continuous socializing agency, is, in America, also *de*socializing.

As a consequence,

> What finally relates the average person to life, space and people is his own personal, intimate economy: family, house and car. He has labelled his occupational world 'not involved', and turned inward upon his little world of family, hobbies and living standard. [66]

Thus, if leisure and home-centredness are important features of contemporary life this is not simply a result of people's having more spare time in which to occupy themselves; rather it is the generally unsatisfactory character of work itself, for most people, that gives leisure its significance. We should remember that, despite progressive reductions in the agreed working week, and despite longer holidays with pay, with overtime many still work more than forty-eight hours a week. In America it is quite common for men to take a second job to augment the family income. What is more, one third of all married women also work – a much higher proportion than at the beginning of the century.

It is important to realize, too, that the retreat into private experiences and home-centredness need not imply a total withdrawal from the social world beyond the family. Indeed we know that more people than ever before are now visiting museums and art galleries, listening to concerts or taking holidays abroad. And despite the massive increase in television viewing more people are also involved in active recreational pastimes. Naturally there are educational and social class differences in respect of the ways in which people choose to spend their leisure time. And doubtless it is more or less satisfying to them not only in relation to the satisfactoriness of their jobs, or their intellectual background, but also according to the opportunities that are available to them where they live. Privatization, then, is not to be seen necessarily as a negative response. It may be the result of a positive attraction to better home surroundings and it may result in higher levels of understanding and co-operation between husband and wife, parents and children.

AN OVERVIEW OF INDUSTRIALIZATION

It will be clear from our discussion of urban and industrial growth, and of the social and economic policies which have accompanied them, that urbanization and industrialism are not once-and-for-all processes. Equally the sequence of development from traditional-rural to urban-industrial society does not occur in a simple progression from cause to effect. Social organizations and human responses are complex and variable. Institutions change and evolve; new standards are set and new aspirations are created. They change, however, against the background of a pre-existing culture. Hence there are numerous points of conflict and accommodation. 'The battleground is at a variety of points and levels: religious and ethical values, family systems, class alignments, educational system, government structure, and legal system.' [67] What is of chief concern to both the sociologist and the social historian, therefore, is to see which institutions of the traditional society are preserved over time, and which transformed and modified – or entirely superseded. This involves a critical examination of the mutually adjusting relationships between institutions, ideas and ideals. It also involves a search for the truths which lie behind the apparent historical or contemporary reality.

35 Homes at West Wittering.

So far our description of the transition from traditional-rural to urban-industrial society has been mainly historical. What we want to consider in the remaining chapters is the way in which the culmination of these developments in contemporary society has affected social class and family relationships, the educational and political systems, and the network of mass communication. We shall also try to assess the direction of future changes in these institutions, and in their meaning for various groups and types of individual. Before we proceed to this, however, perhaps it would be useful to summarize the major changes in social structure that have taken place over the last 200 years.

As we have already seen, it is impossible to describe the 'industrial revolution' in terms of an exact causal sequence, since most of the events and processes involved are both cause and consequence of other related events. For instance, the growth of an efficient national transport system was the result of certain major developments in technology and in industrial organization; on the other hand, certain industries were entirely dependent upon good transport for their establishment and continued success. It would be equally rash for us to try to rank in terms of their relative importance the difference agencies of social development. Military and economic changes, scientific and technological innovations, religious and moral values, and the political and communication systems are far too closely interwoven and mutually interdependent to enable individual factors to be isolated in the overall process of social change. It is clear, for example, that industrialization owed part of its original impetus to developments in science and technology. But the exploitation of the industrial and marketing potential of these discoveries required the existence of businessmen who were prepared to supply the capital for large-scale development, as well as professional men and engineers who were able to cope with the complicated tasks of surveying, land purchase and building and with the relevant commercial and administrative transactions. A readily mobile and intelligent labour force was also indispensable – as was the existence of a network of communications capable of bringing together all the necessary people, services, goods and ideas. Given this complexity of contributory events in the process of industrialization, any summary such as the one that follows must, therefore, remain highly generalized.

Probably the most obvious consequence of industrialization has been the increase in scale not only of factories and workplaces themselves but also of banks and financial corporations, shops and offices, and public and private agencies of administration (including central and local government). Within industry, largeness of scale has resulted in – and from – mass marketing and mass production techniques, as well as from new patterns of ownership and management. These changes have, in turn, given rise to a more detailed division of labour, to greater specialization of skills and to new patterns of industrial relations and new forms of industrial arbitration and conciliation. The improved pay and working conditions won by trade union agitation, mass consumption, easier credit facilities, government contributions to public health, housing and welfare services, the widening of the electorate and the growth of the mass media have all led to changes in the pattern of social class relationships in industrial societies and to changes in political allegiances. They have also been responsible for raised living standards, as measured, for instance, in terms of health, education and leisure.

The higher levels of skill which modern industry demands (in contrast to the early nineteenth-century requirement for sheer manual labour) create a need for prolonged training. As a consequence, education becomes a vital constituent both in present technological success and in future industrial innovation. It also provides – with the changing structure of job opportunities and the creation of new skills – a major means of social (and geographic) mobility. The development of industry has proceeded hand-in-hand with the growth of new urban centres, and many of the traditional patterns of rural community life have been lost on the way.

The importance of the extended family has diminished and the roles of its members have changed considerably. The small nuclear family, on the other hand, now more democratically managed and voluntarily contracted, has ceased to be a major (and self-sufficient) economic unit. Instead, having gradually come to share some of its responsibilities – education and child welfare, for instance – with the State, it acts increasingly as an intermediary, protecting its members from the impersonal and bureaucratic institutions of the wider society. Because of the weakening of the bonds of kinship and community, there is an increasing reliance upon the State in times of family crisis – sickness, unemployment or old age. There is also a tendency for people to rely increasingly upon the mass media as a source of information and guidance on appropriate expectations and styles of life. With the collapse of traditional religious beliefs and the bewildering range of different values available from other societies (now open to our inspection much more readily as a consequence of the speed and efficiency of contemporary communication systems), most of the old moral certainties have disappeared. There is anxiety and confusion in the face of this plurality of values. Social control passes inevitably into the hands of 'official' agencies – law, judiciary, police. Personal and group sanctions are no longer adequate.

If largeness of scale, increasing mechanization and bureaucratic principles are the main characteristics of modern industry and government, and if impersonal and instrumental relationships are typical of contemporary urban life, the key feature of modern society is, nevertheless, not 'massification' or State control or dominance by the mass media. It is change itself. As we stressed at the very beginning, the period of 1750 to 1850 was distinguished from any previous historical epoch because people learnt on a greater scale than ever before to accept, to adapt to, and to expect change. Society was no longer settled, stable and certain. As the French Revolution demonstrated only too clearly, the pattern for the future was to be one of conflict and innovation. The result was a series of profound shifts in the existing social structure. We have already described most of these changes as they occurred in the nineteenth and early twentieth centuries. What we now need to explore is their effect on contemporary social relationships.

NOTES

1 There are, of course, distinct regional and social class variations. See MARSH *The Changing Social Structure of England and Wales*, Chs. 1 and 2. This is the major source of the statistics quoted in this and future chapters, together with the *Annual Abstract of Statistics* published by H.M.S.O.

2 Whereas in 1900 only 9 per cent of the total world population was living in towns, in 1960 that proportion had increased to almost one third. Projections into the twenty-first century assume an even faster rate of growth, resulting in an estimated world urban population of 45 per cent in the year 2000 and 90 per cent in 2050. See further LEONARD REISSMAN *The Urban Process: Cities in Industrial Societies,* Chs. VII and VIII (New York, 1964).

3 See RONALD FRANKENBERG *Communities in Britain* (Harmondsworth, 1965) for a comparison of the findings of a number of recent British surveys and for a theoretical model describing 'rural' and 'urban' patterns of social organization (Ch. 11).

4 Between the purely 'urban' and the purely 'rural' types, for instance, there is an intermediate category – the pre-industrial city. See S. SJOBERG *The Pre-Industrial City* (New York, 1960).

5 See, for example, RICHARD HOGGART *The Uses of Literacy*, especially pp. 41–52 (London, 1957; 1958 edition). See also BRIAN JACKSON *Working Class Community* (London, 1968).

6 R. M. MACIVER and CHARLES H. PAGE *Society,* p. 332 (London, 1950; 1962 edition).

7 'Urban sociology', in WELFORD *et al.* (eds.) *Society,* pp. 486–7.

8 See COLIN ROSSER and CHRISTOPHER HARRIS *The Family and Social Change,* pp. 66–72 (London, 1965), for a discussion of Swansea's various 'urban villages'.

9 C. A. MOSER and WOLF SCOTT *British Towns,* Ch. VI (London and Glasgow, 1961). For a comparable American study, see O. D. DUNCAN and A. J. REISS *Social Characteristics of Urban and Rural Communities* (New York, 1956).

10 i.e. a higher proportion of women per 1,000 of men in the population.

11 *British Towns,* pp. 43–5.

12 PETER MANN *An Approach to Urban Sociology,* pp. 105–6 (London, 1965).

13 A useful overview of these surveys can be found in JOSEPHINE KLEIN'S two-volume study *Samples from English Cultures* (London, 1965).

14 Macro-social surveys are those which take as their subject the whole of a society or social system, while micro-social surveys concentrate on more local patterns of behaviour.

15 An American group, including Lewis Mumford and Clarence Stein, who adopted Howard's and Geddes's views during the 1920s.

16 For a useful summary of the theory of the city, see Don Martindale's introduction to MAX WEBER *The City* (London, 1960).

17 'Urbanism as a way of life', in P. K. HATT and A. J. REISS (eds.) *Cities and Society*, pp. 46–63 (New York, 1957).

18 *Urban Society* (London, 1968). This book contains a very full discussion and evaluation of Wirth's theory.

19 See further MYRA WOOLF *The Housing Survey in England and Wales 1964* (H.M.S.O., 1967).

20 *Samples from English Cultures*, p. 251.

21 LIVERPOOL UNIVERSITY DEPARTMENT OF SOCIAL SCIENCE *Neighbourhood and Community* (1954).

22 'Urban sociology', in WELFORD *et al.* (eds.) *Society*.

23 *The New Towns: the Answer to Megalopolis*, pp. 15–16 (London, 1963).

24 See *The Death and Life of Great American Cities* (London, 1962).

25 *Social Aspects of Urban Development*, p. 74 (London, 1966).

26 See further J. H. NICHOLSON *New Communities in Britain* (London, 1961).

27 WOOLF *The Housing Survey in England and Wales 1964*, p. 21.

28 Ibid., p. 8.

29 See STANLEY ALDERSON *Britain in the Sixties: Housing* (Harmondsworth, 1962).

30 *The Levittowners* (London, 1967). Summarized in *New Society*, 28 September 1967.

31 Nearly all of these findings are the reverse of what Michael Young and Peter Willmott found in Greenleigh. See *Family and Class in a London Suburb* (London, 1960).

32 *Societies in the Making* (London, 1962).

33 Durkheim, who first introduced this concept into sociological thought, defined 'anomie' as a situation in which there is a lack of agreement on socially recognized means or patterns of behaviour.

34 *Communities in Britain*, pp. 199–201.

35 *Neighbours*, p. 184 (London, 1964).

36 'Urban change: can we adapt?', *New Society*, 5 December 1963.

37 *Traffic in Towns*, a shortened edition of the Buchanan Report, p. 13 (Harmondsworth, 1963).

38 DAVID LOCKWOOD *Black Coated Worker*, p. 205 (London, 1958).

39 CLARK KERR *et al. Industrialism and Industrial Man*, p. 38 (London, 1962).

40 *The Changing Social Structure of England and Wales*, pp. 148–9.

41 *The New Industrial State*, B.B.C. Reith Lectures for 1966 (London, 1967).

42 See P. SARGANT FLORENCE *Ownership, Control and Success of Large Companies* (London, 1961).

43 WILLIAM ROBSON (ed.) *Problems of Nationalised Industry*, p. 275 (London, 1952).

44 Ibid., p. 366.

45 HANS GERTH and C. WRIGHT MILLS (eds.) *From Max Weber*, p. 214 (London, 1948). For a fuller discussion of the characteristics of bureaucracies, see PETER BLAU *Bureaucracy in Modern society*, pp. 28–32 (New York, 1956).

46 See, for example, A. W. GOULDNER *Patterns of Industrial Bureaucracy* (New York, 1954) and C. ARGYRIS *Integrating the Individual and the Organization* (New York, 1964).

47 *The Management of Innovation* (London, 1961).

48 See further SIR LEON BAGRITT *The Age of Automation* (London, 1966). See also STEPHEN ARIS 'Automation: its effects on the labour force', in REX MALIK (ed.) *Penguin Survey of Business and Industry 1965* (Harmondsworth, 1965).

49 See further ALAN FOX 'Managerial ideology and labour relations', *British Journal of Industrial Relations*, Vol. IV (3), 1966, for an excellent discussion.

50 *Experiments in Industrial Democracy*, pp. 192–3 (London, 1968).

51 *Modern Organizations*, p. 42 (New Jersey, 1964).

52 See further GRAHAM WOOTTON *Workers, Unions and the State* (London, 1966).

53 See RALF DAHRENDORF *Class and Class Conflict in Industrial Society*, Ch. VII (London, 1959).

54 *The Meaning of Work*, p. 2, Fabian Tract No. 349, 1963.

55 *Workers' Attitudes to Technical Change*, p. 52 (Paris, 1965).

56 RALPH ROSS and ERNEST VAN DEN HAAG *The Fabric of Society*, p. 168 (New York, 1957).

57 *The Human Shape of Work*, pp. 215–16 (New York, 1964).

58 See further HOWARD M. VOLLMER and DONALD L. MILLS (eds.) *Professionalization* (New Jersey, 1966).

59 *Work and Leisure*, p. 26 (London, 1961).

60 See further GEORGES FRIEDMANN *The Anatomy of Work*, pp. 139–45 (London, 1961).

61 *Alienation and Freedom*, pp. 33–4 (Chicago, 1964).

62 *The Worker in an Affluent Society* (London, 1961). See also JOHN GOLDTHORPE et al. *The Affluent Worker, Vol. I: Industrial Attitudes and Behaviour* (Cambridge, 1968).

63 *Towards a Society of Leisure*, p. 3 (New York, 1967).

64 See further MAX KAPLAN *Leisure in America* (New York, 1960).

65 'A meaning in everyday life', *New Society*, 25 May 1967.

66 *Culture Against Man*, pp. 28–9 (London, 1966).

67 KERR *Industrialism and Industrial Man*, p. 19.

Industrial and economic growth was previously discussed in Chapters 1, 3 and 5, the growth of towns in Chapters 2 and 4, housing in Chapters 2, 4 and 5, trade unions and industrial relations in Chapters 3 and 5, leisure in Chapters 3 and 5, and town planning in Chapter 4. Population (discussed in Chapters 1, 4 and 5) is also discussed in Chapter 7.

7

Social Class, Social Conflict and Social Change

In the previous chapter we saw how changes in modern urban and industrial life have resulted in altered living and working conditions. These conditions led, in turn, to the growth of new patterns of social relationship and new forms of political awareness. In the process, a more complex – yet flexible – system of social stratification was created.

We have described the early growth of the urban working class and the expansion of new middle-class commercial and professional groups. We have also discussed the development of class consciousness and the emergence of new patterns of rivalry and conflict in nineteenth-century society. This pattern of social relationships, indeed, the very word 'class' itself – together with the mass political movements which the new social situation generated – was a new phenomenon, rooted in the institutions of industrial capitalism. Because its basis was almost entirely economic, the nineteenth-century system of stratification entailed a different pattern of social relations from those associated with earlier forms of ranking. In contrast to the basically militaristic system of feudal estates and the hereditary order of religious castes in India, social position in the class system was no longer rigidly determined by birth. Increasingly, it came to depend on the individual's relationship to those in power over or under him in the major processes of economic production and exchange. In the absence of legal or religious sanctions limiting movement between the various strata, these relationships were not static, and mobility within and between the main social classes became increasingly possible – even though it was often limited in terms of the actual distances moved. Today, with the greater diversification of the economic system and the removal of most earlier barriers to the free movement of 'talent', class position is to a large extent based on achievement. There are of course some sections of the population – especially those at the top and bottom of the social hierarchy – whose position is still dictated by heredity. However, their position does not necessarily confer *formal* civil or political privileges any longer (except, for example, the right of the aristocracy to sit in the House of Lords).

If the present system of stratification is less rigid than earlier forms of social ranking, however, class position nevertheless exerts a very important influence, both within the structure of society as a whole and in the life of its individual members. As we shall see, class position is likely to reflect working relationships and working conditions; it affects opportunities in both health and education; it also influences patterns of marriage and child-rearing, neighbourhood values and personal aspirations.

We have previously suggested that social class can best be understood in terms of *relationships*. We also emphasized the importance of understanding these relationships within a changing socio-historical context. To talk, as we shall in this chapter, about the present-day pattern of stratification, implying a relatively fixed order of more or less stable social class relationships, may therefore seem contradictory. However, in order to analyse occupational and status groups in more detail, and in order to understand the implications of such distinctions on those based on the possession of certain types of power, prestige, income and education, the sociologist is obliged to work with a more static model. In this chapter, while recognizing that class is to be understood primarily in terms of changing historical relationships between various groups of people in the population, we shall nevertheless adopt the view that particular modes of stratification and the characteristics of particular kinds of class and status group can – and must – be isolated for examination at particular points in time.

THEORIES OF SOCIAL STRATIFICATION

This position can perhaps be clarified by reference to the two main theoretical approaches to social class and stratification which have emerged in the last century: those of the functionalist school and those of Marxist sociologists. [1] The functionalist view, which has been most popular among American theorists like Talcott Parsons and Kingsley Davis, is basically conservative and static. It starts from the assumption that social stratification is a necessary condition for maintaining the stability of the social structure and that a network of reciprocal class positions have an integrating function in societies based on the division of labour and on the unequal distribution of 'natural' talents. It also asserts that 'men have a sense of justice fulfilled and of virtue rewarded when they feel that they are fairly ranked as superior and inferior by the value standards of their own moral community'. [2] Class consciousness and class rivalries, on the other hand, are seen as having potential dysfunctions and even as being 'unjustified disturbance-symptoms' in society.

Marxist theories, by contrast, are more explicitly historical in emphasis and their viewpoint is dynamic. Thus, instead of accepting that the existing social structure is a given and unalterable fact to which particular forms of stratification must necessarily adapt themselves, Marxist theory asserts that it is the economic system that is primary and that particular legal, political and cultural systems arise only secondarily, in response to the structure of economic and social class relations. Class consciousness is fundamental to this theory (and welcomed), for it is seen as being the main agency by which individuals organize themselves to promote future social change.

Both of these theoretical schools have produced valuable insights into the workings of the system of social stratification but, as several critics have pointed out, neither of them is adequate on its own. It is questionable, for instance, whether the terms in which functionalists justify particular systems of stratification would command the assent of more than a tiny minority of the population for whom they are held to apply. Such an approach ignores the existence of conflicting evaluations, and overlooks the experience of the past century of working-class agitation. Indeed, as Cotgrove aptly comments, the main concern of the functionalist view has been to argue the necessity of unequal rewards for positions of unequal importance. It has failed to establish that differences of any specific magnitude are essential, and it has neglected to explore those sources of inequality which derive either from the organized efforts of individual groups to improve their shares or from the intervention of the political system in the distribution of rewards. [3] Marxist theories, however, also have their weaknesses. Not only have many of Marx's own specific predictions failed to come true, but the simple polarity between the owners of the means of production and those without access to property, which Marx suggested to be the basis of class consciousness and group action, ignores the considerable complexity (and contradictions) of competing class interests at all levels in society.

A more adequate theory of social stratification, then, must concern itself both with the static and with the dynamic historical aspects of social class relations. It must also add a psychological perspective, in order to describe 'the larger economic and political situation in terms of its meaning for the inner life and the external career of the individual'. [4] Finally, it must take into account the various separate dimensions of stratification — those based on prestige and social status, as well as those related to economic differences.

THE DIMENSIONS OF STRATIFICATION

As we saw in previous chapters, since the nineteenth century occupation has normally been taken as the main index of the individual's position in society. Recently, following Weber and T. H. Marshall, for example, sociologists have begun to react against a too exclusive insistence on social *class* and on economic criteria as the most central elements in the stratification system. They argue that social ranking is not always correlated with income or occupation but rests also on vaguer criteria associated with an individual's social *status*, his 'way of life', his social habits and manners, and his general pattern of consumption. Status ranking is not, however, in itself a new phenomenon. Status rivalry – particularly between the middle and upper classes – was already very prominent in Victorian Britain. The only difference is that today this rivalry has also extended to the working class, and it has been much more deliberately exploited.

The criteria of social status relate to several different hierarchies of prestige, each evaluated according to the individual's own particular standpoint and frame of reference (compare, for instance, the alternative hierarchies of the 'pop' world, of the academic community, of management executives, and so on). What is more, although they are closely related to social class criteria, the criteria of social status are not synonymous with them. Nor are class position and status position necessarily congruent for the individual (for example, whereas most manual working-class families adopt a traditional working-class way of life, others, with higher aspirations, emulate more typically middle-class patterns of consumption). In one respect, however, class and status do coincide, for both are prescribed by the distribution of power and authority in society. Thus, in general, lack of power (political or economic) implies a low or middle-class position and a corresponding status situation – such differences between class and status, as we have mentioned, being only marginal in this context.

The existence of three different modes of ranking and the wide range of alternative evaluative orders means that the individual's position in relation to the stratification system today is extremely complicated. [5] Indeed, as T. H. Marshall comments, we are witnessing 'the gradual replacement of a simple, clear and institutionalized structure by a complex, nebulous and largely informal one'. [6] Thus, in place of the simple dichotomy between working- and middle-class patterns of life, a whole range of alternative life styles has now been created whose rival attractions and advantages are persistently exploited by advertising men and by the mass media. These styles are also continually undergoing change.

Because of the complexity of the present-day pattern of stratification, then, the traditional way of looking at the division of society simply in terms of two or three major classes provides an increasingly inadequate picture of the situation which in fact exists. Within the various main class divisions it is possible to distinguish a whole variety of different groups, each with its own characteristic sub-cultural styles. Even in the nineteenth century, we must remember, the definition of social class posed considerable difficulties. Thus, in attempting to answer the question, 'Who were the Victorian middle class?' Kitson Clark rehearses many of the problems with which we shall be concerned in the analysis of contemporary social stratification. He points out that

Certain trades and functions were considered to be definitely middle class, but unfortunately opinion on this point altered as the century went forward ... Whether a man might be considered to be middle class might be decided by the education he had received, by the style of his life, by his manners, by the district in which he lived, by whether he went to church or chapel on Sunday, by the way he dressed, or by any number of possible tests some of which it would be quite impossible to recover. [7]

His conclusion, however, is that, despite the difficulty of achieving a precise and stable definition, the concept of the middle class was 'too important and significant to be abandoned, and too insignificant and subjective to be used with any comfort'. Virtually the same kind of statement could be made about contemporary definitions of social class. Nevertheless, as well as being significant in terms of individual life expectations and group patterns of conflict or co-operation, class is still significant to the sociologist because of its association with such factors as birth and death rates, marriage ages, family size, educational attainment and so on.

We have to begin therefore by recognizing that simple class labels do not tell us enough about the way the population is split up. 'Class' and 'status' are extremely complex phenomena based on a very wide cluster of attributes. Some conceptual clarification has emerged in recent sociological discussions of stratification, however, and with the help of computers more sensitive measurement techniques are gradually becoming available.

Among the new concepts that have been introduced to clarify the divisions within the major social classes (and in particular to distinguish the 'newer' from the 'older' occupational groups) are those used, for example, by Margaret Stacey. In her research in Banbury, Mrs Stacey found it useful to make a distinction between what she calls the 'traditionalists' and the 'non-traditionalists' [8] (a similar distinction is implied in Mogey's comparison of 'status assenters' and 'status dissenters'). [9] The former are defined (in both cases) as those who are part of the traditional social structure in a given community and who live by traditional values. They have a large proportion of geographically circumscribed marriages and a low rate of emigration. 'Non-traditionalists', on the other hand, are those who have no fixed roots and who have a tendency to be both socially and geographically more mobile. Using this broad categorization, Mrs Stacey located two main upper-class groups in Banbury: the 'county' and the 'gentry'; two middle-class groups: the 'burgesses' (local tradesmen, professionals and small business owners) and the 'spiralists' (persons engaged in professional and managerial work in large-scale organizations); and three working-class groups: the 'roughs', the 'ordinary' and the 'respectable'.

As we shall see, this kind of distinction between the different sub-groups within the main social strata is very useful, not only for diagnostic purposes but also because of the close links it reveals between class consciousness and political action, and between social aspirations, mobility and achievement. Within the major classes, however, and in different parts of the country, there are other equally important distinctions which might be made. These relate, for instance, to the prestige of different kinds of political and community commitments. Consider the status of two unskilled men, for example, one of whom has no outside interests and the other, as in an actual case quoted by Watson, who is chairman of the local branch of a national political party, a magistrate, a director of the football club, an elder of the church, owns his own home and has three children who have achieved a university education. [10] The label 'working class' is clearly inadequate in describing the social position of both of these men.

For the purposes of social planning, however, as well as in attempting to explore the way in which different individuals and groups respond, say, to the educational opportunities that are available in society, it is necessary to establish some kind of objectively measurable criteria of social status and a commonly agreed ranking order. Normally occupation has been chosen as the main criterion, although some sociologists like Lloyd Warner have used a combined index of status characteristics, linking occupation to area and type of residence and to income. [11] Recently market research firms have elaborated even more complex indices not only based on objective criteria like income and occupation but also related to spending and entertaining habits, leisure pursuits and various psychological characteristics (for example, flexibility, ambitiousness and extravagance). Until more satisfactory clustering techniques become generally available, however, there are several good reasons for sticking to occupation on its own. Not only is information about a person's job relatively easy to obtain (as compared with accurate details on income, for instance), but the difficulties of devising recognizable and generally acceptable occupational scales are fewer than is the case when evaluating the rank of particular residential neighbourhoods or the status of certain types of educational attainment. The evaluation of personality characteristics is, of course, even harder and, as yet, scarcely developed. There is the added advantage that occupation is, in any case, very closely linked to a large number of other factors, including income, educational background and residence. [12]

SCALES OF SOCIAL STRATIFICATION

Despite the practicality of choosing occupational criteria, the resulting ranking scales are not always entirely satisfactory – quite apart from the fact that they ignore the more subtle distinctions of status. On the fivefold occupational scale used by the Registrar General, for example, 51 per cent of the population in 1961 were assigned to Social Class III. [13] Inevitably, in such a large grouping, there were considerable differences between the levels of occupational skill represented within the group, as well as a wide range of types of job, both manual and non-manual.

The second type of classification used by the Registrar General provides a much better breakdown. It distinguishes specifically between agricultural and non-agricultural, manual and non-manual, supervisory and non-supervisory

	1931			1961	
Social class	*Occupation*	*Percentage*	*Socio-economic group*	*Occupation*	*Percentage*
I	Higher professional and managerial	2	1	Employers and managers, etc. large establishments	3·6
II	Intermediate non-manual	13	2	Employers and managers etc. small establishments	5·9
III	Skilled manual and routine non-manual	49	3	Professional workers – self employed	0·8
IV	Semi-skilled	18	4	Professional workers – employees	2·8
V	Unskilled	18	5	Intermediate non-manual workers	3·8
		100	6	Junior non-manual	12·5
			7	Personal service	0·9
			8	Foreman and supervisors – manual	3·3
			9	Skilled manual workers	30·4
			10	Semi-skilled manual workers	14·7
			11	Unskilled „ „	8·6
			12	Own account workers (not professional)	3.6
			13	Farmers – employers and managers	1·0
			14	Farmers – own account	1·0
			15	Agricultural workers	2·3
			16	Members armed forces	1·9
				Unclassified	2·9
					100

Classification of occupied males in England and Wales. After D. C. Marsh, 1965

occupations so that the resulting scale comprises sixteen separate socio-economic groups. But even with this degree of selectiveness, one group – that of the skilled manual workers – still contains almost one third of the total population. Again, therefore, there is considerable heterogeneity within the group. [14]

Once particular criteria of social class have been selected, the second major difficulty in mapping the pattern of stratification is that of devising an acceptable scale. There are several problems here. In the first place, the ranking of occupations in terms of their prestige (even assuming that everyone agreed on this procedure, which is not necessarily the case) does not correspond exactly to their ranking in terms of income or education. [15] And although these three factors are normally fairly closely related, other variables (birth, for example, or inborn qualities, such as physical appearance and skin colour, or personal authority) are also important.

Among the most prominent assumptions which seem to affect status perceptions and status evaluation, Theodore Caplow notes the following:

1 White collar work is superior to manual work
2 Self-employment is superior to employment by others
3 Clean occupations are superior to dirty ones
4 The importance of business occupations depends on the size of the business
5 Personal service is degrading and it is better to be employed by an enterprise that to be employed in the same work by a person. [16]

These, of course, are middle-class assumptions, and this means that most of the scales which are in use today tend to perpetuate a view of society which is not necessarily consistent with the view that would be taken by the majority of the population.

One of the most systematic attempts which has been made to test the acceptability of a particular ranking scale was that carried out by Moser and Hall in preparation for the various surveys of social mobility conducted by David Glass and his team. [17] Not surprisingly, the researchers found that there was a fairly wide measure of agreement over the ranking of occupations at the extremes of their scale. Thus, more than four-fifths of the sample agreed on the grades which should be allocated to the medical officer of health, the company director, the dock labourer and the roadsweeper. And for about half of the occupations listed at least 60 per cent of the sample were in agreement. Occupations like fitter, coal hewer, civil servant, minister, actor, policeman and school teacher, on the other hand, showed a very wide spread of views. In the case of such occupations as civil servant and actor, the lack of consensus was perhaps justified, in view of the wide range of jobs which may be included under these titles. In the case of some of the other jobs over which respondents disagreed, real differences in status perceptions seem to have been in operation.

Such differences were certainly evident in the survey which Willmott and Young carried out among a working-class sample in East London. [18] Their respondents fell into two categories: the so-called 'normal' and the 'deviants'. Among the latter, who formed about a quarter of the total, there was a marked tendency for skilled manual jobs to be elevated in status while certain marginal non-manual occupations were lowered. The reasons for this, the authors suggest, is that in their evaluations the 'deviants' overestimated 'social contribution', at the expense of other criteria like 'ability', 'education', 'remuneration' and 'social milieu'. Here we see the operation of a particular kind of working-class ideology and of what sociologists call the 'halo effect' − i.e. the tendency to exaggerate the importance of one's own position or that of others who are similarly placed at the expense of groups who are seen, rightly or wrongly, to be more distant (it should be remembered that the distortion in perception which this example reveals is not necessarily greater than that which affects middle-class research workers).

SUBJECTIVE ASSESSMENTS OF SOCIAL STRATIFICATION

In an effort to overcome some of the difficulties involved in working with occupational scales, and because no single standard seems to fit everyone or to be agreed upon by all of the population, some sociologists have abandoned the use of objective criteria. Instead, or in addition, they have asked their respondents to assess their own class position – and sometimes that of their neighbours as well. This has proved particularly helpful in trying to distinguish between those who belong to the upper-working class from those who are lower-middle class – groups which together add up to almost half of the total population. But there are disadvantages with this method, too. In the first place, people's responses are likely to depend on the number and names of the alternative ranks among which they are told to locate themselves. There is a big difference, for example, between offering the choice 'upper, middle and *lower*', as against 'upper, middle and *working*' – and also between either of these scales and one comprising 'aristocracy, bourgeoisie and proletariat', or the more complicated 'upper-upper, lower-upper, upper-middle . . .' type of scale. A further difficulty is that of knowing whether two people who assess themselves as belonging to a particular class regard the term as meaning the same thing. For instance, a school teacher may assign herself to the middle class and think of it as consisting of educated, well-spoken, non-manual workers, while a car assembly worker does the same thing on the grounds that he considers anyone who earns over £1,000 a year to be middle class. The third difficulty is that of bias and upgrading. A *Socialist Commentary* survey, for example, found that 47 per cent of objectively described working-class Conservatives thought of themselves as middle class, and so did 30 per cent of working-class Labour supporters. [19]

The way in which class perspectives vary according to the distance between the respondent and the groups of people whose position he is being asked to assess is dealt with very fully by Williams in his study of the North Country village of Gosforth. This investigation confirms the very wide margin of distortion which exists in judgements of marginal status – i.e. of those immediately above or below an individual on the social scale. Thus, whereas the upper-upper class in Gosforth saw themselves as the 'better class', ranking their immediate inferiors, the lower-upper class, as 'social climbers', the members of the lower-upper class considered themselves to be 'ambitious, go-ahead people', in contrast with the upper-uppers who, they said, 'have more breeding than sense'. [20]

Elizabeth Bott offers an explanation of how this kind of distortion comes about. Her suggestion is that

> there are three steps in an individual's creation of a class reference group: first, he internalizes the norms of his primary membership groups – place of work, colleagues, friends, neighbourhood, family – together with other notions assimilated from books and the various mass media; second, he performs an act of conceptualization in reducing these relatively unconnected and often contradictory norms to a common denominator; third, he projects his conceptualization back on to society at large. [21]

In other words, the individual himself is an active agent in this process of class assessment. He does not simply internalize the norms of classes that have an independent existence. He takes in the norms of certain actual groups, especially his own and those close to him, evaluates them on the basis of the kinds of relationship they involve him in, and then constructs a hierarchy of wider reference groups.

We shall return to the discussion of reference groups and subjective perceptions of status, but meanwhile we need to consider the actual differences in income and social status which exist between the various social strata in England today.

INCOMES AND OCCUPATIONS SINCE 1945

Goldthorpe and Lockwood, in their analysis of 'Affluence and the British Class Structure', [22] point to four main areas of change in the pattern of social stratification in the last century: the gap separating property-owning groups and manual wage-earners has been reduced; the range of differentiation in income and wealth has narrowed; mobility – both within and between the various social classes – has increased; and differences in consumption standards have been blurred.

Several factors, both economic and social, have been responsible for these changes. Continuing material prosperity, 'full' employment, the techniques of mass production and mass distribution, and the development of the social welfare services have been of major importance, together with various fiscal measures like the extension of hire purchase facilities and a more redistributive tax policy. Better education, the spread of advertising and the mass media, holidays with pay, and greater leisure time have also contributed significantly.

Despite the overall improvement in social conditions and the narrowing of extreme differences in wealth and opportunity, however, some groups of the population are still relatively much less privileged than others. In fact the statistics of income and capital distribution reveal marked differences between the various social levels. Let us, therefore, look at the evidence on 'equalization' more carefully.

The information which we have on income differentials between the various social classes does at first sight suggest a certain amount of levelling – especially between the lower grades of white collar workers and some skilled manual groups. For instance, in 1960 weekly paid clerical workers were averaging about a shilling a week less than adult manual workers (the average

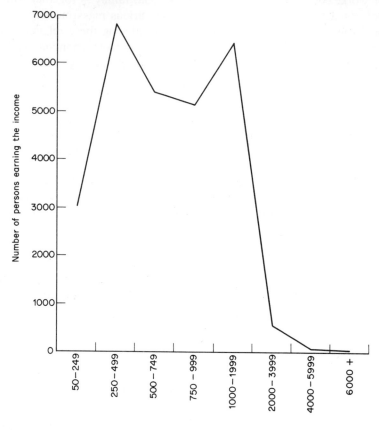

Fig. 13 Distribution of personal incomes in the United Kingdom, 1966. (See also Table 20, p. 327.) After Board of Inland Revenue statistics.

for monthly paid clerical workers was, on the other hand, higher than for all except the very highest paid manual workers). These statistics, however, do not tell the full story. [23] It is important to remember that figures on income differentials take no account of such trends as the rise in the proportion of married people, the increasing number of working wives, the decline of unemployment, the larger average family size of the working class and the higher wages of juveniles. Because of these factors, despite an overall improvement in the real standard of living (between 1938 and 1958, for example, the authors of the Crowther Report estimated an improvement of about 10 per cent per head in the real standard of living), the relative positions of the working and middle classes were virtually unchanged. The persisting inequality between occupational groups is underlined by other longer-term comparisons. Thus, while unskilled workers received approximately 19 per cent of the average earnings of higher professional workers in 1913–14, in 1960 they earned 26 per cent. They earned 31 per cent of the average income of managers in the earlier period but only 29 per cent in 1960.

The statistics of capital ownership reveal an even more striking disparity. Less than 10 per cent of the population owns 80 per cent of all private wealth in Britain, the richest one per cent of these receiving over 12 per cent of the total incomes. At the other end of the scale, one third of all income units have no liquid assets at all.' But it is not only in an economic sense that these differences are important. The possession of capital confers other advantages, freeing the individual from many of the hazards of life which most ordinary people face. It allows the best possible education and professional training. It also confers security and the freedom to take risks, as well as permitting a wider range of choice between occupations and between work and leisure.

The present-day tax structure does little to remedy inequalities in personal wealth. There is, to be sure, a net distribution in favour of the less well-to-do. And some of the more notorious manipulations of the tax system occur only among those in the highest ranks of surtax. But the total effect of perquisites like a company car and telephone bills paid, of tax avoidance and of tax relief subsidies to owner-occupiers, is to reinforce the inequalities of class between manual and non-manual workers. [24]

If the upper classes are still conspicuously better off in all these respects, at least the proportion of the population living in poverty has diminished to some extent since the time of Booth, as we have seen in our discussion of Beveridge and the Rowntree surveys. Using the standard of 40 per cent above National Assistance rates as a measure of minimum subsistence, Townsend estimated that in 1964 three million members of families whose head was in full-time work, two and half million persons of pensionable age, three-quarters of a million fatherless families, three-quarters of a million chronic sick or disabled and over half a million families of unemployed fathers, were in poverty. This amounts to about 14 per cent of the total population. By *basic* National Assistance standards about one third of these groups were in acute poverty. Yet many of them, for reasons of pride or ignorance, failed to take advantage of all of the benefits to which they were entitled under the National Assistance Act. Despite their greater objective needs, these poorer groups often fail to get their fair share of other kinds of allowances as well. Thus, only a very small proportion of families entitled to rent rebates actually obtain them. And nearly half of the children eligible for free school meals in fact pay for them. These families also make fewer demands on the National Health Service and derive fewer returns from the State educational system. [25]

These statistics on income distribution reveal a state of affairs which is very much at variance with the view that 'we are all equal now'. The narrowing of differences in economic terms between the main social classes has not been as extensive as many people – middle and working class alike – seem to believe. John Westergaard sums up the situation by suggesting that inequalities 'have only been marginally reduced'. However, since they operate in areas of expenditure increasingly removed from those of bare subsistence living, and against a background of generally rising levels of real income, their effect is 'less transparent'. [26]

CONSUMPTION AND SOCIAL STATUS SINCE 1945

A part of this reduced 'transparency' can be accounted for in terms of new consumption standards. Mark Abrams, writing in 1959, summarized the main changes in consumer spending as follows:

> Much more money is now being spent on household goods. The proportion of families with a vacuum cleaner has doubled, ownership of refrigerators has trebled, owners of washing machines have increased tenfold; we have stocked our homes with vastly more furniture, radiograms, carpets, space heaters, water heaters, armchairs, light fittings, lawn mowers, television sets, and now tape recorders and film projectors . . . And all this means that for the first time in modern British history the working-class home, as well as the middle-class home, has become a place that is warm, comfortable . . . in fact, pleasant to live in. [27]

That was over ten years ago. Not only is the contrast with the pre-war period quite remarkable, but since then the consumer bonanza has continued unabated, and its products have spread even wider through the community. Whether we can infer from this that 'we are all middle class now' is, however, highly debatable, for incomes and consumption do not constitute the whole of the economic aspect of class, nor do they alone signify a particular social status, as Brian Jackson points out. 'Almost everyone shops sometimes at Marks and Spencer,' he says; furthermore, 'almost everybody might have the same washing powder in their kitchen. Four million people might buy the *Daily Mirror* one morning, ten million might watch a big programme on ITV that evening.' However,

> if the crucial element in class is income and work, it is hard to see how using the same mass products as people more prosperous and powerful than yourself breaks the class barriers . . . the merest glance at half-a-dozen of the major London stores – Harrods, Heals, Liberty's, Selfridges, John Lewis, C and A, tells you that they reflect, serve, and perhaps reinforce quite different social groups. [28]

So, although the mass market in goods and entertainment has undoubtedly lifted standards within the working class and has sometimes made us all own identical objects, it has not had anything to do with dissolving class or status differences. Similarly, although television, for example, has offered an entirely new range of experiences to the working-class community – experiences which they can share with other groups in the population – we cannot conclude that the use made of television is identical in all social classes, or that it has created equality.

The bulk of the evidence which has been used to support the thesis of working-class 'embourgeoisement' (that is, the adoption by the working class of middle-class standards and styles of living) is based on the various studies of community rehousing which we mentioned in the last chapter. According to Goldthorpe and Lockwood, what such surveys stress is that

> in these new communities working-class life is no longer characterized, as it was in the old, by its intimacy and gregariousness . . . Having been torn away from their former tightly-knit networks of kinship and neighbour-hood relations, families tend to keep themselves to themselves; and in place of a sense of communal solidarity there is, rather, a pervasive concern with status distinctions. A home-centred society emerges . . . At the same time, moreover, attitudes towards work and money also change . . . As he becomes more affluent [the worker] becomes more security minded, less prone to expenditure of an unplanned and extravagant kind. [29]

Such changes do not necessarily indicate any widespread adoption by the working class of middle-class norms and aspirations – except perhaps in the area of consumer spending. Rather, the traditional working-class sub-culture which was associated with life in the now declining areas of heavy industry has gradually been modified to meet the needs of a new environment. Even in the inter-war period a fair proportion of working-class families were already living in better homes and in less cohesive communities. Today, the majority – in most parts of the country – share these conditions.

On the new estates some of the old, 'rough' behaviour patterns have been abandoned. The alternative values which have emerged – respect for privacy and pride in one's home and children, for example – are not entirely new values to the working class. They simply take on new significance in a more 'home-centred' society. Differences between working-class and middle-class families remain. Indeed, it is striking that certain characteristic patterns of middle-class behaviour which might have been expected to become established on the new estates have not – at least so far – made any appearance in this country. Despite better home surroundings, for instance, there is little evidence of working-class family entertaining, and a marked lack of support for joining formal community organizations. On the whole, working-class residents have not emerged as leaders or activists, nor have they developed nursery schools and play groups, baby-minding pools, women's guilds, bridge parties and other essentially middle-class institutions. The retention of strong links with 'Mum' and the relatively high degree of contact between members of the old and new generations − even when they live quite far apart − is further evidence of the continued strength of shared working-class loyalties, certainly among the 'traditionalists'.

More damaging evidence against the thesis of 'embourgeoisement' is perhaps the complete collapse of schemes for mixed communities. As we remarked in the previous chapter, status distinctions tend to be exaggerated, not reduced, on the new estates. And even in communities where families of different classes do live in close proximity, there is little evidence of any degree of close contact between them; quite the reverse. Thus, even the upwardly aspiring 'status dissenters' among the working class, although they may successfully imitate middle-class consumption patterns, are not seen to be 'middle class' by their professional neighbours and are rarely invited into their homes. Nor are they seen as equals at work. Indeed, class distinctions as expressed in the works-staff relationship remain fundamental.

We have already commented on inequalities of income between white collar workers and those in manual occupations. These are reinforced by unequal opportunities in respect of hours and conditions of work, prospects for promotion and for improvement in wages, the risk of unemployment, retirement and pension schemes, fringe concessions and tax remissions from the Exchequer. In the ordinary amenities of eating, washing, ventilation, noise and so on, workers also tend to get a worse deal. Thus, as Harvey Swados points out, even if the worker 'earns like the middle class, votes like the middle class, dresses like the middle class, dreams like the middle class', there is one thing that the worker doesn't do like the middle class:

> he works like a worker. The steel-mill puddler does not yet sort memos, the coal miner does not yet sit in conferences, the cotton millhand does not yet sip martinis from his lunchbox. [30]

A closer look at the evidence on 'embourgeoisement', then, does not support the thesis of a complete merging between the middle and working classes. There are still important economic distinctions between the two groups and these have wider social and psychological implications. Working-class families, lacking capital or any substantial chances for improving their earnings and still subject to the recurring cycles of poverty that Rowntree classically analysed (for example, during the years of family building and in old age), must turn to each other for help. This is the basis of their solidarity (whether they actually perceive their relationships self-consciously or not), and it has no parallel in the middle class. Communal ties are also strengthened in other ways.

> The working-class family is less mobile, less 'national', than others. Their jobs, opportunities and aspirations make them stick to the local scene . . .

customarily the working-class man has less access to forms of long distance communication. He does not have a telephone, and may be ill-at-ease using one. Coming from an oral tradition, and with a background over many generations of second-class education, he is not a letter-writer. [31]

For all these reasons, working-class families are bound to their neighbourhood, to wider kin and to other working-class families in a way that is simply not the case for members of the middle class.

'LIFE CHANCES' OF DIFFERENT SOCIAL GROUPS

Not only do middle- and working-class families differ generally from each other in terms of their economic situation and their relational patterns, but their 'life chances' also vary. Differences in infant mortality, for instance, are still quite marked, although since 1960 regional differences have become more significant than those based on social class alone. In 1950 the infant mortality rate was 16·9 per 1,000 in Social Class I, while in Social Classes IV and V the comparable rates were 31·7 and 36·0 respectively. But by 1965 this margin had been considerably reduced. The neonatal death rate [32] was 9·2 per 1,000 for Social Classes I and II combined, compared with a rate of 13·2 for Social Classes IV and V. Only in the Northern region did the traditional type of social class gradient exist, showing statistically significant differences between each of the social class groups. Elsewhere in the country the effects of poverty in maintaining social class differences in infant mortality appear, for the first time, to have been seriously weakened. [33]

Infectious diseases in childhood, and morbidity and mortality rates in general, show parallel social class and regional variations, just as they did in the 1840s or 1910s or 1930s. They also reveal changing and socially mobile fashions in treatment and diagnosis. [34] These variations hinge on the whole pattern of living of the different social classes. Since these patterns are changing, so is the incidence of disease. The development of preventive measures like sanitation, vaccination and immunization, improved living standards and nutrition, school and factory inspection, advances in curative medicine and surgery, and more effective drugs and antibiotics, have all been important in reducing the overall incidence of deaths from infectious diseases and from degenerative organic conditions. But because of changing working conditions, the faster pace of life in contemporary society and changed eating, transport and leisure habits there has been an increase in deaths from other kinds of illness. Among middle-aged, middle-class males, for example, deaths from cardio-vascular diseases and from cancer have increased considerably.

While there have been great changes in the treatment and care of the mentally ill in recent years significant social class differences remain here, too. One American study, for instance, suggested that the incidence of schizophrenia in the lowest social class was ten times that in the highest social class. [35] Whether or not it was actually schizophrenia from which all of these patients were suffering is questionable, for there appears to be a considerable amount of middle-class bias in doctors' diagnostic assessments. But, whatever the diagnosis, there is no doubt that chronic sickness is more prevalent in the lower social groups. It is also interesting to note that the lower down the social scale one goes, the higher is the number of mental patients who are referred to hospital by courts and probation officers and the fewer the number of 'self selecting' patients. The kind of treatment which is available for the mentally ill is also likely to depend on social class. Thus, middle- and upper-class patients can usually resort to private care, either in an institution or through personal therapy, while working-class patients have to make do with the over-crowded and often old-fashioned State-run hospitals which may in fact confirm and exacerbate their illness rather than cure it. [36]

According to many sociologists today who reject the medical illness analogy, mental illness is just as much a form of deviance as are the more obvious kinds of crime and deliquency. Moreover, it often grows out of the same conditions – some kind of breakdown in the individual's primary group relations – that is, the conditions of 'anomie'. Not surprisingly, then, crime and deliquency again show characteristic social patterns – in relation to both the kinds of offences committed and the forms of treatment (or punishment) imposed. Thus, whereas most working-class offences are offences against property, 'white-collar crimes' include tax evasion, fraud and – most prominent of all – motoring offences. [37] And while the majority of working-class 'criminals' are sent to prison or put on probation, many middle-class 'offenders' are either fined or sent off with a recommendation to take a rest or look for psychiatric help.

STATUS DIFFERENCES

In all of these respects, then, we have clear evidence of the persisting influence of social class differences. We shall be referring in the next two chapters to further differences – in respect of educational opportunities and child-rearing practices – both of which add to the picture of fundamental social divisions which we have been describing. But how are these divisions perceived by various groups in society today and what are their implications for political action and possible social conflict?

As we have seen, most of the earlier gross inequalities between the different social classes have been eliminated in the last twenty-five years – except in the case of a minority of very rich and very poor families at the two extremes of the scale. More subtle status differences remain very much in evidence, however. Willmott and Young attribute this to the fact that 'the nearer the classes are drawn by the objective facts of income, style of life and housing, the more are middle-class people liable to pull them apart by exaggerating the differences subjectively regarded'. [38] Differences in dress, speech, entertaining habits and social manners, patterns of leisure activities and the preference for various brands of consumer goods are all capable of being exploited in this way – as the advertising men have learnt to their advantage. Consider simply the effect of language differences, for example. T. H. Pear stresses the importance of the choice of words and phrases, accent, intonation, sentence structure and gesture made by different groups. Each class, he claims, 'uses characteristic terms of approval, disapproval, intimacy, endearment, enthusiasm and boredom, and each ignores or ridicules the choice of others'. [39]

Social differences in the form of material 'status symbols' are also prominent in our society today. Caplow, for instance, draws attention to the kinds of visible appurtenances available to various grades of personnel in the executive hierarchy of a large American chemicals company. This is the company's guide to brief cases and desks:

Brief cases   Top dogs: None – they ask the questions.
                  V.I.P.s: Use backs of envelopes.
                  Brass: Someone goes along to carry theirs.
                  No.2s: Carry their own – empty.
                  Eager beavers: Daily carry their own – filled with work.
                  Hoi-polloi: Too poor to own one.
Office desks   Top dogs: Custom made (to order).
                  V.I.P.s: Executive style (to order).
                  Brass: Type A 'Director'.
                  No.2s: Type B 'Manager'.
                  Eager beavers: Cast-offs from No.2s.
                  Hoi-polloi: Yellow Oak. [40]

Such a list may seem almost quaint to the English reader, but these kinds of status symbol have their equivalents in this country – not least in the Civil Service and in the public corporations.

CLASS, STATUS AND POWER

Subjective status distinctions, then, as well as differences in external circumstances, still exist as a barrier between the working and middle classes – and to a lesser extent between the middle and upper classes. Indeed, it is perhaps only in relation to the hierarchy of power that there are still grounds for doubting the importance of working-class/middle-class distinctions. Although the middle class may have more power in, say, the sense of being free to choose whether or not to purchase a private education for their children or private medical care, ultimately their position in relation to the vital issues of national economic and political strategy is very similar to that of the working class. In fact, the opposition between those in possession of the instruments of power (that is, the owners of the means of production) and those without – highlighted by Marx in the *Communist Manifesto* in 1848 – has remained virtually unaltered in the twentieth century, even though there have been very far-reaching changes in almost every other area of social life.

It is true that we now have universal suffrage. We also have formal equality for men and women before the law. The various services organized under the Welfare State, including education and health, are also available equally to all members of society – even if they are not always equally used. In the industrial situation, however, power is very far from being equally distributed. Nor is it, as we shall see in the final chapter, in political terms.

There are of course many ways in which non-manual workers are more closely associated with the running of industry than are men on the shop floor. When it comes to major policy decisions, though, they have no more influence over what happens in a particular enterprise – either to themselves or to other grades of employees – than do manual workers. Indeed they may even have less since they are less likely to belong to a trade union or to a professional association which might be able to bring pressure to bear on their employers. Or, if they are members of such bodies, they may – by virtue of the kind of work they do – find it more difficult to take effective action.

Since 1945 a number of different kinds of attempt have been made to redress this imbalance in the industrial hierarchy. But workers' control on, for example, the Yugoslavian model and joint participation on management councils are still the exception in British industry and, as we have seen, even where they exist the role of the workers' representatives has usually been limited to the discussion of questions of discipline and working conditions. They have not, for example, given workers the right to choose their managers or directors. Nor has nationalization produced any dramatic changes in this respect. Indeed, it may have made communication between the bosses and workers more difficult. Because of the principle of 'ministerial accountability' and the remoteness of Civil Service administration, for instance, the process of decision-making has been retarded and the scope for delegation of authority much reduced.

None of these changes in industrial organization, therefore, has altered the fundamental power structure. They have merely had the effect of institutionalizing the conflict between competing interests and provided more apparently democratic means of conciliation. But if the power of the industrial capitalist and of the anonymous company board is still paramount, that of the trade unions has also increased. As we have seen, many important concessions have been won for trade union members. However, the extent to which trade unions are capable of exercising real power is ultimately quite circumscribed. It is true that their presence in wages and productivity negotiations provides a countervailing source of influence. The intervention of 'respectable' trade union pressure groups in the different stages of political decision-making may also serve to check the worst abuses of autocratic power, as they have done since, in particular, 1867. Yet even the authority of the government is not always supreme. Often its policies have to be modified in the light of the interests of strong commercial and financial groups, and occasionally, as in the campaign for the establishment of I.T.V., it is defeated by them. [41]

Although the overall distribution of power in this country has not altered to any great extent in the twentieth century, people's perceptions of social class relations do seem to have changed. Most people appear to believe that 'we are all middle class now'. On the other hand, among some middle- and upper-class groups it is felt that the hitherto subjected classes – workers and immigrant minorities – now constitute a 'threat' in political and economic terms. [42] Such perceptions not only ignore the actual distribution of wealth and power in society today, they also fail to take into account the balance of political allegiances between the two major social classes.

As we have seen, objective social class and the individual's own perception of where he feels himself to belong in the social hierarchy do not necessarily coincide. It follows that the dominant and subjected classes of industry need no longer be part of the corresponding political classes. Indeed, for class consciousness to develop at all a number of factors are necessary: a sense of common identity, a distinctive sub-culture of shared beliefs and values and, more importantly, a concerted and organized political programme of action directed towards the pursuit of the group's common interests. We witnessed the growth of the labour movement in the late nineteenth and early twentieth centuries in precisely these terms. What seems increasingly to be happening at present, however, is that this kind of *class* consciousness is declining in favour of more complex and subtle forms of *status* consciousness. At the same time, party politics are becoming less an expression of fundamental class antagonisms and more orientated towards 'tension management' and consensus.

To try to link voting behaviour to social class, and to construe from this relationship facts about the relative distribution of power between different groups in society, may have some historical relevance (although research on nineteenth-century voting behaviour is very little advanced). In the altered circumstances of contemporary society, however, it is totally misleading. [43] Voting behaviour is, in fact, determined by many different and sometimes arbitrary and conflicting pressures, among which accident and habit are probably not much less important than ideological commitment or economic self-interest (witness the large proportion of working-class conservatives). Objective social class background is not a systematic variable. Nor do political allegiances remain constant over long periods of time as they used to do (witness the large number of so-called 'floating voters' in recent national elections). [44]

SOCIAL CONFLICT AND SOCIAL CHANGE

We have seen that the phenomena of class, status and power in contemporary society are full of complexity and often seeming contradictions. Not surprisingly, therefore, sociological interpretations of what these phenomena add up to represent a wide range of different ideological views. Some of these are more or less explicit, as in the case of the opposition between functionalist and Marxist theories of social stratification which we outlined at the beginning of this chapter. Others are less easily identifiable. Whatever the differences in viewpoint on this subject, however, two themes are common: that of equalization and that of political domination, and the real or apparent consequences which can be adduced from these.

It would appear, superficially, that those arguing in favour of the view that the sharp dichotomy between the major classes has been replaced in the twentieth century by a growing tendency towards equality have had the better of the argument so far. [45] Certainly, as we have already suggested, a large proportion of British people are themselves apparently prepared to assent to the proposition that 'we are all middle class now'. They would presumably also feel that we live in a fully democratic society. But as we have shown, despite the obvious real improvements in the standard of living which have occurred during the last century, distinctions between the various social strata remain. This being the case, theories of working-class embourgeoisement seem rather to have missed the point. Such theories are also based on very dubious historical comparisons, as Lockwood points out:

> The contrast between the 'poverty' of the pre-war and the prosperity of the post-war manual wage-labourer, between an earlier class solidarity and a new class fluidity, between radicalism then and conservatism now, is a superficial contrast, not only because it deals with an undifferentiated working class, but also because it fails to take into account the social as well as the economic determinants of working-class consciousness. [46]

If, however, there has not been a merging between the two main social classes, what have in fact been the effects of greater affluence and the growing power of the labour movement? Here again there are a number of alternative theories. Goldthorpe and Lockwood, for instance, argue in favour of a view of 'independent convergence', which they characterize as follows:

> On the side of the working-class, twenty years of near full employment, the gradual erosion of the traditional work-based community, the progressive bureaucratization of trade unionism and the institutionalization of industrial conflict, have all operated in the same direction to reduce the solidary nature of communal attachments and collective action. At the same time, there has been greater scope so far as expenditure, use of leisure time and general levels of aspiration are concerned. Within the white-collar group, on the other hand, a trend in the opposite direction has been going

on. Under conditions of rising prices, increasingly large-scale units of bureaucratic administration and reduced chances of upward 'career' mobility, lower level white-collar workers, at any rate, have now become manifestly less attached to an unqualified belief in the virtues of 'individualism' and more prone to collective, trade union action. [47]

If this analysis is correct, if there has in some respects been a convergence between those on the borders between the working and middle classes, and if industrial conflicts have been insulated from the sphere of politics (for example, through new forms of arbitration and consultation), this in itself does not imply an *identity* of class interests and experiences. Nor can it be taken as evidence of the complete identification of the working class with existing society. Manual workers still see themselves as being different from non-manual groups and are still treated differently by the latter. What is more, the ways in which they view society also tend to be different. Non-manual workers describe the stratification system in terms of levels of strata up which it is possible (and desirable) to move through individual effort. Among manual workers, on the other hand, it is usually seen as being dichotomous (*them* and *us*). [48] Consequently, for manual workers any major improvement in their social position can only come about through concerted group action. This being the case, the theory that we have now reached the 'end of ideology' must also be discarded.

It is true that new political issues have emerged in the last twenty years which are in some measure detached from the class issue: urban traffic problems, State patronage of the arts, homosexuality, abortion and divorce, for example. But these cannot be taken to imply the collapse of issues related to competing power interests. As Dahrendorf points out, 'there still are dichotomies', as between bosses and workers, black and white, educated and non-educated, developed and underdeveloped nations, 'and they are very real to those who experience society in terms of them'. [49] The interests of subjected groups still find expression in radical ideologies and are still the subject of very dramatic public demonstrations.

How do these conflicts relate to social class conflict? It is clear that the simple polarity of interests between bourgeoisie and proletariat has been very much modified in the twentieth century, both as a result of growing material prosperity and as a result of the intervention of the State in industrial relations and in social welfare. Because of these changes Dahrendorf suggests a reformulation of Marxist theory in terms of competing 'role interests'. [50] These, he says, are not to be seen as having the same character as class interests. Indeed, the two will only join in a situation where one class has a monopoly of access to opportunity, thus creating the need for concerted opposition. Because no such complete monopoly of power exists today, at least in Dahrendorf's own view, individuals can be expected to struggle on their own; for instance, by getting higher educational qualifications, without the aid of formal organizations. Through lack of use these same organizations will tend to fragment and lose their power. Thus, the class war will 'go off the boil'. And because social change can only be a product of class conflict or of institutional conflict, and not of limited individual role conflicts, the resulting condition will be one of social and political stagnation. This, in Dahrendorf's opinion, is the current situation, both in Britain and in the United States.

In some respects this account of contemporary social relations rings true. It explains perhaps the existence of intense short-range status rivalry ('keeping up with the Joneses') [51] and it would also account for the presence of large numbers of uncommitted voters in the electorate, the convergence of the two major political parties, and the general mood of apathy among rank and file trade-union members. On the other hand, Dahrendorf's analysis seems to ignore some of the very real political divisions which do still exist in British society – if only latently. It also fails to recognize some of the more hidden sources of potential conflict. Here we can look to Marcuse's theory for further elucidation. He starts where Dahrendorf's argument stops – namely with the absence or, as Marcuse sees it, the impossibility of class conflict in modern society. Marcuse's picture is of a monolithic set of political and economic institutions which coerce both bourgeoisie and proletariat alike, and which eliminate any possible 'outside' point of reference from which conflict or change can be generated. In his chapter on 'One-Dimensional Society', for example, Marcuse suggests that

> culture, politics, and the economy merge into an omnipresent system which swallows up or repulses all alternatives. The productivity and growth potential of this system stabilize the society and contain technical progress within the framework of domination. [52]

But if Marcuse's theory is correct – and it is certainly important as a demonstration of the least visible and most subtly coercive forms of power in modern society – there is a sense in which it has itself now become a pretext for future social change. The strategies adopted in 1968, for example, by the German Student Socialist League (S.D.S.) and by the students in Paris, were formulated as an explicit response to what Marcuse discusses in terms of 'integration'. By providing an ideology which united such disparate groups as trade unionists, university students and various left-wing activist organizations in a combined struggle against political domination and oppression of every kind, his theory has helped to provide a renewed impetus to social conflict. It has regenerated a sense of political consciousness still largely, although not exclusively, based on the consciousness of class relationships (students, for example, are not a social class), and it has promoted a new sense of urgency (at least among some groups of the population) in the pursuit of social change.

Here we find ourselves with a very concrete example of the link between historical and sociological facts and ideology; an example which would confirm Lucien Goldmann's view that social theory 'is not made from without but from within society'. It is a part of the intellectual life of that society and, through it, of social life as a whole. Hence 'to the selfsame extent to which thought is part of social life, its very development transforms that social life itself'. [53]

NOTES

1 See further R. BENDIX and S. LIPSET (eds.) *Class, Status and Power* (New York, 1953), Pt I 'Theories of class structure'.

2 BERNARD BARBER *Social Stratification*, p. 7 (New York, 1957).

3 *The Science of Society*, pp. 235–7.

4 C. WRIGHT MILLS *White Collar*, p. xx (New York, 1951).

5 See WILLIAMS *The Long Revolution*, pp. 343–63 (1963 edition), for a discussion of contemporary ways of thinking about 'class'.

6 *Sociology at the Crossroads*, p. 132 (London, 1963).

7 *The Making of Victorian England*, p. 119.

8 *Tradition and Change*, Ch. 8 (London, 1960). These terms originate from W. WATSON 'Social mobility and social class in industrial communities', in MAX GLUCKMAN (ed.) *Closed Systems and Open Minds* (Edinburgh and London, 1964).

9 *Family and Neighbourhood* (London, 1956).

10 'Social mobility and social class in industrial communities', p. 142.

11 *Social Class in America* (New York, 1960).

12 See MARGARET STACEY *Tradition and Change*, p. 150, for a table giving some distinctive characteristics of class and status groups and relating education, occupation, source of income, social circles and verbal patterns.

13 The distribution of the population between the other social classes in 1961 was as follows: Class I, 4 per cent; Class II, 15 per cent; Class IV, 21 per cent; and Class V, 9 per cent.

14 For a further discussion of occupational scales, see ALBERT J. REISS *et al. Occupations and Social Status* (New York, 1961).

15 See further PETER M. BLAU and OTIS DUDLEY DUNCAN *The American Occupational Structure*, Ch. 2 (New York, 1967).

16 *The Sociology of Work*, pp. 42–9 (New York, 1964 edition).

17 DAVID GLASS (ed.) *Social Mobility in Britain*, Ch. 2 (London, 1954).

18 'Social grading by manual workers', *British Journal of Sociology*, December 1956.

19 Quoted in MARK ABRAMS *et al. Must Labour Lose?*, p. 79 (Harmondsworth, 1960).

20 *The Sociology of an English Village*, pp. 107–9 (London, 1956).

21 *Family and Social Network*, p. 167 (London, 1957).

22 *The Sociological Review*, Vol. 11, 1963. See also JOHN H. GOLDTHORPE *et al. The Affluent Worker in the Class Structure* (Cambridge, 1969). For a review of American findings, see GAVIN MACKENZIE 'The economic dimensions of embourgeoisement', *British Journal of Sociology*, Vol. 18, 1967.

23 See further JOHN WESTERGAARD 'The withering away of class: a contemporary

myth', in PERRY ANDERSON and ROBIN BLACKBURN (eds.) *Towards Socialism* (London, 1965).

24　See further RICHARD TITMUSS *Income Distribution and Social Change* (London, 1962).

25　See further TITMUSS *Essays on 'The Welfare State'*, Ch. 2.

26　'The withering away of class', p. 84.

27　'The home-centred society', *The Listener*, 26 November 1959.

28　*Working Class Community*, p. 164.

29　'Not so bourgeois after all', *New Society*, 18 October 1962.

30　'The happy worker', in STEIN *et al.* (eds.) *Identity and Anxiety*, p. 199.

31　JACKSON *Working Class Community*, p. 156.

32　That is, deaths at birth and during the first week of life. Post-neonatal deaths are those occurring for the remainder of the first year of life. The infant mortality rate is equal to neonatal plus post-neonatal deaths.

33　See C. C. SPICER and L. LIPWORTH *Regional and Social Factors in Infant Mortality* (General Register Office, 1966).

34　See further MICHAEL SUSSER 'Social medicine in Britain: studies of social class', in WELFORD *et al.* (eds.) *Society*.

35　See A. B. HOLLINGSHEAD and F. C. REDLICH *Social Class and Mental Illness* (New York, 1958).

36　See THOMAS SCHEFF *Being Mentally Ill* (London, 1966).

37　See EDWIN H. SUTHERLAND 'White collar crime', in ALEX INKELES (ed.) *Readings on Modern Sociology* (New Jersey, 1966); and DAVID M. DOWNES *The Delinquent Solution* (London, 1966).

38　*Family and Class in a London Suburb*, p. 122.

39　*English Social Differences*, p. 69 (London, 1958).

40　*The Sociology of Work*, p. 156.

41　See H. H. WILSON *Pressure Group* (London, 1961) for an account of this campaign.

42　See W. G. RUNCIMAN *Relative Deprivation and Social Justice*, Pt 3 (London, 1966).

43　See GOLDTHORPE *et al. The Affluent Worker*, Vol. 2. *Political Attitudes and Behaviour*.

44　See further HENRY DURANT 'Voting behaviour in Britain, 1945–64', in RICHARD ROSE (ed.) *Studies in British Politics* (London, 1966).

45　In illustration of this view, see ROBERT MILLAR *The New Classes* (London, 1966).

46　'The "new working class"',' *European Archives of Sociology*, Vol. I, 1960, p. 249.

47　'Affluence and the British class structure', p. 152.

48　See, for example, R. S. MILNE and H. C. MACKENZIE *Marginal Seat*, p. 132 (London, 1958).

49　*Class and Class Conflict in Industrial Society*, p. 289.

50　*Conflict After Class* (Colchester, 1967).

51　See further THOMAS LUCKMAN and PETER BERGER 'Social mobility and personal identity', *European Archives of Sociology*, Vol. V, 1964.

52　*One Dimensional Man*, p. xvi (London, 1964).

53 'The sociology of literature', *International Social Science Journal,* Vol. XIX, No. 4, 1967.

Population was previously discussed in Chapters 1 and 4–6, social status in Chapter 3, social class (previously discussed in Chapter 3) is continued in Chapter 8, and power and politics (discussed in Chapter 3) are also discussed in Chapter 10.

8

Education and Social Mobility

The realities of power and social status and the character of the underlying economic and political organization of society are perhaps nowhere more clearly revealed than in a country's educational institutions. Political choices determine the formal outlines of the educational system, the requirements of the national economy impose limitations on the content and direction of teaching, and social class factors affect not only the supply of recruits to schools and universities, but also opportunities for success within them. Because of the way in which they define access to the various sectors of the educational system, all three kinds of forces – political, social and economic – contribute to the overall degree of mobility in society.

These are not the only links between the educational system and the wider social structure, however. The family, neighbourhood groups and the various media of mass communication all play a crucial part in the process of learning. It is true that with the establishment of a national network of free primary and secondary schools, the formal responsibilities of the family in education are no longer as important as they were in the nineteenth century – nor are those of the Church. Other factors have also altered: the average size of families has fallen, leisure time has increased and the average standard of living has risen. As a consequence there has been a growth both in 'home-centredness' and in the amount of attention devoted to children in the home. These changes have given parents a new role. Family and neighbourhood are the source of the child's linguistic and cultural traditions, and the response of the family to the shared experience of television, radio, films, magazines and newspapers inevitably affects the kinds of values and attitudes he comes to hold. These, in turn, influence the degree of parental encouragement that the child receives while he is at school. Bernstein, for instance, has drawn attention to the importance of patterns of discipline in middle- and working-class families and of parental attitudes towards the educational possibilities of play and toys. He suggests that working-class children often have to learn at school what is part of the day-to-day experience of the middle-class child. [1] Thus, in most middle-class families where the values of the school and those of the home usually reinforce each other, few problems of adaptation occur. Where there is discontinuity between these two sets of values, however, as tends to be the case for children from 'rough' working-class homes, the educational task is a much more difficult one.

CHANGING FUNCTIONS OF THE EDUCATIONAL SYSTEM

Given its focal position in this wider network of social pressures, the educational system is uniquely equipped both to maintain the existing framework of order and social consensus and also to promote mobility and change. But although it is one of the main agents in the transmission of cultural values and is itself an important source of social transformation, the educational system is also very much affected by changes in the economic and political organization of society. Jean Floud and A. H. Halsey, for example, comment on the fact that

> the traditional business of education with the process of cultural trans-
> mission is performed in quite new terms under the new conditions of
> technological society. No longer is it a question of handing on an unchanging
> or only slowly changing, body of knowledge and belief. On the contrary,
> education in modern societies has more to do with changing knowledge
> than with conserving it, and more to do with diffusing culture to wider
> social circles, or from one society to another, than with preserving the
> particular culture of a particular group. [2]

Since the end of the nineteenth century many of the earlier conservative functions of the educational system, such as the 'gentling of the masses' and the preservation of the aristocratic élite, have been replaced by more radical and comprehensive objectives. There are two main reasons for this change of emphasis. On the one hand a new pattern of demands has had to be met, and on the other hand changing assumptions about 'educability' and new aspirations on the part of the mass of the population have created a larger potential supply of school recruits.

On the 'demand' side, probably the most important determining influence on the educational system is the state of development of the national economy. Very schematically it is possible to characterize four stages in the transformation of the educational needs of a society. In the first stage, that of a predominantly agrarian economy, the main requirement is for unskilled farm labourers; they need little or no formal education, and popular educational institutions therefore remain almost entirely undeveloped (the élite, meanwhile, receive their education privately or in the existing endowed grammar schools). During the second stage, that of manufacturing industry, a need arises for skilled and semi-skilled, as well as for unskilled workers; universal literacy and social pacification consequently become the central objectives of educational policy, and opportunities also have to be found for specialized technical training (it is at this stage that new middle-class public schools, for girls and boys, are established as well — both to provide professional training and to provide rival or complementary institutions to those of the upper class). In the third stage, when an increasingly important part in the economy comes to be played by such service industries as advertising, market research, transport and communications, and when there is also a need for highly skilled scientists and engineers, the educational system has to find means of training a whole new range of specialists; radical expansion of the number and capacity of the institutions of secondary and, above all, of higher education is therefore essential. A fourth stage is reached with the advent of advanced automation. The primacy of educational institutions in the functioning of the economy is now fully established, and the changes that remain to be carried through are changes in the content and timing of teaching. Marshall McLuhan, for instance, suggests that since 'the older mechanistic idea of "jobs" or fragmented tasks and specialized slots for "workers" becomes meaningless under automation', automation not only 'ends jobs in the world of work, it ends subjects in the world of learning'. [3] Whether this is entirely true remains to be seen, but McLuhan is probably right in his suggestion that automation may involve a reversal, rather than an intensification, of some of the forms of specialization which have come to dominate the educational system (and life itself) in modern society. In science in particular in the 1960s (as the Dainton and Swann Reports, for example, on scientific training and manpower showed), a radical reappraisal of scientific specialization became of considerable social importance. Indeed, the whole trend of present-day science and industrial organization necessitates greater opportunities for deferred training, particularly for women, and greater facilities for retraining.

These economic and technological factors, then, are the most important variables to have shaped the development of educational policy on the 'demand side', but they are not the only ones. Another powerful influence has been the change which has occurred in political assumptions about the scope and purposes of education for various groups within the community. [4] Demands for the widening of educational opportunity have been voiced by the socialist movement and by individual educationists. They have received useful support from the example of those more progressive schools where a new kind of pedagogy has been put into practice. They have also been linked, more narrowly, with the efforts of particular occupational groups to attain professional and social goals which formerly were beyond their horizon.

Perhaps the most important influence on political attitudes towards education, however, has been the change in the structure of social life itself over the last century. The pressures of urbanism, the growth of bureaucracy, the greater leisure and affluence of the average working man and the weakening of traditional religious and moral beliefs have made a new approach to the content and direction of the educational process essential. The need has also been recognized, in some quarters at least, for an education which will be conducive to 'humanization, or the preservation of whole human beings in a machine-dominated society', [5] as well as providing for the needs of a rapidly changing technology.

Factors on the 'supply' side have been secondary in the transformation of the educational structure up to the present time. One influence which may assume considerable importance in the near future, however, is the feed-back effect of various post-war developments – both in education itself and in work and welfare generally. Wider opportunities of all kinds have been available since 1945, and it seems likely that the educational aspirations of the mass of the population will grow quite dramatically in the latter part of this century as a result of the new social climate which the Robbins Committee Report of 1963 both analysed and itself helped to promote. With the elimination of the harsher kinds of poverty and class discrimination, furthermore, the chances of success of the 'new students' at school and university are also likely to improve.

The impact of these changes in supply and demand carries with it two main consequences: first, education assumes a position of unpredecented importance in the national economy; secondly, it becomes a more important factor than ever before in the lives of individual people. Indeed, 'society must be an "educated society" today – to progress, to grow, even to survive'. [6]

The dominant characteristics of the contemporary educational system – the increasing specialization of educational roles and organizations in particular – and the growing unification and interrelation of different educational activities within a single common structure – bear witness to the needs of an 'educated society'. But the more integrated educational system which we now have is not a harmonious one. There is still a great deal of tension between the many interests concerned in education today, in particular between the values of the school and the values of the home (and between both of these sets of values and those of the mass media), between political and pedagogic policies, between religious and secular philosophies of life and between the so-called 'two cultures'. The conflict between the requirements of expansion on the one hand and of preserving a civilized and humane tradition in education on the other is also very strong at the present time. Jean Floud, in analysing this conflict, considers that:

The disruption of social consensus and integration consequent on rapid social change, urbanization, increased social mobility, the multiplication of secondary groups and associations, and the generally enhanced scale and rationalization of social and economic life, leads to the demand that schools and universities should undertake broad educative functions for the mass of the people which were formerly fulfilled by the weakened 'primary' groups of family, neighbourhood and church. At the same time, the growing economic significance of educated manpower, the continually rising educational threshold of employment and the public thirst for formal educational qualifications, bring about the bureaucratization of education and its conversion into an increasingly rationalized system of mass instruction in the service of a modern labour force. [7]

Expansion and democratization, vocational specialization and the preservation of more liberal and humane values in education – these are the intertwined objectives of the present school and university system in this country and all have become increasingly questioned and challenged from one quarter or another. We must now consider the ways in which they have been accommodated into the formal system of educational administration, and in order to do this we must examine more closely the structural changes which have occurred since the end of the nineteenth century.

THE SCHOOL SYSTEM IN THE TWENTIETH CENTURY

As we saw in Chapter 5, the first steps towards the organization of a national education system were taken in England and Wales in the last quarter of the nineteenth century. The principle of universal elementary education was established in 1870, although it was not until 1880 that the School Boards were obliged to make attendance compulsory and not until 1891 that elementary education became virtually free. In 1902, following the recommendations of the Bryce Commission, the State and local authorities became involved in secondary education. There continued, however, to be little formal connection between these two parts of the educational structure (nor was there any link between the State system and the independent schools). Furthermore, whereas the newly created local education authorities were put under a statutory obligation to provide facilities for elementary education as a result of the 1902 Act, their powers to provide facilities or grant aid for education 'other than elementary' were at first no more than permissive, a fact which helps to account for the continuing disparity in the provision of grammar school places in different parts of the country.

The first real link between the two separate systems of public education was created in 1907 in the form of the free place system. This was in response to the pressure which had mounted since the Bryce Commission a decade before, and called for the extension of the small-scale system of scholarships, whereby the 'less well-to-do classes of our population may be enabled to obtain such Secondary Education as may be suitable and needful for them'. [8]

An increase in the number of free places enabled a small proportion of pupils from the elementary schools to transfer to grammar schools at the age of eleven or twelve (usually up to a quarter of the grammar school places were reserved in this way, the remainder being allocated to fee-paying pupils). The opportunities of brighter working-class and particularly lower-middle-class children were somewhat improved by this scheme, but those of the older pupils who stayed on in the elementary schools continued in most areas to be severely limited. The 'ladder' created for working-class children was, in fact, very narrow. By the First World War, for example, Stockport provided forty scholarships annually, thirty-five of which went to children attending elementary schools. They were tenable at the local municipal secondary school, girls' high school and boys' grammar school. A scholarship entitled the holder to free education, a grant of up to £1 a year for books, and an annual maintenance grant of £5 in suitable cases. [9]

There are two important facts to note about these developments. The first is that they strengthened the conception of *secondary* education as *grammar school* education, and left technical and vocational education as sub-secondary. The creation of Central Schools, following the tradition of the 'higher grade' schools of the late nineteenth century, and experiments in practical education at the top end of the elementary school, offered many working-class children a poor status substitute for the secondary education to which they did not have access. The Bryce Commission had recognized that the 'higher-grade elementary' schools were 'really secondary in their character', teaching science, languages and in some cases a 'literary curriculum'. [10] The free place system, however, after 1907, undermined attempts to strengthen technical and scientific education through the symbolic ladder to a 'real' secondary education, the more traditional grammar school education which Morant had felt it necessary to rescue.

The second important fact about these developments is that they heightened the awareness of the conflict at the heart of an educational system which sought explicitly − though not necessarily with great success − to compensate for the class rigidities of British society. Professor Glass points out that the relative position of middle-class and working-class children born between 1910 and 1929 remained substantially different (39 per cent of those from the middle class and one tenth of those from the working class went to a secondary school). There is no doubt, in his view, 'that the middle classes benefited greatly from the expansion of secondary and university education between the wars, and that they were aided in this by the more generous public provision after the 1902 Act.' Economic considerations, intelligence tests and the 'social class image of the secondary school and its purpose', all helped to hold back the rate of improvement of the educational chances of working-class children. [11] The framework of selective secondary education had been firmly established as, in Lord Eustace Percy's phrase, 'a lift or stairway to the higher storeys of the social structure'. [12]

The Taunton Commission, which reported on the Grammar Schools in 1868, had proposed three different grades of school for roughly three different classes of the community. 'The schools of the third grade are not,' it pointed out, however, 'and are not intended to be, preparatory to schools of the second; nor schools of the second to schools of the first.' Only very reluctantly did it concede the need 'to arrange that real ability shall find its proper opening'. [13] Only since that date had Huxley's concept of a ladder and Percy's of a lift gained popular credence. The conflict involved was that of the bright working-class child caught between the values and life-chances of his own class and those which grammar school education mainly represented. The ladder, in Raymond Williams's analysis, was an 'alternative to solidarity . . . it is a device which can only be used individually: you go up the ladder alone'. He finds the 'ladder version of society' objectionable because it both 'weakens the principle of common betterment' and 'sweetens the pill of hierarchy'. The ladder was, he explains, a substitute for a better common educational provision, a product of a divided society. [14]

The efficiency of the structure was gradually strengthened. Under the provision of the 1918 Act the administrative framework set up in 1902 was not altered, but the school-leaving age was raised to the end of the school year in which pupils attained their fourteenth birthday, and all previous exemptions were abolished (the school-leaving age, that is, the age at which children could be exempted altogether, or partly, from attendance, had been raised from ten in 1880 to twelve in 1899 and to fourteen in 1900; but until 1918 its enforcement had been difficult). The 1918 Act also proposed the establishment of compulsory part-time education for all children between the ages of fifteen and eighteen. With the exception of Rugby, however, local education authorities were reluctant or unable to implement this proposal and the part-time system never materialized. It has never, in fact, been fully reinstated since, despite the subsequent endorsement of the principle both by the 1944 Education Act and the report of the Crowther Committee (1959). The day-release system is our present substitute.

In the inter-war period the need to ensure some measure of uniformity and coherence in the expanding educational system prompted the reform of other aspects of educational administration. It led, for example, to the creation of the Secondary Schools Examinations Council and to the introduction of State scholarships to the universities. Better conditions were established for the training and remuneration of teachers. 'Special Places' ousted the free place system, both increasing the number of places available and introducing the criterion of the means test. The grammar school population increased substantially over the years after 1902 and a greater proportion of free and special places was made available. By 1938, 53 per cent of pupils had free places and 16 per cent had special places. One in twelve children attended a grammar school. More pupils were also encouraged to stay on in the senior forms of the elementary schools or to enrol for courses at local technical colleges and art schools. There continued, however, to be a great deal of dissatisfaction with the existing opportunities. One of the most outspoken criticisms was in a Labour Party policy statement, edited by R. H. Tawney in 1922, which expressed the need both for the improvement of primary and elementary education and also for

> the development of public secondary education to such a point that all normal children, irrespective of the income, class, or occupation of their parents, may be transferred at the age of eleven+ from the primary or preparatory school to one type or another of secondary school, and remain in the latter until sixteen. [15]

Advances in educational psychology and, in particular, research on child development and on intelligence and learning provided additional support for the principle of selective secondary education by emphasizing the varying needs of the adolescent personality and – consequently – the need for different kinds of schools and separate kinds of training.

The report of the Hadow Committee on *The Education of the Adolescent*, published in 1926, reflected both of these currents of opinion. Its recommendation for the division of education into two separate stages was a consummation of previous tendencies in educational reform. It also laid down the ideological foundations for the institutional changes which were to follow in 1944. Some reorganization of the school system began immediately, but with the outbreak of war in 1939 the process was interrupted. The war also brought to light a number of previously unrecognized deficiencies. The poor physical and intellectual condition of most of the evacuee children from the big cities, as well as of a large proportion of army recruits, for instance, dispelled a good many illusions as to the adequacy of the piecemeal modifications which had so far been introduced.

THE TRIPARTITE SYSTEM

During the war planning for reconstruction was given special priority. A plethora of detailed schemes and recommendations representing the ideas of individuals and groups from every segment of British life were presented at public meetings, in the press and in books and pamphlets. Lobbying by teachers' organizations and by a variety of religious groups was especially intense. It was the report of the Norwood Committee, however, which contained the blue-print for the system which was to come into being at the end of the war. At the heart of the plan was the provision of free secondary education. The proposed system was to be tripartite in arrangement, comprising the existing grammar schools, together with secondary modern schools (as proposed by the Hadow Committee) and secondary technical schools (as proposed in the Spens Report of 1938). Each school was to cater for different 'types' of pupil: the grammar school for those children 'interested in learning for its own sake', the secondary modern school for those who 'deal more easily with concrete things than with ideas', and the secondary technical school for those 'whose abilities lie markedly in the field of applied science or applied art'. [16] Selection for secondary education was to take place at the age of eleven and was to be based on diagnostic 'intelligence' tests.

With the passing of the 1944 Education Act the legacy of inter-war reforms and experiments was at last made over into a fully articulated national system, under the direct supervision of a cabinet minister. It covered primary and secondary education as well as the wide range of full- and part-time training available in colleges of further education, technical, commercial and art colleges and in evening institutes. Provisions for a full range of school welfare services (dating back to 1906 and 1907) were also extended: these included free milk, free or subsidized school meals, free dental and medical inspection, grants for travel and clothing, and special schools and facilities for handicapped children. To match these developments an extensive programme of rebuilding was set in motion, and there was also a large increase in the numbers of teachers admitted for training. Apart from the inevitable transitional difficulties, therefore, the basic objectives of expansion now seemed secure. There was less satisfaction with the actual content of teaching in the different types of school, however, and it was not long before criticism was also being directed at the tripartite system itself. [17]

Throughout the 1920s and 1930s, while instruction in 'the three Rs' continued to dominate in the classroom, the debate about the content of education, begun at the time of the Fisher Act (1918), went on. As before, and as is still the case today, the argument turned principally on the rival merits of the liberal and technical functions of training. Wider pedagogic issues, such as school discipline, classroom organization and teacher—pupil relations, were also raised. New approaches for curriculum reform were being called for from a number of different directions: by individual educationists, by organizations such as the New Ideals Group and the New Education Fellowship, and by societies like the Workers Educational Association and the Council for Educational Advance. Few of their recommendations were implemented in the short run, however, since the developing requirements of the economy and the shortages and set-backs which resulted from the First World War and from the depression meant that scarce resources were concentrated mainly on vocational and technical training.

In the primary school, where such economic pressures were less restricting, some changes were under way. The popularization of the psychoanalytic study of childhood, and the work of such educational thinkers as Maria Montessori and John Dewey, for example, resulted in the adoption of more flexible and 'open' patterns of school organization, and in the encouragement of more expressive and child-centred modes of learning. In the post-war years similar developments have also spread into the secondary schools, and are reflected, for instance, in the extension of project methods, interdisciplinary inquiry and

group activities, the relaxation of rigid streaming, experiments in school democracy, psychological counselling, and the encouragement of free expression
in activities like music, painting and drama. [18] These have their counterpart
in the newer universities, in the form of more progressive teaching techniques
(tutorials, seminars and group learning situations) and in the breakdown of
traditional subject boundaries, although here, as in the secondary schools,
the requirements of the formal examination system and the emphasis on
specialization and vocational training militate against their complete success.

One of the main objects of the 1944 Education Act had been to secure an
educational system which would provide equal opportunities for children from
all kinds of social background, irrespective of their abilities. It rapidly became
clear, however, that the three different types of secondary school were not
in fact offering equal opportunities at all. The schools, quite naturally, offered
different kinds of training: this was the whole point of the system. But what
had not been intended – somewhat naively perhaps – was that the different
kinds of training should be differently valued in the society at large. Given
the fact, however, that different types and amounts of education are still rewarded in very different ways in terms of income, status and prestige, parity
of esteem was likely to (and did) remain a pious ideal. The differences were
accentuated by the fact that the physical condition of the buildings, the
locality, the facilities for science and games, and the qualifications of the
staff were very often inferior in the secondary modern schools.

Disillusion over the functioning of the tripartite system in the early 1950s
led first to a concentrated attack on the main instrument of selection, the
eleven-plus tests. Apart from anything else, critics argued, the tests were
arbitrary. The existence of a wide disparity in the number of grammar and
technical school places available in different parts of the country, and even
within different parts of a single local education authority area, resulted in
variable definitions of 'aptitude' and 'ability'. [19] Perhaps most damning,
however, from the point of view of their intended purpose, was the discovery
that the eleven-plus tests were unreliable predictors of achievement. This was
especially serious in view of the very limited opportunities for transfer
between the various parts of the secondary school system.

Evidence of social class bias in the tests provided a further argument
against selection. It also gave a new focus to the controversy about equal
opportunities. A survey conducted by Jean Floud, for instance, revealed that
while 59 per cent of the eleven-year-olds from business and professional homes
in south-west Hertfordshire and 18 per cent from similar backgrounds in
Middlesbrough had found grammar school places, the proportion of
children from unskilled working-class families who went to grammar
schools in these two areas was only 9 per cent. [20]

The adverse effect of the eleven-plus tests on the children themselves
was also increasingly recognized. Robin Pedley, for instance, claimed not
only that selection was based on the evidence of 'blatantly imperfect knowledge

and faulty techniques', but that it possessed far-reaching emotional consequences as well: 'the rupture of a child's closest ties, of the common interests,
friendship and solidarity of a happy family'. [21] The disclosure of an
alarmingly wide variation in the marking of essay questions, together with
criticisms of the limiting effect which preparation for the eleven-plus was
having on the curriculum of the junior schools, of the unfairness of coaching
for middle-class children and of the disadvantages experienced by 'late
developers', added further evidence of the necessity of reform. [22]

POST-WAR MODIFICATIONS

In order to overcome some of these deficiencies in the selection system, a
number of education authorities began to introduce important modifications
in the administration of the eleven-plus tests (they gave spaced tests, for
example, and spot tests, as well as making more use of primary school record
cards and teachers' assessments). Changes were also made in the organization
of the secondary school system. One of the more radical of these alternatives
was the system adopted since 1956 in Leicestershire. Under this scheme, the
child himself, at the age of fourteen, was allowed to choose whether or not
he wished to go on to a senior school (the grammar school equivalent).

By the early 1960s it began to appear that perhaps the only real alternative
to selection, and the only real means to the realization of what John Vaizey
called the 'new definition of equality', [23] was the adoption of some type of
comprehensive system. This was the solution which, in various forms, an increasing number of education authorities adopted. It was also the solution
proposed formally by the Labour government when it came into power in
1964. The arguments in favour of the comprehensive school system derived
not only from the failure of the eleven-plus tests but also from changes in
school organization. The increase in the volume of G.C.E. preparation in good
secondary modern schools, for example, the increasing proportion of children
staying on at school voluntarily up to and beyond the age of sixteen, [24]
and the introduction into the grammar school curriculum of commercial and
even craft subjects, together with the establishment of multilateral and
bilateral schools, had all led to a blurring of the outlines of the old tripartite
system.

UNEQUAL EDUCATIONAL OPPORTUNITIES

If modifications in the structure of secondary school organization have led
to the elimination of some of the worst failures of the early post-war system
of public education, it is clear that many inequalities of opportunities still
exist. The continued existence of the public and private schools which cater

for about 10 per cent of the secondary school population perpetuate inequalities of another kind, of course. Most of these inequalities are still rooted in social class differences. We have mentioned already the fact that working-class children tend to win fewer grammar school places than middle-class children. They also tend to leave school earlier. Figures for children leaving grammar schools, for instance, where early leaving is the lowest – although perhaps the most distressing – show that whereas the wastage is a mere one per cent for boys from upper-middle-class homes, it is 14 per cent for working-class boys. [25]

The detailed explanation of these social differences lies in a variety of background factors. Formerly, poverty, lack of incentive and ambition, and irregular attendance were the commonest causes of early leaving and poor school performance on the part of working-class children. A higher standard of living does not of itself, of course, mean that more children will want to stay on at school. More will be able to, but they may be equally attracted by the rival opportunities offered by the commercial 'youth culture' outside of the schools. The existence of greater affluence, however, and the fact that, formally at least, educational opportunities are now equally available to all classes in society, has directed attention to the existence of more subtle influences on school performance. Of these, language is perhaps the most important. Basil Bernstein, for instance, suggests that there are two main linguistic structures, which he terms the 'restricted' and the 'elaborated' codes. [26] Everybody, he claims, has access to some kind of restricted code, but only children from middle-class homes are likely to learn the more complex elaborated code as well. This fact has important pedagogic consequences. In purely practical terms it explains the lower scores of working-class children in verbal intelligence tests and consequently their relatively poor performance in the tests which precede streaming in the primary school and in the eleven-plus. More importantly, however, Bernstein shows that linguistic skills provide the basis of particular modes of perception and styles of thinking: for example, they affect the child's attention span, his curiosity and his motivation to learn. Because so much current educational practice depends on the abilities which go together with a highly sophisticated language code, therefore, working-class children – unless they can be given special remedial treatment by teachers sympathetic to their difficulties – are bound to be at a disadvantage. Fred Flower has suggested that the only way to release the intellectual potential of children who have come from a cultural tradition that is shaped and constrained by a restricted code is for teachers to 'provide experience that in warmth and depth in some way approaches that of the family. Somehow the schools and colleges must learn to preserve for their students the links with the old culture and the old background while helping them reorientate their outlook on the world, to adjust their existing relationship and to establish new ones.' [27]

Research on streaming in the primary school highlights a further handicap which working-class children encounter, and this may also have its origin in poor verbal ability. Brian Jackson has shown not only that working-class children frequently attend schools which are badly equipped and inadequately staffed, but that the effects of streaming are such that the performance of children selected for 'C' streams actually tends to deteriorate between the ages of seven and eleven. Those children fortunate enough to be placed in 'A' streams, on the other hand (and the majority of these tend to come from middle-class homes for reasons already suggested), improve their 'intelligence' scores. [28] In other words, streaming seems to be self-validating, and at least partly manufactures the differences on which it is justified by its proponents. One of the most important reasons for this is connected with teachers' attitudes. Recent American research, [29] for example, suggests that where teachers expect children to do well they tend, whether consciously or not, to give extra help and encouragement; as a result, the performance of the favoured children improves. The reverse is the case when children are seen, rightly or wrongly, as being of less than average intelligence.

Other pressures, particularly those of the child's home environment, can also operate in such a way as to complicate or interfere with the school career. J. W. B. Douglas has demonstrated the effects of a large number of adverse conditions: poor housing, irregular health, larger families, less reliance on the social and medical welfare services, fewer visits by the parents to the school and less positive encouragement and help given to learning. [30] All these factors militate against the successful performance of the working-class child. The existence of an alien kind of moral ethos in the school may also create difficulties, as Brian Jackson and Dennis Marsden have shown in their comparative study of the grammar school experience of working- and middle-class pupils. [31] Similar problems exist in the secondary modern school. Thus, David Hargreaves was able to discern the existence of two quite different sub-cultures in the particular school he studied. The upper stream sub-culture was characterized by values which were positively orientated to the school and to the teachers. The lower stream 'delinquescent' sub-culture, on the other hand, rejected the system which confers status in academic terms and replaced it with an autonomous and independent peer culture very closely related to the commercial teenage culture of the world outside the school. Membership of the delinquescent group, as might be expected, was predominantly lower-working class. [32]

Despite the achievement of formal equality in the contemporary educational structure, then, the system continues to foster differences of opportunity – including the opportunity to acquire measured intelligence. This, as we shall see, remains true at the stage of further education.

FURTHER AND HIGHER EDUCATION

In the universities, the colleges of education, the technical and commercial colleges and evening institutes, as in the secondary schools, the legacy of nineteenth-century developments – both in the form of the institutions and in the form of the courses and qualifications that they offer – is still apparent. Political decisions concerning the manpower requirements of the national economy have had an equally marked effect on the structure of this sector of the educational system.

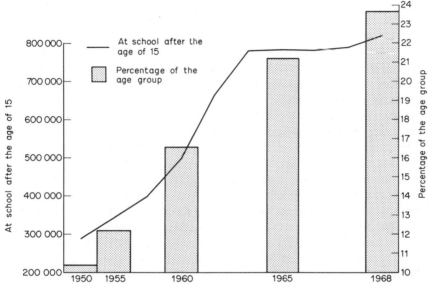

Fig. 14 *Children remaining at school in England and Wales after the age of fifteen, 1950–68. (See also Table 21, p. 328.) After* Statistics of Education, *1968, Vol. 1.*

During the post-war period a number of different kinds of attempt have been made to rationalize the organization of further education. New types of colleges have been established: for example, the Colleges of Advanced Technology (absorbed after the Robbins Report into the university system), the 'new' universities and the polytechnics. New courses and qualifications have also been evolved, and there has been a considerable expansion in the numbers of students attending further educational establishments. The number of day-time students in 1963–4, for instance, was three times that in 1946–7, and the output of scientists and engineers has quadrupled since the end of the war. But there have also been failures and set-backs. Commercial education has lagged (although not in the private sphere), art education has actually been cut, compulsory day attendance at County Colleges for the under-eighteens, or even release on demand, seem as remote as ever, and the examination system remains chaotic – despite some streamlining in the range of advanced awards for both artists and technologists. It became necessary in the late 1960s for an official committee to examine the reasons for a 'swing away from science', which was causing concern, in relation both to man-power and the status of science in education. [33]

In addition to all these difficulties and inadequacies, there is an acute shortage of places in colleges and universities for the increasing proportion of qualified school leavers who would like to continue with some form of higher education. As a consequence, the 'wastage' of potential talent is very serious. [34] In 1964–5 nearly half of the fifteen- to nineteen-year-olds received no organized education at all. Only 40 per cent of the age group got any kind of day-time education and less than 10 per cent of the age group entered full-time advanced courses. As well as limiting the opportunities for qualified applicants, the pressure of scarcity in higher and further education produces very unfortunate effects on the organization of secondary schools. It puts an altogether undue weight on examinations, whose prognostic value is in any case dubious; it limits the scope for flexibility within the curriculum, and it encourages premature specialization.

The very complexity of the further and higher educational system is an additional source of difficulties and potential inefficiency. In terms of institu-tions, for example, the range is considerable: from the universities and the promoted C.A.T.s on the one hand (and even among these institutions there is a recognizable hierarchy of academic and social prestige), to the vast network of polytechnics, national and regional colleges, colleges of education and local technical, commercial and art colleges, on the other. The range of quali-fications which is offered is equally wide, including university degrees and diplomas, the awards given by the Council for National Academic Awards, by the City and Guilds Institute and by the Royal Society of Arts, the various professional qualifications of different occupational groups, National Certificate and National Diploma awards (at ordinary and higher levels), and G.C.E. and C.S.E. qualifications.

Tyrrell Burgess likens this diversity to the 'vegetation of South America: it contains anything you can think of. Much of it is jungle; there are weird and exotic growths and there are some very large areas of desert.' [35] Perhaps this is a slight overstatement, but it remains the case that, despite a consider-able overlap of functions, the various institutions of further and higher education differ widely in respect of wealth, social status, mode of govern-ance, degree of autonomy, facilities for advanced study and research, and in the range of educational opportunities which they offer. For the most part they are rigidly separate, and indeed the 'binary' policy, initiated by Anthony Crosland as Minister of Education in 1965, was developed precisely to achieve this end. [36] What is more, these institutions are stratified in terms of the social class origin of their students. This is partly due to the existence of private fee-paying routes through the further educational system. But even within the publicly provided sector of further and higher education working-class children tend to be proportionately less well represented as the ladder of prestige is ascended – from evening and day release classes at one extreme to Oxford and Cambridge colleges at the other. The pattern of 'wastage' is linked to social class also – or at least linked to the kinds of opportunities available and the conditions under which work proceeds in the various types of colleges. Whereas, for example, the overall failure rate for students graduating from the universities in 1966 was 15 per cent (although there were big differences between different universities and between different faculties), 62 per cent of those studying for degrees at C.A.T.s and in regional colleges (a high proportion of whom were, of course, external students) failed – as did 37 per cent of those studying for Diplomas in Technology. [37] The wastage from part-time day and evening courses is even higher.

Inequalities in respect of social class are not the only barriers to a fully efficient and socially just further and higher educational system, however. Girls have considerably fewer opportunities than boys have – at all levels. Thus, although they outnumber male students by two to one in colleges of education, they represent only one quarter of university students and one fifth of full-time and sandwich students aged over eighteen in technical, commercial and art colleges. If we take the entrants to higher education as a whole, girls are in a minority of about one to four. Their chances of apprenticeship and day-release are also much smaller than those of boys.

Opportunities for full- and part-time education also fall off markedly as people get older, so that there are few chances for 'delayed' students to try again or change their specialization. Rigid restrictions on apprenticeship are one cause of this difficulty, but the reluctance of employers to release adult workers is perhaps just as important. Evening classes, the industrial training boards, residential colleges for mature students, such as Ruskin and Coleg Harlech, and institutions such as the Open University and the Free University at Cambridge have at different stages been designed to fill some of these gaps.

Overall, then, the restrictions imposed by the present structure of secondary and further education, as well as by particular modes of educational assessment, result in a system which is far from being either equal or democratic, whatever the pretensions to the contrary. It is a system, furthermore, in which conservative functions still tend to predominate over its more radical potentialities.

THE SCHOOL AS A SOCIAL SYSTEM

In our description of the post-war educational system we have so far been mainly concerned with establishing the links between the opportunities which the structure permits for educational achievements and such background factors as the child's family and social class position. Before we explore the way in which these factors also affect the pattern of mobility, however, it is necessary to return to our discussion of the internal organization of educational institutions, as these are an equally important influence on the educational process. Just as the family and neighbourhood environment of pupils send them into school with a variety of interpretations of, and attitudes towards, the situation inside its walls, so a particular educational system affects the opportunities available for various types of academic progress, and the social and professional background of teachers and school administrators equips them with particular attitudes and assumptions about their role. The internal life of the school and its relative success or failure (in either educational or social terms) centres on this conjuncture of individual values and institutional possibilities. [39]

The primary function of the school, university or college is, of course, education, and all of the personnel present are involved in furthering that function. This sets the overall tone of the institution and imposes certain limits to its activities. For instance, education in the school, as compared with that in the family or in the peer group, is conducted in relatively formal ways, and even those activities that are least formal – such as games, music and extra-curricular events – are normally evaluated in terms of their contribution to the basic learning situation. Furthermore, educational groupings are formed not on the basis of voluntary choice but in terms of aptitudes for learning and teaching – that is, they are always to some extent coercive.

Above all, the school is concerned with motivating children to learn. Its main task is to enable pupils to achieve positions within the role structure of adult society. Learning in the primary school proceeds along two lines, normally quite closely related – the cognitive and the social (or moral). The emphasis in the secondary school, on the other hand, and to a much greater extent in further and higher education, is on special types of learning, usually with a specific cognitive or vocational reference. How a particular educational institution performs these functions may vary considerably, though. Indeed, even within the unified English school system which was established in 1944, different institutions have pursued their tasks in quite separate fashions – a situation which, in Britain, is almost deliberately built into the structure of local administration and reflects an autonomy for the educational system which contrasts very sharply with that of, say, the United States of America or France.

Ignoring, however, the high degree of variability within the different parts of the English educational system, it is possible to discern a quite marked overall change in emphasis in the internal organization of our schools and universities over the last half-century. This shift has been characterized by Basil Bernstein in terms of the development of what he calls 'open' as opposed to the former 'closed' systems of control within the school. [40] At the

36 Individual and small group work, Prior Western Primary School, London.

extremes these two different types of school organization have the following characteristics. In the 'closed' school, as in the typical grammar school, for example, the instrumental order (that is, the formal arrangements for teaching and learning) is strong. Teaching groups tend to be homogeneous, their size and composition remaining fixed for all activities. Teaching methods emphasize solution-giving and *contents* or states of knowledge. Subject boundaries are rigidly defined and there is a tendency towards education in depth (specialization). Teaching roles in the 'closed' system are insulated from one another and pupils are taught in graded ability groups. Informal interaction between pupils and staff (at least at the formal level) is at a minimum. The instrumental order in 'open' schools, on the other hand, an example of which would be the private progressive schools like Bedales and Dartington or the best of the comprehensives, functions quite differently. Teaching groups are heterogeneous, their size and composition varying for different activities. Teaching methods, as, for instance, in Nuffield Science courses, emphasize heuristic principles and *ways* of knowing. There is a considerable amount of blurring in subject boundaries, and a move towards education in breadth, usually based on a common core curriculum. Teachers remain in close contact with their students and co-operate with them and with their colleagues in deciding on the teaching programme.

Differences in the expressive order (that is, the formal and informal network of personal relations) of these two school systems are also different. In the 'closed' system the ritual order is strongly maintained. Boundary relationships with the outside world are sharply drawn and there are few opportunities for pupils to influence staff decisions. Rewards and punishment are public and ritualized. In the 'open' system, on the other hand, even the architecture of the schools is less enclosed. What is of greater significance, though, is that the boundary relationship between the home and the school has changed:

> parents (their beliefs and socializing styles) are incorporated within the school in a way unheard-of in the older schools. The range and number of non-school adults who visit the school and talk to the pupils have increased. The barrier between the informal teenage subcultures and the culture of the school has weakened; often the non-school age-group sub-culture becomes a content of a syllabus.

Summarizing these changes of emphasis at a more general level, Bernstein suggests that there has been a shift from schools whose symbolic orders point up or celebrate the idea of purity of categories (whether these categories be values, subjects in a curriculum, teaching groups or teachers) to schools whose symbolic orders celebrate the idea of mixture or diversity of categories. Until recently, as we have seen, the English educational system – and certainly its élite institutions – epitomized the concept of purity of categories. The grammar and public schools and the civic universities were almost exclusively 'closed' systems. Their organization was formal and ritualized. There was a firm distinction between the arts and the sciences, and between the 'pure' and the 'applied' subjects of learning. Today, on the other hand, despite a lingering nostalgia for 'purity' in certain sectors of the system, because of the demand for more and more trained scientists, technologists and 'social engineers' who will be capable of adapting themselves to the accelerating pace of change in the advancing society of the late twentieth century, and because of the demand for greater democratization in the educational system, education in breadth and more flexible systems of control are beginning to gain favour. [41] Indeed, where they are not yet formally established, signs began to appear emphatically in 1968 that at the university level and in the technical and art colleges students and junior members of staff were prepared to organize to force such changes. The focus of such pressures was the demand for student representation on university academic councils and for modifications in the structure of courses and examinations, notably in art education. The more flexible degree courses recommended in the Robbins Report, and more 'socially relevant' senior classes in the secondary modern schools recommended in the Newsom Report, also point in the direction of greater openness.

THE DETERMINANTS OF MOBILITY

Because of recent developments in the structure of industry and in the distribution of occupations, the educational system has increasingly become the main arbiter of how opportunities are distributed in adult society. [42] In other words, we have moved from a situation in which most jobs were ascribed by birth to one in which they are achieved on the basis of educational qualifications. Yet in the various types of secondary school and at the various levels of further and higher education opportunities for achievement differ quite markedly, as we have noted. They also differ between boys and girls, and between different parts of the country. For this and other reasons mobility cannot simply be seen as a function of educational opportunity, just as it cannot be measured exclusively in terms of changes in occupational status.

If educational opportunities only partly influence the amount and direction of mobility in contemporary society, however, the structure of academic rewards and the various criteria of educational selection do have an important effect on mobility. Ralph Turner, for instance, compares two patterns of social ascent: 'sponsored' and 'contest' mobility. [43] He takes these to be characteristic both of differences between national educational systems (America versus England or France, for example) and between particular systems at different points of time. Under the system of sponsored mobility, such as existed in England before 1944, élite recruits are chosen by the already existing élite on the basis of some supposed criterion of merit. Thus, upward mobility is like entry into a private club, the ideal credentials being special skills – usually professional or academic – which require the scrutiny of the élite for their recognition. Contest mobility, on the other hand, a system which has been more characteristic of the American educational system, although it is gradually gaining in importance in this country also, offers élite status as a prize in an open competition. Under this system, society at large establishes and interprets the criteria of élite status – hence they must be highly visible and require no special skill for their evaluation (material possessions and mass popularity are ideal credentials). There are other differences between these two systems. Under sponsored mobility the selection point tends to be placed as early in life as possible – even at birth, in some cases – while under contest mobility the final reward is delayed for as long as practicable in order to permit a fair race. What is more, whereas sponsored mobility depends almost exclusively on the attainment of a particular occupational or professional status, contest mobility relates to many different goals, including high income and consumption standards, and political power.

Although educational achievement and the structure of examinations and other kinds of academic reward are important in determining particular forms of mobility, it is important not to lose sight of other variables which also affect the very complicated process of social selection in modern society. David Lockwood, for instance, suggests that 'the problem of who moves where, when and how' in occupational terms, is in principle reducible to the operation of seven distinct factors [44]: (1) the ratio of 'higher' to 'lower' jobs in the occupational structure; (2) the degree to which occupations call for highly specific skills or for the application of more diffuse criteria of ability; (3) differential fertility (together with the first two factors, this determines the total number of vacancies available at any time); (4) the structure of educational opportunities and educational institutions; (5) the distribution of innate abilities in the different occupational strata; (6) the distribution of 'information' and 'influence', both in connection with education and jobs; and (7) the distribution of the motivation to achieve. A number of additional factors may also serve either to promote or hinder mobility. Large-scale immigration, for example, promotes a certain amount of mobility at the lowest occupational levels. Trade-union restrictions on apprenticeship and job demarcations, on the other hand, and more subtle factors like race, religion or lack of the necessary 'cultural prerequisites' or 'social manners' may limit opportunities for advancement in some types of occupation. An exception to this rule, of course, is the world of 'pop' entertainers and professional sportsmen, although there are in fact clear status distinctions between different kinds of sports − as footballers aspiring to knighthoods have always known.

MEASURING SOCIAL MOBILITY

The overall pattern of social stratification in contemporary society includes, as we saw in the last chapter, not only occupational criteria but also dimensions of status and power. Thus, theoretically, social mobility can refer to changes in income, political power, social relations (social distance or deference), skill or occupational prestige, consumption patterns and styles of life, as well as to simple changes in job status. [45] Because of the practical difficulties involved in working with all of these criteria together, and especially in view of the fact that each of them has its own separate indicators, most attempts to measure mobility have employed occupation as their main index. Changes in occupational status have consequently been calculated either *inter*generationally, by comparing the occupational status of fathers and sons, or by comparing the *intra*generational changes in the occupational position of a single individual.

The evidence on intergenerational mobility shows that, over all, the proportion of men who are in the same jobs as their fathers is around 25 per cent (according to 1951 census data [46]). Considering, however, the very extensive changes which have taken place in the structure of the economy over the last century even this figure is perhaps quite high, although the scale of self-recruitment varies between particular groups in the population to quite a considerable extent. Thus, among the professional groups in Social Class I, where sons have traditionally followed their fathers' occupations, self-recruitment is high – and is, of course, perpetuated by the process of sponsored mobility. [47] It is also high in some of the more traditional occupational groups. In agriculture, for example, 50 per cent of sons had inherited their fathers' occupations in 1951, and in mining and quarrying the equivalent figure was 35 per cent. Self-recruitment was lowest among skilled manual workers and in the routine grades of non-manual occupations, although the actual distances moved to new occupational positions were usually relatively small. [48] It appears from these findings that, while there is evidence of some increase in occupational mobility over the last fifty years, most of it has probably been due to changes in the occupational structure and has been largely confined to social levels which are already close together.

EDUCATIONAL OPPORTUNITY AND SOCIAL MOBILITY

What, then, have been the effects of greater educational opportunity? These have been the subject of a number of studies of intragenerational mobility, as well as of research into the present structure and future requirements of the educational system. Although it is too soon yet to assess the full effects of post-war extensions in educational opportunity as far as the pattern of university recruitment is concerned some changes are already discernible. It has been demonstrated, for example, that whereas the proportion of university students from professional and managerial homes has increased from 3 per cent for the generation born before 1910, to 14·5 per cent for those born in the late 1930s, the number from lower-middle-class backgrounds, though relatively much smaller, has increased at a similar rate. The proportion of working-class students in English universities, on the other hand, has remained steady since the 1930s at about half a per cent of the age group. [49] This means that for a child of given ability the differentials between social classes were as great in 1960 as in the earlier period. There has, however, more recently been a considerable increase in the lower-middle-class entry – especially to the less prestigious universities, to the former C.A.T.s and to the polytechnics.

One of the few studies of intragenerational mobility provides comparative data relating to the mid-1950s on the occupational origins of a group of managers. [50] This survey revealed that 27 per cent of those interviewed had started their careers as manual wage earners; 30 per cent had been clerical workers and only 11 per cent had begun specifically as management trainees. Twenty-eight per cent of these men had received a grammar school education, but only one in five of all the managers possessed a degree (the proportion for 'top' managers was one in three). By the 1960s this relatively open pattern of management recruitment had changed, educational qualifications having assumed much greater importance by this time. Thus, David Clark's survey of managers in the North-West region revealed that three-quarters of the managers aged under forty in his sample had received a grammar school education. [51] Over half were graduates. It is also interesting to note that whereas the percentage of Oxbridge graduates was almost half in the case of the 'top' managers, among the lower ranks of management the proportion with an Oxbridge degree was less than a quarter. This suggests that while the educational achievement of entrants to managerial positions in industry has gone up appreciably during the post-war period, a very large element of selectiveness and social class bias still exists at the higher levels. Similar conclusions can be drawn from research which has been conducted into the recruitment patterns for the higher Civil Service, among bishops, and in the House of Commons. Oxbridge graduates dominate in all of these groups, and a majority of them are former public school boys. Hence, according to the majority report of the Public Schools Commission published in 1968, [52] while the public schools take only 2·5 per cent of the nation's children they take 35 per cent of the places at Oxbridge. They provided 42 per cent of Harold Wilson's Labour Cabinet in 1967, 71 per cent of the directors of our most prominent firms, 91 per cent of Lord Home's Conservative Cabinet in 1963, and 'their share of recruitment to senior grades in the Civil Service is growing stronger, not weaker'. [53]

While there has been some increase in mobility as a result of recent extensions of educational opportunity, therefore, and while the extension in the range of middle-class occupations has provided further possibilities for upward mobility, it still cannot be said that, overall, the degree of social mobility is very great. Since the improvements in opportunities have applied equally to all groups of the population, the relative positions of the different social classes have remained substantially unchanged. [54] It is true that there has been a tremendous expansion in both the 'higher' and 'lower' professional groups. It is also true that three new élite groups, which have often been singled out as the inheritors of the functions of the earlier ruling class, have emerged in the twentieth century: the intellectuals (including scientists and technologists), the managers and bureaucrats. But, as Bottomore points out in *Élites and Society,* none of these groups can be seriously regarded as contenders for the position of the governing élite. In the first place, their autonomy is too limited. Class affiliations among the members of these separate groups are in no sense cohesive, and the groups are also divided against each other. In fact, 'they are not a single establishment but a ring of establishments, with slender connections'. [55]

All of the evidence which we have considered on education and social mobility, then, tends to suggest that, despite the extension of the ideal of 'equality of opportunity' and despite the expansion of the various groups comprising the upper and middle classes, no very fundamental changes have occurred in the structure of social class relations, or in the balance of power in contemporary society. Indeed, it seems doubtful whether increased educational opportunity could, on its own, ever make very much difference — for even the term itself contains something of a contradiction. 'Opportunity' must imply 'the opportunity to rise to higher levels in a stratified society'. But at the same time it also presupposes the objective of a degree of 'equality', for it implies that the inequalities embedded in the existing structure of society have to be counteracted so that, in every generation, individuals can really develop their personal abilities to the maximum. As we have seen, 'equality' in this sense is far from having been achieved in England today, in terms either of income, living conditions, education or health. Family back ground and social class are still the most important determinants both of 'educability' and of educational 'achievement'.

NOTES

1 See B. BERNSTEIN and D. HENDERSON 'Social class differences in the relevance of language to socialisation', *Sociology*, Vol. 3, 1969.

2 A. H. HALSEY, JEAN FLOUD and C. ARNOLD ANDERSON (eds.) *Education, Economy and Society*, p. 3 (New York, 1961).

3 *Understanding Media*, pp. 350–1 (London, 1964).

4 See WILLIAMS *The Long Revolution*, Pt 3, Ch. 1.

5 A. K. C. OTTAWAY *Education and Society*, p. 100 (London, 1953; 1968 edition).

6 PETER DRUCKER *Landmarks of Tomorrow*, p. 87 (New York, 1959).

7 'The sociology of education', in WELFORD *et al.* (eds.) *Society*, pp. 521–2.

8 *Report*, p. 299.

9 THISELTON MARK *Modern Views on Education*, pp. 82–3 (London, undated).

10 *Report*, pp. 10, 52–4.

11 D. V. GLASS 'Education', in MORRIS GINSBERG (ed.) *Law and Opinion in England in the 20th Century*, pp. 330–2.

12 Quoted in ibid., p. 336.

13 SCHOOLS INQUIRY COMMISSION *Report*, Vol. I, p. 95.

14 *Culture and Society*, pp. 317–18 (1961 edition).

15 *Secondary Education for All*, p. 7 (London, undated).

16 *Curriculum and Examinations in Secondary Schools*, pp. 2–3 (London, 1941).

17 See further H. C. DENT *The Education Act, 1944* (London, 1944).

18 See further CHARITY JAMES *Young Lives at Stake* (London, 1968).

19 The variation in the proportion of grammar school places available was from 50 to 60 per cent in some places (mainly the Welsh counties) to 12 to 15 per cent in others. In all areas there were fewer 'selective' places for girls than for boys.

20 *Social Class and Educational Opportunity* (London, 1956).

21 *Comprehensive Education: a New Approach,* p. 56 (London, 1956).

22 See further PHILIP VERNON (ed.) *Secondary School Selection* (London, 1957).

23 i.e. a situation in which 'subject to differences in heredity and infantile experience, every child should have the same opportunity for *acquiring* measured intelligence'. See *Education for Tomorrow,* p. 16 (Harmondsworth, 1962).

24 In 1952 the proportion of all pupils aged fifteen to nineteen who were at school or college was one in ten. By 1962 it had increased to one in six. It is estimated that by 1972 it will be about two in five.

25 See J. W. B. DOUGLAS *The Home and the School* (London, 1964).

26 For a review of all of Bernstein's papers on this subject, see DENIS LAWTON *Social Class, Language and Education* (London, 1968).

27 F. D. FLOWER *Language and Education,* pp. 267–8 (London, 1966).

28 *Streaming* (London, 1964). See also the Plowden Report, *Children and their Primary Schools* (London, 1967), for a review of recent research on streaming.

29 See ROBERT ROSENTHAL and LEONORE JACOBSON *Pygmalion in the Classroom* (New York, 1968).

30 *The Home and the School.*

31 *Education and the Working Class* (London, 1962).

32 *Social Relations in a Secondary School* (London, 1967).

33 See COUNCIL FOR SCIENTIFIC POLICY *Enquiry into the Flow of Candidates in Science and Technology into Higher Education* (London, 1968).

34 See the Robbins Committee Report, *Higher Education,* Appendix One (London, 1963).

35 *A Guide to English Schools,* p. 156 (Harmondsworth, 1964).

36 Crosland's policy speech is reproduced as an appendix in ERIC ROBINSON *The New Polytechnics* (London, 1968).

37 See further U.G.C. *Enquiry into Student Progress* (H.M.S.O., 1968).

38 See GERTRUDE WILLIAMS *Recruitment to Skilled Trades* (London, 1957); and KATE LIEPMAN *Apprenticeship* (London, 1960).

39 See ROBERT HAVIGHURST and BERNICE NEUGARTEN *Society and Education* (Boston, 1962).

40 'Open schools, open society?', *New Society,* 14 September 1967.

41 See EDMUND LEACH 'Men and learning', in *A Runaway World?,* Ch. 5 (London, 1968).

42 See A. H. HALSEY 'Education and mobility', in T. R. FYVEL (ed.) *The Frontiers of Sociology* (London, 1964).

43 'Modes of social ascent through education', in HALSEY et al. (eds.) *Education, Economy and Society.*

44 'Social mobility', in WELFORD et al. (eds.) *Society.*

45 S. M. MILLER 'Comparative social mobility', *Current Sociology,* Vol. IX, November 1960.

46 See B. BENJAMIN 'Inter-generation differences in occupation', *Population Studies,* Vol. 11, 1957–8.

47 See R. K. KELSALL 'Self-recruitment to four professions', in GLASS (ed.) *Social Mobility.*

48 See GLASS and HALL 'A study of intergenerational mobility', in GLASS (ed.) *Social Mobility.*

49 ALAN LITTLE and JOHN WESTERGAARD 'The trend of class differentials in educational opportunity in England and Wales', *British Journal of Sociology*, Vol. XV (IV), 1961.

50 ACTON SOCIETY TRUST *Management Succession* (London, 1956).

51 *The Industrial Manager* (London, 1966).

52 The report covered all the independent schools in membership of the Head-masters' Conference, the Association of Governing Bodies of Public Schools and the Association of Governing Bodies of Girls' Public Schools.

53 *Report*, Vol. I, p. 59 (H.M.S.O., 1968).

54 See C. ARNOLD ANDERSON 'A skeptical note on mobility', in HALSEY *et al.* (eds.) *Education, Economy and Society*.

55 ANTHONY SAMPSON *Anatomy of Britain*, p. 624 (London, 1962).

Social mobility was previously discussed in Chapters 1 and 3, education in Chapters 1 and 4, and social class in Chapters 3 and 7.

9

The Family and the Social System

THE FAMILY AND OTHER SOCIAL INSTITUTIONS

In the complex environment of modern Britain perhaps the most important role that the family performs is to mediate between its members and the wider social structure. With the disruption of the settled community traditions of pre-industrial and rural forms of society, with the increasing size and impersonality of industrial and bureaucratic organizations and the continual assault on the individual by the mass communication media, the family today is for most people the one relatively stable and secure focus of meaning and identity. It creates for the individual 'the sort of order in which he can experience his life as making sense', [1] and it equips him with appropriate models of behaviour.

We have already discussed the importance of the family as a source of primary learning for the child, and we have also seen how the family furnishes its members with certain kinds of status (not only in the sense of social class rankings but also in terms of marital and kinship statuses), as well as providing for their care and protection – both in infancy and old age. As a result of the process of socialization, the family also serves to internalize in its younger members a whole range of cultural, political and religious values and attitudes which are vital for the continuity of the various social traditions that go to make up a particular historical 'construction of reality'. [2]

Although the family performs these functions, however, on behalf of the wider social system (in addition, of course, to regulating the personal sexual and emotional needs of its individual members), it is itself very much influenced by other institutions in society. [3] Thus, at different points in time, particular cultural and social class traditions define the form of the family relationship between husbands and wives and between parents and children. They also prescribe what come to be regarded as the acceptable patterns of individual and co-operative group behaviour, as can be seen in a comparison between the 'paternalistic' middle-class family of the mid-nineteenth century and the more permissive, child-centred family system which is typical today. These patterns of behaviour are in turn reinforced by corresponding legal and religious sanctions, although there may be a time-lag during which legal and religious conventions fail to keep up with the changing standards of social behaviour. The extent of the differences in such sanctions can be seen, for example, in the contrast between the inferior legal status of women in the Victorian period and their more equal formal status in the mid-twentieth century. The pattern of urban and industrial organization, the structure of the various social welfare agencies and the system of education also have an important influence on family relationships. Each makes different sorts of demands on the individual family members and each offers different kinds of opportunity or reward. This is evident from a comparison between the economic and educational responsibilities of the early nineteenth-century family under the cottage industry system, for example, and those of the aristocratic family of that time, or the present-day family of whatever social class.

CHANGES IN FAMILY ORGANIZATION

This intimate network of connections, linking the family to the wider institutional framework of society, has always existed. The actual structure of family relationships and the different functions which the family performs have, however, altered quite dramatically in the last century – just as, at the end of the eighteenth century, with industrial and urban growth, earlier patterns of family organization were also disrupted. In fact, although some form of biological kinship grouping seems to be universal in all human societies, the family as we know it today is in some respects a recent phenomenon – dating only from the seventeenth century. Before then, in the towns and in those villages large enough to possess a manor and a wealthy squire, family members were usually part of a wider community. Households were often large and contained within them, in addition to the families of the gentry or aristocracy who were at their head, members of the labouring and servant classes and sometimes apprentices and clerks as well. It is true that the servants were wage earners, not family retainers. But while they were subjected to closer discipline than the actual kin relatives of the head of the household, they were nevertheless treated as members of the family, with rights to be looked after beyond the basic payments called for in their formal contracts. There was little privacy – even architecturally – among this extended community of people; however, each member of the family enjoyed a great deal of sociability and a strong sense of security and 'belonging'. The family was 'a centre of social relations, the capital of a little complex and graduated society under the command of the paterfamilias.' [4]

With the growth of capitalism and early forms of industrial employment, important changes began to take place to disrupt this traditional pattern among the gentry. The changes began in the aristocracy and in the newly forming middle classes. They were a consequence of two factors – the recognition of childhood as a phase of life and as a social status quite distinct from adult social status, and the search for privacy and independence which led to the creation of the home as the now typical household unit. Discussing this transition, David Cooper suggests that:

> the early development of the basic contradictions of capitalist society limited the blurring of class distinctions, which became less tolerable to the upper classes, who began to withdraw socially, geographically (to special districts), and in terms of the upbringing of children. Henceforth values of privacy, the immuration of the family, reigned. [5]

If the diffuse groupings of the large medieval family household began to give way to a more limited concept of the family in the seventeenth century, however, further important modifications in the family patterns characteristic of the various social classes resulted from the intensification of industrialization and from the beginnings of the Welfare State in the later nineteenth and early twentieth centuries.

The most important of these more recent changes has been the decline in the relative importance of the extended family, [6] and the corresponding increase in the reliance of the nuclear family on the State and on other specialized external agencies for the fulfilment of certain of its functions. There has also been a reduction of social class differences in the patterns of family organization. But, while few would deny the fact of changes of this kind, sociologists are far from being agreed on what their consequences are – or on what the implications for the future are likely to be. Some of the apparent confusion which surrounds this subject is based on misleading historical comparisons and on the imprecise use of terminology. Other differences arise because of opposed ideological views. Thus, while most sociologists assume that the family is a functionally necessary, and basically unalterable, social institution, it has also been argued that it is 'possible for the advanced industrial societies of the world to do away with the family and substitute other social arrangements that impose fewer unnecessary and painful restrictions on humanity'. [7] These two positions are totally at odds with each other and it is not difficult to see how they are likely to affect particular judgements concerning the consequences of recent changes in family structure. Individual religious and moral views also prejudice the interpretation of these changes. [8]

FUNCTIONS OF THE FAMILY

The debate about the modern family usually centres on the assertion that, as a consequence of industrialism, the family has lost many of its former functions and is, therefore, rapidly on the way to disintegration and moral collapse – or that, at best, the family today only serves to 'preserve mankind from an intolerable moral solitude'. [9] But these statements are altogether too sweeping and imprecise to be acceptable to the sociologist who understands the lessons of history and cultural anthropology. In the first place, it is not always clear which functions it is that the family is said to have lost, or when lost them. Nor is it clear whether it is the functions of the extended family which are being referred to, or those of the nuclear family. There is the added difficulty that, within any given society, the functions of both the extended and the nuclear family, and the typical patterns of family relationships which they embody, differ – or used to differ – quite markedly between the various social classes and between different local communities. Vogel and Bell illustrate some of these points in detail:

> In some primitive and agrarian societies the family is said to have (or have had) major economic, political, religious and educational duties, but in many cases they are (or were) functions of the extended family, not the nuclear family. In more complex societies, these functions are performed not by the extended family, but by specialized institutions organized on other bases than kinship; the nuclear family's relationship with the extended family has become less important . . . Moreover certain activities and functions performed by the nuclear family in industrial societies have increased in recent decades. For example, the care of infants, household maintenance, and individual tension management, formerly performed in large part by the extended family or the community. [10]

It is over the question of the inevitability of the 'collapse' of the extended family and over the future implications of changes in family life that the biggest differences in interpretation emerge. At one extreme there are those sociologists like Talcott Parsons and Ruth Anshen who appear to take for granted the isolation of the modern nuclear family. They seem either to ignore or to dismiss kinship ties beyond this primary unit. Urban-industrial life in their view inevitably leads to a shrinkage of the wider family because the extended family is no longer functionally useful to its members. It is no longer responsible for assigning individuals to particular statuses in the social hierarchy and it does not help individuals in the process of 'role bargaining', [11] except perhaps in the upper social classes where nepotism and the old boy establishment still exert considerable influence in England.

A number of alternative arguments have been advanced against this strictly functionalist view. Raymond Williams, for example, suggests that the present structure of family and community relationships is only a temporary phenomenon, and that as it adapts to the present changes the extended family may be expected to reconstruct itself. [12] At the other extreme altogether, some sociologists – and particularly those associated with the Institute of Community Studies, for example – would appear to deny that urbanization necessarily causes any family disruption at all. [13] Their work points to the continued vigour and vitality of the extended family – at least in some areas.

Perhaps the view which fits most closely with the results of recent empirical investigations of family life and neighbourhood relations is that argued by Eugene Litwak. [14] Litwak accepts Parsons's argument that the classical extended family is incompatible with the needs of modern industrial society, but he rejects the view that the isolated nuclear family can be the only meaningful alternative. Litwak's own opinion, rather, is that while the extended family has changed in some very important ways, it still performs useful functions for its members, and still exists as a meaningful entity for them.

This theory would certainly accord with the findings of Rosser and Harris, who conclude their review of changing family patterns in Swansea as follows:

> The facts seem to point to the emergence of a modified form of extended family, more widely dispersed, more loosely knit in contact, with the women involved less sharply segregated in role and less compulsively 'domesticated', and with much lower levels of familial solidarity and a greater internal heterogeneity than was formerly the case in the traditional 'Bethnal Green' pattern. It is a form of family structure in which expectations about roles and attitudes are radically altered – and in particular, in which physical and social mobility are accepted. It is the form of extended family which is adjusted to the needs of the mobile society. [15]

We shall return at the end of this chapter to the discussion of recent changes in the structure of the family and to speculations about the future of the family. Meanwhile we need to examine contemporary family patterns in more detail. We shall describe these first of all in general terms, looking particularly at the kinds of relationship which exist between individual family members and between the family as a whole and the wider community. We shall then go on to consider changing demographic trends in relation to child-bearing, marriage and divorce.

CHARACTERISTICS OF THE CONTEMPORARY FAMILY

Compared to the very marked social class variations which existed in the nineteenth century, one of the most outstanding characteristics of contemporary family patterns is their general similarity. This is not to say that social class differences in family behaviour no longer exist: we have already commented, for example, on the extent to which family encouragement of a particular kind helps the child in his school career, and we have seen that this type of encouragement is more typical of middle-class than of working-class families. There are also differences in the child-rearing patterns adopted by the various social classes, and in the structure of relations between husband and wife. [16] On the whole, however, these variations are marginal and there are indications that they will be even further reduced in the future. [17] All of the following characteristics of the contemporary family, for example, apply with only slightly varying degrees of emphasis to each of the social strata.

In Britain today marriages are no longer arranged. They are entered into voluntarily, by individuals who have equal legal status. Most important family decisions are shared and roles are allocated on a more democratic basis than was typical in the past. Social control within the family has been considerably weakened; while this has brought a greater measure of independence for all the family members, it also implies the possibility of greater tension and conflict. Typically, the nuclear family today forms both a single household unit and a single economic unit – although wider kin may be called on, or supported, in times of crisis or difficulty, and most families are also prepared to accept help from external welfare agencies. Geographical and social mobility are quite common nowadays, and the various generations (and wider relatives) often live far apart. Work and residence are also separated – again, often by quite considerable distances – particularly in the major cities. Most families are planned (especially after the first baby) and they are usually small (average family size is now between two and three children). As a consequence children have a very central place in the home and while, on the one hand, new forms of entertainment and recreational facilities have been established which cater for (and separate off) specific age groups, there has also been a proliferation of shared family leisure pursuits. A suburban house and garden (or their equivalent on a new estate or in a new town), the acquisition of material consumer goods – car, television, washing machine and so on – and the search for well-being and success (particularly educational success for the children) are typical goals of the modern family.

Ernest Burgess sums up these characteristics in terms of the development of 'companionship' or partnership in place of the 'institutional' or paternalistic family patterns of the nineteenth century. He adds some further observations on the quality of inter-personal relationships in these two different types of family. In the companionship marriage, claims Burgess, relationships are adaptive and creative rather than static and conventional, and feelings of personal happiness and affection are more important than those of duty and respect. What is more, the idea of companionship relieves the wife of her former 'chattel' status, so that the family becomes 'more the private holding of its members than a collective possession of many relatives'. [18] It is important now to consider what these changes in the structure of the family have meant in more precise terms, and to examine some statistics of marriage and divorce and the new patterns of husband–wife and parent–child relations.

MARRIAGE PATTERNS

In Britain the period since 1945 has been characterized by high marriage rates and earlier ages at marriage. Whereas 552 of every 1,000 women in the age group twenty to thirty-nine were married in 1911, in 1931 the figure was 572; in 1951 it was 731 and in 1961 it had reached 808 — which is practically as high as it can ever be expected to go, according to most demographers.[19] Taking a slightly longer age span, we find that, while in 1921 88 per cent of men and 83 per cent of women were or had been married by the age of forty-five, by the mid-1960s these percentages were 95 and 96 respectively.

There are a number of easily discernible social and economic factors which

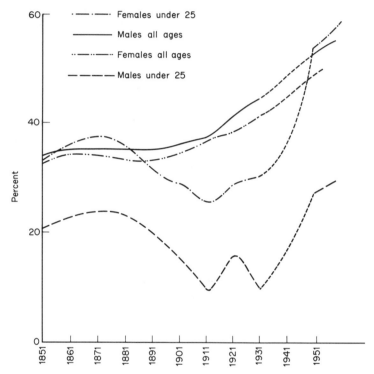

Fig. 15 *Proportion of the population married in England and Wales, 1851–1961. (See also Table 9, p. 319.) After Mitchell and Deane, 1962.*

have been responsible for this change, but part of the increase is undoubtedly due to the equalization in the numbers of spinsters and bachelors at the relevant combination of ages. Male emigration and male war losses are much lower than they were fifty years ago, and so are male infant mortality rates and deaths occurring at work. Today, in fact, in contrast with the Victorian period, there is an excess of males in the younger age groups (for every 1,000 males aged twenty to thirty-nine in 1961, for instance, there were only 976 females). This fact may also help to account for the earlier age at marriage. In 1921 the proportion of husbands who had married before they were twenty-one was less than 5 per cent; it was 15 per cent for wives. By 1968, however, these percentages had trebled — despite the fact that parental consent was still required for those marrying below the age of twenty-one. The mean age at marriage for women in 1965 was 22·6 and for men twenty-five (in America more girls marry at eighteen than at any other age and it has been estimated that half of all young men are married before they are twenty-five). But while similar proportions of men and women marry today from all social classes, age at marriage varies considerably according to educational and occupational background. It is comparatively low in Social Class V and comparatively high in Social Class I where, especially for young men, the period of training for professional and other specialist occupations and the subsequent period of establishing a secure economic position within the profession tend to result in the postponement of marriage.

One of the reasons for the younger age of working-class marriages is the improved standard of living which teenagers now enjoy. As a group they are relatively much better off than they have ever been [20] and, with the extension of easier hire purchase facilities and the improvement in opportunities for women's work, many of the former economic barriers to early marriage have now been removed. The earlier onset of puberty [21] and the larger number of pre-nuptial conceptions are perhaps even more significant factors. For instance, of brides aged under twenty-one approximately one third are already pregnant at the time of marriage, and in the youngest age groups this figure is even higher; in 1964, 11,000 of the 18,000 brides aged between sixteen and seventeen who were married in England and Wales gave birth to children within seven months of their marriage. Conception does not always, however, lead to marriage, and illegitimate maternities have also increased in recent years; while 5 per cent of all the children born in 1955 were illegitimate, that proportion had risen to around 8 per cent by 1967.

CHANGES IN FAMILY SIZE

If more people are now marrying than ever before, and more children are being born in the early years of marriage, this cannot necessarily be taken to imply that the average size of completed families is also on the increase. The very marked rise in the birth rate immediately following the Second World War, for example, was not sustained during the 1950s, although there were signs of another upward movement by the mid-1960s. It seems likely that average family size is now stabilizing at between two and three children. This figure is, of course, much smaller than for the typical Victorian family (over half of married women had five or more live children, and nearly one fifth bore ten or more), but it represents an increase over the very small families characteristic of the 1920s and 1930s. What is more, these changes in family size conceal quite significant social class variations. According to Glass and Grebenik, [22] throughout the period 1900 to 1924 the wives of manual workers had consistently higher fertility than wives of white collar workers (although the absolute differences in family size fell considerably, of course). Since the end of the war a new trend has appeared. It is among the professional classes that increases in family size are most noticeable today, although fertility is still, in fact, highest in Social Class V. Kelsall, [23] for example, demonstrates that whereas the average number of children born to marriages which had

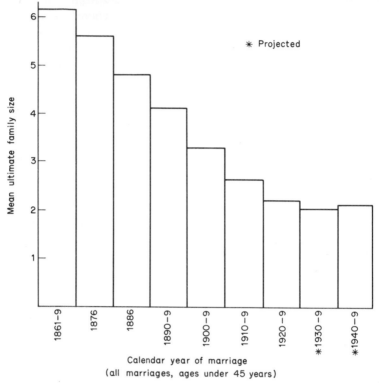

Fig. 16 Mean ultimate family size of cohorts in England and Wales since 1861.
(See also Table 6, p. 315.) After the Registrar-General's Statistical Review
of England and Wales for 1960.

only lasted five years at the time of the 1961 Census was 1·74 for parents in Social Class V, the comparable figure for wives of self-employed professional men was 1·69. The lowest average figure, on the other hand, was for the families of routine grades of non-manual workers, clerks and shop assistants who, in 1961, had had only just over 1·2 children.

The reasons for the recovery in fertility since 1945 (and for some of the social class variations in fertility) are, in many cases, the same as those for higher marriage rates: improved real wages, the extension of the social welfare services and of health, housing, educational and recreation facilities, and the availability of easy credit and hire purchase. Changing, less superstitious and less sentimental attitudes towards pregnancy and childbirth, improved hospital facilities for confinement and the alleviation of some of the drudgery associated with the care of infants and small children (because of the availability – for those who can afford them – of cheaper baby foods, launderettes, washing machines, disposable nappies and so on) have also helped to create a more favourable climate for young parents wanting to have bigger families.

DIVORCE PATTERNS

In quite a different way some of these changes have also been partly responsible for the higher incidence of divorce in recent years. Ideals of marital harmony and of the happiness of children in the home are much higher than they have ever been – in all the social classes. The status of women in the family and the prevailing notions of desirable familial, parental and sexual relations have changed accordingly. Yet if more couples now seem to want to achieve the 'ideal' two-children family so widely popularized in advertisements and on television, they are also more ready to abandon it should the reality not match up to what they had hoped for (or feel to be 'normal'). Thus, Rowntree and Carrier suggest that – of the fiftyfold increase in divorce over the last century – a fivefold rise is due to the lowering of formal barriers, while the remaining tenfold rise is a consequence of society's growing acceptance of divorce as an appropriate end to unhappy marriages. [24] This change of opinion, reflected in the press and on television, and buttressed by new psychological theories deriving from the work of Freud and his successors, can be seen not only in the slow but persistent rise in the rate of petitioning over all, but also in the high rates of remarriage among divorcees. Whereas the proportion of marriages terminated by divorce was 0·2 per cent in 1911, for example, by 1937 it had risen to 1·6 per cent. Immediately after the Second World War the figure reached a peak of over 7 per cent but – while it dropped again slightly in the middle and late 1950s – it has now increased again to about 10 per cent (in the United States about one in five marriages end in divorce). [25]

Some people have argued that this increasing rate of divorce (together with a growing illegitimacy rate, the increasing proportion of pre-nuptial pregnancies and the higher incidence of venereal disease – particularly among teenagers) is evidence of the 'decay' and disintegration of traditional family patterns and of an irresponsible attitude towards marriage and sexual relations in general. While it is important not to underestimate the hardship and suffering which may be caused, especially to the children of divorcing couples, it is just as important to note that almost one third of divorces occur in childless marriages, and that in at least 40 per cent of the cases where children are involved they have already reached the age of sixteen when their parents' divorce takes place. The exceptionally high remarriage rates for divorcees

(75 per cent remarry) would, furthermore, hardly support the view that marriage is a decaying institution. Indeed, it might be said that, rather than being held in any lower repute today than formerly, marriage is more popular than it has ever been. The increase in divorce petitions implies no more than an increasing desire and ability on the part of estranged couples to seek a complete legal termination to their marriage, where earlier they might have separated only on a partial or informal basis or continued to live together without affection and with many of the blunter consequences experienced by families before the divorce arrangements and legal aid of the twentieth century.

Seen in this light, the lament for the lost authority and presumed stability of the nineteenth-century family appears to be totally misplaced. As Christopher Lash observes, criticisms of the contemporary family have their roots in deep-seated prejudices about the sanctity of the home and mother-hood and 'in an underlying despair . . . about the innumerable irritations and confinements of the marital condition'. [26] Such criticisms, however, exploit a myth of domesticity and home-centredness which is both sentimental and – to the extent that it denies the equal status of women in the family – cynical. What is more, they seem to be made in ignorance of the very funda-mental changes which have occurred not only in family life but in every other aspect of social organization over the last century.

The first point to be borne in mind about these changes is, as we saw earlier, that relationships between individual family members and the corres-ponding behaviour norms which come to be accepted at any particular time are a product of changing cultural conditions. They also reflect changing ideological attitudes towards paternal authority, the status of women and children and the degree of integration between the members of the elementary family and their wider kin.

HUSBAND–WIFE RELATIONSHIPS

In the face of the prevailing bureaucratic atmosphere which dominates the wider society today, it is commonly felt that the main task of the family should be to provide a secure basis of emotional support for its various members. But whereas in the nineteenth and early twentieth centuries it was the women of the family who were expected to fulfil the supportive roles (the menfolk existing as more remote authority figures), husbands are now also beginning to take a share in such tasks. In other words, what were formerly segregated roles within the family are now more often seen as joint or shared roles. At the same time, for reasons we have discussed earlier, family life has for most groups in society become more home-centred and more 'privatized'.

In traditional working-class areas such as those described by Young and Wilmott in *Family and Kinship in East London* and by Madeline Kerr in *The*

People of Ship Street, married daughters remain closely tied to their mothers while husbands spend much of their free time outside the home. The same is true in the case of the family life of men in 'extreme' occupations like coal mining and deep-water fishing where, because of the exacting nature of the husband's work and the strong tradition of working men's clubs and drinking in non-work hours, wives are often left alone in the home. On new housing estates, however, as in the middle-class suburbs, relations between husbands and wives are changing. Mogey, for example, in his study of Oxford families, showed that on the new estate of Barton the rigid division of labour between husbands and wives had been considerably weakened since their move from the city. Meetings with members of the wider family also occurred much less frequently. Hannah Gavron's *The Captive Wife,* based on research in the Kentish Town area of London, confirmed the trend towards a growing degree of equality between husbands and wives. For instance, of the working-class husbands in her sample 62 per cent claimed to share all of the tasks of 'mothering' with their wives (the corresponding figure for middle-class husbands was 44 per cent), and in both classes a further 25 per cent were rated by their wives as being 'very helpful'. Mrs Gavron noted, however, an interesting social class difference, in that, while for middle-class wives equality meant independence, for working-class wives it meant greater sharing and closeness.

There are several explanations for these changes. Elizabeth Bott suggests that the existence of a closely knit network of kinship and community relations in traditional working-class areas acts as an alternative focus of attraction to that of the home and family. Thus, even after marriage, each spouse continues to be drawn into activities outside the home, so that the development of shared marital responsibilities is inhibited. Removal to a new housing estate results in the disruption of these former community ties, making it more likely – especially in view of the comparative attractiveness of the new home environment and the greater amount of leisure time which the husband now enjoys – that husband and wife will turn to each other for support and that they will share more domestic responsibilities together. [27] The unattractiveness of the contemporary work environment and its failure to supply many of the men who are engaged in routine manual (and even non-manual) jobs with any meaningful sense of purpose or identity may be a further reason for this change in family relations.

The growing tendency for married women to find work outside the home is another reason for changing attitudes. As Rosser and Harris comment, the more women are involved in domestic affairs, the more likely they are to lead separate lives from their husbands. But when they too have a job, not only is their (and their family's) economic status enhanced, but they have more to share with their husbands in other ways and can more legitimately expect help from them in the home and with the children. It is interesting to note that there are marked social class differences with regard to the husband's attitude to his wife's work. Both professional and (although for different reasons) manual working-class husbands on the whole tend to be co-operative and support their working partners. But the 'status aspiring' lower-middle-class and upper-working-class husbands are more reluctant to see their wives go out to work.

In the past, discussion about the subject of working wives has tended to centre on the conflict between women's two roles — as housewives and mothers and as workers outside the home. [28] Today, however, the scope of this discussion is gradually being enlarged to encompass also the two roles of men and the conflict between the demands of the 'instrumental' order of the world of work and the more 'expressive' demands made by the family. But there remains a considerable amount of prejudice and confusion in judgements of the married women's status in the family. Edmund Dahlström and Rota Liljeström [29] suggest that the prevailing view of the isolation of the elementary family and the expectation that women will be primarily responsible for the therapeutic and affective functions of the family (with the latent mistrust of help provided by external agencies which these assumptions imply) create considerable difficulties for married women wanting to return to work. Thus, while many of the legal and political barriers to equal status between men and women have been removed and many of the restrictions on the employment of married women have similarly disappeared, other barriers of a different kind still remain. They involve deep-rooted attitudes, ideals and expectations held not only among husbands and wives but also among employers and co-workers. They are ideals which are continually being reinforced by the mass media, and especially by the cheaper women's magazines. The origin of this ambiguity and confusion of views lies partly in the existence of two quite distinct ideals of womanhood — both of which date from the nineteenth century. The first of these is the idealization of the middle-class lady of leisure, still sanctified in some lower-middle-class families. The second is based on the ideal of the hard-working wife. Today women are expected to combine both of these roles. Another, and possibly more frustrating legacy from the nineteenth century, is the idea that it is basically wrong (that is, unwomanly) to be a career woman, since this threatens the sanctity of the home and appears to deny the ideal of the child-centred family.

If difficulties and prejudices of this kind still exist, and if many women also experience a crisis of loyalties, however, this has not prevented an increasing proportion of them from going out to work. Whereas in the 1930s only 10 per cent of married women were employed the figure today is over one third. One of the obvious explanations for this trend is that because of higher marriage rates and the earlier age at marriage, the number of single women available for recruitment is much lower than it was formerly. The growth of family planning, smaller average family sizes and the concentration of child-bearing during the early years of marriage also mean that, whereas at the end of the nineteenth century a mother spent about twelve to fifteen years of her life in a state of pregnancy or lactation, today this period is over after only four or five years on average. [30] Compulsory schooling after the age of five (and for the fortunate few, the existence of nursery play schools before this age) also helps to reduce maternal responsibilities to some extent. Taking all of these changes into consideration, and remembering the increased longevity of women today, most mothers can look forward to at least thirty years of active working life after the completion of their families.

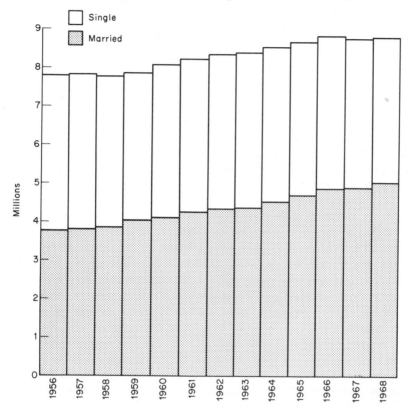

Fig. 17 Women in employment in the United Kingdom. (See also Table 11, p. 320.) After Annual Abstract of Statistics, *1969.*

Economic changes have also contributed to the increased employment of married women. Indeed, in some sectors of the economy, future developments in productivity depend entirely on there being an adequate and ready supply of female workers: teaching is a good example. The growth of retail trading, light manufacturing industries and office work has been the most important factor in the increasing employment of married women. Opportunities are provided for more shop assistants, secretaries, clerks, typists, machine operators, assembly workers and packers. There has also been an increase in the number of women – and especially married women – employed as social workers and medical and teaching auxiliaries. But although nearly half of all women workers are in non-manual jobs, their representation among the higher ranks of professional and administrative occupations is disproportionately small. Less than five in 1,000 women are in the higher professions and, while women make up one third of those employed in the manufacturing industries, not more than one in a hundred is in a supervisory post. What is more, women in most occupations still do not receive the same pay as men. In offices, for example, women receive only two-thirds of the men's rate even when they are engaged on equivalent work. [31] Although legislation and trade union and parliamentary policies in the 1950s and 1960s aimed to eliminate differentials, equal pay had only been achieved in relatively few sectors by 1970.

If the demand for women workers has increased considerably since 1945, however, and if more girls are better qualified educationally than at any time in the past, perhaps the most important reason for the increasing popularity of employment among married women has to do with changing attitudes on the part of these women themselves. It seems doubtful whether married women, except those who have received a professional training – and these are a very small minority and mainly middle-class – actually prefer employment to their traditional roles as wives and mothers. Indeed, most of them see employment as an extension of their family duties. [32] Among the reasons they give for wanting to return to work the most important is that their earnings can be devoted to buying more goods for the home, more clothes and toys for the children and more holidays. The reduction in boredom and isolation which results from going out to work, and the fact that their husbands sometimes find them more interesting as companions when they possess another focus in their lives than simply the home and family, are seen only as secondary gratifications.

It does not appear to be the case, therefore, as some sentimentalists have argued, that women work only in order to accumulate selfish luxuries. If they do accumulate 'luxuries' then these are luxuries which are shared throughout the family – often the children being the main beneficiaries. Nor is it the case, as has also been asserted, that working mothers, by being absent from the home for large parts of the day, starve their children of affection and contribute to the moral decline of the family. Most of them make very careful arrangements to see that someone is there to look after the younger members of the family while they are out at work (i.e. at school lunch-times and after 4 p.m.), and many deliberately choose shift-work jobs that enable them not to have to be away at the crucial times. [33] The high rate of female absenteeism from work – nearly all of it due to the need for the mother to care for her sick children or for her husband – further testifies to the responsibility of working wives, even if it does not please their employers. In fact, in returning to paid employment and in contributing to the family economy, women today are merely reasserting a status that until the end of the eighteenth century, as we have previously seen, had always been theirs. Before industrialization removed many jobs from the home, there was hardly any man's job that was not also performed by women. Indeed, even during the early years of the factory system many women continued to do much hard and strenuous work, for example, in the mines and in the cotton mills. The bourgeois ideal of idleness in married women was entirely a product of the growing veneration of wealth and conspicuous consumption among the Victorian upper and middle classes. Gradually this ideal spread to other social classes, and although it is still quite tenaciously held in certain lower-middle-class groups, more and more women above and below this position in the social scale are returning to work. They are also clamouring for more equal educational opportunities and for more equal earnings.

PARENT–CHILD RELATIONSHIPS

All these developments have, of course, affected relations between parents and children. The main changes which have occurred in the pattern of such relations in the post-war period depend mainly on the fact that families today are much smaller than were their Victorian counterparts. This has inevitably resulted in a closer concentration of parental affection and attention. The decline in paternal authority and the greater sharing of parental roles have reinforced the trend towards 'child-centred' family relations. They have also resulted in a more liberal and democratic climate of feeling within the family, and in more 'natural' child-rearing techniques. [34]

Although this emphasis on greater naturalness has spread throughout English society today, it is possible to detect quite marked differences in the way that it is interpreted by parents in the different social classes. Working-class mothers are on the whole more indulgent than those in middle-class and professional families. They are more likely to allow the extensive use of bottles and dummies; they are less strict about getting the children to bed early and less likely to have toilet-trained their children during their first year. They are also more punitive, as is indicated by a greater use of smacking and less permissiveness in genital play. Middle-class mothers, on the other hand, expect more from their children in the way of self-control, deferred gratification and willingness to please or make an effort.

All of these changes have had both advantages and disadvantages for the various family members. Other things being equal, for instance, small families offer a far less diverse range of emotional experiences to their members, although those relationships which do exist may be much deeper and more fully integrated than was ever possible in the larger families of the past. Where there are only one or two children, particularly in middle-class families which are cut off from any close neighbourhood contacts, these children often tend to suffer from over-protectiveness and over-ambition on the part of their parents (notably, for example, in the case of secondary school selection, university entrance, and examinations in general) or from the lack of companionship with other children of their own or similar ages. Another consequence of small families is that there tends to be a much greater gulf between the generations – the dichotomy between children and grown-ups being much more apparent than when there was a progressive chain of older brothers and sisters to bridge the gap.

The decline in the importance of the extended family, and the tendency for the individual members of the smaller nuclear family to develop and express their own personalities and to follow their own private interests (made possible by improved economic conditions and further encouraged by the specialized appeals to separate age groups made by the media of mass communication), has made parent–child relations more vulnerable. If the smaller number of children in the contemporary family enjoy improved educational opportunities, more pocket money and a wider range of commercial entertainment facilities on which to spend their money and free time, in other ways they are much less secure and self-reliant than children were in the larger families of the early twentieth century.

We have already suggested that the 'discovery' of childhood was one of the major factors leading to the creation of the modern concept of the family. Adolescence is equally central to contemporary discussions of the future of the family. There are a number of reasons for its predominance, one of the most important being the expansion in the size of the adolescent population. According to Mark Abrams, who defines adolescents as 'anyone between fifteen and twenty-four who is unmarried', this group now forms about one tenth of the total population. [35] Another important fact is that once they begin work, many adolescents are now much more affluent than was the case in the past (average real wages of adults increased by 25 per cent between 1938 and 1958, but those of adolescents by twice this amount). What is more, their income, unlike that of adult workers, is normally relatively 'free' (unless they are married) and while affluence has increased so also have the various opportunities and outlets for spending. Indeed, in just about every area of social experience today, from commercial entertainment to private leisure pursuits and religious and secular philosophies of life, the range of choice with which young people are confronted is unprecedentedly wide.

The status of adolescents within the family has changed too. Many of them reach full sexual maturity at a much younger age than in the nineteenth century, but because of the extension of formal schooling the period during which they are economically dependent upon their parents has been prolonged. However, as in the case of primary education (and perhaps even more so, in view of the present concentration on specialization and intensive vocational training), parents are less and less able to take an informed interest in what their children are learning – quite apart from giving them any help or advice.

Parents, like most other representatives of the older generation, then, are often seen to be ineffective and 'out of date'. [36] This means that adolescents, in the absence of any very meaningful contacts with their wider relatives and often lacking older brothers or sisters, have no alternative to the society of their peers. In this situation a certain amount of conflict is inevitable since teenagers, as Peter Laurie comments, 'stand in the same relationship with adults as explorers do to settlers – the one has to travel light, acquire information, react flexibly to any chance; the other has to stay put, narrow his gaze, concentrate his energies, and hoe his furrow'. [37] The growing rationalization of modern urban-industrial life adds to the strains imposed on adolescents today, and it is perhaps not surprising that some of the young people who become 'drop outs' in the selective educational system, and who fail to make the grade in a satisfying job of work once they leave school, are also tempted to drop out in social terms.

The extent to which these changes in the family and wider social status of adolescents have exacerbated what in psychological terms is almost inevitably a period of emotional turmoil and insecurity is difficult to gauge. To generalize is, in any case, dangerous, for, as J. B. Mays points out, there are several quite distinct adolescent sub-groups in existence today. [38] Mays isolates six of these: the 'roughs', 'toughs' and delinquents; the 'street corner boys'; the 'beats' (and their contemporary equivalents, the 'hippies'); the youthful idealists – and those who are political activists; the newly affluent proletarians (for example, the 'mods' and the 'greasers'); and middle-class public school and university types. We should perhaps add the growing number of newly marrieds among the teenage group as well. It is salutary to remember that, despite the impression sometimes created in the popular press, and despite middle-class and middle-aged complaints about the worthlessness of 'pop' culture, according to a Gallup Poll survey published in 1966, only one in 500 teenagers is actually delinquent; one in three go to church regularly; one in three attend evening classes, and not more than one in twelve are really restless and continually changing jobs. In addition, it is only a minority who are sexually experienced. [39] Indeed, as the authors of the Latey Committee Report on *The Age of Majority* observed in 1967, what is most surprising about the younger generation (and in this they are presumably not much different from their predecessors) is their conformity. Most adolescents, it would appear, barely differ at all from their elders in any important political or ideological respect. [40] At the time of the prominent drugs trial in 1967, for example, when a member of the Rolling Stones pop group was sentenced to imprisonment, 85 per cent of the teenagers interviewed in a National Opinion Poll either agreed with the sentence or wanted a more severe sentence imposed. Yet if the vociferous student activists, the delinquents and the 'weirdies' represent only a small minority of adolescents today, they are nevertheless an important minority, and their rebelliousness cannot simply be put down to youthful high spirits. For most of them it represents a serious and committed opposition to forms of social life and kinds of social institution which they feel they can no longer respect.

At the other end of the age scale there are, of course, salient problems relating to the position of old people, who today represent one in seven of the population. For those who retain their health, the role of grandparent is still an important one, in working- and middle-class families alike. Family visiting and joint entertaining are still quite widely maintained too – especially

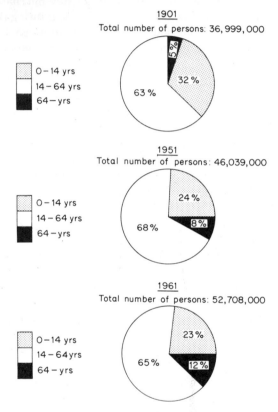

1901
Total number of persons: 36,999,000

0 – 14 yrs
14 – 64 yrs
64 – yrs

5%
32%
63%

1951
Total number of persons: 46,039,000

0 – 14 yrs
14 – 64 yrs
64 – yrs

24%
8%
68%

1961
Total number of persons: 52,708,000

0 – 14 yrs
14 – 64 yrs
64 – yrs

23%
12%
65%

Fig. 18 Age composition of the population of the United Kingdom, 1901–61. After Mitchell and Deane, 1962, and Annual Abstract of Statistics, *1967.*

in the more closely knit traditional neighbourhoods. [41] In addition to their family ties, old people are also perhaps more involved now in outside recreational activities, in travelling, in clubs and in evening classes than at any time in the past. But although more people are now able to enjoy a fully creative life in their old age, the strains imposed by enforced retirement (often at an age when many are still fully capable of work) and by housing and economic dificulties should not be overlooked. Nor should the effects of changing family patterns.

Because the members of the extended family are more widely dispersed geographically and because, in any case, modern houses are often not big enough to accommodate extra people living in permanently, old people may be increasingly obliged to seek support from the State or from the various voluntary organizations in times of hardship. If they do this, however, we should not necessarily take it as evidence of a lack of responsibility on the part of younger generations. Many old people do, of course, prefer to be independent. The more important point is that when so much else has changed in contemporary society, it is irrelevant to bewail the lost functions of the extended family. It is much more important to understand how they have been modified and why.

Most of our discussion in this chapter has been devoted to the way in which changes in the external order of society have influenced the pattern of family and kinship relations in modern Britain. But, as we saw in the opening section, the family performs a number of very important functions more or less independently of its connections with other wider social institutions. It is responsible for the reproduction of the population and for providing a secure emotional setting for its members. It is also concerned with the socialization of new generations – with the transmission to small children of particular cultural traditions and behavioural norms.

THE FAMILY AND SOCIALIZATION

Many theories have been advanced to explain how this process of socialization works. [42] Some of these, like Jean Piaget's study of *The Language and Thought of the Child,* derive from the observation of normal children; others, such as Bruno Bettelheim's study of autistic children, *The Empty Fortress,* have their roots in the study of emotionally disturbed infants – or in laboratory experiments with both animals and children. Still other theories, notably those of Ruth Benedict and Margaret Mead, have focused on the investigation of child-rearing practices and initiation rituals in primitive tribes. But perhaps the most useful approach from our point of view is that based on social role theory and the concept of 'symbolic interaction'.

According to this theory, as the child passes through a sequence of age statuses, varying patterns of behaviour are demanded of him, and other people modify their behaviour in accordance with his needs and capabilities. Thus, a baby is expected (and allowed) to cry when he is uncomfortable, to sleep when he is sleepy and to excrete without restraint. He has no clear sense of himself as a separate identity, nor is he very much aware of what goes on around him in the outside world. He is entirely dependent upon other people – particularly his mother – for care and protection. As his experience and capabilities increase, and as he learns to integrate the changes in his physical growth with developments in his cognitive skills and in his emotional relationships within the family, however, the child's role situation changes, and it does this in predetermined ways, according to the prevailing cultural norms in his particular segment of society.

How does this development occur? The child learns the ways of his group – not, of course, through meeting the culture in the abstract, but mediated to him through other people who already know and carry the patterns of the society to him. His parents are, in G. H. Mead's term, the most important 'significant others', [43] at least in the western family (although on the Israeli kibbutzim, in Caribbean communities and in certain primitive societies this role is often performed by other individuals). By their attitudes and behaviour, parents define the world for their children. They also serve as models for them. They teach the appropriate roles and values by bestowing rewards and inflicting punishments, not only overtly but by their gestures and facial expressions. For example, when a little girl offers to help clear away her toys, her parents beam their approval with warm nods and smiles – they are rewarding her for having learnt their norm of 'tidiness' and for having adopted an appropriate 'feminine' role. The primary mechanism, then, is language and gesture (itself a kind of 'symbolic language'). Learning social behaviour is not, however, just a cognitive process and it does not rest simply on the development of linguistic skills. It is also closely associated with the child's emotional development, as psychoanalysts have shown. [44] Because a child seeks approval and love from his significant others, he is motivated to think and behave as they wish, and to model his behaviour on theirs. Thus, he may suppress his own immediate impulses and learn to gratify his parents' wishes instead, or he may seek to do well in school, knowing that he will gain thereby the goodwill not only of his parents but also of his teachers and possibly his peers.

Gradually some of the patterns which are learnt in this way will become habits and more stable personality traits, and others – such as striving for success – may become part of an internalized value system. But although these patterns nearly always develop in the first place as a response to parental stimuli, the specific impact of any particular interaction is always a function of what the child has already become and of the expectations and relationships which he has already formed. This means that as his own personality develops he becomes better equipped to assess and interpret the meaning of given situations for himself, and is less and less the relatively passive instrument of his parents' wishes and expectations.

Initially, the child's emotional attachments are limited to his relationship with his mother, as we have seen. As he grows older he gradually becomes involved with an ever-widening range of social groups: with his father and siblings and with more distant relatives; with friends and teachers, and possibly with popular heroes or imaginary figures. Finally, at adolescence, meaningful relationships are established with various neighbourhood groups, with work teams and even with national groups. Each of these inclusive reference groups implies the existence of a 'non-we' group from which it is distinguished, and it is by reference to his different groups of origin, his 'we-groups', that the child acquires his developing sense of self and his growing capacity for independent judgement. This concept of self is basic to role theory – just as it is to the individual in his day-to-day life. In order to function in the society, the child must know what behaviour is expected from him in the whole range of roles which he has to fulfil: brother, son, pupil, cousin, Boy Scout, choir boy, butterfly collector, football player, cyclist, book-borrower, classroom monitor, etc. [45] He must also be able, through language and insight, to tell whether or not he is acting appropriately in any specific situation. Only by seeing himself as an object (i.e. by knowing his 'looking-glass self', as C. H. Cooley calls it [46]) can he know how to check, guide and judge his own behaviour and act according to others' expectations.

Knowing how he 'ought' to behave does not, of course, guarantee that the individual will necessarily do what is expected of him. He may not be capable of this, or he may have personal reasons – either conscious or unconscious – for failing to conform. This means that cultural influences and institutional pressures are only ever partially integrated in the members of a society – unless that society is a dictatorship and all learning is conditioned on the basis of the appropriate propaganda. Indeed, it is important, to most of us in the western world at least, that this disjunction should continue to exist. As we shall see in the next chapter, too great a degree of conformity and adaptation to existing social norms may be positively harmful for future social development – quite apart from the fact that it impairs the individual's own personality development and restricts his opportunity to live creatively. [47]

Although the family is undoubtedly the most important agency in socialization, other groups also play a considerable part in this process. Thus, the school contributes to the child's formal education and is ultimately responsible for his allocation to adult occupational statuses. It also helps the child to gain emotional independence from his parents by providing an environment in which he can make friends not only with others of his own age but also with more neutral representatives of the older generation. The peer group, which usually has its basis either in a particular neighbourhood locality or in a collection of school friends, is important in the socialization process for other reasons. It provides the child with his first experience of egalitarian types of relationship (as distinct from the various kinds of authority relationship met with in the home and in the school classroom). It also provides him with a context in which to try out new experimental role identities and to exchange information on otherwise 'taboo' subjects. Wider neighbourhood institutions, including the church and, in the case of minority peoples, the ethnic group, add their particular codes and traditions to the child's growing vocabulary of social conduct.

Beyond this network of primary groups, the institutions of mass communication – and especially television – also play an increasingly significant role in the process of socialization, even though their influence is relatively impersonal and remote. For instance, they do not themselves evoke feelings of love and approval, nor do they impart punishments or rewards or necessitate day-to-day adjustments in the behaviour of their audience. However, they not only portray aspects of popular culture which other agencies do not often (or so successfully) transmit, but also generate new fashions in entertainment and – to a far greater extent than is possible in the school or peer group – introduce individuals to a wider knowledge of the world and of the society in which they live. Nevertheless, important and perhaps valuable as these functions are, they do not supplant the very crucial processes of social learning which occur within the family.

THE FUTURE OF THE FAMILY

Most sociologists today, as we have suggested, regard it as axiomatic that the family is a necessary and enduring social institution. This does not mean that they ignore the very fundamental changes which have taken place in its structure over the past century, but such an assumption does influence their conclusions about what such changes imply. Peter Townsend, for instance, summarizes the altered structure of family relationships in these terms:

> More marriages may mean fewer isolated people in old age, but fewer uncommitted aunts who can, whenever they are needed, run to the aid of their kin. Smaller family size may mean not only small sibling groups, more manageable tasks for mother and grandmother, and the concentration of the responsibilities of parenthood into a shorter span of years, but that aged people will have fewer, and more elderly, children to look after them. [48]

He goes on to suggest that the longer survival and the greater incidence of marriage has 'given greater prominence to the relationship between man and wife in society'. As a consequence, as compared with fifty years ago, 'family relationships now seem to be deeper (in generation depth), more symmetrical, and less collaterally extended'.

Many would agree with Townsend's analysis. The American sociologist J. Barrington Moore, however, considers that this kind of appraisal reflects the projection of 'certain middle-class hopes and ideals', rather than a dispassionate analysis of the kinds of relationship that actually exist within the contemporary family. It is his view that, in the context of modern urban-industrial society, the family is prevented from performing the social and social-psychological functions ascribed to it by writers like Townsend. He contends, for instance, that the obligation 'to give affection as a duty to a particular set of persons on account of the accident of birth' is a 'true relic of barbarism'. [49] And he points to a number of trends in present-day society which, he suggests, have sharply reduced, rather than increased, the effectiveness of the family as an agency for bringing up children. When the father was head of a joint family economic unit, Moore claims, and when the children could see and value what he did, the father had a role to be copied, and the source of his authority was clear. Today this is much less true. Moore also instances the conflict faced by working wives and mothers, [50] the disillusionment of some young people with what they take to be entirely unacceptable values in adult life – conspicuous consumption, status seeking, apathy, graft, corruption – and the high rate of divorce, as further evidence of the obsolescence of the family. The work of psychiatrists like Ronald Laing contains similar indictments, although its frame of reference is quite different. [51] For Laing, the 'barbarity' of the family is to be seen in its failure to help its members to develop truly authentic personalities, by 'binding' them in immature and potentially 'schizophrenogenic' relationships.

What are we to conclude from these two different kinds of analysis ? One thing at least seems fairly clear ; the family is still of vital strategic significance in contemporary society (as can be evinced from the failure of attempts in the 1930s to abolish the family in the Soviet Union, for instance). It is true that some families seem ill-equipped to help in the socialization of their younger members and that in some families the marital relationship is far from 'ideal' (whatever that may mean). But in this they probably do not differ to any great extent from certain families in the past. Dr Leach may even be correct when he suggests that 'the family, with its narrow privacy and tawdry secrets, is the source of all our discontents'. [52] The important point is, however, that only if individuals are motivated to serve the needs of the society will it be capable of survival. At present the family alone seems capable of supplying that motivation. Formal agencies of social control are not enough. What is needed is a 'set of social forces that responds to the individual whenever he does well or poorly, supporting his internal controls as well as the controls of the formal agencies'. [53] By implanting such controls in the individual as a result of the process of socialization we have described, and by continuing to influence the individual through most of his adult life, the family is uniquely equipped to provide that set of forces. [54] It remains the essential mediating agency between the individual and the wider social structure.

NOTES

1 PETER BERGER and HANSFRIED KELLER 'Marriage and the construction of reality', *Diogenes*, 46, 1964.
2 See THOMAS LUCKMANN and PETER BERGER *The Social Construction of Reality* (London, 1967).
3 See further CHRISTOPHER TURNER *Family and Kinship in Modern Britain*, Ch. 5 (London, 1969).

4 See PHILIPE ARIÈS *Centuries of Childhood,* p. 404 (London, 1962); and, for an alternative view of the family in the seventeenth century, PETER LASLETT *The World We Have Lost.*

5 *Psychiatry and Anti-Psychiatry,* p. 30 (London, 1967).

6 The extended family refers to any persistent kinship grouping of persons related by descent, marriage, or adoption, which is wider than the elementary (or nuclear) family, in that it characteristically spans three generations.

7 J. BARRINGTON MOORE. JR 'Thoughts on the future of the family', in STEIN *et al.* (eds.) *Identity and Anxiety,* p. 392. See also LEACH *A Runaway World.*

8 See FLETCHER *The Family and Marriage,* Ch. 1.

9 ARIÈS *Centuries of Childhood,* p. 406.

10 *A Modern Introduction to the Family,* p. 6 (New York, 1960; 1966 edition).

11 See WILLIAM GOODE 'The process of role bargaining in the impact of urbanisation and industrialisation on family systems', *Current Sociology,* Vol. XII (1), 1963–4.

12 *The Long Revolution,* pp. 331–2.

13 See, for example, MICHAEL YOUNG and PETER WILLMOTT *Family and Kinship in East London* (London, 1957); and PETER TOWNSEND *The Family Life of Old People* (London, 1957).

14 'Occupational mobility and extended family cohesion', *American Sociological Review,* Vol. 25, 1960.

15 *The Family and Social Change,* p. 301.

16 See D. G. MCKINLEY *Social Class and Family Life* (New York, 1964).

17 Minority groups (religious and ethnic) are an exception to this general pattern if they continue to preserve their traditional customs.

18 *The Family: from Institution to Companionship* (New York, 1963).

19 See R. K. KELSALL *Population,* p. 21 (London, 1967).

20 See MARK ABRAMS *Teenage Consumer Spending in 1959* (London, 1961).

21 Estimates for the average age of the onset of puberty are notoriously difficult to arrive at. However, whereas the present age is around thirteen for girls and fifteen for boys, in 1854 puberty for girls seems generally to have occurred between fourteen and sixteen years of age (see GEORGE R. DRYSDALE *The Elements of Social Science,* p. 65 (London, 1854; 1881 edition)).

22 *The Trend and Pattern of Fertility in Great Britain* (London, 1954).

23 *Population,* pp. 56–7.

24 'The resort to divorce in England and Wales, 1858–1957', *Population Studies,* Vol. 11, 1957–8.

25 See further MCGREGOR *Divorce in England.*

26 'Divorce American style', *New York Review of Books,* 17 February 1966.

27 See further KLEIN *Samples from English Cultures,* pp. 155–66.

28 See ALVA MYRDAL and VIOLA KLEIN *Women's Two Roles* (London, 1956).

29 *The Changing Roles of Men and Women,* Ch. 5 (London, 1967).

30 See TITMUSS 'The position of women', in *Essays on 'The Welfare State'.*

31 See NAN BERGER *and* JOAN MAIZELS *Woman – Fancy or Free?,* Ch. VI (London, 1962).

32 See PEARL JEPHCOTT *et al. Married Women Working* (London, 1962).

33 See S. YUDKIN and A. HOLME *Working Mothers and their Children* (London, 1965).

34 See JOHN and ELIZABETH NEWSOM *Patterns of Infant Care* (Harmondsworth, 1965).
35 *Teenage Consumer Spending in 1959*, p. 3.
36 See further BARRY SUGARMAN 'Youth culture, academic achievement and conformity', *British Journal of Sociology*, Vol. 18, 1967.
37 *Teenage Revolution*, p. 11 (London, 1965).
38 *The Young Pretenders*, pp. 169–71 (Liverpool, 1965).
39 See further MICHAEL SCHOFIELD *The Sexual Behaviour of Young People* (London, 1965).
40 See also EDGAR FRIEDENBERG *The Vanishing Adolescent* (Boston, 1959).
41 See further TOWNSEND *The Family Life of Old People*.
42 For a general survey see F. ELKIN *The Child and Society* (New York, 1960).
43 *Mind, Self and Society* (Chicago, 1934).
44 See ERIK ERIKSON *Childhood and Society* (Harmondsworth, 1965).
45 See ERVING GOFFMAN *The Presentation of Self in Everyday Life* (Edinburgh, 1957).
46 *Human Nature and the Social Order* (Boston, 1902).
47 See HENRY *Culture Against Man* and R. D. LAING *The Politics of Experience* (Harmondsworth, 1967).
48 *The Family Life of Old People*, pp. 232–3.
49 'Thoughts on the future of the family', p. 393.
50 See further BETTY FRIEDAN *The Feminine Mystique* (New York, 1963).
51 See *The Divided Self* (London, 1960); and with A. ESTERSON *Sanity, Madness and the Family* (London, 1964). See also PETER LOMAS (ed.) *The Predicament of the Family* (London, 1967).
52 *A Runaway World?*, p. 44.
53 WILLIAM GOODE *The Family*, p. 2 (New York, 1964).
54 For two accounts of the Israeli kibbutzim which provide an alternative mode of socialization (although one which has not yet proved satisfactory from every point of view), see M. E. SPIRO *Children of the Kibbutz* (New York, 1965), and BRUNO BETTELHEIM *The Children of the Dream* (London, 1969).

Questions of women and of the family were previously discussed in Chapter 4.

10

Politics and Communications

In previous chapters we have tried to trace the consequences of modern urban and industrial growth for the structure of contemporary work relations, for the educational system, for the family, and for community life more generally. In this brief survey we have not been able to cover every aspect of modern social structure; nor have we taken up all of the earlier historical threads. However, in view of the importance of the theme of power and communications in modern society and because, in one way or another, the institutions of government and social control, and the impact of mass markets and of the mass media, permeate the entire fabric of contemporary life, we shall in this chapter attempt to give a very general account of these phenomena. We shall also try to suggest some of the ways in which they may be expected to influence the future development of British society.

Two elements are of crucial importance for an explanation of the distribution of power in contemporary society: one is an understanding of British political culture, the other is a knowledge of the historical context out of which the present-day structure of government has grown. At the beginning of the nineteenth century political philosophers and social theorists, prompted by the violent social and political upheavals generated by the American and French revolutions, attempted to analyse the links between particular political systems and what was then called 'national character' (what we would now term the nation's political culture). These investigations were based almost entirely on subjective evidence, and they tended to reflect highly biased ideological views. In the twentieth century, however, as a result of the development of survey techniques and opinion polls, it is possible to study political behaviour much more objectively. We can, for example, ask individuals to describe their feelings about what governments should or should not do in arbitrating between the interests of various groups in the society (as well as finding out more precisely, in quantitative terms, what the particular needs of such groups are). We can ask people to describe the way in which they see their own political role – either as participants or as passive subjects of government, and also to say how they think particular systems of control ought to be altered or improved. At the same time, we can amass helpful comparative data on the ways in which alternative systems actually work out in practice. The answers to exercises like these – although often unsophisticated – enable us to assess the prevailing political climate much more precisely than was possible a century ago. They also make it possible to discern subcultural variations within an overall political system and, therefore, to predict the potentialities of different groups for different types of political action. In a similar manner, by comparing what we know about British political attitudes and British institutions with those in other countries, we are able to construct national 'profiles' and comparative typologies. These are of particular value in helping us to understand better the central question of how political systems are linked to given forms of social system, [1] for although, as Richard Rose points out, the political culture is in one sense 'the sum total of individual political outlooks', these outlooks are themselves very much influenced by 'the cultural values, beliefs and emotions which are taught persons in the process of political socialization.' [2] What this means, as Philip Abrams suggests, is that

> When a man enters a polling booth he does not suddenly become a Benthamite calculating machine; he remains the creature of his social experience, his family background, his occupation, his education and his friends. His vote distils the conjunction of his political and social roles. [3]

The importance of the historical context is directly connected to this point about socialization, since it is within a particular historical context that particular cultural systems are created and transmitted. All stable societies, as we have seen, contrive to implant in the growing child orientations to his society which are suited to perpetuating its own distinctive institutions. Thus, the child learns, tacitly from his family and friends, and more explicitly from representatives of the government and church, to recognize the workings of his political system and to see himself as a subject and citizen. He also learns some of the techniques and limits of rejection and protest, of course; just as in states with a multi-party system he learns to be a partisan of one group rather than another. In fact, what the child learns are precisely the political dispositions that the system requires him to possess, and these are based on earlier political traditions and values.

CHANGES IN THE STRUCTURE OF POWER

The question we must ask firstly then is how the contemporary structure of power in Britain emerged. Up to the end of the eighteenth century, the landed aristocracy exercised virtually complete control over English society; they were the State. Their authority was shared between three agencies: those of government, the army and the Church. Then, with the expansion of industry and commerce in the early nineteenth century, a new class of wealthy business-men and independent property owners took shape and challenged the supremacy of the established élite. In England, unlike France or Italy, no revolution was necessary for this new class of men to gain a share of power in the existing political hierarchy. The more successful of them were simply absorbed into the dominant class, while the remainder were appeased by an extension of the franchise. This at least enabled them to be more marginally involved than hitherto in the processes of government. As they moved up-wards, the successful burghers took with them the capitalist ideals of self-help and *laissez-faire* which had already, in large part, secured them their economic strength. These ideals too were absorbed by the ruling élite, until, as we have previously seen, they became the very cornerstone not only of late nineteenth-century social policy generally but also of the continued stability and political effectiveness of the upper class itself. [4]

The established aristocracy managed to maintain its former positions of authority even into the twentieth century (for instance, it was not until 1923 that a non-aristocrat held the position of Foreign Secretary for the first time since the 1832 Reform Act, and not until 1929 that a government was elected on the basis of universal suffrage). But new power groups have also emerged in the last fifty years: those of the large corporation, of organized labour and of the mass communications industry, for example. At the same time, the influ-ence of the army and of the established Church has been considerably eroded.

In some societies the legitimacy of particular political institutions is secured by force. This has not been the case in Britain. The continued survival of some political groups and the attrition of others is, therefore, to be explained as part of a continuous process of revaluation in which members of the society assess the relative usefulness to them of different modes of authority and sub-mission, and distribute their allegiances accordingly. Survival also depends, of course, on the relative financial strength of the various groups contending for power.

With the decline of the authority of the army and the Church, the major resources of power in contemporary British society have become concentrated within the parliamentary and economic spheres. Yet despite the democratiza-tion of election procedures, the growth of mass political parties, the creation of a national education system, of nationalized industries and of the various agencies of the Welfare State – all of which have contributed towards a level-ling of social differences – membership of the élite in the government, as in the army and in the established Church, is still very largely based on the possession of private wealth and a private education. [5] The continued strength of this very narrowly constituted ruling class owes its existence to a number of peculiarly British political traditions.

CONFLICT AND CONSENSUS POLITICS

If the English public had not learnt to value the symbolic authority of the Crown, if they had not believed in gradualism and in respect for law and order, and if they had not been willing to compromise and make concessions, the structure of our political institutions would almost certainly have assumed a very different character. As we have seen, in the nineteenth century a number of popular demands for reform were acceded to − in education, in public health, and in working conditions and labour relations (thereby containing the potential revolutionary challenge of the urban working class and, in the process, securing valuable electoral support from some of them). Most members of the working class, while continuing to agitate for further extensions to their democratic rights, nevertheless persisted in holding to traditional patterns of deference and submission (thus undermining their own collective strength and confirming the power of the élite).

Here we have a clear example of the British amalgam of conflict and consensus politics. Both are crucial to our system of government. Conflict means that there will be 'a struggle over ruling positions, challenges to parties in power, and shifts of parties in office'. Consensus, on the other hand, 'a system allowing the peaceful "play" of power, the adherence of the "outs" to the decisions of the "ins", and the recognition by the "ins" of the rights of the "outs" ', is important because without it 'there can be no democracy'. [6] We have seen earlier how the debate about equality has shifted its focus since the Second World War. The discussion of democracy has also taken a new direction. With the achievement, at least theoretically, of equal educational opportunities, and with equal access for all citizens to medical care, pensions, industrial insurance and so on, attention is now turned towards the investigation of more fundamental sources of social inequality. How much 'real' freedom of action do different individuals and groups possess in contemporary society? How far are the institutions of government 'really' democratic? What degrees of freedom of choice exist within modern bureaucratic organizations? What rights do minority groups possess? How effective is public opinion in influencing those who take the major political decisions? How far are we 'manipulated' by the mass media? To what extent do consensus politics imply 'managed' politics, the 'institutionalization of opposition' and the coercion of the majority? These are the kinds of questions which concern political sociologists today. They involve two main areas of discussion. On the one hand we need to examine the degree of effective democracy which exists within the formal system of government as such. And on the other hand we have to consider the structure of power within industrial organizations and the system of mass communications.

THE CONCEPT OF DEMOCRACY

Before embarking on these various issues of political power it is perhaps necessary to return to our earlier attempt to define the concept of democracy. It
is a term, as we have seen, which can convey a whole range of meanings, some
of which carry wider 'democratic' implications than others. For Burke, the
Conservative political theorist, and for Ostrogorski, one of the earliest writers
to attempt a study of party organization, it was a sufficient condition for
democracy that:

> a group of citizens first organize themselves into a political party on the
> basis of some principle or set of principles; they then deduce a political
> programme from these principles and their candidates proceed to lay this
> programme before the electorate; if the party secures a majority in
> Parliament, it then implements the 'mandate' given it by the electors. If
> issues arise not covered by the 'mandate', then it is for the M.P.s to use
> their own judgement in deciding what to do. [7]

To more radically minded political thinkers, however, this model lacks what
is perhaps the most important characteristic of democratic processes: the
element of continuous accountability and participation. Robert McKenzie, for
example, asserts that any explanation of the democratic process which ignores
the role of organized interest groups 'is hopelessly inadequate and sterile in
that it leaves out of account the principal channels though which the mass
of the citizenry bring influence to bear on the decision makers whom they
have elected'. [8] This difference is crucial, for, according to the second model,
voters undertake to do far more than simply choose their elected representatives. McKenzie suggests that they have the further right, via the enormous
range of pressure groups which exist in this society, to advise, cajole and
argue with the government about the policies that it seeks to adopt. A wider
extension of this principle would also imply that they have the right, as
citizens and as workers, to participate in the day-to-day management of their
living and working conditions.

But if this second model gives us our definition of the ideal conditions for
democracy, how closely do the workings of the present social system in Britain
approximate to it? And, in particular, how effective is the participation of
different sorts of groups in the various processes of decision-making which
mould the day-to-day conditions of life in our society?

THE ELECTORAL SYSTEM

Let us look at the electoral system first. The pre-industrial pattern of
constituencies, including the 'rotten boroughs', has been reformed, although
there are still some border anomalies – especially in the fast-growing urban

conglomerations. Hence, in 1951, for example, a Conservative government took office, having obtained fewer votes than the Labour Party which it ousted. The ballot is conducted in secret, and the electorate has expanded on the basis of universal suffrage from one of about 220,000 (3 per cent of the adult population) in 1830 to one of over 40 million today (it should be noted, however, that the principle of 'one man one vote' was not in fact applied until 1950: before then certain categories of people, such as university graduates and the owners of business premises, had extra votes). The House of Lords, on the other hand, is still overwhelmingly recruited on a hereditary basis. Although the nomination of life peers and peeresses, and wider plans for the reform of the Lords, in one sense represent steps towards the creation of a more democratically constituted second chamber, they tend nevertheless to confirm the existing structure of power (by rewarding those who already occupy 'top' positions) rather than to involve representatives from the wider society.

Today, then, everybody over the age of eighteen has the right to vote. The question we have to ask is how they actually use this right. Over the last twenty-five years participation in parliamentary elections has been high – with 85 per cent of the electorate voting. But, according to a number of recent investigations of voters' attitudes, it has not been an especially informed or committed kind of participation. At any one time up to one third of the electorate apparently knows nothing about the major political parties, and the proportion who are able to state a particular government policy and give reasons for supporting or rejecting it is no more than one in ten. Even during the heat of an election campaign, less than half of the population describes itself as seriously interested in the struggle. [9] In our earlier discussion of class consciousness and social change we referred to a number of possible explanations for the existence of this mood of political apathy. Alasdair MacIntyre suggests another, which, while it certainly cannot be said to hold true for the mass of the electorate, may explain the reaction of certain middle of the road and left wing intellectuals. In MacIntyre's view a part of the feeling of apathy is a reaction to what he calls 'the strange death of social democratic England'. [10] In the immediate post-war period, MacIntyre argues, the belief was very strongly expressed and acted upon that

> the interests of the working class can be expressed by a political party which would both adhere to the conventions of parliamentary democracy and also accept the fact that the interests of the working class must conflict with the goals which dominate the economic system.

By the 1960s, however, 'the Labour Party and the Labour government [had] accepted definitions of political reality and political possibility according to which social democracy can no longer exist'. As a consequence, the working class no longer has a party, and because of the present system of 'managed' politics no conventional political remedies or channels of communication appear to be relevant to them.

The general lack of public involvement in political questions in this country, and the low level of active participation in community affairs and in the work of the trade union movement, are also reflected in a basically weak sense of commitment to the major political parties. While the total membership of the Conservative and Labour Parties is high – their combined membership is over 9 million – the number of active members who do the work of the parties in the constituences, canvass new members, draft the resolutions debated in the party conferences and choose the constituency candidates for their respective parties, is not more than a few hundred per constituency of 50,000 to 60,000 electors. It should be noted, furthermore, that of the 6 million members of the Labour Party, 5 million or more are included simply by virtue of trade union membership and a failure to contract out of the political levy. Signed-up members amount to only some 800,000, compared to over 2·5 million members of the Conservative party. This small 'stage army of the politically active', as McKenzie calls it, contains perhaps the only people to take full advantage of their democratic electoral rights. However, at least in theory, the structure does permit the participation of the majority. The structure of party politics within parliament, on the other hand, does not.

PARLIAMENTARY PARTIES

In the early days of the Labour Party it was an article of faith that no party could call itself democratic unless its parliamentary leaders were responsible to the mass organization. Once it achieved office, though, this kind of accountability to the mass party proved unworkable. The Conservative Party, because of its different history, did not meet with the same problem. Until well into the nineteenth century, as we have seen, it had no need of a mass organization, although the rapid expansion of the electorate after 1867, the tightening of the law against electoral corruption and the growth of public education and increased literacy – as well, of course, as the growing strength of the labour movement – eventually forced the Conservative parliamentarians to organize a mass party in the constituences. They never committed themselves to the principle of accountability, however.

These basic differences in the origins and principles of the two major parties are still evident in their present-day structure. Officially, the Conservative leader has sole responsibility for almost every aspect of party activity. Once elected, he is not required to submit himself for periodic re-election. As in any other party when in office, the leader chooses the cabinet. But even in opposition the Conservative leader chooses his 'shadow cabinet'. Whether in power or in opposition, he has sole responsibility for the formulation of policies, the resolutions of the national conference are in no way binding on him. What is more, the Central Office (the party bureaucracy and research organization) is also under his personal control. This means that he can direct all the main instruments of propaganda, research and finance. Increasingly, however, the Conservative leader is not nearly as free in practice as this model suggests. He must rely on the support both of his parliamentary party and of the mass movement (the pressure of constituency party opinion on such subjects as capital punishment and the control of immigration is a good example of the way in which parliamentary policies have been modified to suit the mood of the mass party).

Theoretically the Labour Party has an internal system which is very differently organized from that of the Conservative Party. Members of the parliamentary party, for example, are considered by many in the labour movement to be servants of that movement and directly responsible to it; the leader is seen as little more than a spokesman for his parliamentary colleagues. But although the Labour shadow cabinet is democratically elected, when Labour is in office the Prime Minister chooses his own cabinet. The leader does not hold himself under any obligation to consult the opinions of the constituency parties or to respect the decisions taken at the annual party conferences. Even so, the mass organization of the Labour Party and the elected National Executive do play a larger (even if not a major) part in the affairs of the parliamentary party than is the case with their Conservative equivalents.

The remoteness of the British parliamentary parties and the absence of any direct channels of accountability constitute, for some political theorists, direct evidence of the failure of democracy. But perhaps this situation is unavoidable: Robert Michels has suggested that all large-scale decision-making bodies – whether in business, in the trade unions or in government – must because of their size inevitably be undemocratic, since they are susceptible to what he terms 'the iron law of oligarchy', that is, the rule of officials. [11] McKenzie and Beer, two of the most serious and objective students of the contemporary political system in Britain, would seem to support this conclusion. [12] In their view, democracy can only be safeguarded if there are channels through which organized interest groups can intervene in the formal processes of government.

INTEREST GROUPS

Interest groups have been in existence in Britain since long before the days of the democratic franchise. Some of them, such as the Anti-Corn-Law League, expired once their purposes were achieved, leaving behind, however, important traditions of popular organization. Others, such as the T.U.C., which was founded in 1868, have gained in importance over the years. New groups come into existence almost daily so that scarcely an interest or cause does not now have its body of organized defenders (or opponents) – and very often they have several such bodies to represent them. In fact, approximately half of the electorate belong to one or more interest groups. Not all of these groups have equal influence; nor is a very large proportion of their membership especially active. [13]

The strongest interest groups in Britain today are those of the sectional organizations. In the mid-1960s, for example, the Federation of British Industries represented the interests of some 50,000 firms (roughly six-sevenths of all those firms employing more than eleven workers), and the British Employers' Confederation united over 250 individual bodies which, together, negotiated with about three-quarters of the employed population. The labour lobby, which was even stronger in numerical terms (even if not in terms of its power), was in 1967 made up of nearly 600 unions of employees and had a total membership of over 9·5 million. As we saw earlier, however, many of these unions were quite tiny, and therefore, individually could exert very little power. On matters of common concern to all of the unions negotiations are conducted by the T.U.C., which has an affiliated membership of about 8·5 million. These business and occupational groups, together with the professional associations, such as the British Medical Association and the National Union of Teachers, are by far the most influential ones, especially taking into account their associated propaganda organizations. Many of these latter organizations, the Aims of Industry organization, the Fabian Society, the Socialist Educational Association and the Co-operative Movement, for example, focus their activities on the production of journals and propagandist literature. In this they demonstrate the operation of earlier radical traditions in the modern context of the domination by monopoly organizations of the media of communication.

In addition to the major sectional groups there are a large number of important civic promotional groups, like the Howard League for Penal Reform, the National Council for Civil Liberties and the Consumers' Association. There are groups representing special sections of the population, such as the British Legion and the Automobile Association. There are religious and evangelical groups, and a multitude of educational, cultural and recreational groups, including, for example, the Victorian Society, the Society for the Preservation of Rural England, the National Trust and the National Playing Fields Association.

The day-to-day activities of these various groups pervade every sphere of the government's domestic policy – and sometimes its foreign policies as well, as in the case of the Anti-Apartheid Movement, the Anti-Common Market League and the organizations which, since the Second World War, have sought to recruit public support against, for example, German rearmament, nuclear weapons and the wars in Korea and Vietnam. Their methods and tactics vary considerably, however – from ministerial consultation, the sponsorship of M.P.s, lobbying, tabling amendments, parliamentary questions and private members' bills, to campaigns and public demonstrations, press publicity, broadcasts and advertising – depending on what the group hopes to achieve and which institutions or people it aims to influence. [14] Tactics are also, of course, limited by the power and influence of the particular groups concerned and by their funds. Thus, while the T.U.C. and the Employers' Confederation can, and do, expect to be consulted by the government, smaller and less influential groups have to be content with writing letters to M.P.s and with local campaigning for funds and support.

There is no question, then, that pressure groups do permit the establishment of intermediate links between government and electorate. They help to check and balance the power of the ruling élite and they are also able to supply both M.P.s and civil servants with vital specialized advice and information. In several respects, however, the system is imperfect. As we have already commented, not all groups have equal influence – some are less well organized than others, they are not so wealthy, nor so well staffed or so well represented in parliament. It should also be noted that some sections of the population are simply not represented at all in this way – the poor and those living in backward, underdeveloped regions of the country, for example. What is more, despite the effectiveness of some of the larger interest groups, there is a danger that their organizational requirements (the need for a trained leadership, specialized research and a bureaucratic hierarchy of control), like those of the major parliamentary parties, are susceptible to Michel's 'iron law of oligarchy'. As a consequence, the general public – and even the mass membership of these organizations – are cut off from the places where important decisions are made. [15] In these latter ways the democratic process is compromised – or perhaps fails altogether.

CORPORATIONS

The parliamentary system which we have described, with its formal democratic channels of communication between Leader and cabinet, cabinet and parliamentary party, parliamentary party and constituency organizations, and between the parliamentary parties and organized interest groups outside, is connected in other ways to the wider social structure. The government is also subject to other countervailing sources of influence: to the banks, the financial corporations, the Civil Service, foreign governments and international trading or defensive alliances, and national press and television networks. Indeed, in the last twenty years, these institutions have come to hold a much more central place in the processes of government decision-making than ever before. This means that the task of the leading politicians to-day is not so much to administer the policies put to them by the mass of the population (or their representatives) – or even to fulfil a particular electoral mandate – it is, rather, to negotiate with the various states within the state – the banks, the industrial giants, the 'experts', the Civil Service and so on. They bargain and compromise in this way to achieve a coalition among the different major interests concerned. This, and not equalization or a 'responsible' form of government, is the present meaning of consensus politics in Britain. It is a form of 'managed' government, and as such it has a deeply undemocratic side to it.

The key to the creation of stable government in these new conditions lies in the use of the modern communications system and, here again, the contrast with the nineteenth century is marked. A hundred years ago dissenting minorities had, if not equality, at least some comparative opportunity of access to the places where opinion was formed – the cheap printing press, the hustings, the soap-box, the chapel, the public hall. Although many of these means are still available today, the main channels of fact and persuasion are very different. They are the television networks, the mass circulation daily papers, and the advertising media – all of which have now to a very important extent been absorbed into the major structures of power. It is true, of course, that on television opposition and minority groups are by law allowed an occasional hearing, but normally the terms on which they are given this hearing are those of the established system. Dissident views, therefore, tend to be 'processed' or 'neutralized'. [16]

CENTRAL AND LOCAL GOVERNMENT

Full and equal participation in the present system of government in this country seems, then, to be less and less of a reality. Elections do occur, but only at long intervals. Parliamentary candidates are chosen by party members in the constituencies, but only certain nominations are acceptable and only a tiny minority of the public is involved on the selection committees: 'inner circles are not photographic images of outer circles.' [17] In local Conservative associations the inner caucus is generally composed of employers, small shopkeepers, junior executives and white collar workers with, in some areas, a scattering of retired military officers and landed gentry. On the Labour side selection tends to be controlled by trade unionists, members of cooperative organizations, teachers and employees. It is interesting to note, however, that in both parties the central office has less power to place candidates than is usually supposed, and is often (though within certain limits) obliged to accept the decision of the local branch, even when it would prefer another candidate. [18] Once a government is elected it is virtually autonomous. The day-to-day pattern of political decision-making and administration, therefore, becomes a closed style of politics. Most of the vital debates are held in private – either in the cabinet or in committees away from the floor of the House – and although what ordinary people want and the policies for which they vote are obviously seen as one factor in what is decided, and although the advice and opinion of the more powerful pressure groups are not in-frequently sought, the major conflict of interests occurs on another level altogether. In this process the role of the elected government is frequently reduced to little more than that of a broker. It acts as the co-ordinator of all these external interests, but is unable to defy their power. Andrew Hacker, referring to the power of 'the corporate élite', illustrates the implications of just one aspect of this situation. Investment decisions, he reminds us, are very sweeping in their ramifications, and no one is unaffected by their con-sequences:

> Yet this is an area where neither the public nor the government is able to participate. If the contours of the economy and society are being shaped in a hundred or so board rooms, so far as the average citizen is con-cerned these decisions are in the lap of the gods. [19]

To the 'average citizen' decisions of this magnitude are in the lap of the gods whether they are taken in the board room, Westminster or the local Town or County Hall. The local government structure has become, since the nineteenth century, more efficient and more all-embracing but, in most senses, more remote. Many of the battles of the nineteenth century (over health or education, for example) concerned with public administration were fought out in terms of State versus local control, and this remains true of a substantial number of issues in the mid-twentieth century. The Englishman's pride in local institutions is a commonplace of English history, and is adduced at every turn in attempts to resolve tensions between national and local authority. In such fields as housing and education policy, and most conspicuously where national finance is channelled through local government, the tensions have at times been very profound. The very nature of the tensions, the party loyalties in-volved and the sense that local autonomy is in the last analysis circumscribed by national policy-making, all contribute to a popular cynicism about local government and local officialdom.

Local government to the 'average citizen' is merely another form of government. The very history of the services has strengthened this view, given the relentless widening of their scope. The vision of Sidney and Beatrice Webb and the Fabians of all-purpose local authorities, to replace less efficient, less well co-ordinated *ad hoc* authorities, has been realized, but a real sense of local democracy has not been achieved. The all-purpose authorities ab-sorbed, in 1902, the functions of the School Boards, and in 1929 those of the Poor Law guardians. Since the Local Government Acts of 1929 and 1933, in fact, local government machinery has been highly ordered and com-plete. Boundary disputes with national government (over block grants, air-ports or comprehensive education) have not disturbed an underlying popular apathy about the activities of local government. Local issues, like national ones, can momentarily flare into life, but the Aldermanic Bench is in reality as close to the citizen as is the Woolsack or the House of Lords. The mass media have probably, in fact, brought Westminster much nearer. Local council membership is not widely seen as important or prestigious. The importance is seen to rest with the Education Officer, the Medical Officer of Health, the Borough Treasurer — the bureaucrat. Candidates for local elections are, in most areas, not particularly highly qualified in educational terms and their average age is at least fifty-five or over. Turnout for local elections is a measure of the place of local government in the popular imagination (it often falls as low as 40 or 30 per cent). [20]

The point here is not to consider how an efficient system of local administrative and political machinery could have grown up otherwise. It is to ask how such a system of local, and national, government survives. How does it assure its legitimacy? The answers lie in the history of the British political system and in the particular cultural attitudes which have grown up alongside it. Philip Abrams, for instance, suggests that in Britain people are on the whole both proud and complacent about their political system. They believe it to be basically democratic and have 'faith', for the most part, in their leaders. Most of them have a moderate sense of civic duty but compared, say, with the German people they are not very well informed politically. What is more, they do not often seek to take an active part in politics, nor do they believe that top positions should necessarily be open to all comers. Because of this, Abrams concludes, our political culture is 'quite well suited to maintaining, in a mass society, a rather élitist version of parliamentary government'. [21]

Simply to rely on public complacency is a dangerous tactic for any government (witness the failure of the Conservative government in 1964 after thirteen years of the people 'never having had it so good'). The public must continually be courted and cajoled into submission. It must also be given the impression that its views are being listened to. The way in which this is done is described, perhaps over-cynically, by the authors of the *May Day Manifesto*. They suggest that, in its internal mechanisms, government today has replaced what used to be understood as democratic processes by the 'methods which it uses in its economic activities: market research, the taking of consumer opinion'. It takes account of public opinion not in active ways, by offering direct choices, but in 'planned ways' which allow 'the governing bureaucracy to know its room for manœuvre, and to estimate what is necessary in building a public opinion which is organized only in relation to itself'. [22] In order to be effective at all this kind of political persuasion depends on the role played by the mass media, the consideration of which brings us to the wider political characteristics of modern mass society.

THE POWER OF THE MASS MEDIA

The essential characteristics of the modern media of communication are their scale and concentration. Television, radio, the popular press, all today penetrate a truly mass audience. Yet the range of choice within this vast network of communications is seriously limited. Let us briefly consider the history of this development.

The modern daily national newspaper was made possible by technology and transport. Before the mid-nineteenth century newspapers were mostly local or, as in the case of the metropolitan papers, dependent for their national circulation on slow and expensive postal services. The radical press, weekly for the most part, circulated through the channels of radical political organizations, and the cheap publications of religious and evangelical bodies were distributed through informal agencies. The final ending of the 'taxes on knowledge' (which had been designed to restrict the organs of political agitation) in 1855 also resulted in the appearance of the *Daily Telegraph* which took over the lead from the older *Times*-type of commentary newspaper and whose 140,000 daily sale resulted from, among other things, the speed of the railways. The Sunday newspaper established itself as a mass circulation institution at the same time (the *News of the World*, founded in 1843, was selling 100,000 copies weekly in 1850). From the mid-1840s the electric telegraph was in regular use, and journalism began to take on a new efficiency. Steam-printing had been evolved by the late 1850s to the point at which 20,000 news sheets an hour could be produced (*The Times* had been producing 250 an hour before steam-printing was introduced in 1814, and only four times that number immediately after). The major turning point, however, came in the 1880s and 1890s. Papermaking was revolutionized through the use of wood pulp in the 1860s. In the same decade provincial and London evening papers became firmly established mass media, maintaining a strong reliance on up-to-date gossip news. The Newnes *Tit-bits* and Northcliffe *Answers* appeared in the 1880s, as did the first modern circulation campaigns (initiated by the *Daily Telegraph*).

Greater efficiency in news-gathering, the new tradition of snippet-presentation, the greater scale and monopolization of industry and commerce and the attendant ability to exploit possibilities of newspaper advertising on a large scale, and advances in printing (most notably the rotary press) all contributed to the development of the mass circulation newspaper as we now know it. Northcliffe's halfpenny *Daily Mail*, exploiting these new possibilities, rolled off the press at the rate of 200,000 copies an hour in 1896. At the beginning of the twentieth century the *News of the World* reached a Sunday circulation of 3 million. The *Daily Mail* passed the million mark and the *Daily Express* was to be the first daily to reach 2 million. Circulation had become vital, less for the direct income than for its reflection in advertising revenue. In 1938 national daily newspaper sales totalled 11·5 million.

Thirty million papers are now bought each morning, 10 million of which are accounted for by the *Daily Mirror* and the *Daily Express*. Comics are seen by 98 per cent of the nation's children and whereas magazines and periodicals had a circulation of about 26 million in 1938 that figure has practically doubled today. Lending by public libraries has also doubled since 1938, so that the average number of books borrowed per head of the population is now around fifteen a year. The annual average of new books published has risen by about four times since the beginning of the century, and while the majority of this increase represents new fiction titles, more educational and technical books are also being published.

Dramatic as these increases in popular readership are, however, they

37 1930s Regal.

do not match the even more striking increase in television viewing. Whereas in 1948, for example, only 1 per cent of the population owned a television set, today the proportion is over 80 per cent, and average peak audience figures often top the 10 million mark. Sound radio broadcasts still have extremely large audiences too. And about half of the population regularly listen to at least one programme (usually many more) each day. Because of the rival attraction of radio and television (as well as for reasons connected with the financial structure of these institutions), the theatre and the cinema have experienced something of a decline in the last fifteen years. There are fewer new productions and there has also been a contraction in the number of theatres and cinemas. The weekly cinema audience is nevertheless still high (between 8 and 9 million), and more money is spent on this form of entertainment – especially by young people – than on any other. The record-buying market is also largely dominated by a teenage audience. Yet, while there has been a vast increase in the output of popular music, minority tastes – in jazz or classical music, for example – have been more widely catered for as well. Fine art exhibitions, live orchestral concerts, opera and ballet also reach a wider audience today than ever before.

Important as these distribution and audience figures are in providing us with information about how people spend their leisure time and where they acquire (or consolidate) their political, aesthetic and cultural standards, what is more significant for us here is the structure of ownership and control in the various mass communication industries, and their links with the advertising world. Since the end of the Second World War the ownership of the means of communication has passed, or is passing, to a kind of financial organization unknown in earlier periods: the modern corporation. In this process, the methods and attitudes of capitalist business have become embedded right at the centre of the communications system – just as they have also become an important part of the political system. What this means, in particular, is a widespread dependence on advertising money. It also means that the 'selling' emphasis extends into the very substance of the communications themselves. In the expanding world of advertising and publicity, Raymond Williams argues, there can be 'a kind of manufacture and marketing of personalities ... There can also be a kind of packaging of experience: putting it out with the right gloss, or even making the gloss a substitute for the experience.' [23] We cannot here consider the content of the media in any detail, nor can we examine the effects of sales pressures and advertising needs. Before we consider the broad effects of modern mass communications, however, it may be helpful to have some idea of the scale of operations of the modern advertising industry.

By the late 1960s, annual advertising revenue in this country was some £525 million (about 2·5 per cent of the total national income). This was not far short of the entire cost of old age pensions and it was many times more than government expenditure on the arts or on nursery schools. Not all of this money, of course, went on television advertising, on glossy magazines or neon lights. Some of it was spent by the government itself in the process of persuading us to buy premium bonds, to drive more carefully, to export more or to join the army. A further fairly substantial sum was spent on the advertising which manufacturers and traders undertake for each other's benefit in trade and technical journals; and classified advertisements in newspapers accounted for another 6 or 7 per cent of the total revenue. But even after making all these deductions we are still left with two-thirds of that bill which was not devoted to the simple provision, or exchange, of information. This is the controversial sum – the money which goes on television and press advertisements – which rival firms (or even the same firm) use to boost virtually identical products by a variety of subtle 'hidden persuasion' methods. [24]

As we have already remarked, the dependence of the popular press and of commercial television on advertising revenue implies that the paramount need is to please the advertiser rather than to satisfy the reader or the viewer (in the battle to maintain audience figures in competition with the commercial channels, the B.B.C. is, of course, also drawn into this vicious circle). At a fairly trivial level the dependence on advertising revenue is manifested, for example, in 'the editorial puff for the advertised product, the special supplement concerned with holiday travel or with some particular industry, the colour section shrewdly constructed according to the space salesman's specification in order to tap for the *Sunday Times* certain new sources of advertising revenue'. [25] But the negative effect of the link between advertising and the mass media also operates in other ways. It inhibits most newspapers, for instance, from any attempt to review ordinary commercial products critically, in the same way that they review new books or films. It also ensures that one will never hear, from either the press or commercial television, any radical criticism of the advertising industry itself – however much this might be in the public interest. Daniel Bell sums up the situation in these terms:

> the cost of reaching a mass audience fosters oligopoly [26] ... and reinforces the unique position and power of the modern patron, the commercial sponsor. In effect, Big Business sits at the control of mass communication, and becomes one of the main arbiters of taste. [27]

Questionable as the ethics of this form of communications system are, especially in view of the limitations which they impose on techniques of presentation and on the quality of information and entertainment provided, it is important to remind ourselves that not all of the effects of the mass communications industry are necessarily deleterious.

THE EFFECTS OF THE MASS MEDIA

In the complex circumstances of modern society, the mass media are capable of performing important mediating functions. Because of the rapidity of change today, there is a confusion of choice among the rival kinds of life style, values, modes of behaviour, dress and speech. A socially mobile person has no ready source of new knowledge on how to live 'better' than before. His guides become the cinema, the television, popular magazines and advertisements. The media not only affect changes in life styles and enable people to adjust more readily to their changing social environment, but also gradually affect the structure of existing institutions. They have a particular impact on children and adolescents since these age groups have now become the focus of a very high-powered commercial market in 'pop' records, clothes and entertainment. Ultimately, they affect the different goals of achievement in society. Hilde Himmelweit, in *Television and the Child*, demonstrates the improved 'general knowledge' and the heightened job aspirations of working-class children which result from their watching television. Approval of these wider kinds of influence which the mass media exert depends very much on subjective feelings about the 'sanctity' of the family, the 'proper' place of children in the home and the 'freedom' of the individual. They are, however, influences which cannot be denied (even if sociologists are still at the very early stages of measuring their precise and more subtle effects [28]).

By virtue of the enormous fund of shared experiences which they provide, mass communications make another kind of contribution to life in contemporary society. Ross and Van den Haag, for instance, point out that 'movies, television programs, newspapers, and magazines link vast heterogeneous publics and establish constant contact among people even if they stay put. They bring about some uniformity of attitude and a blending of customs and beliefs.' Most of these contacts are, they observe, casual and transitory and, in the case of more popular forms of mass communication, 'generalized, vicarious, and abstract . . . They do not replace personal relationships to things or people but make it harder for them to grow.' [29] What is implied in this judgement is that television and the other mass media have the effect of increasing conformity and restricting individual freedom. At one level this seems indisputable but, as we have seen, some degree of consensus and conformity is essential in any social organization – as are shared ritual experiences. So long, therefore, as conformity does not become synonymous with uncritical acceptance of any and every experience provided by the mass media, and so long as there are adequate channels of participation and protest for those 'outside' the system (which, as we saw, is not in fact the case in our society at present), the conditions of democracy may tend to be reinforced rather than destroyed once there are broad areas of common interest and understanding.

Against those who stress the tendency of the mass media to reduce all of their output to the level of the 'lowest common denominator', it is important to stress the comparative resilience of the audience – at least in response to certain of the more overt challenges and appeals that the media make to their audience. [30] Joseph Klapper, in one of the most important pieces of research yet published on the effects of mass communications, concludes that rather than changing attitudes, 'persuasive mass communication is in general more likely to reinforce the existing opinions of its audience'. He does concede, however, that 'this is not to say . . . that conversion does not occur nor that under certain conditions it may not be widespread'. What seems to be important in determining attitude change is not so much the content of the media themselves as certain 'extra-communication factors and conditions';

38 *Hyde Park pop concert, 1969.*

among these Klapper lists peoples' existing predispositions and 'the derived processes of selective retention', 'the group, and the norms of groups, to which the audience member belongs', the influence of 'opinion leaders' and the effect of 'inter-personal dissemination of communication content'. [31]

The fact that the advertisers and programme producers themselves spend so much on finding out about how people react to different sorts of products (or programmes) itself suggests that they do not have complete control of the media. On the other hand, the use of the communication system by totalitarian régimes is a salutary reminder of the extreme coercive potentiality of the media when they are used in harness with an oppressive political and military machine.

The reality in modern English society seems to be that the mass media do not produce complacency and conformity – or not uniquely and not necessarily so. They also create opportunities for people to acquire new knowledge and new tastes. However, the reinforcement effect of mass communications, which Klapper describes, has considerable consequences for society. Given the fact that the effects of mass communications depend primarily on how the society – and, in particular, such institutions as the family, schools and churches – moulds the tastes and interests of the audience members, any improvement (for example, in the direction of greater individual autonomy or more egalitarian political attitudes) must depend upon the conscious re-education of that society itself. The main responsibility here lies with parents and teachers, although the backing of a responsible – and responsive – government is indispensable.

While there are good grounds for concern, therefore, about many aspects of advertising, about the structure of ownership and power in the mass communications industry and about the content of some of its products, it may be the case that a number of the fears which have been expressed by critics of the media are excessive. Nevertheless, if democracy has profited or could profit in some respects by the extension of the mass media – at the same time, admittedly, that these institutions have profited by reducing individual freedoms in other ways – conditions of life in contemporary society have given rise to a considerable amount of pessimism and gloom. This is often summed up in the use of terms like 'alienation' and 'anomie', or in the expression 'the threat of mass society'. In our concluding chapter we shall examine the meaning of these concepts and attempt to weigh up the balance of social developments over the last 150 years.

NOTES

1 See GABRIEL ALMOND and SIDNEY VERBA *The Civic Culture* (Princeton, 1963), for a comparative empirical study of the political cultures of Britain, America, Germany, Italy and Mexico.

2 *Studies in British Politics*, p. 1.

3 'The sociology of political life', in FYVEL (ed.) *The Frontiers of Sociology*, pp. 45–6.

4 See further PETER WORSLEY 'The distribution of power in industrial society', *Sociological Review Monograph* No. 8 (1964).

5 See C. S. WILSON and T. LUPTON'S survey 'Social background and connections of top decision-makers', quoted in J. BLONDEL *Voters, Parties and Leaders*, p. 239 (Harmondsworth, 1963). See also R. WILKINSON *The Prefects: British Leadership and the Public School Tradition* (London, 1964).

6 S. M. LIPSET *Political Man*, p. 21 (London, 1959).

7 'Parties and pressure groups', in ROSE *Studies in British Politics*, p. 257.

8 Ibid., pp. 258–9.

9 See further ABRAMS *Must Labour Lose?* and BLONDEL *Voters, Parties and Leaders*.

10 'The strange death of social democratic England', *The Listener*, 4 July 1968.

11 *Political Parties*, Pt 6, Ch. II (Glencoe edition, 1949).

12 See ROBERT MCKENZIE *British Political Parties* (London, 1963) and S. H. BEER *Modern British Politics* (London, 1965).

13 For a general account of the history and tactics of various kinds of pressure groups, see S. E. FINER *Anonymous Empire* (London, 1958) and J. D. STEWART *British Pressure Groups* (London, 1958).

14 For a full account of the operation of pressure group politics, see WILSON *Pressure Group* and H. ECKSTEIN *Pressure Group Politics* (London, 1960).

15 See J. GOLDSTEIN *The Government of British Trade Unions* (London, 1952).

16 See further PHILIP ABRAMS 'Radio and television', in DENYS THOMPSON (ed.) *Discrimination and Popular Culture* (Harmondsworth, 1964).

17 BLONDEL *Voters, Parties and Leaders*, p. 100.

18 See AUSTIN RANNEY *Pathways to Parliament* (London, 1965) for a detailed discussion of the selection of parliamentary candidates.

19 'Power to do what', in IRVING HOROWITZ (ed.) *The New Sociology*, p. 140 (New York, 1965).

20 See BLONDEL *Voters, Parties and Leaders*, pp. 52–6.

21 'The sociology of political life', p. 56.

22 WILLIAMS (ed.), p. 154.

23 *Communications*, p. 24 (Harmondsworth, 1962).

24 See further RALPH HARRIS and ARTHUR SELDON *Advertising in Action* (London, 1962) and MARTIN MAYER *Madison Avenue, U.S.A.* (Harmondsworth, 1961).

25 FRANK WHITEHEAD 'Advertising', in THOMPSON (ed.) *Discrimination and Popular Culture*, p. 41.

26 i.e. the domination of the market by a few large firms.

27 'Advertising: the impact on society', *The Listener*, 27 December 1956.

28 See, for example, J. D. HALLORAN *The Effects of Mass Communication* (Leicester, 1964).
29 *The Fabric of Society*, p. 168.
30 See, for example, JACKSON *Working Class Community*, pp. 150–1, for an account of the survival of brass band music in an age of pop. See also JAY BLUMLER and DENIS MCQUAIL *Television and Politics* (London, 1968) for a description of the effectiveness of party political broadcasts.
31 *The Effects of Mass Communication*, pp. 49–52 (New York, 1966).

Democracy was previously discussed in Chapters 1 and 3, local government in Chapters 2 and 5, and power and politics in Chapters 3 and 7.

Conclusion: Man in Mass Society

Since the middle of the nineteenth century, when industrialism began to establish itself not only in England but also in other parts of Western Europe and in North America, social scientists have been keenly preoccupied with the definition of 'industrial' and, latterly, of 'mass' society. They have also been concerned with the problem of identifying the main agencies and mechanisms of social change within these societies. Investigations of this kind present serious difficulties. In the first place, definitions – and the words used to describe phenomena like 'class', 'freedom' and 'democracy' – are rooted in historical experiences. This means that simply to list the attributes of 'industrial' society creates the impression of an internal uniformity and coherence which bears little resemblance to the continually changing and variable characteristics of particular industrial societies at different historical periods. Another difficulty arises from the existence of differing ideological viewpoints. These alter the perspective from which the phenomena of industrial society are described, as well as affecting the way in which different social theorists explain (and justify or criticize) the processes of social change. But despite these theoretical difficulties and differences, most social scientists do, in fact, agree upon the central features of industrial societies and upon the main mechanisms involved in the transformation from the much simpler pattern of existence of traditional rural communities.

As we have seen, the most striking characteristics of social organization in England since the mid-nineteenth century are those of large-scale complexity and rapid change. In the industrial sphere this has meant concentration of ownership, the growth of State control and public property, the development of bureaucratic methods of administration and the intensification of the division of labour. [1] For the individual in his job of work the consequence of industrialism is that he can now only perform one small part in the total production process. Men are no longer entirely self-sufficient; both in personal terms and in industrial and commercial terms we are increasingly dependent upon one another. Yet, because of the size and impersonality of many modern institutions, although we are so closely interdependent, we are – in our subjective experience – more at a distance. Life in large cities, for instance, depends upon the availability of an efficient network of such public services as transport, water, sewage, gas and electricity. These services, however, are for the most part privately consumed; our relationship with those who provide and maintain them remaining distant and formalized.

As the division of labour has become ever more complicated under industrialism, and as industrial and commercial enterprises have continued to grow in size, larger concentrations of capital have become necessary. This has tended to result in the divorce of ownership from management. It is the board which runs business nowadays and the board is composed of experts rather than paternalistic employers. Given the present pattern of shareholding an extraordinary degree of power is, in fact, placed in very few hands (especially if we bear in mind the growth of monopolies, cartels and trusts – in all of which the actual size and extent of property holdings are disguised by the continued use of the old names of the subsidiary firms). The dangers of large-scale power are not confined to private industry, however. The running of the nationalized industries and public corporations also involves disadvantages and diseconomies, although the problems here are somewhat different: the remoteness of the Minister in charge, the principle of accountability and the frustration of rigid bureaucratic controls, and consequent delays in adaptation to new methods and ideas.

With these changes in the division of labour and property ownership, with the growth in size and improved bargaining power of the trade union movement and with the existence of other factors, such as extended educational opportunities and wider political participation, the system of social stratification in England has changed considerably in the last hundred years. It has also become much more complex, less completely based on the traditional polarity between 'bosses' and 'workers' and more related to subtle subjective perceptions of status and style of life. Despite persisting differences, for example in housing, in security of tenure, in pay and retirement benefits and in capital ownership, some of the more marked and unjust divisions between the social classes have been reduced and patterns of family life have become much more similar.

So far, our description of the processes characteristic of industrial societies has been confined to those features which derive immediately from changes in the pattern of industrial organization. But the growth of industry, as we have seen, also resulted in the intensification of urban development, and the urban way of life has given rise to several other distinctive features of modern society. It has led to the isolation of the nuclear family and to the predominance of partial, secondary contacts over deep, personalized relationships. With the development of large-scale factories and the disruption of the traditional family economy, home and job have become separated – often by considerable distances. The journey to work and lonely suburban housewives are only two of the effects of this new pattern of existence. Within the major centres of population, distinctive urban and suburban (as well as 'twilight') areas have tended to become established, each housing particular classes of people and specialized types of commercial and productive activity.

Since the family has ceased to be a major productive unit itself it is no longer an advantage to have large numbers of children. In the smaller contemporary family, however, mobility is quite high. Less informal support tends to be available to the wider kin in times of emergency and, as a consequence, a greater burden is thrown upon the State and voluntary welfare agencies, whose response is very uneven. In our analysis of contemporary English society we have had to ignore the agencies which cater for these emergencies. In our earlier chapters, we used some aspects of social welfare in the nineteenth century to demonstrate focal points around which attitudes could be seen to develop, and which were in themselves revealing of settled and changing aspects of social structure. We have made no attempt to describe the services that have grown up since 1945; their scale and complexity alone would have excluded them from our discussion. There is, however, an important point that needs to be made. Services have become more sophisticated and more all-embracing. They have developed on an explicit basis of removing various kinds of obstacle to a full and normal life. They have, therefore, a philosophy which announces minimum standards below which people should not be permitted to fall. At the back of most services, especially those concerned with children, there are also more positive values.

At the end of the Second World War, society appeared to have shouldered the collective responsibility for integrating the range of social provisions. The enormous advances made cannot, however, disguise glaring discrepancies between the philosophy and the reality. The social services form a complex structure for which the building work has never been completed. In one sense, of course, the work can never be completed because standards of medical and social protection themselves rise, but even within the terms of the 1940s the achievement has been limited. Let us take two illustrations.

In 1965 Margot Jefferys completed work on a detailed analysis of the social services available in the county of Buckinghamshire, in an effort to 'provide a picture of the work of the staff of social welfare services . . . and of those who are served by them'. The aim was to pin-point the strengths and weaknesses of individual services and the problems of relationships between them. Society is irrevocably committed, the survey points out,

> to trying to prevent illness and mitigate the effects of physical or mental handicap among people of all ages and economic circumstances. It recognized that this can only be done by bringing a variety of medical and social skills to the aid of the afflicted and those who care for them. It is committed to the rehabilitation of offenders as well as to the protection of society from them, and it has also an interest in the quality and stability of

family units because marital and parent-child relationships help to determine the actual dependence of children on the state. These commitments and interests are so broad, and becoming broader, that no absolute limits can be set to the needs which welfare services could meet.

This is a comprehensive statement of the philosophy of welfare. From such a starting point certain assumptions can be made about needs that society is committed to meet, and the resources that have to be made available. Margot Jefferys makes a very precise point about one aspect of the resources available to meet the needs:

> In 1960–1, nearly every service in Bucks had vacancies for staff which had been unfilled for some months, and workers complained of their inability to give sufficient time to individual clients. Society, in short, was unable to mobilize resources to meet its recognized commitments. [2]

Since the formulation of the Welfare State there have been many readaptations of individual services, and readjustments of relations between services, but such basic points of overall failure have remained.

The child poverty campaign would provide a second precise illustration of the position, reaching out as it does to the weaknesses in many aspects of social policy, perhaps most notably housing. A simpler illustration, however, will suffice. In their book, *Children in Distress,* Sir Alec Clegg and Barbara Megson demonstrated, in 1968, the extent of society's neglect of children's problems which could be, but to a large extent are not tackled. Using the experience of the West Riding of Yorkshire they show that 'there are very many children struggling against conditions which are adverse in the extreme; only a fraction of this army of distressed and deprived children will reveal their need by some form of aberrant behaviour and of this fraction only the few that do harm to themselves or offend society in some way will be offered help'. Very frequently the help is not forthcoming because responsibility for providing it is not clearly defined, and the work of the various agencies is not adequately co-ordinated. In other cases the resources are lacking. More often than not the problems go unrecognized. The machinery is lacking or imperfect:

> There are, for instance, many occasions when children have all the symptoms of maladjustment but cannot be treated because there are no places available for them in the schools which cater for their needs. One education officer was once heard to say that he could state at any given moment how many such children there were in the borough which he served. When challenged, he gave the number forty-two and when his confidence was questioned he asserted with some irony that this was the number of places available in the school for such pupils at his disposal. [3]

The response of Buckinghamshire's social services to their clients in general, and of this borough to problems of maladjustment, is governed very fundamentally by the scale of the resources available.

For this discussion to be complete it would be necessary, of course, to survey in detail what resources *are* made available, and the strengths of the services that exist. The point here is not to deny the strengths, but simply to indicate that an important element in our overall discussion of the relationship of individuals and families to the structure of mass society is the extent of human needs and the quality of society's response.

In political terms, industrialization and urbanism have resulted in the growth of organized mass parties. [4] It was the appearance of an educated urban working class (already partially organized in the craft unions) which made mass parties a necessity from the point of view of the traditional ruling élite. The development of mass communications – including cheap forms of rapid transport – in the last quarter of the nineteenth century made such parties a firm possibility. But even the most efficient communications system is incapable of cementing groups once they grow beyond a certain size. Hence, it has been the fate of the mass parties – like that of the trade unions and the larger pressure groups – that they have tended to split into two unequal parts, the leadership and the led: the officials, belonging to a trained and specialized bureaucracy, and the rank-and-file members. The widening of this gap in contemporary society has been at the expense of any shared sense of representative government.

The separation of home and work, the disruption of many neighbourhood and kinship loyalties and the dominance of the mass media in modern urban—industrial societies mean that none of the certainties of the rural way of life – and few of its intimate rituals – are any longer available. An immense range of alternative, and continually changing, job opportunities and life styles now exists. There is an equally large – and probably even more perplexing – variety in the patterns of moral standards and values. Amid this instability and confusion, the Church – once the sole source of moral authority and support – is today unable to provide guidance. Science and technology are the contemporary deities. But they offer no easy solutions either; rather they have added to people's fears and confusion, as have the horrifying spectacle of two world wars, Nazism, a series of colonial atrocities and the constant threat of nuclear destruction.

Ideally we might expect the communications system to help provide a feeling of community and shared values. However, in this society the mass media are so remote and impersonal (as well as being mainly profit orientated), that they yield no easy pointers and no deeply shared values – although there are admittedly opportunities for shared vicarious release and entertainment. The knowledge and skills imparted by the contemporary educational system are not much better at producing a sense of belonging. Indeed, secondary and higher education have become so highly bureaucratized that, instead of diminishing social differences and helping people to find a way through the vast range of modern ideas and values, they are tending to create new barriers and specialisms of their own.

Wherever we look, then, in exploring the consequences of urban and industrial growth we find the same dichotomies: impersonal cities – isolated families; big factories – alienated workers; bureaucratic administrations – remote citizens. Yet in England, at least, over the last 150 years large-scale and violent forms of protest, which were very prominent in the early stages of industrialization, have tended to decline. How can we explain this? Is it because workers have become more familiar with the ways of industrial and urban life, because they have become more tolerant of the bureaucratic formalities which hedge their daily activities, because they are more motivated by private and monetary considerations, or because they are seduced into conformity and are powerless to rebel? It is over questions like these that social theorists begin to disagree. Here the analysis of industrial and mass societies becomes more complicated.

As we have seen, Durkheim, Marx, Tönnies and Weber were all engaged in the analysis of the new patterns of social organization which followed from industrial and urban changes in the first half of the nineteenth century. They drew attention to such phenomena as the intensification of the division of labour, new patterns of community relations, new forms of property ownership, new structures of power and new modes of social stratification. Already they were referring to the problems of alienation and anomie. In more directly political terms de Tocqueville and Ortega y Gasset, and from a cultural angle, Matthew Arnold and Karl Mannheim, have emphasized the dangers of what they felt to be the likely 'tyranny of the masses' in modern societies, and the consequent threat of pressures towards conformity, standardization and mediocrity.

Recently the debate about the future of industrial society has taken a different direction. Writers like Hannah Arendt, C. Wright Mills and Herbert Marcuse, for example, have suggested that – far from being too powerful – the masses today are to be seen as the helpless victims of relentless systems of political and economic oppression. They argue that modern man, manipulated through the mass media, lacking communal ties, impotent and frustrated before the complexities of life in our technological environment, is left with a sense of powerlessness and alienation. This analysis, as applied to English society, probably exaggerates the supposed adverse effects of the mass media, and ignores some of the positive advances that have been won under industrialism. In order to clarify the argument – and decide how far it seems justified – it is perhaps necessary to consider what exactly is meant by the term alienation.

Like the phrases 'industrial society' or 'mass society', 'alienation' is a term which has been employed in many different ways. For Marx it arose from the separation of the worker from his product and from the ownership of the means of production. Weber, on the other hand, was more concerned with the kind of alienation which results from bureaucratic methods of administration – a theme more recently taken up by C. Wright Mills and by

W. H. Whyte in his book, *Organisation Man*. Psychoanalysts also use the term alienation, but for them it usually carries the connotation of 'The Fear of Freedom', [5] that is, the reluctance of individuals to advance from the state of childhood dependency to achieve what Sartre has called truly 'authentic' personalities.

The concept of alienation may be separated into several different dimensions. Marvin Seeman, for instance, isolates five of these: powerlessness, meaninglessness, normlessness, isolation or anomie, and self-estrangement. [6] Each of these modes of alienation reflects a different kind of 'split' in man's relationship with his environment. Underlying all of them is the sense that man in modern society has become reduced to an object − a 'thing', isolated, and fragmented − in other words that he has become 'over-socialized', [7] existing more for society than society for him. What is more, as Tönnies pointed out, this society is no longer an organic community. It is a mass society in which relationships are essentially contractual. As a result there can be no true feeling of belonging − even of sharing one's sense of alienation − only a phoney kind of togetherness, what Robert Merton has called a '*pseudo-Gemeinschaft*'. [8]

This diagnosis of the state of alienation, similar in many respects to Durkheim's study of anomie and to Talcott Parsons's analysis of the predominance of instrumental over expressive modes of action in modern society, is sometimes offered as more than an explanation of the loneliness and anxiety which beset individuals today. According to some sociologists, alienation is endemic in industrial societies. In justification of this argument they point to the fact that the fragmentations in man's experience, which are characteristic of the different modes of alienation, all seem to have resulted from basic changes in social organization brought about by the industrial revolution. Hence, the breadth of the concept of alienation − each of its dimensions reflects the combination of particular sets of conditions and consequences produced by the transition from the traditional form of society to urban-industrial society. But if alienation is, indeed, characteristic of certain aspects of life and work in industrial societies, it is not necessarily a permanent condition − nor does it exist uniformly, as Robert Blauner has demonstrated in relation to conditions of work in modern industry. In the more advanced stages of industrialization, he suggests, alienation may be overcome − or at least 'rendered bearable for individuals and relatively harmless for society'. [9]

Here we begin to confront historical niceties and the problems of vocabulary and definition which were mentioned at the beginning of this chapter. Lewis Feuer, for instance, arguing against the view that alienation is endemic in industrial societies, suggests that what stands out from a historical and comparative standpoint is the universal experience of alienation. He claims, moreover, that 'a multitude of alienated persons would be dissatisfied equally

39 Flats for families, London, 1969.

with conditions of power-possession, meaningfulness, norm-orientedness, and self-acknowledgement'. [10] However, what Feuer means by the idea of alienation is 'the will to criticize and polemicize'. This interpretation – although it is clearly related to the various states of powerlessness and so on referred to earlier – is less a description of the state of alienation than of a reaction to it. Percy Cohen adopts a rather similar position to Feuer in this debate. '"Alienation" in work in modern industrial organizations is doubtless a reality', he agrees. But he asks whether there is any reason why most men should enjoy their work, rather than their leisure activities. As for the alienation of man from man, 'it is true that the "organic" communities of rural society no longer exist: but does this mean that the relationships between kinsmen, friends, workers, members of voluntary associations, etc., are without meaning?' [11]

We begin to see, then, that the concept of alienation is used in many different ways and is capable of many different interpretations. This clearly limits its usefulness as a tool in sociological analysis. Because it describes situations and experiences which are at the very core of human existence – situations which ought to provide man with a source of self-identification and a feeling of dignity and worth – the term alienation inevitably becomes coloured with value judgements, and its use tends to reflect different ranges of ideological opinion. Often, however, the concept suffers from being used against an inadequate historical perspective too. Daniel Bell, for example, points out that the loss of community and of a stable system of values has to be balanced against the gain of increased mobility, and a variety of norms as against the monopolistic controls of a single group. [12] Similarly, the mass media have to be seen as reflecting, as well as sometimes shaping, public opinion, as having the potential to educate as well as to manipulate. It is important to remember, too, that the various modes of alienation in present-day society are to a large degree independent of each other. They do not necessarily follow, the one from the other, in an inexorable logic of total oppression. Indeed, it could be argued that many of the forms of dissatisfaction and tension characteristic of the various states of alienation which we have described are fundamental to the striving for economic betterment and political change upon which future developments in the social structure are likely to depend. As Feuer reminds us, it is the critical, polemical element in the state of alienation which provides the necessary dynamic for social transformation.

But despite the necessity of conflict in this sense, and despite the very real gains that have been made possible by modern technological development, societies today do present new and difficult obstacles to the realization of political freedom and individual autonomy, and these cannot be ignored. Bureaucracy, the mass media, and the institutions of modern government make new demands on those who control them – and on those who use them. It is clear, both from the social changes with which we have been concerned and from the continued presence in our society of major social problems and urgent moral dilemmas, that it remains necessary to find new bases for legitimate relations of authority and new means for ensuring that social wants are adequately satisfied. Above all, it is necessary for us to recognize the inevitability of change – and, hence, of conflict too. This involves a willingness to abandon attitudes of nostalgia and of concern with security. Ronald Fletcher has in this respect asked some very real questions.

> Might we not be mistaken in thinking that a good society is one which always enjoys certainty and harmony? Perhaps the good society, in which freedom and equality are realities, is a society institutionally prepared for perennial conflict. . . . Perhaps, too, large scale organization is not a bad thing. Perhaps men are treated far better, and are far happier, in our large industrial organizations than ever they were in small ones? And perhaps men need not feel lost and insignificant in them? Perhaps the intense status-seeking that we now feel is only to be expected as we move towards a greater degree of equality. [13]

Instead of bewailing the lost simplicity and harmony of traditional societies, it is also important for us to recognize the real gains in living standards and personal expectations that have been won as a result of industrialization. It is also important for us to remember the increase in social justice – while we also strive to reduce the continuing inequalities – and, above all, to come to terms with the idea that it is normal for societies to undergo change.

NOTES

1 For an excellent discussion of 'The logic of industrialism', see KERR *Industrialism and Industrial Man*, Ch. 2.
2 MARGOT JEFFERYS *An Anatomy of Social Welfare Services*, pp. 1, 300–1 (London, 1965).
3 ALEC CLEGG and BARBARA MEGSON *Children in Distress*, pp. 14–16 (Harmondsworth, 1968).
4 See further WILIAM KORNHAUSER *The Politics of Mass Society* (London, 1960).
5 ERICH FROMM *The Fear of Freedom* (London, 1955).
6 *American Sociological Review*, 24 December 1959.
7 See DENNIS WRONG 'The over-socialised conception of man', in INKELES *Readings on Modern Sociology*.
8 See *Social Theory and Social Structure*, Ch. V (New York, 3rd edition, 1968).
9 *Alienation and Freedom*, p. 33.
10 FEUER 'Alienation: the career of a concept', in STEIN *et al.* (eds.) *Identity and Anxiety*.
11 *Modern Social Theory*, p. 231 (London, 1968).
12 'America as a mass society: a critique', in *The End of Ideology* (New York, 1961).
13 *Human Needs and the Social Order*, p. 42 (London, 1965).

Guide to Further Reading

The suggested reading below covers the main themes discussed in this book, but does not follow the pattern of the chapters. We have tried to indicate books which are neither too specialized nor too inaccessible. We have given details of sub-titles where these help to clarify the titles of books. In most cases the first date of publication is given, and also – where we have thought this important – the date at which a revised edition has appeared. A very large number of these books are available in recent editions, and in paperback, but it has not been possible to include all this information. Additonal suggestions for reading of a more detailed or specialized kind can be traced in the footnotes at appropriate points in the text.

1 THE INDUSTRIAL REVOLUTION AND BEFORE

ASHTON, T. S. *The Industrial Revolution 1760–1830* (London, 1948; revised edition 1962).

BEALES, H. L. *The Industrial Revolution 1750–1850* (London, 1928; reprinted 1958 with new introductory essay).

CHAMBERS, J. D. and MINGAY, G. E. *The Agricultural Revolution 1750–1880* (London, 1966).

DEANE, PHYLLIS *The First Industrial Revolution* (Cambridge, 1965).

GEORGE, DOROTHY *England in Transition* (London, 1931).

HARTWELL, R. M. *The Causes of the Industrial Revolution in England* (London, 1967).

LASLETT, PETER *The World We Have Lost* (London, 1965).

2 TOWNS

ASHWORTH, W. *The Genesis of Modern British Town Planning* (London, 1954).

BOWLEY, MARION *Housing and the State 1919–1944* (London, 1945).

BRIGGS, ASA *Victorian Cities* (London, 1963).

BURNETT, JOHN *Plenty and Want: a Social History of Diet in England from 1815 to the Present Day* (London, 1966).

CULLINGWORTH, J. B. *Housing in Transition* (London, 1963).

ENGELS, FRIEDRICH *The Condition of the Working Class in England* (first published in German, 1845).

GLASS, RUTH 'Urban sociology', Ch. 26 in WELFORD, A. T. *et al.* (eds.) *Society: Problems and Methods of Study* (London, 1962).

JONES, EMRYS *Towns and Cities* (London, 1966).

LONGMATE, NORMAN *King Cholera* (London, 1966).

MARTIN, GEOFFREY *The Town* (London, 1961).

OSBORN, FREDERIC and WHITTICK, ARNOLD *The New Towns: An Answer to Megalopolis* (London, 1963).

PAHL, R. E. *Patterns of Urban Life* (London, 1970).

PFAUTZ, HAROLD W. (ed.) *Charles Booth on the City* (Chicago, 1967).

REX, JOHN and MOORE, ROBERT *Race, Community and Conflict* (London, 1967).

ROYAL COMMISSION ON THE DISTRIBUTION OF THE INDUSTRIAL POPULATION *Report,* Cmnd 6153 (London, 1940).

WICKHAM, E. R. *Church and People in an Industrial City* (London, 1957).

3 TRANSPORT

DYOS, H. J. and ALDCROFT, D. H. *British Transport: an Economic Survey from the Seventeenth Century to the Twentieth* (Leicester, 1969).

ROBBINS, MICHAEL *The Railway Age* (London, 1962).

SAVAGE, CHRISTOPHER I. *An Economic History of Transport* (London, 1959).

SIMMONS, JACK *Transport* (London, 1962).

Traffic in Towns: The Specially Shortened Edition of the Buchanan Report (London, 1963).

4 INDUSTRY AND ECONOMY

ALLEN, G. C. *The Structure of Industry in Britain* (London, 1966).

ASHWORTH, WILLIAM *An Economic History of England 1870–1939* (London, 1960).

BURNS, TOM (ed.) *Industrial Man* (Harmondsworth, 1969).

CHAMBERS, J. D. *The Workshop of the World: British Economic History from 1820 to 1880* (London, 1961).

KERR, CLARK *et al. Industrialism and Industrial Man* (Cambridge, Mass., 1960).

POLLARD, SIDNEY *The Development of the British Economy 1914–50* (London, 1962).

5 WORK AND INDUSTRIAL RELATIONS

BLAU, PETER M. *Bureaucracy in Modern Society* (New York, 1956).

BLAU, PETER M. and SCOTT, W. RICHARD *Formal Organizations: A Comparative Approach* (San Francisco, 1962).

BLAUNER, ROBERT *Alienation and Freedom: The Manual Worker in Industry* (Chicago, 1963).

BROWN, E. H. PHELPS *The Growth of British Industrial Relations* (London, 1959).

BURNS, TOM and STALKER, GEORGE M. *The Management of Innovation,* (London, 1961).

FRIEDMANN, GEORGES *The Anatomy of Work* (London, 1961).

GOLDTHORPE, JOHN H. *et al. Industrial Attitudes and Behaviour* (Cambridge, 1968).

HOBSBAWM, E. J. *Labouring Men: Studies in the History of Labour* (London, 1964).

MAYHEW, HENRY *London Labour and the London Poor* (London, 1861–2); Selections edited by JOHN L. BRADLEY (London, 1965).

TILLYARD, FRANK *The Worker and the State* (London, 3rd edition, 1948).

WHYTE, WILLIAM H. *The Organization Man* (New York, 1956).

6 DEMOCRACY AND SOCIAL MOVEMENTS

BETAILLE, ANDRÉ (ed.) *Social Inequality* (Harmondsworth, 1969).

BEVAN, ANEURIN *In Place of Fear* (London, 1952).

COLE, G. D. H. *A Short History of the British Working-Class Movement 1789–1947* (first published in one volume, London, 1932; revised edition 1948); *A Century of Co-operation* (London, 1944).

MOORE, J. BARRINGTON *The Social Origins of Dictatorship and Democracy: Lord and Peasant in the Making of the Modern World* (Boston, Mass., 1966).

PELLING, HENRY *A History of British Trade Unionism* (London, 1963).

THOMPSON, E. P. *The Making of the English Working Class* (London, 1963).

WILLIAMS, RAYMOND *The Long Revolution* (London, 1961).

7 POPULATION

BANKS, J. A. *Prosperity and Parenthood: A Study of Family Planning among the Victorian Middle Classes* (London, 1954).

BENJAMIN, BERNARD *The Population Census* (London, 1970).

DRAKE, MICHAEL *Population in Industrialization* (London, 1969).

GLASS, D. V. and EVERSLEY, D. E. C. (eds.) *Population in History,* especially Part II (London, 1965).

KELSALL, R. K. *Population* (London, 1967).

MALTHUS, THOMAS ROBERT *Essay on Population* (first published 1798).

WRIGLEY, E. A. *Population and History* (London, 1969).

WRONG, D. H. *Population and Society* (New York, 1961).

8 SOCIAL STRATIFICATION AND SOCIAL MOBILITY

BELL, COLIN R. *Middle Class Families: Social and Geographical Mobility* (London, 1968).

BOTTOMORE, T. B. *Classes in Modern Society* (London, 1965).

COLE, G. D. H. *Studies in Class Structure* (London, 1955).

GLASS, D. V. (ed.) *Social Mobility in Britain* (London, 1954).

GOLDTHORPE, J. H. *et al. The Affluent Worker in the Class Structure* (Cambridge, 1969).

JACKSON, J. A. (ed.) *Social Stratification* (Cambridge, 1969).

LAWTON, DENIS *Social Class, Language and Education* (London, 1968).

LOCKWOOD, D. 'Social mobility', Ch. 28 in WELFORD, A. T. *et al.* (eds.) *Society* (London, 1962).

MARSHALL, T. H. *Sociology at the Crossroads,* Part II: 'Social Class' (London, 1963).

RUNCIMAN, W. G. *Relative Deprivation and Social Justice* (London, 1966).

9 EDUCATION

ADAMSON, J. W. *English Education, 1789–1902* (Cambridge, 1930).

ARMYTAGE, W. H. G. *Civic Universities: Aspects of a British Tradition* (London, 1955).

BERNBAUM, GERALD *Social Change and the Schools, 1918–1944* (London, 1967).

COTGROVE, S. F. *Technical Education and Social Change* (London, 1958).

DOUGLAS, J. W. B. *The Home and the School* (London, 1964).

HALSEY, A. H. *et al.* (eds.) *Education, Economy and Society* (New York, 1961).

JACKSON, BRIAN and MARSDEN, DENNIS *Education and the Working Class* (London, 1962).

JACKSON, PHILIP W. *Life in Classrooms* (New York, 1968).

MACLURE, J. STUART *Educational Documents, England and Wales, 1816–1963* (London, 1965).

SILVER, HAROLD *The Concept of Popular Education: a Study of Ideas and Social Movements in the Early Nineteenth Century* (London, 1965).

SIMON, BRIAN *Studies in the History of Education 1780–1870* (London, 1960); *Education and the Labour Movement, 1870–1920* (London, 1965).

SWIFT, D. F *The Sociology of Education* (London, 1969).

TAYLOR, GEORGE and AYRES, N. *Born and Bred Unequal* (London, 1969).

VAIZEY, JOHN *Education for Tomorrow* (Harmondsworth, 1962; revised edition 1969).

VERNON, P. E. (ed.) *Secondary School Selection* (London, 1957).

10 THE FAMILY AND SOCIALIZATION

DAHLSTROM. E. (ed.) *The Changing Roles of Men and Women,* trans. G. M. and S. D. ANDERMAN (London, 1967).

FLETCHER, RONALD *The Family and Marriage in Britain* (Harmondsworth, 1962; revised edition 1966).

GRAVESON, R. H. and CRANE, F. R. *A Century of Family Law, 1857–1957* (London, 1957; revised edition 1965).

LOMAS, PETER (ed.) *The Predicament of the Family* (London, 1967).

MCGREGOR, O. R. *Divorce in England* (London, 1957).

MUSGROVE, FRANK *The Family, Education and Society* (London, 1966).

NEWSON, JOHN and ELIZABETH *Patterns of Infant Care in an Urban Community* (London, 1963).

TOWNSEND, PETER *The Family Life of Old People* (London, 1957).

TURNER, CHRISTOPHER *Family and Kinship in Modern Britian* (London, 1969).

11 WOMEN

BERGER, NAN and MAIZELS, JOAN *Woman – Fancy or Free?* (London, 1962).

GAVRON, HANNAH *The Captive Wife: Conflicts of Household Mothers* (London, 1966).

HEWITT, MARGARET *Wives and Mothers in Victorian Industry* (London, 1958).

JEPHCOTT, P. *et al. Married Women Working* (London, 1962).

KAMM, JOSEPHINE *Hope Deferred: Girls' Education in English History* (London, 1965).

KLEIN, V. *Britain's Married Women Workers* (London, 1965).

MILL, JOHN STUART *The Subjection of Women* (1869); WOLLSTONECRAFT, MARY *A Vindication of the Rights of Women* (1792); published together in Everyman edition.

MYRDAL, A. and KLEIN, V. *Women's Two Roles* (London, 1956).

PINCHBECK, IVY *Women Workers and the Industrial Revolution, 1750–1850* (London, 1930).

YUDKIN, SIMON and HOLME, ANTHEA *Working Mothers and their Children* (London, 1963).

12 COMMUNICATIONS AND MASS MEDIA

ALTICK, RICHARD D. *The English Common Reader: a Social History of the Mass Reading Public 1800–1900* (Chicago, 1957).

HALLORAN, J. D. *The Effects of Mass Communication* (Leicester, 1964).

HOGGART, RICHARD *The Uses of Literacy: Aspects of Working Class Life with Special Reference to Publications and Entertainments* (London, 1957).

PILKINGTON, SIR H. *Report of the Committee on Broadcasting,* Cmnd 1753 (London, 1962).

TRENAMON, J. and MCQUAIL, D. *Television and the Political Image* (London, 1961).

TUNSTALL, JEREMY *Advertising Man* (London, 1964).

WILLIAMS, RAYMOND *Communications* (London, 1966).

13 POLITICAL PARTIES AND VOTING

BEER, SAMUEL H. *Modern British Politics* (London, 1965).

BLONDEL, J. *Voters, Parties and Leaders* (Harmondsworth, 1963).

BUTLER, DAVID and STOKES, DONALD *Political Change in Britain* (London, 1969).

FINER, S. E. *Anonymous Empire: a study of the Lobby in Great Britain* (London, 1958).

MCKENZIE, R. T. *British Political Parties* (London, 1955; revised edition 1963).

MCKENZIE, R. T. and SILVER, ALLAN *Angels in Marble: Working Class Conservatives in England* (London, 1968).

GOLDTHORPE, J. H. *et al. The Affluent Worker: Political Attitudes and Behaviour* (Cambridge, 1968).

GUTTSMAN, W. L. *The British Political Elite* (London, 1963).

PELLING, HENRY *A Short History of the Labour Party* (London, 1961); *The Origins of the Labour Party, 1880–1900* (Oxford, 1965).

ROSE, RICHARD (ed.) *Studies in British Politics* (London, 1966).

14 SOCIAL POLICY AND ADMINISTRATION

BRUCE, MAURICE *The Coming of the Welfare State* (London, 1961).

CARR, E. H. *The New Society* (London, 1951).

DONNISON, D. V. and CHAPMAN, VALERIE *Social Policy and Administration* (London, 1965).

GILBERT, BENTLEY B. *The Evolution of National Insurance in Great Britain: the origins of the Welfare State* (London, 1966).

JONES, KATHLEEN *Mental Health and Social Policy 1845–1959* (London, 1960).

MARSHALL, T. H. *Social Policy* (London, 1965).

MIDWINTER, E. C. *Victorian Social Reform* (London, 1968).

MINISTRY OF HEALTH and DEPARTMENT OF HEALTH FOR SCOTLAND *Report of the Working Party on Social Workers in the Local Authority Health and Welfare Services (Younghusband Report)* (London, 1959).

MOWAT, CHARLES LOCH *The Charity Organisation Society 1869–1913* (London, 1961).

ROBERTS, DAVID *Victorian Origins of the British Welfare State* (New Haven, 1960).

SMELLIE, K. B. *One Hundred Years of English Government* (London, 1937); *A History of Local Government* (London, 1946; revised edition 1957).

Social Insurance and Allied Services (Beveridge Report) (H.M.S.O., London, 1942).

TITMUSS, RICHARD M. *Essays on 'The Welfare State'* (London, 1958); *Commitment to Welfare* (London, 1968).

WOODROOFE, KATHLEEN *From Charity to Social Work in England and the United States* (London, 1962).

WOOTTON, BARBARA *Social Science and Social Policy* (London, 1959).

15 SOME IMPORTANT FIGURES

BOTTOMORE, T. B. and RUBEL, MAXIMILIEN (eds.) *Karl Marx: Selected Writings in Sociology and Social Philosophy* (London, 1956).

BRIGGS, ASA *Social Thought and Social Action: A Study of the Work of Seebohm Rowntree 1871–1954* (London, 1961).

FINER, S. E. *The Life and Times of Sir Edwin Chadwick* (London, 1952).

HAMMOND, J. L. and BARBARA *Lord Shaftesbury* (London, 1923).

LAMBERT, ROYSTON *Sir John Simon 1816–1904 and English Social Administration* (London, 1963).

LEWIS, R. A. *Edwin Chadwick and the Public Health Movement, 1832–1854* (London, 1952).

MILL, JOHN STUART *Autobiography* (London, 1873).

SIMEY, T. S. and M. B. *Charles Booth, Social Scientist* (London, 1960).

16 HISTORY AND SOCIOLOGY

BERGER, PETER *Invitation to Sociology: a Humanistic Perspective* (New York, 1963).

BOTTOMORE, T. B. *Sociology* (London, 1962).

BRIGGS, ASA 'Sociology and history', Ch. 5 in WELFORD, A. T. *et al.* (eds.) *Society* (London, 1962).

CARR, E. H. *What is History?* (London, 1961).

GOLDTHORPE, J. E. *An Introduction to Sociology* (London, 1968).

HUGHES, H. STUART *History as Art and as Science* (New York, 1964).

MARSH, D. C. (ed.) *The Social Sciences: an Outline for the Intending Student* (London, 1965).

MILLS, C. WRIGHT *The Sociological Imagination* (New York, 1959).

STEIN, MAURICE and VIDICH, ARTHUR *Sociology on Trial* (New York, 1963).

17 SOCIAL AND ECONOMIC HISTORIES — GENERAL

CARR-SAUNDERS, A. M. *et al. A Survey of Social Conditions in England and Wales as Illustrated by Statistics* (Oxford, 1958).

CHAMBERS, J. D. and MINGAY, G. E. *The Agricultural Revolution 1750–1800* (London, 1966).

CLARK, G. KITSON *The Making of Victorian England* (London, 1962).

FYRTH, H. J. and GOLDSMITH, M. *Science, History and Technology;* Book I: 1800–1840s (London, 1965); Book II: 3 Pts, 1840s–1960s (London, 1969).

HOBSBAWM, E. J. *Industry and Empire: an Economic History of Britain since 1750* (London, 1968).

MARSH, DAVID C. *Changing Social Structure of England and Wales 1871–1961* (London, 1958; revised edition 1965).

MATTHIAS, PETER *The First Industrial Nation: an Economic History of Britain 1700–1914* (London, 1969).

PYKE, MAGNUS *The Science Century* (London, 1967).

RODERICK, G. W. *The Emergence of a Scientific Society in England 1800–1965* (London, 1967).

TAYLOR, F. SHERWOOD *The Century of Science* (London, 1941).

18 SURVEY METHODS AND SURVEY RESULTS

ABRAMS, MARK *Social Surveys and Social Action* (London, 1951).

BANKS, J. A. (ed.) *Studies in British Society* (London, 1969).

BANTON, MICHAEL (ed.) *The Social Anthropology of Complex Societies* (London, 1966).

BOTT, ELIZABETH *Kinship and Social Network* (London, 1957).

DENNIS, N. *et al. Coal Is Our Life* (London, 1956).

FLOUD, J. E. *et al. Social Class and Educational Opportunity* (London, 1957).

FRANKENBERG, RONALD *Communities in Britain* (Harmondsworth, 1966).

KERR, MADELINE *The People of Ship Street* (London, 1958).

KLEIN, JOSEPHINE *Samples from English Cultures* (London, 1964).

LASSWELL, MARGARET *Wellington Road* (London, 1962).

MADGE, JOHN *The Tools of Social Science* (London, 1953).

MOSER, C. A. *Survey Methods in Social Investigation* (London, 1958).

ROSSER, COLIN and HARRIS, CHRISTOPHER *The Family and Social Change* (London, 1965).

ROWNTREE, B. S. and LAVERS, G. R. *Poverty and the Welfare State* (London, 1951).
TOWNSEND, PETER *The Family Life of Old People* (London, 1957).
WILLIAMS, W. W. *The Sociology of an English Village* (London, 1957); *A West Country Village: Ashworthy* (London, 1963).
WILLMOTT, PETER *The Evolution of a Community* (London, 1963).
WILLMOTT, PETER and YOUNG, MICHAEL *Family and Class in a London Suburb* (London, 1960).
YOUNG, MICHAEL and WILLMOTT, PETER *Family and Kinship in East London* (London, 1957).

19 OTHER READING

ARGYLE, MICHAEL *Religious Behaviour* (London, 1958).
DUMAZEDIER, JOFFRE *Towards a Society of Leisure* (New York, 1967).
GLASS, RUTH *Newcomers* (London, 1961).
INGLIS, K. S. *Churches and the Working Classes in Victorian England* (London, 1963).
LEACH, EDMUND *A Runaway World?* (London, 1969).
MARWICK, ARTHUR *The Deluge: British Society and the First World War* (London, 1965).
MOWAT, CHARLES LOCH *Britain Between the Wars 1918–1940* (London, 1955).
PATTERSON, S. *Immigration and Race Relations 1960–1967* (London, 1959).
PIMLOTT, J. A. R. *The Englishman's Holiday: A Social History* (London, 1947); *Recreations* (London, 1968).
ROBERTSON, ROLAND (ed.) *Sociology of Religion* (Harmondsworth, 1969).

Appendix

Tables 1–7 Population

TABLE 1 *Population growth, 1750–1968 (thousands)*

	United Kingdom	England and Wales	Wales	Scotland	Northern Ireland
1751	—	6,467 [R]	—	1,265 [1755]	3,191 [1754]
1761	—	6,736 [R]	—	—	3,480 [1767]
1771	—	7,428 [R]	—	—	3,584 [1772]
1781	—	7,953 [R]	—	—	4,048
1791	—	8,675 [R]	—	—	4,753
1801	—	8,893	—	1,608	—
1811	—	10,164	—	1,806	—
1821	15,472	12,000	794	2,092	1,380
1831	17,835	13,897	904	2,364	1,574
1841	20,183	15,914	1,046	2,620	1,649
1851	22,259	17,928	1,163	2,889	1,443
1861	24,525	20,066	1,286	3,062	1,396
1871	27,431	22,712	1,413	3,360	1,359
1881	31,015	25,974	1,572	3,736	1,305
1891	34,264	29,003	1,771	4,026	1,236
1901	38,237	32,528	2,013	4,472	1,237
1911	42,082	36,070	2,421	4,761	1,251
1921	44,027	37,887	2,656	4,882	1,258 [e]
1931	46,038	39,952	2,593	4,843	1,243 [e]
1951	50,225	43,758	2,599	5,096	1,371
1961	52,709	46,105	2,644	5,179	1,425
1968 †	55,283	48,593	2,720	5,188	1,502

[R] after Rickman.
[e] Estimates.
Before 1821 Eire is included with the Northern Ireland totals.
† mid-year estimates.
See also Fig. 2, p. 22.

SOURCE: Mitchell and Deane, 1962 (for 1751–1821).
     Annual Abstract of Statistics, 1969 (for 1821–1968)

TABLE 2 *Births in England and Wales, 1870–1968*
          (in thousands)

	Total	Legitimate	Illegitimate	Total per 1,000 population
1870–2	805	761	45	35·5
1880–2	885	842	43	34·1
1890–2	894	856	38	30·8
1900–2	932	896	37	28·7
1910–2	884	846	37	24·5
1920–2	862	823	39	22·8
1930–2	632	603	28	15·8
1951	678	645	33	15·4
1952	674	641	33	15·3
1953	684	652	33	15·4
1954	674	642	32	15·1
1955	668	637	31	15·0
1956	700	667	34	15·6
1957	723	689	35	16·1
1958	741	705	36	16·4
1959	749	710	38	16·5
1960	785	742	43	17·2
1961	811	763	48	17·6
1962	839	783	55	18·0
1963	854	795	59	18·2
1964	876	813	63	18·5
1965	863	796	66	18·1
1966	850	783	67	17·7
1967	832	762	70	17·2
1968	819	749	70	16·9

Until 1930, figures relate to births per calendar year.
See also Fig. 10, p. 158.

SOURCE: *Annual Abstract of Statistics*, 1969.

TABLE 3 *The death rate in England and Wales, 1850–1968*

	Deaths per 1,000 persons	Infant mortality per 1,000 live births	Maternal deaths per 1,000 live births[b]
1850	20·8	162	—
1855	22·6	153	—
1860	21·2	148	—
1865	23·2	160	—
1870	22·9	160	4·8*
1875	22·7	158	—
1880	20·5	153	4·6
1885	19·2	138	—
1890	19·5	151	5·3*
1895	18·7	161	—
1900	18·2	154	4·7*
1905	15·3	128	—
1910	13·5	105	3·7*
1915	15·7[a]	110	—
1920	12·4[a]	80	4·0*
1925	12·1	75	—
1930	11·4	60	4·2
1935	11·7	57	4·3
1940	14·4[a]	57	2·8
1945	12·6[a]	46	1·9
1950	11·8	30	0·9
1955	11·8	25	0·6
1960	11·5	22	0·4
1965	11·6	19	0·3
1966	11·8	19	0·3
1968	11·9	18	0·2

[a] Civilian deaths only.
[b] Deaths in pregnancy and childbirth.
* Figures for 1870–2, 1880–2, 1890–2, 1900–2, 1910–12, 1920–2.
See also Fig. 10, p. 158.
SOURCE: Mitchell and Deane, 1962, and *Annual Abstract of Statistics*, 1969.

TABLE 4 *Expectation of life at birth in England and Wales*

	Male	Female
1841	40	42
1871–80	41	45
1881–90	43	48
1901–10	49	52
1910–12	52	55
1920–22	56	59
1930–32	59	63
1950–52	66	72
1960–62	68	74
1964–66	69	75

See also Fig. 11, p. 158

SOURCE: *The Population of Britain*, B.I.S., 1968.

TABLE 5 *Infant mortality rates, 1870–1968, deaths of infants under one year old per 1,000 live births*

	United Kingdom	England and Wales	Scotland
1870–2	150	156	126
1880–2	137	141	118
1890–2	145	149	125
1900–2	142	146	124
1910–2	110	110	109
1920–2	82	80	94
1930–2	67	64	84
1935	60	51	77
1936	62	59	82
1937	61	58	80
1938	56	53	70
1939	54	51	69
1940	61	57	78
1941	63	60	83
1942	53	51	69
1943	52	49	65
1944	48	45	65
1945	49	46	56
1946	43	43	54
1947	44	41	56
1948	36	34	45
1949	34	32	41
1950	31	30	39
1951	31	30	37
1952	29	28	35
1953	28	27	31
1954	26	25	31
1955	26	25	30
1956	24	24	29
1957	24	23	29
1958	23	23	28
1959	23	22	28
1960	22	22	26
1961	22	21	26
1962	22	22	27
1963	22	21	26
1964	21	20	24
1965	20	19	23
1966	20	19	23
1967	19	18	21
1968	19	18	21

From 1935 to 1956 death rates are based on the births to which they relate in the current and preceding years.
See also Fig. 8, p. 143

SOURCE: Mitchell and Deane, 1962, and *Annual Abstract of Statistics*, 1969.

TABLE 6 *Mean ultimate family size of cohorts in England and Wales. since 1861*

Calendar year of marriage	Mean ultimate family size
1861–9	6·16
1876	5·62
1886	4·81
1890–9	4·13
1900–9	3·30
1910–19	2·64
1920–9	2·23
1930–9	2·06[p]
1940–9	2·15[p]

[p] Projected.
All marriages, ages under 45 years.
See also Fig. 16, p. 252.

SOURCE: *Registrar-General's Statistical Review of England and Wales for 1960.*

TABLE 7 *Proportions of each age group (by sex) according to marital condition, England and Wales, 1851–1961 (per thousand of the appropriate sex in each age group)*

A. Males

		1851	1871	1901	1921	1951	1961
All ages	S	625	613	608	550	438	437
	M	337	351	357	414	523	530
	W	38	36	35	36	39	33
15–19	S	996	995	997	996	995	989
	M	4	5	3	4	5	11
	W	–	–	–	–	–	–
20–24	S	797	767	826	822	762	691
	M	200	230	173	177	237	309
	W	3	3	1	1	1	—
25–34	S	356	316	359	341	272	235
	M	627	668	631	649	720	760
	W	17	16	10	10	8	5
35–44	S	162	137	158	150	120	120
	M	795	826	812	827	862	866
	W	43	37	30	23	18	14
45–54	S	115	97	110	120	92	92
	M	802	832	819	831	877	881
	W	83	71	71	49	31	27
55–64	S	98	89	89	104	78	83
	M	748	772	764	782	850	860
	W	154	139	147	114	72	57
65–74	S	85	82	78	91	84	75
	M	626	638	630	654	733	773
	W	289	280	292	255	183	152
75–84	S	74	71	66	73	79	78
	M	458	444	444	468	530	556
	W	468	485	490	459	391	366
85 and over	S	76	62	62	70	65	73
	M	290	270	263	272	311	337
	W	634	668	675	658	624	590

B. Females

		1851	*1871*	*1901*	*1921*	*1951*	*1961*
All ages	S	598	586	586	535	405	388
	M	330	339	340	383	487	498
	W	72	75	74	82	108	114
15–19	S	975	968	985	982	956	934
	M	25	32	15	18	44	66
	W	–	–	–	–	–	–
20–24	S	687	652	726	726	518	420
	M	308	343	272	270	480	577
	W	5	5	2	4	2	31
25–34	S	329	295	340	337	182	133
	M	643	675	643	631	798	855
	W	28	30	17	32	20	12
35–44	S	163	156	185	192	137	98
	M	757	762	751	746	821	867
	W	80	82	64	62	42	35
45–54	S	122	121	136	164	151	114
	M	716	716	705	721	759	803
	W	162	163	159	115	90	83
55–64	S	115	109	117	153	155	141
	M	589	589	569	600	624	658
	W	296	302	314	247	221	201
65–74	S	111	104	111	139	156	154
	M	400	393	368	393	428	430
	W	489	503	521	468	416	416
75–84	S	109	97	111	132	164	158
	M	211	204	176	187	222	201
	W	680	699	713	681	614	641
85 and over	S	107	91	119	130	172	172
	M	81	74	59	67	77	71
	W	812	835	822	803	751	757

S = single. M = married. W = widowed and divorced.
See also Fig. 15, p. 250.
SOURCE: Mitchell and Deane, 1962, and the 1961 Census.

Tables 8–12 Employment

TABLE 8 *Size of the labour force in Great Britain, 1857–1967 (thousands)*

Year	Total	Male	Female
1851	9,377	6,545	2,832
1861	10,520	7,266	3,254
1871	11,870	8,220	3,650
1881	12,739	8,852	3,887
1891	14,499	10,010	4,489
1901	16,299	11,548	4,751
1911	18,340	12,927	5,413
1921	19,355	13,656	5,699
1931	21,055	14,790	6,265
1951	22,610	15,649	6,961
1960	24,436	16,239	8,197
1967	25,322	16,388	8,935

SOURCE: Mitchell and Deane, 1962, and Butler and Freeman, *British Political Facts, 1900–1968*, 1969.

TABLE 9 *Persons registered as unemployed in Great Britain, 1922–68 (thousands)*

1922	1,543	1938	1,791	1954	285
1923	1,275	1939	1,514	1955	232
1924	1,130	1940[b]	963	1956	257
1925	1,226	1941	350	1957	297
1926	1,385	1942	123	1958	457
1927	1,088	1943	82	1959	475
1928	1,217	1944	75	1960	360
1929	1,216	1945	137	1961	341
1930	1,917	1946	374	1962	463
1931	2,630	1947	480	1963	573
1932	2,745	1948	310	1964	381
1933	2,521	1949	308	1965	329
1934	2,159	1950	314	1966	360
1935	2,036	1951	253	1967	560
1936	1,755	1952	414	1968	564
1937[a]	1,484	1953	342		

[a] Change in accounting method resulting in fall in recorded numbers of about 50,000.

[b] After July 1940 men at Government Training Centres not classed as unemployed.

Figures include those permanently stopped as well as those temporarily unemployed.

See also Fig. 9, p. 145.

SOURCE: Mitchell and Deane, 1962, and *Annual Abstract of Statistics*, 1969.

TABLE 10 *Employment of women in the United Kingdom, 1851–1960*

	Employed (thousands)	Not employed (thousands)	Females as percentage of total labour force
1851	2,832	5,294	30·20
1861	3,254	5,762	30·93
1871	3,650	6,429	30·74
1881	3,887	7,617	30·53
1891	4,849	8,537	33·44
1901	4,751	10,229	29·14
1911	5,413	11,375	29·51
1921	5,699	11,968	29·44
1931	6,265	12,055	29·75
1951	6,961	13,084	30·78
1961	7,782	12,976	32·42

See also Table 11, p. 320.

After Mitchell and Deane, 1962, and the 1961 census.

TABLE 11 *Women in employment in the United Kingdom, 1956–68 (in thousands)*

	1956	1957	1958	1959	1960	1961	1962	1963	1964	1965	1966	1967	1968
Total	7,791	7,847	7,777	7,863	8,097	8,242	8,367	8,413	8,543	8,677	8,845	8,752	8,766
of whom married women	3,776	3,823	3,884	4,055	4,147	4,268	4,350	4,382	4,544	4,700	4,881	4,909	5,026

See also Fig. 17, p. 257.

SOURCE: *Annual Abstract of Statistics*, 1969.

TABLE 12 *Growth and consolidation of trade-union membership (head offices in the United Kingdom), 1892–1969*

	Total number unions	Total number members (thousands)
1892	1,233	1,576
1895	1,340	1,504
1900	1,323	2,022
1905	1,244	1,997
1910	1,269	2,565
1915	1,229	4,359
1920	1,384	8,348
1925	1,176	5,506
1930	1,121	4,842
1935	1,049	4,867
1940	1,004	6,613
1945	781	7,875
1950	732	9,289
1955	694	9,726
1960	646	9,897
1965	574	10,111
1968	555	9,967

See also Fig. 7, p. 136.

SOURCE: Mitchell and Deane, 1962, and Butler and Freeman, *British Political Facts, 1900–1968*, 1969.

Tables 13–17   Characteristics of urban development

TABLE 13 *The geographical distribution of*
the population in England and
Wales (in thousands)

	Urban	Rural
1801	1,506	7,386
1851	8,991	8,937
1861	10,961	9,105
1871	14,041	8,671
1881	17,637	8,338
1891	20,896	8,107
1901	25,058	7,469
1911	28,163	7,908
1921	30,035	7,851
1931	31,952	8,000
1939	34,183	7,277
1951	35,336	8,423
1961	36,872	9,233
1968	38,325	10,268

See also Fig. 5, p. 106.

SOURCE: *Annual Abstract of Statistics,* 1969, and Adna
Ferrin Weber, *The Growth of Cities in the*
Nineteenth Century, New York, 1899. (See
also the latter, pp. 43–7, for criteria used in
apportioning the population.)

TABLE 14 *The growth of conurbations in England and Wales, 1801–1968 (thousands)*

Conurbation	Area in square miles at time of 1961 Census	1801	1811	1821	1831	1841	1851	1861	1871	1901	1921	1931	1939	1951	1961	1968*
Greater London	721·6	1,117	1,327	1,600	1,907	2,239	2,685	3,227	3,890	6,586	7,488	8,216	8,778	8,348	8,183	7,764
South-East Lancashire	379·6								1,386	2,117	2,361	2,427	2,421	2,423	2,428	2,441
West Midlands	268·8								969	1,483	1,773	1,933	2,079	2,237	2,347	2,425
West Yorkshire	480·9								1,064	1,524	1,614	1,655	1,658	1,693	1,704	1,730
Merseyside	148·5								690	1,030	1,263	1,347	1,357	1,382	1,384	1,351
Tyneside	90·1								346	678	816	827	825	836	855	843

* Mid-year estimate.

See also Fig. 3, p. 33.

Conurbations are: 'areas of urban development where a number of separate towns have grown into each other or become linked by such factors as a common industrial or business interest, or a common centre for shopping or education' (*Annual Abstract of Statistics*, 1969, p. 12).

SOURCE: Mitchell and Deane, 1962, and *Annual Abstract of Statistics*, 1969.

TABLE 15 *Permanent houses built in Great Britain, 1856–1968 (in thousands)*

1856	52·6	1895	89·8	1935	350·5
1860	45·2	1900	139·7	1940	95·1
1865	53·6	1905	127·4	1945	13·8
1870	85·9	1910	86·0	1950	198·2
1875	120·3	1915	30·8	1955	317·4
1880	83·1	1920	29·7	1960	297·8
1885	76·7	1925	174·2	1965	382·3
1890	75·8	1930	202·4	1968	413·7

SOURCE: Mitchell and Deane, 1962, and *Annual Abstract of Statistics*, 1969.

TABLE 16 *Population of selected towns of the United Kingdom, 1801–1951 (thousands)*

	1801	1831	1851	1871	1891	1911	1931	1951
Aberdeen	27	57	72	88	125	164	167	183
Belfast	—	53	87	174	256	387	438	444
Birkenhead	φ	3	24	45	100	131	148	143
Birmingham	71	144	233	344	478	526	1,003	1,113
Environs of Birmingham later incorporated	—	—	32	91	156	314	—	—
Blackpool	φ	1	3	6	24	58	102	147
Bournemouth	—	—	—	6	38	79	117	145
Bradford	13	44	104	146	216	288	298	292
Brighton	7	41	66	90	116	131	147	156
Bristol	61	104	137	183	222	357	397	443
Cambridge	10	21	28	30	37	40	67	82
Cardiff	2	6	18	40	129	182	224	244
Chester	15	21	28	35	37	39	41	48
Coventry	16	27	36	38	53	106	167	258
Derby	11	24	41	50	94	123	142	141
Edinburgh (including Leith)	83	162	194	242	332	401	439	467
Exeter	17	28	33	35	37	49	66	76
Glasgow	77	202	345	522	658	784	1,088	1,090
Environs of Glasgow later incorporated		10	18	46	108	169		
Huddersfield	7	19	31	70	95	108	113	129
Hull	30	52	85	122	200	278	314	299
King's Lynn	10	13	19	17	18	20	21	26
Leeds	53	123	172	259	368	446	483	505
Leicester	17	41	61	95	175	227	239	285
Liverpool	82	202	376	493	518	746	856	789
Environs of Liverpool later incorporated		8	19	47	113			
Luton	—	4	11	17	30	50	69	110
Manchester	75	182	303	351	505	714	766	703
Environs of Manchester later incorporated		12	26	57				
environs of Manchester later incorporated			9	36	70			
Newcastle-upon-Tyne	33	54	88	128	186	267	283	292
Nottingham	29	50	57	87	214	260	269	306
Oxford	12	21	28	31	46	53	81	99
Portsmouth	33	50	72	114	159	231	249	234
Sheffield	46	92	135	240	324	455	512	513
Southampton	8	19	35	54	65	119	176	178
Southend-on-Sea				5	12	63	120	152
Stoke-upon-Trent		35	66	101	145	235	277	275
Swansea	10	20	31	52	91	115	165	161
Wigan	11	21	32	39	55	89	85	85
Wolverhampton	13	25	50	68	83	95	133	163
York	17	26	36	44	67	82	85	105

See also Fig. 4, p. 41.   SOURCE: Mitchell and Deane, 1962.

TABLE 17 *Availability of household amenities in London, 1951 and 1961*

1951

Amenity	Exclusive use of amenity	Shared with others	Entirely without use of amenity	Total number of households
Cold-water tap	778,571	332,939	9,157	1,120,667
percentage of total	69·5	29·7	0·8	100
Fixed bath	466,886	205,575	448,206	1,120,667
percentage of total	41·7	18·3	40·0	100
Water closet	729,480	388,473	2,774	1,120,667
percentage of total	65·1	34·7	0·2	100
Kitchen sink	935,895	117,461	67,311	1,120,667
percentage of total	83·5	10·5	6·0	100
Cooking stove	1,026,856	57,864	35,947	1,120,667
percentage of total	91·6	5·2	3·2	100

1961

Amenity	Exclusive use of amenity	Shared with others	Entirely without use of amenity	Total number of households
Cold-water tap	1,024,377	80,295	2,458	1,107,130
percentage of total	92·5	7·3	0·2	100
Hot-water tap	648,897	52,519	405,714	1,107,130
percentage of total	58·6	4·7	36·6	100
Fixed bath	563,000	206,002	338,128	1,107,130
percentage of total	50·9	18·6	30·5	100
Water closet	765,821	334,089	7,220	1,107,130
percentage of total	69·2	30·2	0·7	100

Availability of kitchen sink, cooking stove not known for 1961.
Availability of hot tap not known for 1951.

SOURCE: *Census of England and Wales: County Reports* (London) 1951, Table 13. *Census of England and Wales: County Reports* (London) 1961, Table 23.

Tables 18–20 The economy

TABLE 18   *Coal output, exports and labour employed in Great Britain, 1800–1966*

Year	Total U.K. output	Total exports	%	Total employment (thousands)	Output per man (tons)
1800	11	0·2	2	—	—
1816	16	0·4	3	—	—
1820	17	0·2	1	—	—
1850	49	3	7	—	—
1855–9	67	6	9	—	—
1860–4	85	8	9	308†	276
1865–9	103	10	10	332	310
1870–4	121	12	10	439	277
1875–9	134	15	11	499	268
1880–4	156	20	13	504	313
1885–9	165	24	15	540	306
1890–4	180	29	16	674	267
1895–9	202	35	17	705	286
1900–4	227	44	19	820	277
1905–9	256	60	24	937	273
1910–14	270	63	23	1,094	247
1915–19	243	37	15	1,035	235
1920–4	237	51	22	1,189	199
1925–9	223	47	21	1,014	220
1930–4	220	43	20	839	263
1935–8	230	38	17	780	294
1940	224	27	12	749	299
1945	175	9	5	709	247
1950	204	20	10	687	295
1955	210	16	8	704	298
1960	194	5	3	602	321
1965	187	4	2	466	402
1968	164	3	2	343	478

Amounts in million tons, average per annum, per quinquennium, and selected years.
† In 1864 output per man based on 93m. production for 1864.
See also Fig. 1, p. 20.

SOURCE: Mitchell and Deane, 1962; G. C. Allen, *British Industries and their Organization*, 1966; *Annual Abstract of Statistics*, 1969.

TABLE 19 *Motor-car production, 1923–1968 (thousands)*

Year	Private cars and taxis	Year	Private cars and taxis	Year	Private cars and taxis
1923	71	1945	17	1957	861
1925	132	1946	219	1958	1,052
1929	182	1947	287	1959	1,190
1930	170	1948	335	1960	1,353
1931	159	1949	412	1961	1,004
1932	171	1950	523	1962	1,249
1933	221	1951	476	1963	1,608
1934	257	1952	448	1964	1,868
1935	325	1953	595	1965	1,722
1936	367	1954	769	1966	1,604
1937	379	1955	898	1967	1,552
1938	341	1956	708	1968	1,815
1939	305				

Year ends in September for 1927–34 and the rest are calendar years.
See also Fig. 6, p. 133.

SOURCE: G. C. Allen, *British Industries and their Organization*, Longmans, 1959; *Annual Abstract of Statistics*, 1969 (for 1960–68).

TABLE 20 *Distribution of personal incomes in the United Kingdom, 1966*

Range of net incomes £ per annum	Number of persons earning the income (thousands)	Total income before tax (£ millions)	Income tax and surtax* (£ millions)	Net income after tax (£ millions)
50–249	3,006	616	—	616
250–499	6,841	2,609	74	2,535
500–749	5,431	3,630	272	3,358
750–999	5,153	4,809	401	4,408
1,000–1,999	6,460	9,515	1,129	8,386
2,000–3,999	595	2,100	590	1,510
4,000–5,999	84	682	281	401
6,000 and over	30	548	333	215
Total	27,600	24,509	3,080	21,429

* At rates current in 1965–6.
See also Fig. 13, p. 202.

SOURCE: Board of Inland Revenue statistics.

Table 21 Education

TABLE 21 *Children remaining at school in England and Wales after the age of fifteen, 1950–68*

Year	As percentage of the age-group	Numbers at school after age fifteen (thousands)
1950	10·4	290,000
1955	12·2	346,000
1958	14·1	400,000
1960	16·6	501,000
1963	18·5	668,000
1964	21·1	781,000
1965	21·2	785,000
1966	20·9	782,000
1967	21·7	790,000
1968	23·7	823,000

See also Fig. 14, p. 231.

SOURCE: *Statistics of Education 1968*, Vol. I (Schools), H.M.S.O., 1969.

Table 22 Votes cast in elections since 1900

TABLE 22 *Proportion of votes cast for the major political parties, in elections in the United Kingdom since 1900*

Election year	Conservative party %	Labour party %	Liberal party %	Others %	Total number of votes (millions)
1900	51	2	45	2	3·5
1906	44	6	49	1	5·6
1910 (Jan.)	47	8	43	2	6·7
1910 (Dec.)	46	7	44	3	5·2
1918	36	24	26	14	10·8
1922	38	29	29	4	14·4
1923	38	30	30	2	14·5
1924	48	33	18	1	16·6
1929	38	37	23	2	22·7
1931	55	32	11	2	21·7
1935	54	38	6	2	22·0
1945	40	48	9	3	25·1
1950	43	46	9	2	28·8
1951	48	49	3	—	28·6
1955	50	46	3	1	26·8
1959	49	44	6	1	27·9
1964	43	44	11	2	27·7
1966	42	48	9	1	27·3
1970	46	43	8	3	28·3

SOURCE: Butler and Freeman, *British Political Facts, 1900–1968*, 1969.

Index